# U.S. and CANADA LITERATURE ORDER FORM

NAME: _____

COMPANY: _____

ADDRESS: _____

CITY: _____ STATE: _____ ZIP: _____

COUNTRY: _____

PHONE NO.: ( _____ ) _____

D1806624

| ORDER NO. | TITLE | QTY. | PRICE | TOTAL |
|---|---|---|---|---|
| ☐☐☐☐☐☐ | _____ | ____ × | _____ = | _____ |
| ☐☐☐☐☐☐ | _____ | ____ × | _____ = | _____ |
| ☐☐☐☐☐☐ | _____ | ____ × | _____ = | _____ |
| ☐☐☐☐☐☐ | _____ | ____ × | _____ = | _____ |
| ☐☐☐☐☐☐ | _____ | ____ × | _____ = | _____ |
| ☐☐☐☐☐☐ | _____ | ____ × | _____ = | _____ |
| ☐☐☐☐☐☐ | _____ | ____ × | _____ = | _____ |
| ☐☐☐☐☐☐ | _____ | ____ × | _____ = | _____ |
| ☐☐☐☐☐☐ | _____ | ____ × | _____ = | _____ |
| ☐☐☐☐☐☐ | _____ | ____ × | _____ = | _____ |

Subtotal _____

Must Add Your
Local Sales Tax _____

Postage: add 10% of subtotal ⟶ Postage _____

Total _____

Pay by check, money order, or include company purchase order with this form ($100 minimum). We also accept VISA, MasterCard or American Express. Make payment to Intel Literature Sales. Allow 2-4 weeks for delivery.

☐ VISA  ☐ MasterCard  ☐ American Express  Expiration Date _____

Account No. _____

Signature _____

**Mail To:** Intel Literature Sales
P.O. Box 7641
Mt. Prospect, IL 60056-7641

**International Customers** outside the U.S. and Canada should use the International order form or contact their local Sales Office or Distributor.

**For phone orders in the U.S. and Canada**
**Call Toll Free: (800) 548-4725**

Prices good until 12/31/89.

Source HB

CG/LOF1/081789

# INTERNATIONAL LITERATURE ORDER FORM

NAME: _____

COMPANY: _____

ADDRESS: _____

CITY: _____ STATE: _____ ZIP: _____

COUNTRY: _____

PHONE NO.: (_____) _____

| ORDER NO. | TITLE | QTY. | PRICE | TOTAL |
|---|---|---|---|---|
| ☐☐☐☐☐☐ | _____ | ____ × | ____ = | _____ |
| ☐☐☐☐☐☐ | _____ | ____ × | ____ = | _____ |
| ☐☐☐☐☐☐ | _____ | ____ × | ____ = | _____ |
| ☐☐☐☐☐☐ | _____ | ____ × | ____ = | _____ |
| ☐☐☐☐☐☐ | _____ | ____ × | ____ = | _____ |
| ☐☐☐☐☐☐ | _____ | ____ × | ____ = | _____ |
| ☐☐☐☐☐☐ | _____ | ____ × | ____ = | _____ |
| ☐☐☐☐☐☐ | _____ | ____ × | ____ = | _____ |
| ☐☐☐☐☐☐ | _____ | ____ × | ____ = | _____ |
| ☐☐☐☐☐☐ | _____ | ____ × | ____ = | _____ |

Subtotal _____

Must Add Your
Local Sales Tax _____

Total _____

**PAYMENT**

Cheques should be made payable to your local Intel Sales Office (see inside back cover.)

Other forms of payment may be available in your country. Please contact the Literature Coordinator at your local Intel Sales Office for details.

The completed form should be marked to the attention of the LITERATURE COORDINATOR and returned to your local Intel Sales Office.

# 387™ DX
# PROGRAMMER'S REFERENCE
# MANUAL

### 1989

# CUSTOMER SUPPORT

## INTEL'S COMPLETE SUPPORT SOLUTION WORLDWIDE

Customer Support is Intel's complete support service that provides Intel customers with hardware support, software support, customer training, consulting services and network management services. For detailed information contact your local sales offices.

After a customer purchases any system hardware or software product, service and support become major factors in determining whether that product will continue to meet a customer's expectations. Such support requires an international support organization and a breadth of programs to meet a variety of customer needs. As you might expect, Intel's customer support is quite extensive. It can start with assistance during your development effort to network management. 100 Intel sales and service offices are located worldwide — in the U.S., Canada, Europe and the Far East. So wherever you're using Intel technology, our professional staff is within close reach.

## HARDWARE SUPPORT SERVICES

Intel's hardware maintenance service, starting with complete on-site installation will boost your productivity from the start and keep you running at maximum efficiency. Support for system or board level products can be tailored to match your needs, from complete on-site repair and maintenance support to economical carry-in or mail-in factory service.

Intel can provide support service for not only Intel systems and emulators, but also support for equipment in your development lab or provide service on your product to your end-user/customer.

## SOFTWARE SUPPORT SERVICES

Software products are supported by our Technical Information Service (TIPS) that has a special toll free number to provide you with direct, ready information on known, documented problems and deficiencies, as well as work-arounds, patches and other solutions.

Intel's software support consists of two levels of contracts. Standard support includes TIPS (Technical Information Phone Service), updates and subscription service (product-specific troubleshooting guides and; *COMMENTS Magazine*). Basic support consists of updates and the subscription service. Contracts are sold in environments which represent product groupings (e.g., iRMX® environment).

## CONSULTING SERVICES

Intel provides field system engineering consulting services for any phase of your development or application effort. You can use our system engineers in a variety of ways ranging from assistance in using a new product, developing an application, personalizing training and customizing an Intel product to providing technical and management consulting. Systems Engineers are well versed in technical areas such as microcommunications, real-time applications, embedded microcontrollers, and network services. You know your application needs; we know our products. Working together we can help you get a successful product to market in the least possible time.

## CUSTOMER TRAINING

Intel offers a wide range of instructional programs covering various aspects of system design and implementation. In just three to ten days a limited number of individuals learn more in a single workshop than in weeks of self-study. For optimum convenience, workshops are scheduled regularly at Training Centers worldwide or we can take our workshops to you for on-site instruction. Covering a wide variety of topics, Intel's major course categories include: architecture and assembly language, programming and operating systems, BITBUS™ and LAN applications.

## NETWORK MANAGEMENT SERVICES

Today's networking products are powerful and extremely flexible. The return they can provide on your investment via increased productivity and reduced costs can be very substantial.

Intel offers complete network support, from definition of your network's physical and functional design, to implementation, installation and maintenance. Whether installing your first network or adding to an existing one, Intel's Networking Specialists can optimize network performance for you.

# PREFACE

This manual describes the 387™ DX Math Coprocessor. Understanding the 387 DX requires an understanding of the 386™ DX; therefore, a brief overview of 386 DX concepts is presented first. A detailed discussion of the 386 DX microprocessor can be found in the *386™ DX Programmer's Reference Manual*.

## THE 386™ DX MICROSYSTEM

The 386 DX is the basis of a new VLSI microprocessor system with exceptional capabilities for supporting large-system applications. This powerful microsystem is designed to support multiuser reprogrammable and real-time multitasking applications. Its dedicated system support circuits simplify system hardware; sophisticated hardware and software tools reduce both the time and the cost of product development. The 386 DX microsystem offers a total-solution approach, enabling you to develop high-speed, interactive, multiuser, multitasking—even multiprocessor—systems more rapidly and at higher performance than ever before.

- Reliability and system up-time are becoming increasingly important in all applications. Information must be protected from misuse or accidental loss. The 386 DX includes a sophisticated and flexible four-level protection mechanism that can isolate layers of operating system programs from application programs to maintain a high degree of system integrity.

- The 386 DX addresses up to 4 gigabytes of physical memory to support today's application requirements. This large physical memory enables the 386 DX to keep many large programs and data structures simultaneously in memory for high-speed access.

- For applications with dynamically changing memory requirements, such as multiuser business systems, the 386 DX CPU provides on-chip memory management and virtual memory support. On a 386 DX-based system, each user can have up to 64 terabytes of virtual-address space. This large address space virtually eliminates restrictions on the size of programs that may be part of the system. The memory management features are subject to control of systems software; therefore, systems software designers can choose among a variety of memory-organization models. Systems designers can choose to view memory in terms of fixed-length pages, in terms of variable length segments, or as a combination of pages and segments. The sizes of segments can range from one byte to 4 gigabytes. Virtual memory can be implemented either at the level of segments or at the level of pages.

- Large multiuser or real-time multitasking systems are easily supported by the 386 DX. High-performance features, such as a very high-speed task switch, fast interrupt-response time, intertask protection, page-oriented virtual memory, and a quick and direct operating system interface, make the 386 DX highly suited to multiuser/multitasking applications.

- The 386 DX has two primary operating modes: real-address mode and protected mode. In real-address mode, the 386 DX/387 DX is fully upward compatible from the 8086, 8088, 80186, and 80188 microprocessors and from the 80286 real-address mode; all of the extensive libraries of 8086 and 8088 software execute 15 to 20 times faster on the 386 DX, without any modification.

- In protected-address mode, the advanced memory management and protection features of the 386 DX become available, without any reduction in performance. Upgrading 8086 and 8088 application programs to use these new memory management and protection features usually requires only reassembly or recompilation (some programs may require minor modification). Entire 80286 protected-mode applications can run in this mode without modification.

- The virtual-8086 mode of the 386 DX is available when the primary mode is protected mode. Virtual-8086 mode enables direct execution of multiple 8086/8088 programs within a protected-mode environment. Most 8086 and 8088 application programs can be executed in this environment without alteration (refer to the *386™ DX Programmer's Reference Manual* for differences from 8086). This high degree of compatibility between 386 DX and earlier members of the 8086 processor family reduces both the time and the cost of software development.

## THE ORGANIZATION OF THIS MANUAL

This manual describes the 387 DX Numeric Processor Extension (NPX) for the 386 DX microprocessor. The material in this manual is presented from the perspective of software designers, both at an applications and at a systems software level.

- Chapter 1, "Introduction to the 387™ DX Math Coprocessor," gives an overview of the 387 DX Math Coprocessor and reviews the concepts of numeric computation using the 387 DX.

- Chapter 2, "387™ DX Numerics Processor Architecture," presents the registers and data types of the 387 DX to both applications and systems programmers.

- Chapter 3, "Special Computational Situations," discusses the special values that can be represented in the 387 DX's real formats—denormal numbers, zeros, infinities, NaNs (not a number)—as well as numerics exceptions. This chapter should be read thoroughly by systems programmers, but may be skimmed by applications programmers. Many of these special values and exceptions may never occur in applications programs.

- Chapter 4, "387™ DX Instruction Set," provides functional information for software designers generating applications for systems containing an 386 DX CPU with an 387 DX Math Coprocessor. The 386 DX/387 DX instruction set mnemonics are explained in detail.

- Chapter 5, "Programming Numeric Applications," provides a description of programming facilities for 386 DX/387 DX systems. A comparative 387 DX programming example is given.

- Chapter 6, "System-Level Numeric Programming," provides information of interest to systems software writers, including details of the 387 DX architecture and operational characteristics.

- Chapter 7, "Numeric Programming Examples," provides several detailed programming examples for the 387 DX, including conditional branching, the conversion between floating-point values and their ASCII representations, and the use of trigonometric functions. These examples illustrate assembly-language programming on the 387 DX Math Coprocessor.

- Appendix A, "Machine Instruction Encoding and Decoding," gives reference information on the encoding of NPX instructions. This information is useful to writers of debuggers, exception handlers, and compilers.

- Appendix B, "Exception Summary," provides a list of the exceptions that each instruction can cause. This list is valuable to both applications and systems programmers.

- Appendix C, "Compatability between the 387™ DX and the 80287/8087," describes the differences from the 387 DX that are common to the 80287 and the 8087.

- Appendix D, "Compatability between the 387™ DX and the 8087," describes the additional differences between the 387 DX and the 8087 that are of concern when porting 8086/8087 programs directly to the 386 DX/387 DX.

- Appendix E, "387™ DX 80-Bit CHMOS IV Numeric Processor Extension," reproduces a data sheet of 387 DX specifications that is separately available. The table of instruction timings in this appendix will be of interest to many readers of this manual. (The AC and DC specifications have been deliberately left out.) The specifications in data sheets are subject to change; consult the most recent data sheet for design-in information.

- Appendix F, "PC/AT-Compatible 387™ DX Connection," documents a nonstandard method of connecting an 387 DX to an 386 DX to achieve compatibility with the IBM PC/AT.

- The Glossary defines 387 DX and floating-point terminology. Refer to it as needed.

## RELATED PUBLICATIONS

To best use the material in this manual, readers should be familiar with the operation and architecture of 386 DX systems. The following manuals contain information related to the content of this manual and of interest to programmers of 387 DX systems:

- *Introduction to the 80386*, order number 231252
- *386™ DX Data Sheet*, order number 231630
- *386™ DX Hardware Reference Manual*, order number 231732
- *386™ DX Programmer's Reference Manual*, order number 230985
- *387™ DX Data Sheet*, order number 240448
- *387™ SX Data Sheet*, order number 240225

# TABLE OF CONTENTS

**APPENDIX F**
**PC/AT-COMPATIBLE 387™ DX CONNECTION**

**GLOSSARY**

# Tables

# Figures

# Introduction To The 387™ DX Math Coprocessor

# CHAPTER 1
# INTRODUCTION TO THE 387™ DX
# MATH COPROCESSOR

The 387™ DX Math Coprocessor is a high-performance numerics processing element that extends the 386™ DX architecture by adding significant numeric capabilities and direct support for floating-point, extended-integer, and BCD data types. The 386 DX CPU with 387 DX Math Coprocessor easily supports powerful and accurate numeric applications through its implementation of the IEEE Standard 754 for Binary Floating-Point Arithmetic. The 387 DX provides floating-point performance comparable to that of large minicomputers while offering compatibility with object code for 8087, 80287, and 387 SX.

## 1.1 HISTORY

The 387 DX Math Coprocessor is compatible with its predecessors, the earlier Intel 8087 NPX, 80287 NPX and 387 SX NPX. As the 386 DX runs 8086 programs, so programs designed to use the 8087, 80287 and 387 SX should run unchanged on the 387 DX.

The 8087 Math Coprocessor was designed for use in 8086-family systems. The 8086 was the first microprocessor family to partition the processing unit to permit high-performance numeric capabilities. The 8087 Math Coprocessor for this family implemented a complete numeric processing environment in compliance with an early proposal for the IEEE 754 Floating-Point Standard.

With the 80287 Math Coprocessor, high-speed numeric computations were extended to 80286 high-performance multitasking and multiuser systems. Multiple tasks using the numeric processor extension were afforded the full protection of the 80286 memory management and protection features.

The 387 DX Math Coprocessor is Intel's third generation math coprocessor. The 387 DX implements the final IEEE standard (standard 754), adds new trigonometric instructions, and uses a new design and CHMOS-IV process to allow higher clock rates and require fewer clocks per instruction. Together, the 387 DX with additional instructions and the improved standard bring even more convenience and reliability to numerics programming and make this convenience and reliability available to applications that need the high-speed and large memory capacity of the 32-bit environment of the 386 DX CPU.

Figure 1-1 illustrates the relative performance of 5-MHz 8086/8087, 8-MHz 80286/80287, and 33-MHz 386 DX/387 DX systems in executing numerics-oriented applications.

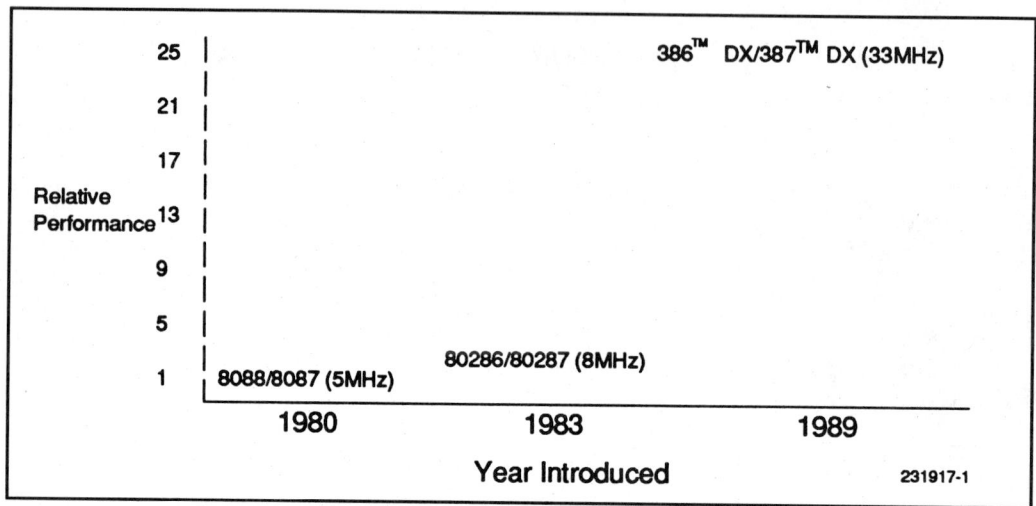

**Figure 1-1. Evolution and Performance of Numeric Processors**

**NOTE**

The 387 DX Math Coprocessor is also referred to as the 387 DX Numeric Processor Extension (NPX) in this document.

## 1.2 PERFORMANCE

Table 1-1 compares the execution times of several 387 DX instructions with the equivalent operations executed on an 8-MHz 80287. As indicated in the table, the 33-MHz 387 DX NPX provides about 10 to 12 times the performance of an 8-MHz 80287 NPX. A 33-MHz 387 DX multiplies 32-bit and 64-bit floating-point numbers in about 0.8 and 1.4 microseconds, respectively. Of course, the actual performance of the NPX in a given system depends on the characteristics of the individual application.

Although the performance figures shown in Table 1-1 refer to operations on real (floating-point) numbers, the 387 DX also manipulates fixed-point binary and decimal integers of up to 64 bits or 18 digits, respectively. The 387 DX can improve the speed of multiple-precision software algorithms for integer operations by 10 to 100 times.

Because the 387 DX NPX is an extension of the 386 DX CPU, no software overhead is incurred in setting up the NPX for computation. The 387 DX and 386 DX processors coordinate their activities in a manner transparent to software. Moreover, built-in coordination facilities allow the 386 DX CPU to proceed with other instructions while the 387 DX NPX is simultaneously executing numeric instructions. Programs can exploit this concurrency of execution to further increase system performance and throughput.

**Table 1-1. Numeric Processing Speed Comparisons**

| Floating-Point Instruction | | | Approximate Performance Ratios: 33 MHz 386™ DX/387™ DX ÷ 8 MHz 80286/80287 |
|---|---|---|---|
| FADD | ST, ST(i) | Addition | 12.5 |
| FDIV | dword_var | Division | 9.5 |
| FYL2X | stack (0), (1) assumed | Logarithm | 12.0 |
| FPATAX | stack (0) assumed | Arctangent | 5.3* |
| F2XM1 | stack (0) assumed | Exponentiation | 5.5* |

*The ration is higher if the operand is not in range of the 80287 instruction.

## 1.3 EASE OF USE

The 387 DX NPX offers more than raw execution speed for computation-intensive tasks. The 387 DX brings the functionality and power of accurate numeric computation into the hands of the general user. These features are available in most high-level languages available for the 386 DX.

Like the 8087 and 80287 that preceded it, the 387 DX is explicitly designed to deliver stable, accurate results when programmed using straightforward "pencil and paper" algorithms. The IEEE standard 754 specifically addresses this issue, recognizing the fundamental importance of making numeric computations both easy and safe to use.

For example, most computers can overflow when two single-precision floating-point numbers are multiplied together and then divided by a third, even if the final result is a perfectly valid 32-bit number. The 387 DX delivers the correctly rounded result. Other typical examples of undesirable machine behavior in straightforward calculations occur when computing financial rate of return, which involves the expression $(1 + i)^n$ or when solving for roots of a quadratic equation:

$$\frac{-b \pm \sqrt{b^2 - 4ac}}{2a}$$

If a does not equal 0, the formula is numerically unstable when the roots are nearly coincident or when their magnitudes are wildly different. The formula is also vulnerable to spurious over/underflows when the coefficients a, b, and c are all very big or all very tiny. When single-precision (4-byte) floating-point coefficients are given as data and the formula is evaluated in the 387 DX's normal way, keeping all intermediate results in its stack, the 387 DX produces impeccable single-precision roots. This happens because, by default and with no effort on the programmer's part, the 387 DX evaluates all those subexpressions with so much extra precision and range as to overwhelm any threat to numerical integrity.

If double-precision data and results were at issue, a better formula would have to be used, and once again the 387 DX's default evaluation of that formula would provide substantially enhanced numerical integrity over mere double-precision evaluation.

On most machines, straightforward algorithms will not deliver consistently correct results (and will not indicate when they are incorrect). To obtain correct results on traditional machines under all conditions usually requires sophisticated numerical techniques that are foreign to most programmers. General application programmers using straightforward algorithms will produce much more reliable programs using the 387 DX. This simple fact greatly reduces the software investment required to develop safe, accurate computation-based products.

Beyond traditional numerics support for scientific applications, the 387 DX has built-in facilities for commercial computing. It can process decimal numbers of up to 18 digits without round-off errors, performing *exact arithmetic* on integers as large as $2^{64}$ or $10^{18}$. Exact arithmetic is vital in accounting applications where rounding errors may introduce monetary losses that cannot be reconciled.

The NPX contains a number of optional facilities that can be invoked by sophisticated users. These advanced features include directed rounding, gradual underflow, and programmed exception-handling facilities.

These automatic exception-handling facilities permit a high degree of flexibility in numeric processing software, without burdening the programmer. While performing numeric calculations, the NPX automatically detects exception conditions that can potentially damage a calculation (for example, $X \div 0$ or $\sqrt{X}$ when $X < 0$). By default, on-chip exception logic handles these exceptions so that a reasonable result is produced and execution may proceed without program interruption. Alternatively, the NPX can signal the CPU, invoking a software exception handler to provide special results whenever various types of exceptions are detected.

## 1.4 APPLICATIONS

The 386 DX's versatility and performance make it appropriate to a broad array of numeric applications. In general, applications that exhibit any of the following characteristics can benefit by implementing numeric processing on the 387 DX:

- Numeric data vary over a wide range of values, or include nonintegral values.

- Algorithms produce very large or very small intermediate results.

- Computations must be very precise; i.e., a large number of significant digits must be maintained.

- Performance requirements exceed the capacity of traditional microprocessors.

- Consistently safe, reliable results must be delivered using a programming staff that is not expert in numerical techniques.

Note also that the 387 DX can reduce software development costs and improve the performance of systems that use not only real numbers, but operate on multiprecision binary or decimal integer values as well.

A few examples, which show how the 387 DX might be used in specific numerics applications, are described below. In many cases, these types of systems have been implemented in the past with minicomputers or small mainframe computers. The advent of the 387 DX brings the size and cost savings of microprocessor technology to these applications for the first time.

- Business data processing — The NPX's ability to accept decimal operands and produce *exact* decimal results of up to 18 digits greatly simplifies accounting programming. Financial calculations that use power functions can take advantage of the 387 DX's exponentiation and logarithmic instructions. Many business software packages can benefit from the speed and accuracy of the 387 DX; for example, Lotus* 1-2-3*, Multiplan*, SuperCalc*, and Framework*.

- Simulation — The large (32-bit) memory space of the 386 DX coupled with the raw speed of the 386 DX and 387 DX processors make 386 DX/387 DX microsystems suitable for attacking large simulation problems, which heretofore could only be executed on expensive mini and mainframe computers. For example, complex electronic circuit simulations using SPICE can now be performed on a microcomputer, the 386 DX/387 DX. Simulation of mechanical systems using finite element analysis can employ more elements, resulting in more detailed analysis or simulation of larger systems.

- Graphics transformations — The 387 DX can be used in graphics terminals to locally perform many functions that normally demand the attention of a main computer; these include rotation, scaling, and interpolation. By also using an 82786 Graphics Display Controller to perform high-speed drawing and window management, very powerful and highly self-sufficient terminals can be built from a relatively small number of 386 DX family parts.

- Process control — The 387 DX solves dynamic range problems automatically, and its extended precision allows control functions to be fine-tuned for more accurate and efficient performance. Control algorithms implemented with the NPX also contribute to improved reliability and safety, while the 387 DX's speed can be exploited in real-time operations.

- Computer numerical control (CNC) — The 387 DX can move and position machine tool heads with accuracy in real-time. Axis positioning also benefits from the hardware trigonometric support provided by the 387 DX.

- Robotics — Coupling small size and modest power requirements with powerful computational abilities, the 387 DX is ideal for on-board six-axis positioning.

- Navigation — Very small, lightweight, and accurate inertial guidance systems can be implemented with the 387 DX. Its built-in trigonometric functions can speed and simplify the calculation of position from bearing data.

- Data acquisition — The 387 DX can be used to scan, scale, and reduce large quantities of data as it is collected, thereby lowering storage requirements and time required to process the data for analysis.

The preceding examples are oriented toward *traditional* numerics applications. There are, in addition, many other types of systems that do not appear to the end user as *computational*, but can employ the 387 DX to advantage. Indeed, the 387 DX presents the imaginative system designer with an opportunity similar to that created by the introduction of the microprocessor itself. Many applications can be viewed as numerically-based if sufficient computational power is available to support this view (e.g., character generation for a laser printer). This is analogous to the thousands of successful products that have been built around "buried" microprocessors, even though the products themselves bear little resemblance to computers.

## 1.5 UPGRADABILITY

The architecture of the 386 DX CPU is specifically adapted to allow easy upgradability to use an 387 DX, simply by plugging in the 387 DX NPX. For this reason, designers of 386 DX systems may wish to incorporate the 387 DX NPX into their designs in order to offer two levels of price and performance at little additional cost.

Two features of the 386 DX CPU make the design and support of upgradable 386 DX systems particularly simple:

- The 386 DX can be programmed to recognize the presence of an 387 DX NPX; that is, software can recognize whether it is running on an 386 DX with or without an 387 DX NPX.

- After determining whether the 387 DX NPX is available, the 386 DX CPU can be instructed to let the NPX execute all numeric instructions. If an 387 DX NPX is not available, the 386 DX CPU can emulate all 387 DX numeric instructions in software. This emulation is completely transparent to the application software — the same object code may be used by 386 DX systems both with and without an 387 DX NPX. No relinking or recompiling of application software is necessary; the same code will simply execute faster with the 387 DX NPX than without.

To facilitate this design of upgradable 386 DX systems, Intel provides a software emulator for the 387 DX that provides the functional equivalent of the 387 DX hardware, implemented in software on the 386 DX. Except for timing, the operation of this 387 DX emulator (EMUL387) is the same as for the 387 DX NPX hardware. When the emulator is combined as part of the systems software, the 386 DX system with 387 DX emulation and the 386 DX with 387 DX hardware are virtually indistinguishable to an application program. This capability makes it easy for software developers to maintain a single set of programs for both systems. System manufacturers can offer the NPX as a simple plug-in performance option without necessitating any changes in the user's software.

## 1.6 PROGRAMMING INTERFACE

The 386 DX/387 DX pair is programmed as a single processor; all of the 387 DX registers appear to a programmer as extensions of the basic 386 DX register set. The 386 DX has a class of instructions known as ESCAPE instructions, all having a common format. These ESC instructions are numeric instructions for the 387 DX NPX. These numeric instructions for the 387 DX are simply encoded into the instruction stream along with 386 DX instructions.

All of the CPU memory-addressing modes may be used in programming the NPX, allowing convenient access to record structures, numeric arrays, and other memory-based data structures. All of the memory management and protection features of the CPU (both paging and segmentation) are extended to the NPX as well.

Numeric processing in the 387 DX centers around the NPX register stack. Programmers can treat these eight 80-bit registers either as a fixed register set, with instructions operating on explicitly-designated registers, or as a classical stack, with instructions operating on the top one or two stack elements.

Internally, the 387 DX holds all numbers in a uniform 80-bit extended format. Operands that may be represented in memory as 16-, 32-, or 64-bit integers, 32-, 64-, or 80-bit floating-point numbers, or 18-digit packed BCD numbers, are automatically converted into extended format as they are loaded into the NPX registers. Computation results are subsequently converted back into one of these destination data formats when they are stored into memory from the NPX registers.

Table 1-2 lists each of the seven data types supported by the 387 DX, showing the data format for each type. All operands are stored in memory with the least significant digits starting at the initial (lowest) memory address. Numeric instructions access and store memory operands using only this initial address. For maximum system performance, all operands should start at memory addresses divisible by four.

Table 1-3 lists the 387 DX instructions by class. No special programming tools are necessary to use the 387 DX, because all of the NPX instructions and data types are directly supported by the ASM386 Assembler, by high-level languages from Intel, and by assemblers and compilers produced by many independent software vendors. Software routines for the 387 DX may be written in ASM386 Assembler or any of the following higher-level languages from Intel:

PL/M-386
C-386
FORTRAN-386
ADA-386

### Table 1-2. Numeric Data Types

| Data Type | Bits | Significant Digits (Decimal) | Approximate Range (Decimal) |
|---|---|---|---|
| Word integer | 16 | 4 | $-32{,}768 \leq X \leq +32{,}767$ |
| Short integer | 32 | 9 | $-2 \times 10^9 \leq X \leq +2 \times 10^9$ |
| Long integer | 64 | 18 | $-9 \times 10^{18} \leq X \leq +9 \times 10^{18}$ |
| Packed decimal | 80 | 18 | $-99...99 \leq X \leq +99...99$ (18 digits) |
| Single real | 32 | 6-7 | $1.18 \times 10^{-38} \leq |X| \leq 3.40 \times 10^{38}$ |
| Double real | 64 | 15-16 | $2.23 \times 10^{-308} \leq |X| \leq 1.80 \times 10^{308}$ |
| Extended real* | 80 | 19 | $3.30 \times 10^{-4932} \leq |X| \leq 1.21 \times 10^{4932}$ |

*Equivalent to *double extended* format of IEEE Std 754.

In addition, all of the development tools supporting the 8086/8087 and 80286/80287 can also be used to develop software for the 386 DX/387 DX.

All of these high-level languages provide programmers with access to the computational power and speed of the 387 DX without requiring an understanding of the architecture of the 386 DX and 387 DX chips. Such architectural considerations as concurrency and synchronization are handled automatically by these high-level languages. For the ASM386 programmer, specific rules for handling these issues are discussed in a later section of this manual.

The following operating systems are known or expected to support the 387 DX: RMX-286/386, MS-DOS, Xenix-286/386, and Unix-286/386. Advanced in-circuit debugging support is provided by ICE-386.

**Table 1-3. Principal NPX Instructions**

| Class | Instruction Types |
|---|---|
| Data Transfer | Load (all data types), Store (all data types), Exchange |
| Arithmetic | Add, Subtract, Multiply, Divide, Subtract Reversed, Divide Reversed, Square Root, Scale, Remainder, Integer Part, Change Sign, Absolute Value, Extract |
| Comparison | Compare, Examine, Test |
| Transcendental | Tangent, Arctangent, Sine, Cosine, Sine and Cosine, $2^x - 1$, Y $\bullet$ $Log_2(X)$, Y $\bullet$ $Log_2 (X+1)$ |
| Constants | 0, 1, $\pi$, $Log_{10}2$, $Log_e 2$, $Log_2 10$, $Log_2 e$ |
| Processor Control | Load Control Word, Store Control Word, Store Status Word, Load Environment, Store Environment, Save, Restore, Clear Exceptions, Initialize |

# 387™ DX Math Coprocessor

2

# CHAPTER 2
# 387™ DX MATH COPROCESSOR

To the programmer, the 387™ DX Math Coprocessor appears as a set of additional registers, data types, and instructions—all of which complement those of the 386™ DX. Refer to Chapter 4 for detailed explanations of the 387 DX instruction set. This chapter explains the new registers and data types that the 387 DX brings to the architecture of the 386 DX.

## 2.1 387™ DX REGISTERS

The additional registers consist of

- Eight individually-addressable 80-bit numeric registers, organized as a register stack

- Three sixteen-bit registers containing:

  the NPX status word
  the NPX control word
  the tag word

- Two 48-bit registers containing pointers to the current instruction and operand (these registers are actually located in the 386 DX)

All of the NPX numeric instructions focus on the contents of these NPX registers.

## 2.1.1 The NPX Register Stack

The 387 DX register stack is shown in Figure 2-1. Each of the eight numeric registers in the 387 DX's register stack is 80 bits wide and is divided into fields corresponding to the NPX's extended real data type.

Numeric instructions address the data registers relative to the register on the top of the stack. At any point in time, this top-of-stack register is indicated by the TOP (stack TOP) field in the NPX status word. Load or push operations decrement TOP by one and load a value into the new top register. A store-and-pop operation stores the value from the current TOP register and then increments TOP by one. Like 386 DX stacks in memory, the 387 DX register stack grows *down* toward lower-addressed registers.

Many numeric instructions have several addressing modes that permit the programmer to implicitly operate on the top of the stack, or to explicitly operate on specific registers relative to the TOP. The ASM386 Assembler supports these register addressing modes, using the expression ST(0), or simply ST, to represent the current Stack Top and ST($i$) to specify the $i$th register from TOP in the stack ($0 \leq i \leq 7$). For example, if TOP contains 011B (register 3 is the top of the stack), the following statement would add the contents of two registers in the stack (registers 3 and 5):

```
FADD   ST, ST(2)
```

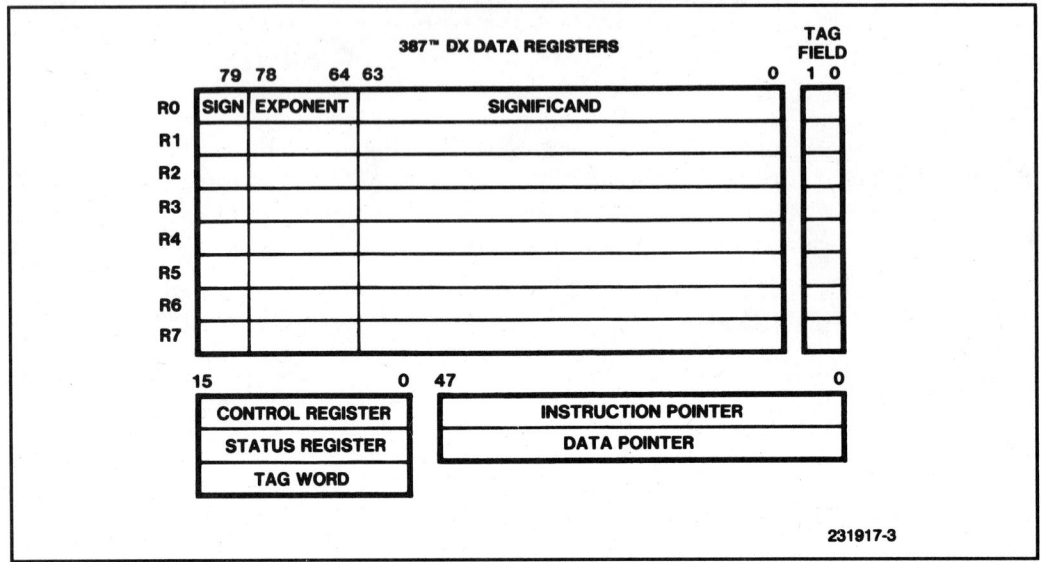

**Figure 2-1. 387™ Register Set**

The stack organization and top-relative addressing of the numeric registers simplify sub-routine programming by allowing routines to pass parameters on the register stack. By using the stack to pass parameters rather than using "dedicated" registers, calling routines gain more flexibility in how they use the stack. As long as the stack is not full, each routine simply loads the parameters onto the stack before calling a particular subroutine to perform a numeric calculation. The subroutine then addresses its parameters as ST, ST(1), etc., even though TOP may, for example, refer to physical register 3 in one invocation and physical register 5 in another.

## 2.1.2 The NPX Status Word

The 16-bit status word shown in Figure 2-2 reflects the overall state of the 387 DX. This status word may be stored into memory using the FSTSW/FNSTSW, FSTENV/ FNSTENV, and FSAVE/FNSAVE instructions, and can be transferred into the 386 DX AX register with the FSTSW AX/FNSTSW AX instructions, allowing the NPX status to be inspected by the CPU.

The B-bit (bit 15) is included for 8087 compatibility only. It reflects the contents of the ES bit (bit 7 of the status word), not the status of the BUSY# output of the 387 DX.

The four NPX condition code bits ($C_3$-$C_0$) are similar to the flags in a CPU: the 387 DX updates these bits to reflect the outcome of arithmetic operations. The effect of these instructions on the condition code bits is summarized in Table 2-1. These condition code bits are used principally for conditional branching. The FSTSW AX instruction stores the NPX status word directly into the CPU AX register, allowing these condition codes

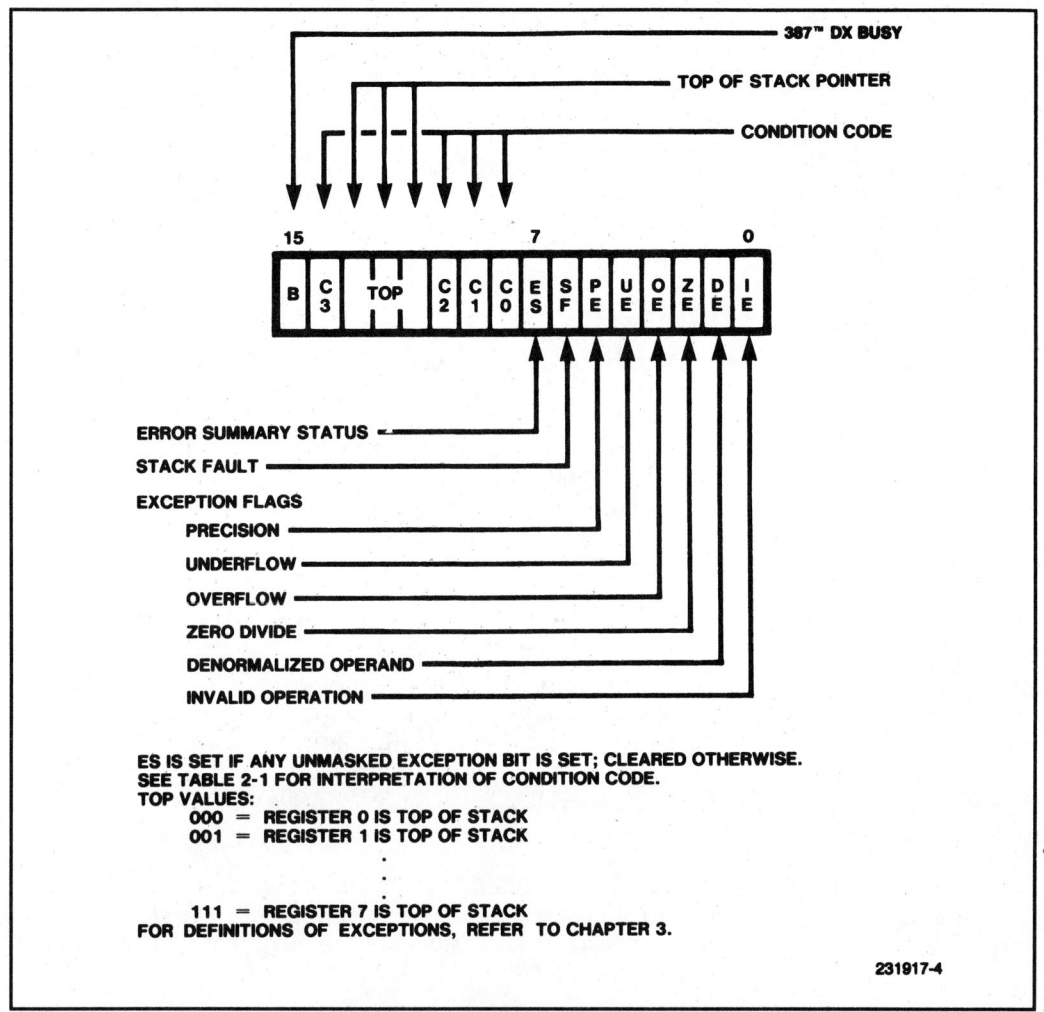

ES IS SET IF ANY UNMASKED EXCEPTION BIT IS SET; CLEARED OTHERWISE.
SEE TABLE 2-1 FOR INTERPRETATION OF CONDITION CODE.
TOP VALUES:
    000 = REGISTER 0 IS TOP OF STACK
    001 = REGISTER 1 IS TOP OF STACK
         .
         .
         .
    111 = REGISTER 7 IS TOP OF STACK
FOR DEFINITIONS OF EXCEPTIONS, REFER TO CHAPTER 3.

231917-4

**Figure 2-2.  387™ DX Status Word**

to be inspected efficiently by 386 DX code. The 386 DX SAHF instruction can copy $C_3$-$C_0$ directly to 386 DX flag bits to simplify conditional branching. Table 2-2 shows the mapping of these bits to the 386 DX flag bits.

Bits 12-14 of the status word point to the 387 DX register that is the current Top of Stack (TOP). The significance of the stack top has been described in the prior section on the register stack.

Figure 2-2 shows the six exception flags in bits 0-5 of the status word. Bit 7 is the exception summary status (ES) bit. ES is set if any unmasked exception bits are set, and is cleared otherwise. If this bit is set, the ERROR# signal is asserted. Bits 0-5 indicate whether the NPX has detected one of six possible exception conditions since these status bits were last cleared or reset. They are "sticky" bits, and can only be cleared by the instructions FINIT, FCLEX, FLDENV, FSAVE, and FRSTOR.

Bit 6 is the stack fault (SF) bit. This bit distinguishes invalid operations due to stack overflow or underflow from other kinds of invalid operations. When SF is set, bit 9 ($C_1$) distinguishes between stack overflow ($C_1 = 1$) and underflow ($C_1 = 0$).

## 2.1.3 Control Word

The NPX provides the programmer with several processing options, which are selected by loading a word from memory into the control word. Figure 2-3 shows the format and encoding of the fields in the control word.

The low-order byte of this control word configures the 387 DX exception masking. Bits 0–5 of the control word contain individual masks for each of the six exception conditions recognized by the 387 DX. The high-order byte of the control word configures the 387 DX processing options, including

- Precision control

- Rounding control

The precision-control bits (bits 8–9) can be used to set the 387 DX internal operating precision at less than the default precision (64-bit significand). These control bits can be used to provide compatibility with the earlier-generation arithmetic processors having less precision than the 387 DX. The precision-control bits affect the results of only the following five arithmetic instructions: ADD, SUB(R), MUL, DIV(R), and SQRT. No other operations are affected by PC.

The rounding-control bits (bits 10–11) provide for the common round-to-nearest mode, as well as directed rounding and true chop. Rounding control affects only the arithmetic instructions (refer to Chapter 3 for lists of arithmetic and nonarithmetic instructions).

## 2.1.4 The NPX Tag Word

The tag word indicates the contents of each register in the register stack, as shown in Figure 2-4. The tag word is used by the NPX itself to distinguish between empty and nonempty register locations. Programmers of exception handlers may use this tag information to check the contents of a numeric register without performing complex decoding of the actual data in the register. The tag values from the tag word correspond to physical registers 0–7. Programmers must use the current top-of-stack (TOP) pointer stored in the NPX status word to associate these tag values with the relative stack registers ST(0) through ST(7).

The exact values of the tags are generated during execution of the FSTENV and FSAVE instructions according to the actual contents of the nonempty stack locations. During execution of other instructions, the 387 DX updates the TW only to indicate whether a stack location is empty or nonempty.

### Table 2-1. Condition Code Interpretation

| Instruction | C0 (S) | C3 (Z) | C1 (A) | C2 (C) |
|---|---|---|---|---|
| FPREM, FPREM1 | Three least significant bits of quotient | | | Reduction<br>0 = complete<br>1 = incomplete |
| | Q2 | Q0 | Q1<br>or O/U# | |
| FCOM, FCOMP, FCOMPP, FTST, FUCOM, FUCOMP, FUCOMPP, FICOM, FICOMP | Result of comparison | | Zero<br>or O/U# | Operand is not comparable |
| FXAM | Operand class | | Sign<br>or O/U# | Operand class |
| FCHS, FABS, FXCH, FINCSTP, FDECSTP, Constant loads, FXTRACT, FLD, FILD, FBLD, FSTP (ext real) | UNDEFINED | | Zero<br>or O/U# | UNDEFINED |
| FIST, FBSTP, FRNDINT, FST, FSTP, FADD, FMUL, FDIV, FDIVR, FSUB, FSUBR, FSCALE, FSQRT, FPATAN, F2XM1, FYL2X, FYL2XP1 | UNDEFINED | | Roundup<br>or O/U# | UNDEFINED |
| FPTAN, FSIN, FCOS, FSINCOS | UNDEFINED | | Roundup<br>or O/U#<br>undefined<br>if C2 = 1 | Reduction<br>0 = complete<br>1 = incomplete |
| FLDENV, FRSTOR | Each bit loaded from memory | | | |
| FLDCW, FSTENV, FSTCW, FSTSW, FCLEX, FINIT, FSAVE | UNDEFINED | | | |

O/U#          When both IE and SF bits of status word are set, indicating a stack exception, this bit distinguishes between stack overflow (C1 = 1) and underflow (C1 = 0).

Reduction     If FPREM and FPREM1 produces a remainder that is less than the modulus, reduction is complete. When reduction is incomplete the value at the top of the stack is a partial remainder, which can be used as input to further reduction. For FPTAN, FSIN, FCOS, and FSINCOS, the reduction bit is set if the operand at the top of the stack is too large. In this case the original operand remains at the top of the stack.

Roundup       When the PE bit of the status word is set, this bit indicates whether the last rounding in the instruction was upward.

UNDEFINED     Do not rely on finding any specific value in these bits.

**Table 2-2. Correspondence between 387™ DX and 386™ DX Flag Bits**

| 387™ DX Flag | 386™ DX Flag |
|:---:|:---:|
| $C_0$ | CF |
| $C_1$ | (none) |
| $C_2$ | PF |
| $C_3$ | ZF |

## 2.1.5 The NPX Instruction and Data Pointers

The instruction and data pointers provide support for programmed exception-handlers. These registers are actually located in the 386 DX, but appear to be located in the 387 DX because they are accessed by the ESC instructions FLDENV, FSTENV, FSAVE, and FRSTOR. Whenever the 386 DX decodes an ESC instruction, it saves the instruction address, the operand address (if present), and the instruction opcode.

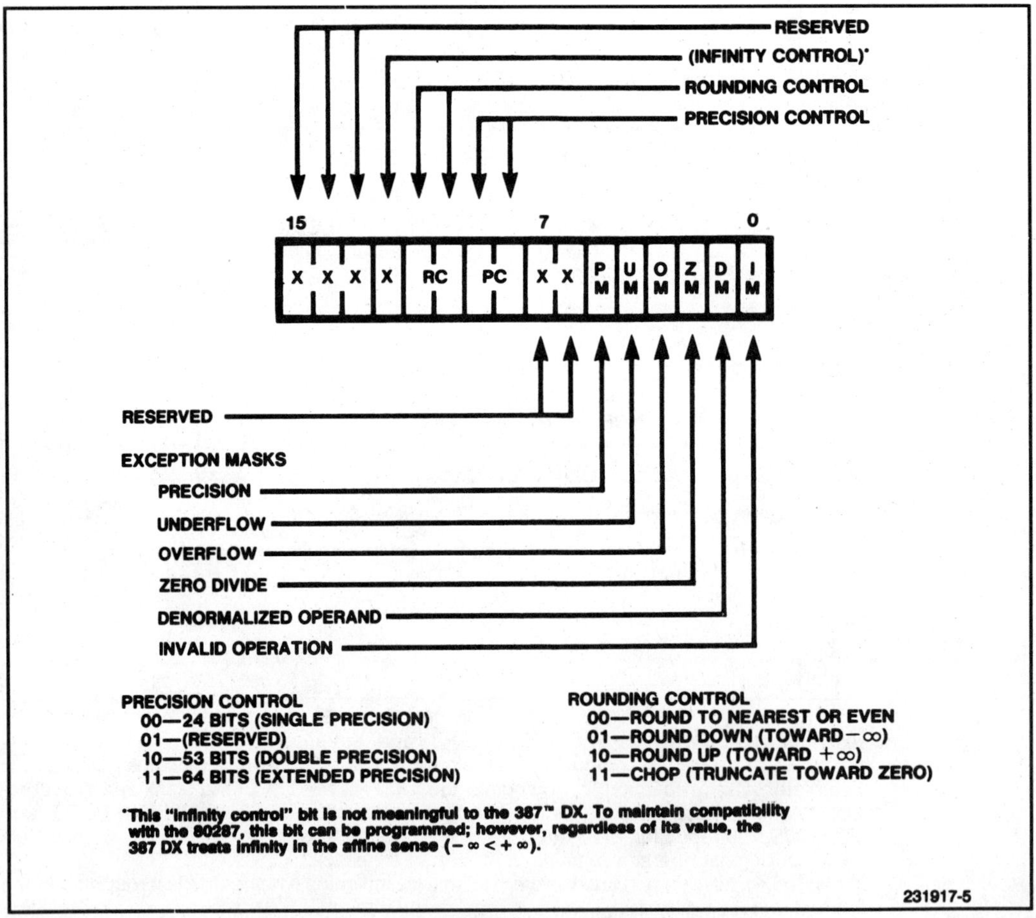

RESERVED
(INFINITY CONTROL)*
ROUNDING CONTROL
PRECISION CONTROL

15    7    0

| X | X | X | X | RC | PC | X | X | P M | U M | O M | Z M | D M | I M |

RESERVED

EXCEPTION MASKS

PRECISION
UNDERFLOW
OVERFLOW
ZERO DIVIDE
DENORMALIZED OPERAND
INVALID OPERATION

PRECISION CONTROL
00—24 BITS (SINGLE PRECISION)
01—(RESERVED)
10—53 BITS (DOUBLE PRECISION)
11—64 BITS (EXTENDED PRECISION)

ROUNDING CONTROL
00—ROUND TO NEAREST OR EVEN
01—ROUND DOWN (TOWARD $-\infty$)
10—ROUND UP (TOWARD $+\infty$)
11—CHOP (TRUNCATE TOWARD ZERO)

*This "infinity control" bit is not meaningful to the 387™ DX. To maintain compatibility with the 80287, this bit can be programmed; however, regardless of its value, the 387 DX treats infinity in the affine sense ($-\infty < +\infty$).

231917-5

**Figure 2-3. 387™ DX Control Word Format**

When stored in memory, the instruction and data pointers appear in one of four formats, depending on the operating mode of the 386 DX (protected mode or real-address mode) and depending on the operand-size attribute in effect (32-bit operand or 16-bit operand). When the 386 DX is in virtual-8086 mode, the real-address mode formats are used.

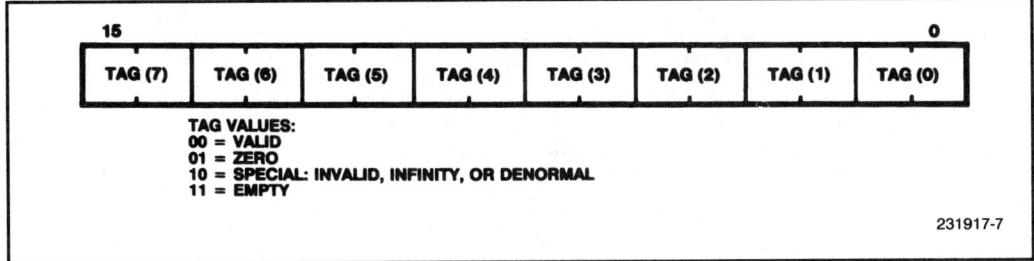

**Figure 2-4. 387™ DX Tag Word Format**

Figures 2-5 through 2-8 show these pointers as they are stored following an FSTENV instruction.

The FSTENV and FSAVE instructions store this data into memory, allowing exception handlers to determine the precise nature of any numeric exceptions that may be encountered.

The instruction address saved in the 386 DX (as in the 80287) points to any prefixes that preceded the instruction. This is different from the 8087, for which the instruction address points only to the ESC instruction opcode.

Note that the processor control instructions FINIT, FLDCW, FSTCW, FSTSW, FCLEX, FSTENV, FLDENV, FSAVE, FRSTOR, and FWAIT do not affect the data pointer. Note also that, except for the instructions just mentioned, the value of the data pointer is *undefined* if the prior ESC instruction did not have a memory operand.

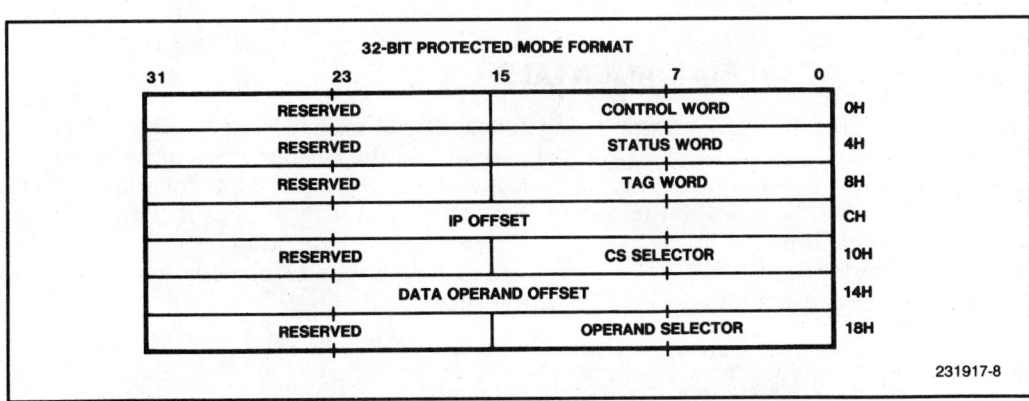

**Figure 2-5. Protected Mode 387™ DX Instruction and Data Pointer Image in Memory, 32-Bit Format**

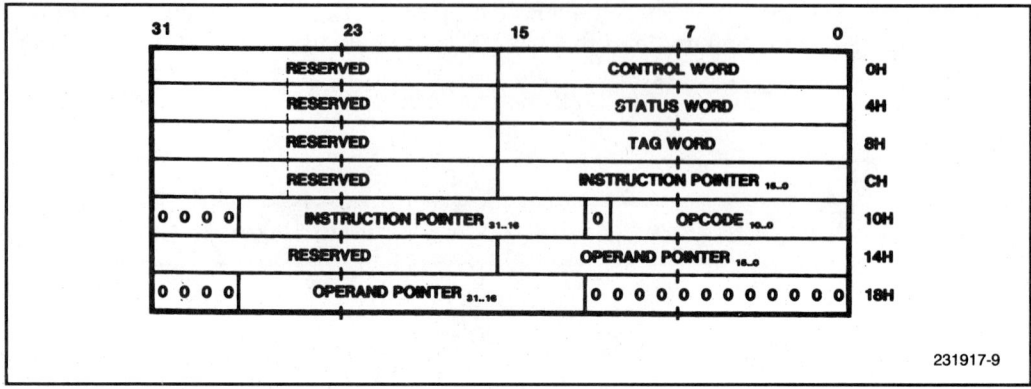

**Figure 2-6. Real Mode 387™ DX Instruction and Data Pointer
Image in Memory, 32-Bit Format**

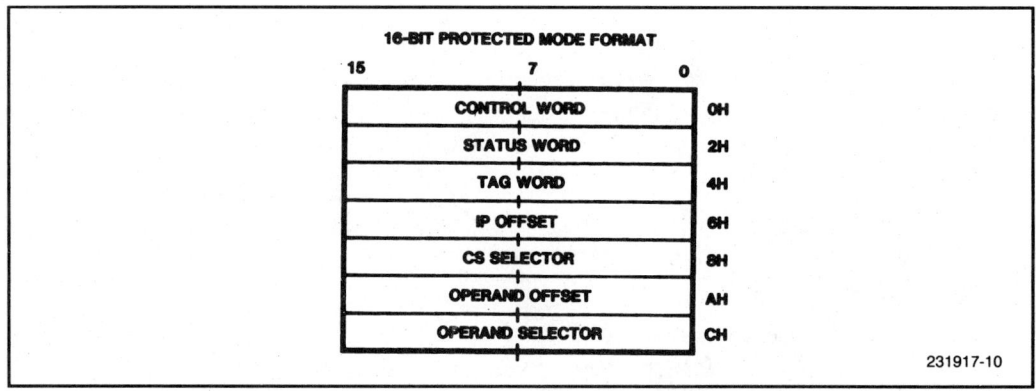

**Figure 2-7. Protected Mode 387™ DX Instruction and Data Pointer Image in Memory,
16-Bit Format**

## 2.2 COMPUTATION FUNDAMENTALS

This section covers 387 DX programming concepts that are common to all applications.
It describes the 387 DX's internal number system and the various types of numbers that
can be employed in NPX programs. The most commonly used options for rounding and
precision (selected by fields in the control word) are described, with exhaustive coverage
of less frequently used facilities deferred to later sections. Exception conditions that may
arise during execution of NPX instructions are also described along with the options that
are available for responding to these exceptions.

### 2.2.1 Number System

The system of real numbers that people use for pencil and paper calculations is concep-
tually infinite and continuous. There is no upper or lower limit to the magnitude of the
numbers one can employ in a calculation, or to the precision (number of significant

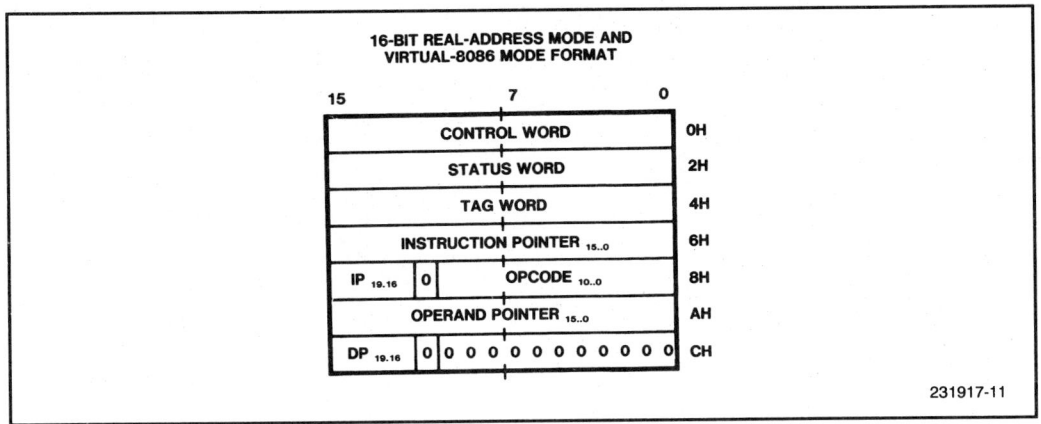

**16-BIT REAL-ADDRESS MODE AND
VIRTUAL-8086 MODE FORMAT**

| 15 | 7 | 0 | |
|---|---|---|---|
| CONTROL WORD | | | 0H |
| STATUS WORD | | | 2H |
| TAG WORD | | | 4H |
| INSTRUCTION POINTER $_{15..0}$ | | | 6H |
| IP $_{19.16}$ | 0 | OPCODE $_{10..0}$ | 8H |
| OPERAND POINTER $_{15..0}$ | | | AH |
| DP $_{19.16}$ | 0 0 0 0 0 0 0 0 0 0 0 0 | | CH |

231917-11

**Figure 2-8. Real Mode 387™ DX Instruction and Data Pointer Image in Memory,
16-Bit Format**

digits) that the numbers can represent. When considering any real number, there are always arbitrarily many numbers both larger and smaller. There are also arbitrarily many numbers between (i.e., with more significant digits than) any two real numbers. For example, between 2.5 and 2.6 are 2.51, 2.5897, 2.500001, etc.

While ideally it would be desirable for a computer to be able to operate on the entire real number system, in practice this is not possible. Computers, no matter how large, ultimately have fixed-size registers and memories that limit the system of numbers that can be accommodated. These limitations determine both the range and the precision of numbers. The result is a set of numbers that is finite and discrete, rather than infinite and continuous. This sequence is a subset of the real numbers that is designed to form a useful *approximation* of the real number system.

Figure 2-9 superimposes the basic 387 DX real number system on a real number line (decimal numbers are shown for clarity, although the 387 DX actually represents numbers in binary). The dots indicate the subset of real numbers the 387 DX can represent as data and final results of calculations. The 387 DX's range of double-precision, normalized numbers is approximately $\pm 2.23 \times 10^{-308}$ to $\pm 1.80 \times 10^{308}$. Applications that are required to deal with data and final results outside this range are rare. For reference, the range of the IBM System 370* is about $\pm 0.54 \times 10^{-78}$ to $\pm 0.72 \times 10^{76}$.

The finite spacing in Figure 2-9 illustrates that the NPX can represent a great many, but not all, of the real numbers in its range. There is always a gap between two adjacent 387 DX numbers, and it is possible for the result of a calculation to fall in this space. When this occurs, the NPX rounds the true result to a number that it can represent. Thus, a real number that requires more digits than the 387 DX can accommodate (e.g., a 20-digit number) is represented with some loss of accuracy. Notice also that the 387 DX's representable numbers are not distributed evenly along the real number line. In fact, an equal number of representable numbers exists between successive powers of 2 (i.e., as many representable numbers exist between 2 and 4 as between 65,536 and 131,072).

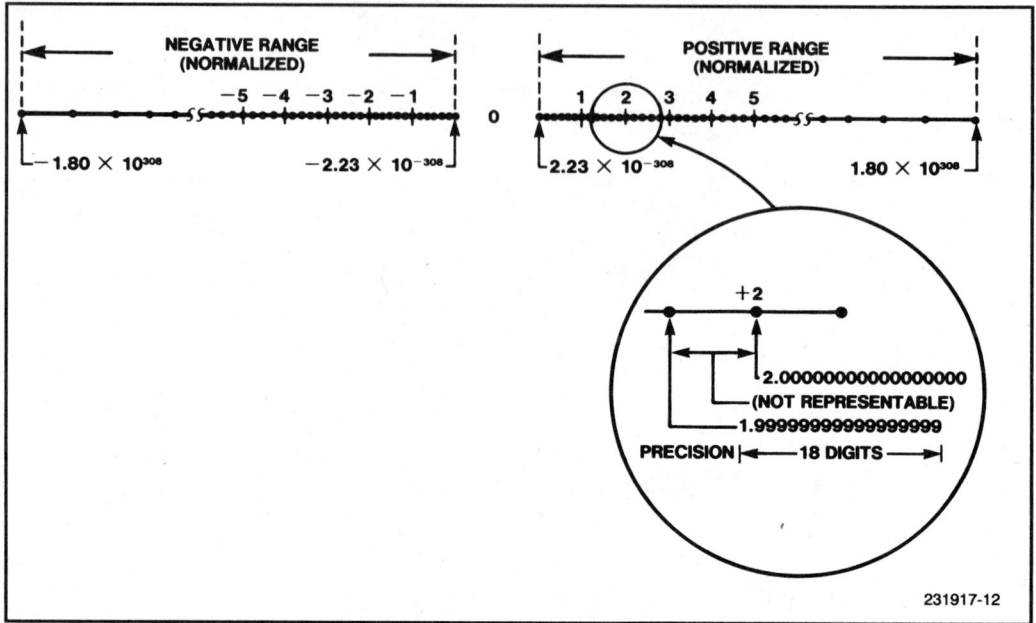

**Figure 2-9. 387™ DX Double-Precision Number System**

Therefore, the gaps between representable numbers are larger as the numbers increase in magnitude. All integers in the range $\pm 2^{64}$ (approximately $\pm 10^{18}$), however, are exactly representable.

In its internal operations, the 387 DX actually employs a number system that is a substantial superset of that shown in Figure 2-9. The internal format (called extended real) extends the 387 DX's range to about $\pm 3.30 \times 10^{-4932}$ to $\pm 1.21 \times 10^{4932}$, and its precision to about 19 (equivalent decimal) digits. This format is designed to provide extra range and precision for constants and intermediate results, and is not normally intended for data or final results.

From a practical standpoint, the 387 DX's set of real numbers is sufficiently large and dense so as not to limit the vast majority of microprocessor applications. Compared to most computers, including mainframes, the NPX provides a very good approximation of the real number system. It is important to remember, however, that it is not an exact representation, and that arithmetic on real numbers is inherently approximate.

Conversely, and equally important, the 387 DX *does* perform exact arithmetic on integer operands. That is, if an operation on two integers is valid and produces a result that is in range, the result is exact. For example, $4 \div 2$ yields an exact integer, $1 \div 3$ does not, and $2^{40} \times 2^{30} + 1$ does not, because the result requires greater than 64 bits of precision.

## 2.2.2 Data Types and Formats

The 387 DX recognizes seven numeric data types for memory-based values, divided into three classes: binary integers, packed decimal integers, and binary reals. A later section describes how these formats are stored in memory (the sign is always located in the highest-addressed byte).

Figure 2-10 summarizes the format of each data type. In the figure, the most significant digits of all numbers (and fields within numbers) are the leftmost digits.

## 2.2.2.1 BINARY INTEGERS

The three binary integer formats are identical except for length, which governs the range that can be accommodated in each format. The leftmost bit is interpreted as the number's sign: 0 = positive and 1 = negative. Negative numbers are represented in standard

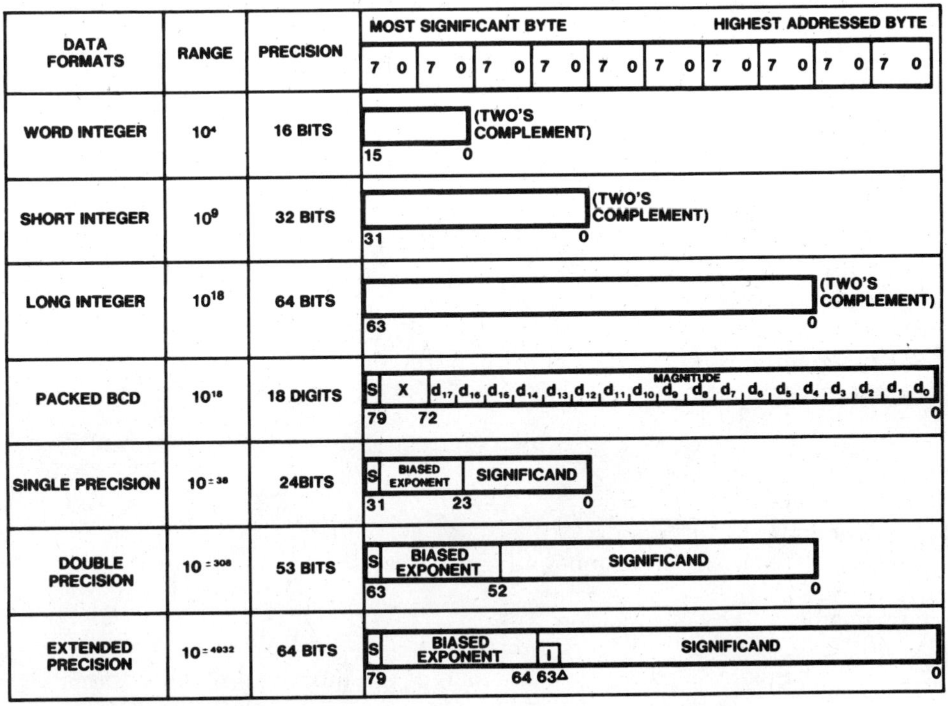

| DATA FORMATS | RANGE | PRECISION | MOST SIGNIFICANT BYTE — HIGHEST ADDRESSED BYTE |
|---|---|---|---|
| WORD INTEGER | $10^4$ | 16 BITS | (TWO'S COMPLEMENT)  15  0 |
| SHORT INTEGER | $10^9$ | 32 BITS | (TWO'S COMPLEMENT)  31  0 |
| LONG INTEGER | $10^{18}$ | 64 BITS | (TWO'S COMPLEMENT)  63  0 |
| PACKED BCD | $10^{18}$ | 18 DIGITS | S  X  $d_{17}$ $d_{16}$ $d_{15}$ $d_{14}$ $d_{13}$ $d_{12}$ $d_{11}$ $d_{10}$ $d_9$ $d_8$ $d_7$ $d_6$ $d_5$ $d_4$ $d_3$ $d_2$ $d_1$ $d_0$ MAGNITUDE  79  72  0 |
| SINGLE PRECISION | $10^{\pm 38}$ | 24 BITS | S  BIASED EXPONENT  SIGNIFICAND  31  23  0 |
| DOUBLE PRECISION | $10^{\pm 308}$ | 53 BITS | S  BIASED EXPONENT  SIGNIFICAND  63  52  0 |
| EXTENDED PRECISION | $10^{\pm 4932}$ | 64 BITS | S  BIASED EXPONENT  I  SIGNIFICAND  79  64 63△  0 |

(1) S = SIGN BIT (0 = positive, 1 = negative)
(2) $d_n$ = DECIMAL DIGIT (TWO PER TYPE)
(3) X = BITS HAVE NO SIGNIFICANCE; 387™ DX IGNORES WHEN LOADING, ZEROS WHEN STORING
(4) △ = POSITION OF IMPLICIT BINARY POINT
(5) I = INTEGER BIT OF SIGNIFICAND; STORED IN TEMPORARY REAL, IMPLICIT IN SINGLE AND DOUBLE PRECISION
(6) EXPONENT BIAS (NORMALIZED VALUES):
    SINGLE: 127 (7FH)
    DOUBLE: 1023 (3FFH)
    EXTENDED REAL: 16383 (3FFFH)
(7) PACKED BCD: $(-1)^S (D_{17}...D_0)$
(8) REAL: $(-1)^S (2^{E-BIAS}) (F_0 F_1...)$

231917-6

**Figure 2-10. 387™ DX Data Formats**

two's complement notation (the binary integers are the only 387 DX format to use two's complement). The quantity zero is represented with a positive sign (all bits are 0). The 387 DX word integer format is identical to the 16-bit signed integer data type of the 386 DX; the 387 DX short integer format is identical to the 32-bit signed integer data type of the 386 DX.

The binary integer formats exist in memory only. When used by the 387 DX, they are automatically converted to the 80-bit extended real format. All binary integers are exactly representable in the extended real format.

### 2.2.2.2 DECIMAL INTEGERS

Decimal integers are stored in packed decimal notation, with two decimal digits "packed" into each byte, except the leftmost byte, which carries the sign bit (0 = positive, 1 = negative). Negative numbers are not stored in two's complement form and are distinguished from positive numbers only by the sign bit. The most significant digit of the number is the leftmost digit. All digits must be in the range 0–9.

The decimal integer format exists in memory only. When used by the 387 DX, it is automatically converted to the 80-bit extended real format. All decimal integers are exactly representable in the extended real format.

### 2.2.2.3 REAL NUMBERS

The 387 DX represents real numbers of the form:

$$(-1)^s 2^E (b_{0_\Delta} b_1 b_2 b_3 .. b_{p-1})$$

...where...

    s = 0 or 1
    E = any integer between Emin and Emax, inclusive
    $b_i$ = 0 or 1
    p = number of bits of precision

Table 2-3 summarizes the parameters for each of the three real-number formats.

**Table 2-3. Summary of Format Parameters**

| Parameter | Format | | |
|---|---|---|---|
| | **Single** | **Double** | **Extended** |
| Format width in bits | 32 | 64 | 80 |
| p (bits of precision) | 24 | 53 | 64 |
| Exponent width in bits | 8 | 11 | 15 |
| Emax | +127 | +1023 | +16383 |
| Emin | −126 | −1022 | −16382 |
| Exponent bias | +127 | +1023 | +16383 |

The 387 DX stores real numbers in a three-field binary format that resembles scientific, or exponential, notation. The format consists of the following fields:

- The number's significant digits are held in the *significand* field, $b_0{}_\Delta b_1 b_2 b_3..b_{p-1}$. (The term "significand" is analogous to the term "mantissa" used to describe floating point numbers on some computers.)

- The *exponent* field, $e = E + bias$, locates the binary point within the significant digits (and therefore determines the number's magnitude). (The term "exponent" is analogous to the term "characteristic" used to describe floating point numbers on some computers.)

- The 1-bit *sign* field indicates whether the number is positive or negative. Negative numbers differ from positive numbers only in the sign bits of their significands.

Table 2-4 shows how the real number 178.125 (decimal) is stored in the 387 DX single real format. The table lists a progression of equivalent notations that express the same value to show how a number can be converted from one form to another. (The ASM386 and PL/M-386 language translators perform a similar process when they encounter programmer-defined real number constants.) Note that not every decimal fraction has an exact binary equivalent. The decimal number 1/10, for example, cannot be expressed exactly in binary (just as the number 1/3 cannot be expressed exactly in decimal). When a translator encounters such a value, it produces a rounded binary approximation of the decimal value.

**Table 2-4. Real Number Notation**

| Notation | Value | | |
|---|---|---|---|
| Ordinary Decimal | 178.125 | | |
| Scientific Decimal | $1_\Delta 78125E2$ | | |
| Scientific Binary | $1_\Delta 0110010001E111$ | | |
| Scientific Binary (Biased Exponent) | $1_\Delta 011001001E100000110$ | | |
| 387™ DX Single Format (Normalized) | **Sign** | **Biased Exponent** | **Significand** |
| | 0 | 10000110 | 01100100010000000000000 $1_\Delta$ (implicit) |

The NPX usually carries the digits of the significand in normalized form. This means that, except for the value zero, the significand contains an *integer bit* and *fraction bits* as follows:

$$1_\Delta fff...ff$$

where $_\Delta$ indicates an assumed binary point. The number of fraction bits varies according to the real format: 23 for single, 52 for double, and 63 for extended real. By normalizing real numbers so that their integer bit is always a 1, the 387 DX eliminates leading zeros in small values ($|X| < 1$). This technique maximizes the number of significant digits that can be accommodated in a significand of a given width. Note that, in the single and double formats, the integer bit is *implicit* and is not actually stored; the integer bit is physically present in the extended format only.

If one were to examine only the significand with its assumed binary point, all normalized real numbers would have values greater than or equal to 1 and less than 2. The exponent field locates the *actual* binary point in the significant digits. Just as in decimal scientific notation, a positive exponent has the effect of moving the binary point to the right, and a negative exponent effectively moves the binary point to the left, inserting leading zeros as necessary. An unbiased exponent of zero indicates that the position of the assumed binary point is also the position of the actual binary point. The exponent field, then, determines a real number's magnitude.

In order to simplify comparing real numbers (e.g., for sorting), the 387 DX stores exponents in a biased form. This means that a constant is added to the *true exponent* described above. As Table 2-3 shows, the value of this *bias* is different for each real format. It has been chosen so as to force the *biased exponent* to be a positive value. This allows two real numbers (of the same format and sign) to be compared as if they are unsigned binary integers. That is, when comparing them bitwise from left to right (beginning with the leftmost exponent bit), the first bit position that differs orders the numbers; there is no need to proceed further with the comparison. A number's true exponent can be determined simply by subtracting the bias value of its format.

The single and double real formats exist in memory only. If a number in one of these formats is loaded into an 387 DX register, it is automatically converted to extended format, the format used for all internal operations. Likewise, data in registers can be converted to single or double real for storage in memory. The extended real format may be used in memory also, typically to store intermediate results that cannot be held in registers.

Most applications should use the double format to store real-number data and results; it provides sufficient range and precision to return correct results with a minimum of programmer attention. The single real format is appropriate for applications that are constrained by memory, but it should be recognized that this format provides a smaller margin of safety. It is also useful for the debugging of algorithms, because roundoff problems will manifest themselves more quickly in this format. The extended real format should normally be reserved for holding intermediate results, loop accumulations, and constants. Its extra length is designed to shield final results from the effects of rounding and overflow/underflow in intermediate calculations. However, the range and precision of the double format are adequate for most microcomputer applications.

### 2.2.3 Rounding Control

Internally, the 387 DX employs three extra bits (guard, round, and sticky bits) that enable it to round numbers in accord with the infinitely precise true result of a computation; these bits are not accessible to programmers. Whenever the destination can represent the infinitely precise true result, the 387 DX delivers it. Rounding occurs in arithmetic and store operations when the format of the destination cannot exactly represent the infinitely precise true result. For example, a real number may be rounded if it is stored in a shorter real format, or in an integer format. Or, the infinitely precise true result may be rounded when it is returned to a register.

The NPX has four rounding modes, selectable by the RC field in the control word (see Figure 2-3). Given a true result $b$ that cannot be represented by the target data type, the 387 DX determines the two representable numbers $a$ and $c$ that most closely bracket $b$ in value ($a < b < c$). The processor then rounds (changes) $b$ to $a$ or to $c$ according to the mode selected by the RC field as shown in Table 2-5. Rounding introduces an error in a result that is less than one unit in the last place to which the result is rounded.

- "Round to nearest" is the default mode and is suitable for most applications; it provides the most accurate and statistically unbiased estimate of the true result.
- The "chop" or "round toward zero" mode is provided for integer arithmetic applications.
- "Round up" and "round down" are termed *directed rounding* and can be used to implement interval arithmetic. Interval arithmetic generates a certifiable result independent of the occurrence of rounding and other errors. The upper and lower bounds of an interval may be computed by executing an algorithm twice, rounding up in one pass and down in the other.

Rounding control affects only the arithmetic instructions (refer to Chapter 3 for lists of arithmetic and nonarithmetic instructions).

### 2.2.4 Precision Control

The 387 DX allows results to be calculated with either 64, 53, or 24 bits of precision in the significand as selected by the precision control (PC) field of the control word. The default setting, and the one that is best suited for most applications, is the full 64 bits of significance provided by the extended real format. The other settings are required by the IEEE 754 standard and are provided to obtain compatibility with the specifications of certain existing programming languages. Specifying less precision nullifies the advantages of the extended format's extended fraction length. When reduced precision is specified, the rounding of the fractional value clears the unused bits on the right to zeros. Precision control affects only the instructions FADD, FSUB, FMUL, FDIV, and FSQRT.

**Table 2-5. Rounding Modes**

| RC Field | Rounding Mode | Rounding Action |
|----------|---------------|-----------------|
| 00 | Round to nearest | Closer to $b$ of $a$ or $c$; if equally close, select even number (the one whose least significant bit is zero). |
| 01 | Round down (toward $-\infty$) | $a$ |
| 10 | Round up (toward $+\infty$) | $c$ |
| 11 | Chop (toward 0) | Smaller in magnitude of $a$ or $c$ |

**NOTE:** $a < b < c$; $a$ and $c$ are successive representable numbers; $b$ is not representable.

# Special Computational Situations

3

# CHAPTER 3
# SPECIAL COMPUTATIONAL SITUATIONS

Besides being able to represent positive and negative numbers, the 387™ DX data formats may be used to describe other entities. These special values provide extra flexibility, but most users will not need to understand them in order to use the 387 DX successfully. This section describes the special values that may occur in certain cases and the significance of each. The 387 DX exceptions are also described, for writers of exception handlers and for those interested in probing the limits of computation using the 387 DX.

The material presented in this section is mainly of interest to programmers concerned with writing exception handlers. Many readers will only need to skim this section.

When discussing these special computational situations, it is useful to distinguish between *arithmetic instructions* and *nonarithmetic instructions*. Nonarithmetic instructions are those that have no operands or transfer their operands without substantial change; arithmetic instructions are those that make significant changes to their operands. Table 3-1 defines these two classes of instructions.

## 3.1 SPECIAL NUMERIC VALUES

The 387 DX data formats encompass encodings for a variety of special values in addition to the typical real or integer data values that result from normal calculations. These special values have significance and can express relevant information about the computations or operations that produced them. The various types of special values are

- Denormal real numbers
- Zeros
- Positive and negative infinity
- NaN (Not-a-Number)
- Indefinite
- Unsupported formats

The following sections explain the origins and significance of each of these special values. Tables 3-6 through 3-10 at the end of this section show how each of these special values is encoded for each of the numeric data types.

### 3.1.1 Denormal Real Numbers

The 387 DX generally stores nonzero real numbers in normalized floating-point form; that is, the integer (leading) bit of the significand is always a one. (Refer to Chapter 2 for a review of operand formats.) This bit is explicitly stored in the extended format, and is implicitly assumed to be a one $(1_\Delta)$ in the single and double formats. Since leading zeros are eliminated, normalized storage allows the maximum number of significant digits to be held in a significand of a given width.

### Table 3-1. Arithmetic and Nonarithmetic Instructions

| Nonarithmetic Instructions | Arithmetic Instructions |
| --- | --- |
| FABS | F2XM1 |
| FCHS | FADD (P) |
| FCLEX | FBLD |
| FDECSTP | FBSTP |
| FFREE | FCOMP(P)(P) |
| FINCSTP | FCOS |
| FINIT | FDIV(R)(P) |
| FLD (register-to-register) | FIADD |
| FLD (extended format from memory) | FICOM(P) |
| FLD constant | FIDIV(R) |
| FLDCW | FILD |
| FLDENV | FIMUL |
| FNOP | FIST(P) |
| FRSTOR | FISUB(R) |
| FSAVE | FLD (conversion) |
| FST(P) (register-to-register) | FMUL(P) |
| FSTP (extended format to memory) | FPATAN |
| FSTCW | FPREM |
| FSTENV | FPREM1 |
| FSTSW | FPTAN |
| FWAIT | FRNDINT |
| FXAM | FSCALE |
| FXCH | FSIN |
| | FSINCOS |
| | FSQRT |
| | FST(P) (conversion) |
| | FSUB(R)(P) |
| | FTST |
| | FUCOM(P)(P) |
| | FXTRACT |
| | FYL2X |
| | FYL2XP1 |

When a numeric value becomes very close to zero, normalized floating-point storage cannot be used to express the value accurately. The term *tiny* is used here to precisely define what values require special handling by the 387 DX. A number R is said to be *tiny* when $-2^{Emin} < R < 0$ or $0 < R < +2^{Emin}$. (As defined in Chapter 2, Emin is $-126$ for single format, $-1022$ for double format, and $-16382$ for extended format.) In other words, a nonzero number is *tiny* if its exponent would be too negative to store in the destination format.

To accommodate these instances, the 387 DX can store and operate on reals that are not normalized, i.e., whose significands contain one or more leading zeros. Denormals typically arise when the result of a calculation yields a value that is *tiny*.

Denormal values have the following properties:

- The biased floating-point exponent is stored at its smallest value (zero)
- The integer bit of the significand (whether explicit or implicit) is zero

The leading zeros of denormals permit smaller numbers to be represented, at the possible cost of some lost precision (the number of significant bits is reduced by the leading zeros). In typical algorithms, extremely small values are most likely to be generated as intermediate, rather than final, results. By using the NPX's extended real format for holding intermediate values, quantities as small as $\pm 3.4 \times 10^{-4932}$ can be represented; this makes the occurrence of denormal numbers a rare phenomenon in 387 DX applications. Nevertheless, the NPX can load, store, and operate on denormalized real numbers when they do occur.

Denormals receive special treatment by the 387 DX in three respects:

- The 387 DX avoids creating denormals whenever possible. In other words, it always normalizes real numbers except in the case of tiny numbers.
- The 387 DX provides the unmasked underflow exception to permit programmers to detect cases when denormals would be created.
- The 387 DX provides the denormal exception to permit programmers to detect cases when denormals enter into further calculations.

Denormalizing means incrementing the true result's exponent and inserting a corresponding leading zero in the significand, shifting the rest of the significand one place to the right. Denormal values may occur in any of the single, double, or extended formats. Table 3-2 illustrates how a result might be denormalized to fit a single format destination.

Denormalization produces either a denormal or a zero. Denormals are readily identified by their exponents, which are always the minimum for their formats; in biased form, this is always the bit string: 00..00. This same exponent value is also assigned to the zeros, but a denormal has a nonzero significand. A denormal in a register is tagged *special*. Tables 3-8 and 3-9 later in this chapter show how denormal values are encoded in each of the real data formats.

The denormalization process causes loss of significance if low-order one-bits bits are shifted off the right of the significand. In a severe case, *all* the significand bits of the true result are shifted out and replaced by the leading zeros. In this case, the result of denormalization is a true zero, and, if the value is in a register, it is tagged as a zero.

**Table 3-2. Denormalization Process**

| Operation | Sign | Exponent | Significand |
|-----------|------|----------|-------------|
| True Result | 0 | −129 | 1△01011100..00 |
| Denormalize | 0 | −128 | 0△101011100..00 |
| Denormalize | 0 | −127 | 0△0101011100..00 |
| Denormalize | 0 | −126 | 0△00101011100..00 |
| Denormal Result | 0 | −126 | 0△00101011100..00 |

Denormals are rarely encountered in most applications. Typical debugged algorithms generate extremely small results during the evaluation of intermediate subexpressions; the final result is usually of an appropriate magnitude for its single or double format real destination. If intermediate results are held in temporary real, as is recommended, the great range of this format makes underflow very unlikely. Denormals are likely to arise only when an application generates a great many intermediates, so many that they cannot be held on the register stack or in extended format memory variables. If storage limitations force the use of single or double format reals for intermediates, and small values are produced, underflow may occur, and, if masked, may generate denormals.

When a denormal number is single or double format is used as a source operand and the denormal exception is masked, the 387 DX automatically *normalizes* the number when it is converted to extended format.

## 3.1.1.1 DENORMALS AND GRADUAL UNDERFLOW

Floating-pont arithmetic cannot carry out all operations exactly for all operands; approximation is unavoidable when the exact result is not representable as a floating-point variable. To keep the approximation mathematically tractable, the hardware is made to conform to accuracy standards that can be modeled by certain inequalities instead of equations. Let the assignment

$$X \leftarrow Y @ Z \qquad \text{(where @ is some operation)}$$

represent a typical operation. In the default rounding mode (round to nearest), each operation is carried out with an absolute error no larger than half the separation between the two floating-point numbers closest to the exact results. Let $x$ be the value stored for the variable whose name in the program is X, and similarly $y$ for Y, and $z$ for Z. Normally $y$ and $z$ will differ by accumulated errors from what is desired and from what would have been obtained in the absence of error. For the calculation of $x$ we assume that $y$ and $z$ are the best approximations available, and we seek to compute $x$ as well as we can. If $y@z$ is representable exactly, then we expect $x = y@z$, and that is what we get for every algebraic operation on the 387 DX (i.e., when $y@z$ is one of $y+z$, $y-z$, $y \times z$, $y \div z$, *sqrt z*). But if $y@z$ must be approximated, as is usually the case, then $x$ must differ from $y@z$ by no more than half the difference between the two representable numbers that straddle $y@z$. That difference depends on two factors:

1. The precision to which the calculation is carried out, as determined either by the precision control bits or by the format used in memory. On the 387 DX, the precisions are single (24 significant bits), double (53 significant bits), and extended (64 significant bits).

2. How close $y@z$ is to zero. In this respect the presence of denormal numbers on the 387 DX provides a distinct advantage over systems that do not admit denormal numbers.

In any floating-point number system, the density of representable numbers is greater near zero than near the largest representable magnitudes. However, machines that do not use denormal numbers suffer from an enormous gap between zero and its closest neighbors. Figures 3-1 and 3-2 show what happens near zero in two kinds of floating-point number systems.

Figure 3-1 shows a floating-point number system that (like the 387 DX) admits denormal numbers. For simplicity, only the non-negative numbers appear and the figure illustrates a number system that carries just four significant bits instead of the 24, 53, or 64 significant bits that the 387 DX offers.

Each vertical mark stands for a number representable in four significant bits, and the bolder marks stand for the normal powers of 2. The denormal numbers lie between 0 and the nearest normal power of 2. They are no less dense than the remaining normal nonzero numbers.

Figure 3-2 shows a floating-point number system that (unlike the 387 DX) does not admit denormal numbers. There are two yawning gaps, one on the positive side of zero (as illustrated) and one on the negative side of zero (not illustrated). The gap between zero and the nearest neighbor of zero differs from the gap between that neighbor and the next bigger number by a factor of about $8.4 \times 10^6$ for single, $4.5 \times 10^{15}$ for double, and $9.2 \times 10^{18}$ for extended format. Those gaps would horribly complicate error analysis.

The advantage of denormal numbers is apparent when one considers what happens in either case when the underflow exception is masked and $y@z$ falls into the space between zero and the smallest normal magnitude. The 387 DX returns the nearest denormal number. This action might be called "gradual underflow." The effect is no different than the rounding that can occur when $y@z$ falls in the normal range.

On the other hand, the system that does not have denormal numbers returns zero as the result, an action that can be much more inaccurate than rounding. This action could be called "abrupt underflow."

### 3.1.2 Zeros

The value *zero* in the real and decimal integer formats may be signed either positive or negative, although the sign of a binary integer zero is always positive. For computational purposes, the value of zero always behaves identically, regardless of sign, and typically the fact that a zero may be signed is transparent to the programmer. If necessary, the FXAM instruction may be used to determine a zero's sign.

If a zero is loaded or generated in a register, the register is tagged zero. Table 3-3 lists the results of instructions executed with zero operands and also shows how a zero may be created from nonzero operands.

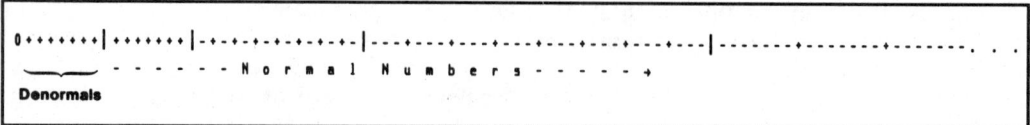

**Figure 3-1. Floating-Point System with Denormals**

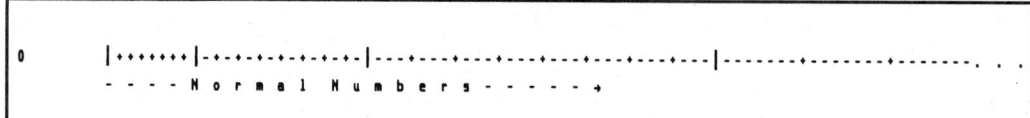

**Figure 3-2. Floating-Point System without Denormals**

### Table 3-3. Zero Operands and Results

| Operation | Operands | Result |
|---|---|---|
| FLD,FBLD | $\pm 0$ | #0 |
| FILD | $+0$ | $+0$ |
| FST,FSTP | $\pm 0$ | #0 |
|  | $+X$ | $+0^1$ |
|  | $-X$ | $-0^1$ |
| FBST | $\pm 0$ | #0 |
| FIST,FISTP | $\pm 0$ | #0 |
|  | $+X$ | $+0^3$ |
|  | $-X$ | $-0^3$ |
| FCHS | $+0$ | $-0$ |
|  | $-0$ | $+0$ |
| FABS | $\pm 0$ | $+0$ |
| Addition | $+0$ plus $+0$ | $+0$ |
|  | $-0$ plus $-0$ | $-0$ |
|  | $+0$ plus $-0$, $-0$ plus $+0$ | $\pm 0^2$ |
|  | $-X$ plus $+X$, $+X$ plus $-X$ | $\pm 0^2$ |
|  | $\pm 0$ plus $\pm X$, $\pm X$ plus $\pm 0$ | #X |
| Subtraction | $+0$ minus $-0$ | $+0$ |
|  | $-0$ minus $+0$ | $-0$ |
|  | $+0$ minus $+0$, $-0$ minus $-0$ | $\pm 0^2$ |
|  | $+X$ minus $+X$, $-X$ minus $-X$ | $\pm 0^2$ |
|  | $\pm 0$ minus $\pm X$ | $-$#X |
|  | $\pm X$ minus $\pm 0$ | #X |
| Multiplication | $\pm 0 \times \pm 0$ | O0 |
|  | $\pm 0 \times \pm X$, $\pm X \times \pm 0$ | O0 |
|  | $+X \times +Y$, $-X \times -Y$ | $+0^1$ |
|  | $+X \times -Y$, $-X \times +Y$ | $-0^1$ |

| X and Y | denote nonzero, positive, finite, operands. |
|---|---|
| 1 | When extreme underflow denormalizes the result to zero. |
| 2 | Sign determined by rounding mode: $+$ for nearest, up, or chop, $-$ for down. |
| 3 | When $0 < X < 1$ and the magnitude is not rounded up. |
| # | Sign of original X operand. |
| $-$# | Complement of sign of original X operand. |
| O | Exclusive OR of the signs of the operands. |

## Table 3-3. Zero Operands and Results (Cont'd.)

| Operation | Operands | Result |
|---|---|---|
| Division | ±0 ÷ ±0 | Invalid Operation |
| | ±X ÷ ±0 | O ∞ (Zero Divide) |
| | ±X ÷ ±∞ | O 0 |
| | +0 ÷ +X, −0 ÷ −X | +0 |
| | +0 ÷ −X, −0 ÷ +X | −0 |
| | −X ÷ −Y, +X ÷ +Y | +0[1] |
| | −X ÷ +Y, +X ÷ −Y | −0[1] |
| FPREM, FPREM1 | ±0 rem ±0 | Invalid Operation |
| | ±X rem ±0 | Invalid Operation |
| | +0 rem ±X | +0 |
| | −0 rem ±X | −0 |
| | +X rem ±Y | +0 Y exactly divides X |
| | −X rem ±Y | −0 Y exactly divides X |
| FSQRT | ±0 | #0 |
| Compare | ±0 : +X | ±0 < +X |
| | ±0 : ±0 | ±0 = ±0 |
| | ±0 : −X | ±0 > −X |
| FTST | ±0 | ±0 ± 0 |
| FXAM | +0 | C3 = 1;C2 = C1 = C0 = 0 |
| | −0 | C3 = C1 = 1; C2 = C0 = 0 |
| FRNDINT | ±0 | #0 |
| FSCALE | ±0 scaled by −∞ | *0 |
| | ±0 scaled by +∞ | Invalid Operation |
| | ±0 scaled by X | *0 |
| FXTRACT | +0 | ST = +0,ST(1) = −∞, Zero divide |
| | −0 | ST = −0,ST(1) = −∞, Zero divide |
| FPTAN | ±0 | *0 |
| FSIN (or SIN result of FSINCOS) | ±0 | *0 |
| FCOS (or COS result of FSINCOS) | ±0 | +1 |
| FPATAN | ±0 ÷ +X | *0 |
| | ±0 ÷ −X | *π |
| | ±X ÷ ±0 | #π/2 |
| | ±0 ÷ +0 | *0 |
| | ±0 ÷ −0 | *π |
| | +∞ ÷ ±0 | +π/2 |
| | −∞ ÷ ±0 | −π/2 |
| | ±0 ÷ +∞ | *0 |
| | ±0 ÷ −∞ | *π |
| F2XM1 | ±0 | #0 |
| FYL2X | ±Y × log(±0) | Zero Divide |
| | ±0 × log(±0) | Invalid Operation |
| FYL2XP1 | +Y × log(±0+1) | *0 |
| | −Y × log(±0+1) | −*0 |

| | |
|---|---|
| X and Y | denote nonzero, positive, finite operands. |
| 1 | When extreme underflow denormalizes the result to zero. |
| 2 | Sign determined by rounding mode: + for nearest, up, or chop, − for down. |
| 3 | When 0 < X < 1 and the magnitude is not rounded up. |
| * | Sign of original zero operand. |
| # | Sign of original X operand. |
| −# | Complement of sign of original X operand. |
| O | Exclusive OR of the signs of the operands. |

## 3.1.3 Infinity

The real formats support signed representations of infinities. These values are encoded with a biased exponent of all ones and a significand of $1_\Delta00..00$; if the infinity is in a register, it is tagged special.

A programmer may code an infinity, or it may be created by the NPX as its masked response to an overflow or a zero divide exception. Note that depending on rounding mode, the masked response may create the largest valid value representable in the destination rather than infinity.

The signs of the infinities are observed, and comparisons are possible. Infinities are always interpreted in the affine sense; that is, $-\infty <$ (any finite number) $< +\infty$. Arithmetic on infinities is always exact and, therefore, signals no exceptions, except for the invalid operations specified in Table 3-4.

**Table 3-4. Infinity Operands and Results**

| Operation | Operands | Result |
|---|---|---|
| FLD,FBLD | $\pm \infty$ | $^*\infty$ |
| FST,FSTP,FRNDINT | $\pm \infty$ | $^*\infty$ |
| FCHS | $+ \infty$ | $- \infty$ |
| | $- \infty$ | $+ \infty$ |
| FABS | $\pm \infty$ | $+ \infty$ |
| Addition | $+ \infty$ plus $+ \infty$ | $+ \infty$ |
| | $- \infty$ plus $- \infty$ | $- \infty$ |
| | $+ \infty$ plus $- \infty$ | Invalid Operation |
| | $- \infty$ plus $+ \infty$ | Invalid Operation |
| | $\pm \infty$ plus $\pm X$ | $^*\infty$ |
| | $\pm X$ plus $\pm \infty$ | $^*\infty$ |
| Subtraction | $+ \infty$ minus $- \infty$ | $+ \infty$ |
| | $- \infty$ minus $+ \infty$ | $- \infty$ |
| | $+ \infty$ minus $+ \infty$ | Invalid Operation |
| | $- \infty$ minus $- \infty$ | Invalid Operation |
| | $\pm \infty$ minus $\pm X$ | $^*\infty$ |
| | $\pm X$ minus $\pm \infty$ | $-^*\infty$ |
| Multiplication | $\pm \infty \times \pm \infty$ | $\mathrm{O}\infty$ |
| | $\pm \infty \times \pm Y, \pm Y \times \pm \infty$ | $\mathrm{O}\infty$ |
| | $\pm 0 \times \pm \infty, \pm \infty \times \pm 0$ | Invalid Operation |
| Division | $\pm \infty \div \pm \infty$ | Invalid Operation |
| | $\pm \infty \div \pm X$ | $\mathrm{O}\infty$ |
| | $\pm X \div \pm \infty$ | $\mathrm{O}0$ |
| | $\pm \infty \div \pm 0$ | $\mathrm{O}\infty$ |

| | |
|---|---|
| X | Zero or nonzero, positive, finite, operand. |
| Y | Nonzero positive operand. |
| * | Sign of original infinity operand. |
| $-$* | Complement of sign of original infinity operand. |
| $ | Sign of original operand. |
| O | Exclusive OR of signs of operands. |

### Table 3-4. Infinity Operands and Results (Cont'd.)

| Operation | Operands | Result |
|---|---|---|
| FPREM,FPREM1 | $\pm \infty$ rem $\pm \infty$ | Invalid Operation |
| | $\pm \infty$ rem $\pm X$ | Invalid Operation |
| | $\pm X$ rem $\pm \infty$ | $X, Q = 0 |
| FSQRT | $- \infty$ | Invalid Operation |
| | $+ \infty$ | $+ \infty$ |
| Compare | $+ \infty : + \infty$ | $+ \infty = + \infty$ |
| | $- \infty : - \infty$ | $- \infty = - \infty$ |
| | $+ \infty : - \infty$ | $+ \infty > - \infty$ |
| | $- \infty : + \infty$ | $- \infty < + \infty$ |
| | $+ \infty : \pm X$ | $+ \infty > X$ |
| | $- \infty : \pm X$ | $- \infty < X$ |
| | $\pm X : + \infty$ | $X < + \infty$ |
| | $\pm X : - \infty$ | $X > + \infty$ |
| FTST | $+ \infty$ | $+ \infty > 0$ |
| | $- \infty$ | $- \infty < 0$ |
| FSCALE | $\pm \infty$ scaled by $- \infty$ | Invalid Operation |
| | $\pm \infty$ scaled by $+ \infty$ | $^* \infty$ |
| | $\pm \infty$ scaled by $\pm X$ | $^* \infty$ |
| | $\pm 0$ scaled by $- \infty$ | $\pm 0^1$ |
| | $\pm 0$ scaled by $\infty$ | Invalid Operation |
| | $\pm Y$ scaled by $+ \infty$ | $\# \infty$ |
| | $\pm Y$ scaled by $- \infty$ | $\# 0$ |
| FXTRACT | $\pm \infty$ | $ST = {}^* \infty, ST(1) = + \infty$ |
| FXAM | $+ \infty$ | $C0 = C2 = 1; C1 = C3 = 0$ |
| | $- \infty$ | $C0 = C1 = C2 = 1; C3 = 0$ |
| FPATAN | $\pm \infty \div \pm X$ | $^* \pi/2$ |
| | $\pm Y \div + \infty$ | $\# 0$ |
| | $\pm Y \div - \infty$ | $\# \pi$ |
| | $\pm \infty \div + \infty$ | $^* \pi/4$ |
| | $\pm \infty \div - \infty$ | $^* 3\pi/4$ |
| | $\pm \infty \div \pm 0$ | $^* \pi/2$ |
| | $+ 0 \div + \infty$ | $+ 0$ |
| | $+ 0 \div - \infty$ | $+ \pi$ |
| | $- 0 \div + \infty$ | $- 0$ |
| | $- 0 \div - \infty$ | $- \pi$ |
| F2XM1 | $+ \infty$ | $+ \infty$ |
| | $- \infty$ | $- 1$ |
| FYL2X | $\pm \infty \times \log(1)$ | Invalid Operation |
| | $\pm \infty \times \log(X > 1)$ | $^* \infty$ |
| | $\pm \infty \times \log(0 < X < 1)$ | $-{}^* \infty$ |
| | $\pm Y \times \log(+ \infty)$ | $\# \infty$ |
| | $\pm 0 \times \log(+ \infty)$ | Invalid Operation |
| | $\pm Y \times \log(- \infty)$ | Invalid Operation |
| FYL2XP1 | $\pm \infty \times \log(1)$ | Invalid Operation |
| | $\pm \infty \times \log(X > 0)$ | $^* \infty$ |
| | $\pm \infty \times \log(-1 < X < 0)$ | $-{}^* \infty$ |
| | $\pm Y \times \log(+ \infty)$ | $\# \infty$ |
| | $\pm 0 \times \log(+ \infty)$ | Invalid Operation |
| | $\pm Y \times \log(- \infty)$ | Invalid Operation |

| | |
|---|---|
| X | Zero or nonzero, positive, finite operand. |
| Y | Nonzero positive, finite operand. |
| * | Sign of original infinity operand. |
| – * | Complement of sign of original infinity operand. |
| $ | Sign of original operand. |
| O | Exclusive OR of signs of operands. |
| # | Sign of the original Y operand. |
| 1 | Sign of original zero operand. |

## 3.1.4 NaN (Not-a-Number)

A NaN (Not a Number) is a member of a class of special values that exists in the real formats only. A NaN has an exponent of 11..11B, may have either sign, and may have any significand except $1_\Delta 00..00B$, which is assigned to the infinities. A NaN in a register is tagged special.

There are two classes of NaNs: signaling (SNaN) and quiet (QNaN). Among the QNaNs, the value *real indefinite* is of special interest.

### 3.1.4.1 SIGNALING NaNs

A signaling NaN is a NaN that has a zero as the most significant bit of its significand. The rest of the significand may be set to any value. The 387 DX never generates a signaling NaN as a result; however, it recognizes signaling NaNs when they appear as operands. Arithmetic operations (as defined at the beginning of this chapter) on a signaling NaN cause an invalid-operation exception (except for load operations, FXCH, FCHS, and FABS).

By unmasking the invalid operation exception, the programmer can use signaling NaNs to trap to the exception handler. The generality of this approach and the large number of NaN values that are available provide the sophisticated programmer with a tool that can be applied to a variety of special situations.

For example, a compiler could use signaling NaNs as references to uninitialized (real) array elements. The compiler could preinitialize each array element with a signaling NaN whose significand contained the index (relative position) of the element. If an application program attempted to access an element that it had not initialized, it would use the NaN placed there by the compiler. If the invalid operation exception were unmasked, an interrupt would occur, and the exception handler would be invoked. The exception handler could determine which element had been accessed, since the operand address field of the exception pointers would point to the NaN, and the NaN would contain the index number of the array element.

### 3.1.4.2 QUIET NaNs

A quiet NaN is a NaN that has a one as the most significant bit of its significand. The 387 DX creates the quiet NaN *real indefinite* (defined below) as its default response to certain exceptional conditions. The 387 DX may derive other QNaNs by converting an SNaN. The 387 DX converts a SNaN by setting the most significant bit of its significand to one, thereby generating an QNaN. The remaining bits of the significand are not changed; therefore, diagnostic information that may be stored in these bits of the SNaN is propagated into the QNaN.

The 387 DX will generate the special QNaN, *real indefinite*, as its masked response to an invalid operation exception. This NaN is signed negative; its significand is encoded $1_\Delta 100..00$. All other NaNs represent values created by programmers or derived from values created by programmers.

Both quiet and signaling NaNs are supported in all operations. A QNaN is generated as the masked response for invalid-operation exceptions and as the result of an operation in which at least one of the operands is a QNaN. The 387 DX applies the rules shown in Table 3-5 when generating a QNaN.

**Table 3-5. Rules for Generating QNaNs**

| Operation | Action |
|---|---|
| Real operation on an SNaN and a QNaN. | Deliver the QNaN operand. |
| Real operation on two SNaNs. | Deliver the QNaN that results from converting the SNaN that has the larger significand. |
| Real operation on two QNaNs. | Deliver the QNaN that has the larger significand. |
| Real operation on an SNaN and another number. | Deliver the QNaN that results from converting the SNaN. |
| Real operation on a QNaN and another number. | Deliver the QNaN. |
| Invalid operation that does not involve NaNs. | Deliver the default QNaN *real indefinite*. |

Note that handling of a QNaN operand has greater priority than all exceptions except certain invalid-operation exceptions (refer to the section "Exception Priority" in this chapter).

Quiet NaNs could be used, for example, to speed up debugging. In its early testing phase, a program often contains multiple errors. An exception handler could be written to save diagnostic information in memory whenever it was invoked. After storing the diagnostic data, it could supply a quiet NaN as the result of the erroneous instruction, and that NaN could point to its associated diagnostic area in memory. The program would then continue, creating a different NaN for each error. When the program ended, the NaN results could be used to access the diagnostic data saved at the time the errors occurred. Many errors could thus be diagnosed and corrected in one test run.

In embedded applications which use computed results in further computations, an undetected QNaN can vitiate all subsequent results. Such applications should therefore periodically check for QNans and provide a recovery mechanism to be used if a QNaN result is detected.

### 3.1.5 Indefinite

For every 387 DX numeric data type, one unique encoding is reserved for representing the special value *indefinite*. The 387 DX produces this encoding as its response to a masked invalid-operation exception.

In the case of reals, the *indefinite* value is a QNaN as discussed in the prior section.

Packed decimal *indefinite* may be stored by the NPX in a FBSTP instruction; attempting to use this encoding in a FBLD instruction, however, will have an undefined result; thus *indefinite* cannot be loaded from a packed decimal integer.

In the binary integers, the same encoding may represent either *indefinite* or the largest negative number supported by the format ($-2^{15}$, $-2^{31}$, or $-2^{63}$). The 387 DX will store this encoding as its masked response to an invalid operation, or when the value in a source register represents or rounds to the largest negative integer representable by the destination. In situations where its origin may be ambiguous, the invalid-operation exception flag can be examined to see if the value was produced by an exception response. When this encoding is loaded or used by an integer arithmetic or compare operation, it is always interpreted as a negative number; thus *indefinite* cannot be loaded from a binary integer.

### 3.1.6 Encoding of Data Types

Tables 3-6 through 3-10 show how each of the special values just described is encoded for each of the numeric data types. In these tables, the least-significant bits are shown to the right and are stored in the lowest memory addresses. The sign bit is always the left-most bit of the highest-addressed byte.

### 3.1.7 Unsupported Formats

The extended format permits many bit patterns that do not fall into any of the previously mentioned categories. Table 3-10 shows these unsupported formats. Some of these encodings were supported by the 80287 NPX; however, most of them are not supported by the 387 DX NPX. These changes are required due to changes made in the final version of the IEEE 754 standard that eliminated these data types.

The categories of encodings formerly known as pseudozeros, pseudo-NaNs, pseudoinfinities, and unnormal numbers are not supported by the 387 DX. The 387 DX raises the invalid- operation exception when they are encountered as operands.

The encodings formerly known as pseudodenormal numbers are not generated by the 387 DX; however, they are correctly utilized when encountered in operands to 387 DX instructions. The exponent is treated as if it were 00..01 and the mantissa is unchanged. The denormal exception is raised.

### Table 3-6. Binary Integer Encodings

| Class | | Sign | Magnitude |
|---|---|---|---|
| Positives | (Largest) | 0 | 11..11 |
| | | . | . |
| | | . | . |
| | | . | . |
| | | . | . |
| | | . | . |
| | | 0 | 00..01 |
| | (Smallest) | | |
| Zero | | 0 | 00..00 |
| Negatives | (Smallest) | 1 | 11..11 |
| | | . | . |
| | | . | . |
| | | . | . |
| | | . | . |
| | | . | . |
| | | 1 | 00..00 |
| | (Largest/Indefinite*) | | |
| | | Word:  Short:  Long: | — 15 bits — <br> — 31 bits — <br> — 63 bits — |

*If this encoding is used as a source operand (as in an integer load or integer arithmetic instruction), the 387™ DX interprets it as the largest negative number representable in the format... $-2^{15}$, $-2^{31}$, or $-2^{63}$. The 387™ DX delivers this encoding to an integer destination in two cases:

1. If the result is the largest negative number.
2. As the response to a masked invalid operation exception, in which case it represents the special value *integer indefinite*.

### Table 3-7. Packed Decimal Encodings

| Class | | Sign | | Magnitude | | | | | |
|---|---|---|---|---|---|---|---|---|---|
| | | | | digit | digit | digit | digit | ... | digit |
| Positives | (Largest) | 0 | 0000000 | 1 0 0 1 | 1 0 0 1 | 1 0 0 1 | 1 0 0 1 | ... | 1 0 0 1 |
| | (Smallest) | 0 | 0000000 | 0 0 0 0 | 0 0 0 0 | 0 0 0 0 | 0 0 0 0 | ... | 0 0 0 1 |
| | Zero | 0 | 0000000 | 0 0 0 0 | 0 0 0 0 | 0 0 0 0 | 0 0 0 0 | ... | 0 0 0 0 |
| Negatives | Zero | 1 | 0000000 | 0 0 0 0 | 0 0 0 0 | 0 0 0 0 | 0 0 0 0 | ... | 0 0 0 0 |
| | (Smallest) | 1 | 0000000 | 0 0 0 0 | 0 0 0 0 | 0 0 0 0 | 0 0 0 0 | ... | 0 0 0 0 |
| | (Largest) | 1 | 0000000 | 1 0 0 1 | 1 0 0 1 | 1 0 0 1 | 1 0 0 1 | ... | 1 0 0 1 |
| Indefinite* | | 1 | 1111111 | 1 1 1 1 | 1 1 1 1 | U U U U** | U U U U | ... | U U U U |
| | | — 1 byte — | | — 9 bytes — | | | | | |

*The *packed decimal indefinite* is stored by FBSTP in response to a masked invalid operation exception.
Attempting to load this value via FBLD produces an undefined result.
**UUUU means bit values are undefined and may contain any value.

### Table 3-8. Single and Double Real Encodings

| Class | | | Sign | Biased Exponent | Significand ff-ff* |
|---|---|---|---|---|---|
| **Positives** | **NaNs** | Quiet | 0 | 11..11 | 11..11 |
| | | | 0 | 11..11 | 10..00 |
| | | Signaling | 0 | 11..11 | 01..11 |
| | | | 0 | 11..11 | 00..01 |
| | | Infinity | 0 | 11..11 | 00..00 |
| | **Reals** | Normals | 0 | 11..10 | 11..11 |
| | | | 0 | 00..01 | 00..00 |
| | | Denormals | 0 | 00..00 | 11..11 |
| | | | 0 | 00..00 | 00..01 |
| | | Zero | 0 | 00..00 | 00..00 |
| **Negatives** | **Reals** | Zero | 1 | 00..00 | 00.00 |
| | | Denormals | 1 | 00..00 | 00..01 |
| | | | 1 | 00..00 | 11..11 |
| | | Normals | 1 | 00..01 | 00..00 |
| | | | 1 | 11..10 | 11..11 |
| | | Infinity | 1 | 11..11 | 00..00 |
| | **NaNs** | Signaling | 1 | 11..11 | 00..01 |
| | | | 1 | 11..11 | 01..11 |
| | | Quiet — Indefinite | 1 | 11..11 | 10..00 |
| | | | 1 | 11..11 | 11..11 |
| | | Single: | | — 8 bits — | — 23 bits — |
| | | Double: | | — 11 bits — | — 52 bits — |

*Integer bit is implied and not stored.

### Table 3-9. Extended Real Encodings

| | | Class | Sign | Biased Exponent | Significand I.ff-ff |
|---|---|---|---|---|---|
| Positives | NaNs | Quiet | 0 <br> . <br> . <br> 0 | 11..11 <br> . <br> . <br> 11..11 | 1 11..11 <br> . <br> . <br> 1 10..00 |
| | | Signaling | 0 <br> . <br> . <br> 0 | 11..11 <br> . <br> . <br> 11..11 | 1 01..11 <br> . <br> . <br> 1 00..01 |
| Positives | Reals | Infinity | 0 | 11..11 | 1 00..00 |
| | | Normals | 0 <br> . <br> . <br> 0 | 11..10 <br> . <br> . <br> 00..01 | 1 11..11 <br> . <br> . <br> 0 00..01 |
| | | Denormals | 0 <br> . <br> . <br> 0 | 00..00 <br> . <br> . <br> 00..00 | 0 11..11 <br> . <br> . <br> 1 00..01 |
| | | Zero | 0 | 00..00 | 0 00..00 |
| Negatives | | Zero | 1 | 00..00 | 0 00..00 |
| | | Denormals | 1 <br> . <br> . <br> 1 | 00..00 <br> . <br> . <br> 00..00 | 0 00..01 <br> . <br> . <br> 0 11..11 |
| | | Normals | 1 <br> . <br> . <br> 1 | 00..01 <br> . <br> . <br> 11..10 | 1 00..00 <br> . <br> . <br> 1 11..11 |
| | | Infinity | 1 | 11..11 | 1 00..00 |
| Negatives | NaNs | Signaling | 1 <br> . <br> . <br> 1 | 11..11 <br> . <br> . <br> 11..11 | 1 00..01 <br> . <br> . <br> 1 01..11 |
| | | Quiet    Indefinite | 1 <br> . <br> . <br> 1 | 11..11 <br> . <br> . <br> 11..11 | 1 10..00 <br> . <br> . <br> 1 11..11 |
| | | | ─ 15 bits ─ | ─ 64 bits ─ |

**Table 3-10. Unsupported Formats**

| | | Class | Sign | Biased Exponent | Significand f.ff--ff |
|---|---|---|---|---|---|
| Positives | Pseudo NaNs | Quiet | 0 · 0 | 11..11 · 11..11 | 0 11..11 · 0 10..00 |
| | | Signaling | 0 · 0 | 11..11 · 11..11 | 0 01..11 · 0 00..01 |
| | | Pseudoinfinity | 0 | 11..11 | 0 00..00 |
| | Reals | Unnormals | 0 · 0 | 11..10 · 00..01 | 0 11..11 · 0 00..00 |
| | | Pseudodenormals | 0 · 0 | 00..00 · 00..00 | 1 11..11 · 1 00..00 |
| Negatives | Reals | Pseudodenormals | 1 · 1 | 00..00 · 00..00 | 1 11..11 · 1 00..00 |
| | | Unnormals | 1 · 1 | 11..10 · 00..01 | 0 11..11 · 0 00..00 |
| | Pseudo NaNs | Pseudoinfinity | 1 | 11..11 | 0 00..00 |
| | | Signaling | 1 · 1 | 11..11 · 11..11 | 0 01..11 · 0 00..01 |
| | | Quiet | 1 · 1 | 11..11 · 11..11 | 0 11..11 · 0 10..00 |
| | | | | — 15 bits — | — 64 bits — |

## 3.2 NUMERIC EXCEPTIONS

The 387 DX can recognize six classes of numeric exception conditions while executing numeric instructions:

1. I — Invalid operation

    • Stack fault

    • IEEE standard invalid operation

2. Z — Divide-by-zero

3. D — Denormalized operand

4. O — Numeric overflow

5. U — Numeric underflow

6. P — Inexact result (precision)

### 3.2.1 Handling Numeric Exceptions

When numeric exceptions occur, the NPX takes one of two possible courses of action:

• The NPX can itself handle the exception, producing the most reasonable result and allowing numeric program execution to continue undisturbed.

• A software exception handler can be invoked by the CPU to handle the exception.

Each of the six exception conditions described above has a corresponding flag bit in the 387 DX status word and a mask bit in the 387 DX control word. If an exception is masked (the corresponding mask bit in the control word = 1), the 387 DX takes an appropriate default action and continues with the computation. If the exception is unmasked (mask = 0), the 387 DX asserts the ERROR# output to the 386 DX to signal the exception and invoke a software exception handler.

Note that when exceptions are masked, the NPX may detect multiple exceptions in a single instruction, because it continues executing the instruction after performing its masked response. For example, the 387 DX could detect a denormalized operand, perform its masked response to this exception, and then detect an underflow.

#### 3.2.1.1 AUTOMATIC EXCEPTION HANDLING

The 387 DX NPX has a default fix-up activity for every possible exception condition it may encounter. These masked-exception responses are designed to be safe and are generally acceptable for most numeric applications.

As an example of how even severe exceptions can be handled safely and automatically using the NPX's default exception responses, consider a calculation of the parallel resistance of several values using only the standard formula (Figure 3-3). If R1 becomes zero, the circuit resistance becomes zero. With the divide-by-zero and precision exceptions masked, the 387 DX NPX will produce the correct result.

By masking or unmasking specific numeric exceptions in the NPX control word, NPX programmers can delegate responsibility for most exceptions to the NPX, reserving the most severe exceptions for programmed exception handlers. Exception-handling software is often difficult to write, and the NPX's masked responses have been tailored to deliver the most reasonable result for each condition. For the majority of applications, masking all exceptions other than invalid-operation yields satisfactory results with the least programming effort. Certain exceptions can be left unmasked during the debugging phase of software development, and then masked when the clean software is actually run. An invalid-operation exception, for example, typically indicates a program error that must be corrected.

The exception flags in the NPX status word provide a cumulative record of exceptions that have occurred since these flags were last cleared. Once set, these flags can be cleared only by executing the FCLEX (clear exceptions) instruction, by reinitializing the NPX, or by overwriting the flags with an FRSTOR or FLDENV instruction. This allows a programmer to mask all exceptions (except invalid operation), run a calculation, and then inspect the status word to see if any exceptions were detected at any point in the calculation.

### 3.2.1.2 SOFTWARE EXCEPTION HANDLING

If the NPX encounters an unmasked exception condition, it signals the exception to the 386 DX CPU using the ERROR# status line between the two processors.

The next time the 386 DX CPU encounters a WAIT or ESC instruction in its instruction stream, the 386 DX will detect the active condition of the ERROR# status line and automatically trap to an exception response routine using interrupt #16, the "processor extension error" exception.

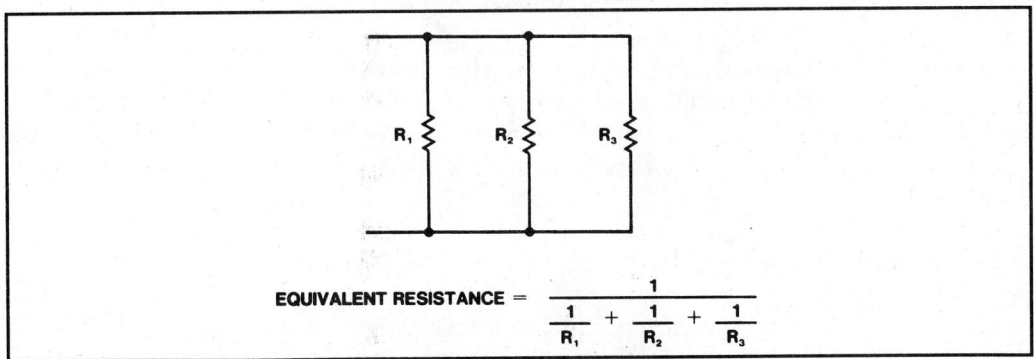

**Figure 3-3. Arithmetic Example Using Infinity**

This exception-handling routine is normally a part of the systems software. Typical exception responses may include:

- Incrementing an exception counter for later display or printing

- Printing or displaying diagnostic information (e.g., the 387 DX environment and registers)

- Aborting further execution

- Using the exception pointers to build an instruction that will run without exception and executing it

For 386 DX systems having systems software support for the 387 DX NPX, applications programmers should consult the operating system's reference manuals for the appropriate system response to NPX exceptions. For systems programmers, specific details on writing software exception handlers are included in Chapter 6.

## 3.2.2 Invalid Operation

This exception may occur in response to two general classes of operations:

1. Stack operations

2. Arithmetic operations

The stack flag (SF) of the status word indicates which class of operation caused the exception. When SF is 1 a stack operation has resulted in stack overflow or underflow; when SF is 0, an arithmetic instruction has encountered an invalid operand.

### 3.2.2.1 STACK EXCEPTION

When SF is 1, indicating a stack operation, the O/U# bit of the condition code (bit $C_1$) distinguishes between stack overflow and underflow as follows:

O/U# = 1        Stack overflow — an instruction attempted to push down a nonempty stack location.

O/U# = 0        Stack underflow — an instruction attempted to read an operand from an empty stack location.

When the invalid-operation exception is masked, the 387 DX returns the QNaN *indefinite*. This value overwrites the destination register, destroying its original contents.

When the invalid-operation exception is not masked, the 386 DX exception "processor extension error" is triggered. TOP is not changed, and the source operands remain unaffected.

### 3.2.2.2 INVALID ARITHMETIC OPERATION

This class includes the invalid operations defined in IEEE Std 754. The 387 DX reports an invalid operation in any of the cases shown in Table 3-11. Also shown in this table are the 387 DX's responses when the invalid exception is masked. When unmasked, the 386 DX exception "processor extension error" is triggered, and the operands remain unaltered. An invalid operation generally indicates a program error.

**Table 3-11. Masked Responses to Invalid Operations**

| Condition | Masked Response |
|---|---|
| Any arithmetic operation on an unsupported format. | Return the QNaN *indefinite*. |
| Any arithmetic operation on a signaling NaN. | Return a QNaN (refer to the section "Rules for Generating QNaNs"). |
| Compare and test operations: one or both operands is a NaN. | Set condition codes "not comparable." |
| Addition of opposite-signed infinities or subtraction of like-signed infinities. | Return the QNaN *indefinite*. |
| Multiplication: $\infty \times 0$; or $0 \times \infty$. | Return theQNaN *indefinite*. |
| Division: $\infty \div \infty$; or $0 \div 0$. | Return the QNaN *indefinite*. |
| Remainder instructions FPREM, FPREM1 when modulus (divisor) is zero or dividend is $\infty$. | Return the QNaN *indefinite*; set $C_2$. |
| Trigonometric instructions FCOS, FPTAN, FSIN, FSINCOS when argument is $\infty$. | Return theQNaN *indefinite*; set $C_2$. |
| FSQRT of negative operand (except FSQRT $(-0) = -0$), FYL2X of negative operand (except FYL2X $(-0) = -\infty$), FYL2XP1 of operand more negative than $-1$. | Return the QNaN *indefinite*. |
| FIST(P) instructions when source register is empty, a NaN, $\infty$, or exceeds representable range of destination. | Store integer *indefinite*. |
| FBSTP instruction when source register is empty, a NaN, $\infty$, or exceeds 18 decimal digits. | Store packed decimal *indefinite*. |
| FXCH instruction when one or both registers are tagged empty. | Change empty registers to the QNaN *indefinite* and then perform exchange. |

### 3.2.3 Division by Zero

If an instruction attempts to divide a finite nonzero operand by zero, the 387 DX will report a zero-divide exception. This is possible for F(I)DIV(R)(P) as well as the other instructions that perform division internally: FYL2X and FXTRACT. The masked response for FDIV and FYL2X is to return an infinity signed with the exclusive OR of the signs of the operands. For FXTRACT, ST(1) is set to $-\infty$; ST is set to zero with the same sign as the original operand. If the divide-by-zero exception is unmasked, the 386 DX exception "processor extension error" is triggered; the operands remain unaltered.

## 3.2.4 Denormal Operand

If an arithmetic instruction attempts to operate on a denormal operand, the NPX reports the denormal-operand exception. Denormal operands may have reduced significance due to lost low-order bits, therefore it may be advisable in certain applications to preclude operations on these operands. This can be accomplished by an exception handler that responds to unmasked denormal exceptions. Most users will mask this exception so that computation may proceed; any loss of accuracy will be analyzed by the user when the final result is delivered.

When this exception is masked, the 387 DX sets the D-bit in the status word, then proceeds with the instruction. Gradual underflow and denormal numbers as handled on the 387 DX will produce results at least as good as, and often better than what could be obtained from a machine that flushes underflows to zero. In fact, a denormal operand in single- or double-precision format will be normalized to the extended-real format when loaded into the 387 DX. Subsequent operations will benefit from the additional precision of the extended-real format used internally.

When this exception is not masked, the D-bit is set and the exception handler is invoked. The operands are not changed by the instruction and are available for inspection by the exception handler.

If an 8087/80287 program uses the denormal exception to automatically normalize denormal operands, then that program can run on an 387 DX by masking the denormal exception. The 8087/80287 denormal exception handler would not be used by the 387 DX in this case. A numerics program runs faster when the 387 DX performs normalization of denormal operands. A program can detect at run-time whether it is running on an 387 DX or 8087/80287 and disable the denormal exception when an 387 DX is used. The following code sequence is recommended to distinguish between an 387 DX and an 8087/80287.

```
        FINIT                   ; Use default infinity mode:
                                ;   projective for 8087/80287,
                                ;   affine for 387 DX
        FLD1                    ; Generate infinty
        FLDZ
        FDIV
        FLD     ST              ; Form negative infinity
        FCHS
        FCOMPP                  ; Compare +infinity with -infinity
        FSTSW   temp            ; 8087/80287 will say they are equal
        MOV     AX, temp
        SAHF
        JNZ     Using_387 DX
```

The denormal-operand exception of the 387 DX permits emulation of arithmetic on unnormal operands as provided by the 8087/80287. The standard does not require the denormal exception nor does it recognize the unnormal data type.

## 3.2.5 Numeric Overflow and Underflow

If the exponent of a numeric result is too large for the destination real format, the 387 DX signals a numeric overflow. Conversely, if the exponent of a result is too small to be represented in the destination format, a numeric underflow is signaled. If either of these exceptions occur, the result of the operation is outside the range of the destination real format.

Typical algorithms are most likely to produce extremely large and small numbers in the calculation of intermediate, rather than final, results. Because of the great range of the extended-precision format (recommended as the destination format for intermediates), overflow and underflow are relatively rare events in most 387 DX applications.

### 3.2.5.1 OVERFLOW

The overflow exception can occur whenever the rounded true result would exceed in magnitude the largest finite number in the destination format. The exception can occur in the execution of most of the arithmetic instructions and in some of the conversion instructions; namely, FST(P), F(I)ADD(P), F(I)SUB(R)(P), F(I)MUL(P), FDIV(R)(P), FSCALE, FYL2X, and FYL2XP1.

The response to an overflow condition depends on whether the overflow exception is masked:

- Overflow exception masked. The value returned depends on the rounding mode as Table 3-12 illustrates.

- Overflow exception not masked. The unmasked response depends on whether the instruction is supposed to store the result on the stack or in memory:

  - Destination is the stack. The true result is divided by $2^{24,576}$ and rounded. (The bias 24,576 is equal to $3 \times 2^{13}$.) The significand is rounded to the appropriate precision (according to the precision control (PC) bit of the control word, for those instructions controlled by PC, otherwise to extended precision). The roundup bit ($C_1$) of the status word is set if the significand was rounded upward.

  The biasing of the exponent by 24,576 normally translates the number as nearly as possible to the middle of the exponent range so that, if desired, it can be used in subsequent scaled operations with less risk of causing further exceptions. With the instruction FSCALE, however, it can happen that the result is too large and overflows even after biasing. In this case, the unmasked response is exactly the same as the masked round-to-nearest response, namely ± infinity. The intention of this feature is to ensure the trap handler will discover that a translation of the exponent by $-24574$ would not work correctly without obliging the programmer of Decimal-to-Binary or Exponential functions to determine which trap handler, if any, should be invoked.

— Destination is memory (this can occur only with the store instructions). No result is stored in memory. Instead, the operand is left intact in the stack. Because the data in the stack is in extended-precision format, the exception handler has the option either of reexecuting the store instruction after proper adjustment of the operand or of rounding the significand on the stack to the destination's precision as the standard requires. The exception handler should ultimately store a value into the destination location in memory if the program is to continue.

**Table 3-12. Masked Overflow Results**

| Rounding Mode | Sign of True Result | Result |
|---|---|---|
| To nearest | +<br>− | $+\infty$<br>$-\infty$ |
| Toward $-\infty$ | +<br>− | Largest finite positive number<br>$-\infty$ |
| Toward $+\infty$ | +<br>− | $+\infty$<br>Largest finite negative number |
| Toward zero | +<br>− | Largest finite positive number<br>Largest finite negative number |

### 3.2.5.2 UNDERFLOW

Underflow can occur in the execution of the instructions FST(P), FADD(P), FSUB(RP), FMUL(P), F(I)DIV(RP), FSCALE, FPREM(1), FPTAN, FSIN, FCOS, FSINCOS, FPATAN, F2XM1, FYL2X, and FYL2XP1.

Two related events contribute to underflow:

1. Creation of a tiny result which, because it is so small, may cause some other exception later (such as overflow upon division).

2. Creation of an inexact result; i.e. the delivered result differs from what would have been computed were both the exponent range and precision unbounded.

Which of these events triggers the underflow exception depends on whether the underflow exception is masked:

1. Underflow exception masked. The underflow exception is signaled when the result is both tiny and inexact.

2. Underflow exception not masked. The underflow exception is signaled when the result is tiny, regardless of inexactness.

The response to an underflow exception also depends on whether the exception is masked:

1. Masked response. The result is denormal or zero. The precision exception is also triggered.

2. Unmasked response. The unmasked response depends on whether the instruction is supposed to store the result on the stack or in memory:

   - Destination is the stack. The true result is multiplied by $2^{24,576}$ and rounded. (The bias 24,576 is equal to $3 \times 2^{13}$.) The significand is rounded to the appropriate precision (according to the precision control (PC) bit of the control word, for those instructions controlled by PC, otherwise to extended precision). The roundup bit ($C_1$) of the status word is set if the significand was rounded upward.

     The biasing of the exponent by 24,576 normally translates the number as nearly as possible to the middle of the exponent range so that, if desired, it can be used in subsequent scaled operations with less risk of causing further exceptions. With the instruction FSCALE, however, it can happen that the result is too tiny and underflows even after biasing. In this case, the unmasked response is exactly the same as the masked round-to-nearest response, namely $\pm 0$. The intention of this feature is to ensure the trap handler will discover that a translation by $+24576$ would not work correctly without obliging the programmer of Decimal-to-Binary or Exponential functions to determine which trap handler, if any, should be invoked.

   - Destination is memory (this can occur only with the store instructions). No result is stored in memory. Instead, the operand is left intact in the stack. Because the data in the stack is in extended-precision format, the exception handler has the option either of reexecuting the store instruction after proper adjustment of the operand or of rounding the significand on the stack to the destination's precision as the standard requires. The exception handler should ultimately store a value into the destination location in memory if the program is to continue.

### 3.2.6 Inexact (Precision)

This exception condition occurs if the result of an operation is not exactly representable in the destination format. For example, the fraction 1/3 cannot be precisely represented in binary form. This exception occurs frequently and indicates that some (generally acceptable) accuracy has been lost.

By their nature, the transcendental instructions typically cause the inexact exception.

The $C_1$ (roundup) bit of the status word indicates whether the inexact result was rounded up ($C_1 = 1$) or chopped ($C_1 = 0$).

The inexact exception accompanies the underflow exception when there is also a loss of accuracy. When underflow is masked, the underflow exception is signaled only when there is a loss of accuracy; therefore the precision flag is always set as well. When underflow is unmasked, there may or may not have been a loss of accuracy; the precision bit indicates which is the case.

This exception is provided for applications that need to perform exact arithmetic only. Most applications will mask this exception. The 387 DX delivers the rounded or over/underflowed result to the destination, regardless of whether a trap occurs.

## 3.2.7 Exception Priority

The 387 DX deals with exceptions according to a predetermined precedence. Precedence in exception handling means that higher-priority exceptions are flagged and results are delivered according to the requirements of that exception. Lower-priority exceptions may not be flagged even if they occur. For example, dividing an SNaN by zero causes an invalid-operand exception (due to the SNaN) and not a zero-divide exception; the masked result is the QNaN *real indefinite*, not ∞. A denormal or inexact (precision) exception, however, can accompany a numeric underflow or overflow exception.

The exception precedence is as follows:

1. Invalid operation exception, subdivided as follows:

    a. Stack underflow.

    b. Stack overflow.

    c. Operand of unsupported format.

    d. SNaN operand.

2. QNaN operand. Though this is not an exception, if one operand is a QNaN, dealing with it has precedence over lower-priority exceptions. For example, a QNaN divided by zero results in a QNaN, not a zero-divide exception.

3. Any other invalid-operation exception not mentioned above or zero divide.

4. Denormal operand. If masked, then instruction execution continues, and a lower-priority exception can occur as well.

5. Numeric overflow and underflow. Inexact result (precision) can be flagged as well.

6. Inexact result (precision).

## 3.2.8 Standard Underflow/Overflow Exception Handler

As long as the underflow and overflow exceptions are masked, no additional software is required to cause the output of the 387 DX to conform to the requirements of IEEE Std 754. When unmasked, these exceptions give the exception handler an additional option in the case of store instructions. No result is stored in memory; instead, the operand is left intact on the stack. The handler may round the significand of the operand on the stack to the destination's precision as the standard requires, or it may adjust the operand and reexecute the faulting instruction.

# The 387™ DX
# Instruction Set

4

# CHAPTER 4
## 387™ DX INSTRUCTION SET

The floating-point instructions available on the 387™ DX NPX can be grouped into six functional classes:

- Data Transfer Instructions

- Nontranscendental Instructions

- Comparison Instructions

- Transcendental Instructions

- Constant Instructions

- Control Instructions

In this chapter, the instruction classes are described as a collection of resources available to ASM386 programmers.

## 4.1 SOURCE AND DESTINATION OPERANDS

The typical floating-point instruction takes one or two operands, which can come from the 387 DX register stack or from memory. Many instructions, such as FSIN, automatically operate on the top 387 DX stack element. Others allow, or require, the programmer to code the operand(s) explicitly along with the instruction mnemonic. Still others accept one explicit operand and one implicit operand (usually the top 387 DX stack element).

Whether specified by the programmer or supplied by default, floating-point operands are of two basic types, *sources* and *destinations*. A source operand provides an input to an instruction, but is not altered by its execution. Even when an instruction converts the source operand from one format to another (e.g., real to integer), the conversion is performed in an internal work area to avoid altering the source operand. A destination operand may also provide an input to an instruction; on execution, however, the instruction returns a result to the destination, overwriting its previous contents.

Many instructions allow their operands to be coded in more than one way. For example, FADD (add real) may be written without operands, with only a source, or with a destination and a source. When both destination and source operands are specified, the destination must precede the source on the command line, and both must come from the 387 DX stack.

Memory operands can be coded with any of the memory-addressing methods provided by the ModR/M byte. To review these methods (BASE = (INDEX × SCALE) + DISPLACEMENT), refer to the 386 DX Data Sheet. Floating-point instructions with memory operands either read from memory or write to it; no floating-point instruction does both.

## 4.2 DATA TRANSFER INSTRUCTIONS

These instructions (summarized in Table 4-1) move operands among elements of the register stack, and between the stack top and memory. Any of the seven data types can be converted to extended-real and loaded (pushed) onto the stack in a single operation; they can be stored to memory in the same manner. The data transfer instructions automatically update the 387 DX tag word to reflect whether the register is empty or full following the instruction.

## 4.3 NONTRANSCENDENTAL INSTRUCTIONS

The nontranscendental instruction set provides a wealth of variations on the basic add, subtract, multiply, and divide operations, and a number of other useful functions. These range from a simple absolute value instruction to instructions which perform exact modulo division, round real numbers to integers, and scale values by powers of two. Table 4-2 shows the nontranscendental operations provided, apart from basic arithmetic.

The basic arithmetic instructions (addition, subtraction, multiplication and division) are designed to encourage the development of very efficient algorithms. In particular, they allow the programmer to reference memory as easily as the FPU register stack. Table 4-3 summarizes the available operation/operand forms that are provided for basic arithmetic. In addition to the four normal operations, there are "reversed" subtraction and division instructions which eliminate the need for many exchanges between ST(0) and ST(1). The variety of instruction and operand forms give the programmer unusual flexibility:

- Operands can be located in registers or memory.

- Results can be deposited in a choice of registers.

- Operands can be a variety of numerical data types: extended real, double real, single real, short integer or word integer, with automatic conversion to extended real performed by the FPU.

Five basic instruction forms can be used across all six operations, as shown in Table 4-3. The classical stack form can be used to make the 387 DX operate like a classical stack machine. No operands are coded in this form, only the instruction mnemonic. The 387 DX picks the source operand from the stack top (ST) and the destination from the next stack element (ST(1)). After performing its calculation, it returns the result to ST(1) and then pops ST, effectively replacing the operands by the result.

### Table 4-1. Data Transfer Instructions

| Real | | Integer | | Packed Decimal | |
|---|---|---|---|---|---|
| FLD | Load Real | FILD | Load Integer | FBLD | Load Packed Decimal |
| FST | Store Real | FIST | Store Integer | | |
| FSTP | Store Real and Pop | FISTP | Store Integer and Pop | FBSTP | Load Packed Decimal and Pop |
| FXCH | Exchange registers | | | | |

**Table 4-2. Nontranscendental Instructions (Besides Basic Arithmetic)**

| Mnemonic | Operation |
|---|---|
| FSQRT | Square Root |
| FSCALE | Scale |
| FXTRACT | Extract Exponent and Significand |
| FPREM | Partial Remainder |
| FPREM1 | IEEE Standard Partial Remainder |
| FRNDINT | Round to Integer |
| FABS | Absolute Value |
| FCHS | Change Sign |

**Table 4-3. Basic Arithmetic Instructions and Operands**

| Instruction Form | Mnemonic Form | Operand Forms: Destination, Source |
|---|---|---|
| Classical Stack | F*op* | {ST(1), ST} |
| Classical Stack, extra pop | F*op*P | {ST(1), ST} |
| Register | F*op* | ST(i), ST or ST, ST(i) |
| Register, pop | F*op*P | ST(i), ST |
| Real Memory | F*op* | {ST} single-real/double-real |
| Integer Memory | FI*op* | {ST} word-integer /short-integer |

**NOTES:**

Braces ({ }) surround implicit operands; these are not coded, but are supplied by the assembler.

*op*=  
  ADD   DEST ← DEST + SRC  
  SUB   DEST ← ST − Other Operand  
  SUBR  DEST ← Other Operand − ST  
  MUL   DEST ← DEST × SRC  
  DIV   DEST ← ST ÷ Other Operand  
  DIVR  DEST ← Other Operand ÷ ST  

The register form is a generalization of the classical stack form; the programmer specifies the stack top as one operand and any register on the stack as the other operand. Coding the stack top as the destination provides a convenient way to access a constant, held elsewhere in the stack, from the top stack. The destination need not always be ST, however. The basic two-operand instructions allow the use of another register as the destination. Using ST as the source allows, for example, adding the stack top into a register used as an accumulator.

Often the operand in the stack top is needed for one operation but then is of no further use in the computation. The register pop form can be used to pick up the stack top as the source operand, and then discard it by popping the stack. Coding operands of ST(1), ST with a register pop mnemonic is equivalent to a classical stack operation: the top is popped and the result is left at the new top.

The two memory forms increase the flexibility of the nontranscendental instructions. They permit a real number or a binary integer in memory to be used directly as a source operand. This is useful in situations where operands are not used frequently enough to justify holding them in registers. Note that any memory-addressing method can be used to define these operands, so they can be elements in arrays, structures, or other data organizations, as well as simple scalars.

## 4.4 COMPARISON INSTRUCTIONS

The instructions of this class allow numbers of all supported real and integer data types to be compared. Each of these instructions (Table 4-4) analyzes the top stack element, often in relationship to another operand, and reports the result as a condition code (flags $C_0$, $C_2$, and $C_3$) in the status word.

The basic operations are compare, test (compare with zero), and examine (report type, sign, and normalization). Special forms of the compare operation are provided to optimize algorithms by allowing direct comparisons with binary integers and real numbers in memory, as well as popping the stack after a comparison.

The FSTSW AX (store status word) instruction can be used after a comparison to transfer the condition code to the AX register for inspection. The TEST instruction is recommended for using the 387 DX flags (once they are in the AX register) to control conditional branching. First check to see if the comparison resulted in *unordered*. This can happen, for instance, if one of the operands is a NaN. TEST the contents of the AX register against the constant 0400H; this will clear ZF (the Zero Flag of the EFLAGS register) if the original comparison was unordered, and set ZF otherwise. The JNZ instruction can now be used to transfer control (if necessary) to code which handles the case of unordered operands. With the unordered case now filtered out, TEST the contents of the AX register against the appropriate constant from Table 4-5, and then use the corresponding conditional branch.

It is not always necessary to filter out the unordered case when using this algorithm for conditional jumps. If the software has been thoroughly tested, and incorporates periodic checks for QNaN results (as recommended in Chapter 3), then it is not necessary to check for *unordered* every time a comparison is made.

Instructions other than those in the comparison group can update the condition code. To ensure that the status word is not altered inadvertently, store it immediately following a comparison operation.

**Table 4-4. Comparison Instructions**

| Mnemonic | Operation |
|---|---|
| FCOM | Compare Real |
| FCOMP | Compare Real and Pop |
| FCOMPP | Compare Real and Pop Twice |
| FICOM | Compare Integer |
| FICOMP | Compare Integer and Pop |
| FTST | Test |
| FUCOM | Unordered Compare Real |
| FUCOMP | Unordered Compare Real and Pop |
| FUCOMPP | Unordered Compare Real and Pop Twice |
| FXAM | Examine |

**Table 4-5. TEST Constants for Conditional Branching**

| Order | Constant | Branch |
|---|---|---|
| ST > Operand | 4500H | JZ |
| ST < Operand | 0100H | JNZ |
| ST = Operand | 4000H | JNZ |
| Unordered | 0400H | JNZ |

## 4.5 TRANSCENDENTAL INSTRUCTIONS

The instructions in this group (Table 4-6) perform the time-consuming core calculations for all common trigonometric, inverse trigonometric, hyperbolic, inverse hyperbolic, logarithmic, and exponential functions. The transcendentals operate on the top one or two stack elements, and they return their results to the stack. The trigonometric operations assume their arguments are expressed in radians. The logarithmic and exponential operations work in base 2.

The results of transcendental instructions are highly accurate. The absolute value of the relative error of the transcendental instructions is guaranteed to be less than $2^{-62}$. (Relative error is the ratio between the absolute error and the exact value.)

The trigonometric functions accept a practically unrestricted range of operands, whereas the other transcendental instructions require that arguments be more restricted in range. FPREM or FPREM1 can be used to bring the otherwise valid operand of a periodic function into range. Prologue and epilogue software can be used to reduce arguments for other instructions to the expected range and to adjust the result to correspond to the original arguments if necessary. The instruction descriptions later in this chapter document the allowed operand range for each instruction.

When the argument of a trigonometric function is in range, it is automatically reduced by the appropriate multiple of $2\pi$ (in 66-bit precision), by means of the same mechanism used in the FPREM and FPREM1 instructions. The value of $\pi$ used in the automatic reduction has been chosen so as to guarantee no loss of significance in the operand, provided it is within the specified range. The internal value of $\pi$ is:

$$4 * 0.\text{C90FDAA2 2168C234 C H}$$

**Table 4-6. Transcendental Instructions**

| Mnemonic | Operation |
|---|---|
| FSIN | Sine |
| FCOS | Cosine |
| FSINCOS | Sine and Cosine |
| FPTAN | Tangent |
| FPATAN | Arctangent of ST(1) ÷ ST |
| F2XM1 | $2^X - 1$; X is in ST |
| FYL2X | Y x $\log_2$X; Y is in ST(1), X is in ST |
| FYL2XP1 | Y x $\log_2$(X + 1); Y is in ST(1), X is in ST |

A program may use an explicit value for $\pi$ in computations whose results later appear as arguments to trigonometric functions. In such a case (in explicit reduction of a trigonometric operand outside the specified range, for example), the value used for $\pi$ should be the same as the full 66-bit internal $\pi$. This will insure that the results are consistent with the automatic argument reduction performed by the trigonometric functions. The 66-bit $\pi$ cannot be represented as an extended-real value, so it must be encoded as two or more numbers. A common solution is to represent $\pi$ as the sum of a high$\pi$ which contains the 33 most-significant bits and a low$\pi$ which contains the 33 least-significant bits. When using this two-part $\pi$, all computations should be performed separately on each part, with the results added only at the end.

The complications of maintaining a consistent value of $\pi$ for argument reduction can be avoided, either by applying the trigonometric functions only to arguments within the range of the automatic reduction mechanism, or by performing all argument reductions (down to a magnitude less than $\pi/4$) explicitly in software.

## 4.6 CONSTANT INSTRUCTIONS

Each of these instructions (Table 4-7) pushes a commonly used constant onto the stack. (ST(7) must be empty to avoid an invalid exception.) The values have full extended real precision (64 bits) and are accurate to approximately 19 decimal digits. Because an external real constant occupies 10 memory bytes, the constant instructions, which are only two bytes long, save storage and improve execution speed, in addition to simplifying programming.

The constants used by these instructions are stored internally in a format more precise than extended real. When loading the constant, the 387 DX rounds the more precise internal constant according the RC (rounding control) bit of the control word. However, in spite of this rounding, the precision exception is not raised (to maintain compatibility). When the rounding control is set to round to nearest, the 387 DX produces the same constant that is produced by the 8087 and 80287 numeric coprocessors.

## 4.7 CONTROL INSTRUCTIONS

The 387 DX control instructions are shown in Table 4-8. The FSTSW instruction is commonly used for conditional branching. The remaining instructions are not typically used in calculations; they provide control over the 387 DX for system-level activities. These activities include initialization of the 387 DX, numeric exception handling, and task switching.

**Table 4-7. Constant Instructions**

| Mnemonic | Operation |
|---|---|
| FLDZ | Load $+0.0$ |
| FLD1 | Load $+1.0$ |
| FLDPI | Load $\pi$ |
| FLDL2T | Load $\log_2 10$ |
| FLDL2E | Load $\log_2 e$ |
| FLDLG2 | Load $\log_{10} 2$ |
| FLDLN2 | Load $\log_e 2$ |

### Table 4-8. Control Instructions

| Mnemonic | Operation |
|----------|-----------|
| FINIT / FNINIT | Initialize FPU |
| FLDCW | Load Control Word |
| FSTCW / FNSTCW | Store Control Word |
| FSTSW / FNSTSW | Store Status Word |
| FSTSW AX / FNSTSW AX | Store Status Word to AX Register |
| FCLEX / FNCLEX | Clear Exceptions |
| FSTENV / FNSTENV | Store Environment |
| FLDENV | Load Environment |
| FSAVE / FNSAVE | Save State |
| FRSTOR | Restore State |
| FINCSTP | Increment Stack-Top Pointer |
| FDECSTP | Decrement Stack-Top Pointer |
| FFREE | Free Register |
| FNOP | No Operation |
| FWAIT | Report FPU Error |

As shown in Table 4-8, certain instructions have alternative mnemonics. The instructions which initialize the 387 DX, clear exceptions, or store (all or part of) the 387 DX environment come in two forms:

- *Wait*—the mnemonic is prefixed only with an F, such as FSTSW. This form checks for unmasked numeric exceptions.

- *No-wait*—the mnemonic is prefixed with an FN, such as FNSTSW. This form ignores unmasked numeric exceptions.

When the control instruction is coded using the no-wait form of the mnemonic, the ASM386 assembler does not precede the ESC instruction with a WAIT instruction, and the processor does not test for a floating-point error condition before executing the control instruction.

The only no-wait instructions are those shown in Table 4-8. All other floating-point instructions are automatically synchronized by the processor; all operands are transferred before the next instruction is initiated. Because of this automatic synchronization, non-control floating-point instructions need not be preceded by a WAIT instruction in order to execute correctly.

Exception synchronization relies on the WAIT instruction. Since the 386 DX and the 387 DX operate in parallel, it is possible in the case of a floating-point exception for the processor to disturb information vital to exception recovery before the exception-handler can be invoked. Coding a WAIT or FWAIT instruction in the proper place can prevent this. See Chapter 5 for details.

It should also be noted that the 8087 instructions FENI and FDISI and the 80287 instruction FSETPM perform no function in the 387 DX processor. If these opcodes are detected in the instruction stream, the 387 DX processor performs no specific operation and no internal states are affected. Appendix C contains a more complete description of the differences between floating-point operations on the 387 DX NPX and on 8087 and 80287 math coprocessors.

## 4.8 387™ DX INSTRUCTIONS

This section presents instructions for the 387 DX NPX in alphabetical order. For each instruction, the forms are given for each operand combination, including object code produced, operands required, execution time, and a description. For each instruction, there is an operational description and a summary of exceptions generated.

Exceptions generated by the 386 DX are abbreviated as follows:

| Abbreviation | Description | Interrupt |
|---|---|---|
| #NM | Numerics Missing | 7 |
| #GP | General Protection | 13 |
| #PF | Page Fault | 14 |
| #SS | Stack Fault | 12 |

# F2XM1 — Computer $2^x - 1$

| Opcode | Instruction | Clocks | Description |
|--------|-------------|--------|-------------|
| D9 F0  | F2XM1       | 211-476 | Replace ST with $(2^{ST} - 1)$. |

## Operation

$ST \leftarrow (2^{ST} - 1);$

## Description

F2XM1 replaces the contents of ST with $(2^{ST} - 1)$. ST must lie in the range $-1 < ST < 1$.

## FPU Flags Affected

$C_1$ as described in Table 2-1; $C_0$, $C_2$, $C_3$ undefined

## Numeric Exceptions

P, U, D, I, IS

## Protected Mode Exceptions

#NM if either EM or TS in CR0 is set

## Real Address Mode Exceptions

Interrupt 7 if either EM or TS in CR0 is set

## Virtual 8086 Mode Exceptions

#NM if either EM or TS in CR0 is set

## Notes

If the operand is outside the acceptable range, the result of F2XM1 is undefined.

The F2XM1 instruction is designed to produce a very accurate result even when the operand is close to zero. Larger errors are incurred for operands with magnitudes very close to 1.

Values other than 2 can be exponentiated using the formula

$x^y = 2^{(y \times \log_2 x)}$

The instructions FLDL2T and FLDL2E load the constants $\log_2 10$ and $\log_2 e$, respectively. FYL2X can be used to calculate $y \times \log_2 x$ for arbitrary positive x.

# FABS — Absolute Value

| Opcode | Instruction | Clocks | Description |
|--------|-------------|--------|-------------|
| D9 E1 | FABS | 22 | Replace ST with its absolute value. |

## Operation

sign bit of ST ← 0

## Description

The absolute value instruction clears the sign bit of ST. This operation leaves a positive value unchanged, or replaces a negative value with a positive value of equal magnitude.

## FPU Flags Affected

$C_1$ as described in Table 2-1; $C_0$, $C_2$, $C_3$ undefined

## Numeric Exceptions

IS

## Protected Mode Exceptions

#NM if either EM or TS in CR0 is set

## Real Address Mode Exceptions

Interrupt 7 if either EM or TS in CR0 is set

## Virtual 8086 Mode Exceptions

#NM if either EM or TS in CR0 is set

## Notes

The invalid-operation exception is raised only on stack underflow, even if the operand is signalling NaN or is in an unsupported format.

# FADD/FADDP/FIADD — Add

| Opcode | Instruction | Clocks | Description |
|--------|-------------|--------|-------------|
| D8 /0 | FADD m32 real | 24-32 | Add m32real to ST. |
| DC /0 | FADD m64real | 29-37 | Add m64real to ST. |
| D8 C0+i | FADD ST, ST(i) | 23-31[1] | Add ST(i) to ST. |
| DC C0+i | FADD ST(i), ST | 23-31[1] | Add ST to ST(i). |
| DE C0+i | FADDP ST(i), ST | 23-31[1] | Add ST to ST(i) and pop ST. |
| DE C1 | FADD | 23-31[1] | Add ST to ST(1) and pop ST. |
| DA /0 | FIADD m32int | 57-72 | Add m32int to ST. |
| DE /0 | FIADD m16int | 71-85 | Add m16int to ST. |

(1) Add 3 clocks to the range when d = 1

## Operation

DEST ← DEST + SRC;
If instruction = FADDP THEN pop ST FI;

## Description

The addition instructions add the source and destination operands and return the sum to the destination. The operand at the stack top can be doubled by coding:

FADD ST, ST(0)

## FPU Flags Affected

$C_1$ as described in Table 2-1; $C_0$, $C_2$, $C_3$ undefined

## Numeric Exceptions

P, U, O, D, I, IS

## Protected Mode Exceptions

#GP(0) for an illegal memory operand effective address in the CS, DS, ES, FS, or GS segments; #SS(0) for an illegal address in the SS segment; #PF (fault-code) for a page fault; #NM if either EM or TS in CR0 is set.

## Real Address Mode Exceptions

Interrupt 13 if any part of the operand would lie outside the effective address space from 0 to 0FFFFH; Interrupt 7 if either EM or TS in CR0 is set

## Virtual 8086 Mode Exceptions

Same exceptions as in Real Address Mode; #PF (fault code) for a page fault.

## Notes

If the source operand is in memory, it is automatically converted to the extended-real format.

# FBLD — Load Binary Coded Decimal

| Opcode | Instruction | Clocks | Description |
|--------|-------------|--------|-------------|
| DF /4 | FBLD m80 dec | 266-275 | Push m80dec onto the 387 DX stack. |

## Operation

Decrement FPU stack-top pointer;
ST(0) ← SRC;

## Description

FBLD converts the BCD source operand into extended-real format, and pushes it onto the 387 DX stack.

## FPU Flags Affected

$C_1$ as described in Table 2-1; $C_0$, $C_2$, $C_3$ undefined

## Numeric Exceptions

IS

## Protected Mode Exceptions

#GP(0) for an illegal memory operand effective address in the CS, DS, ES, FS, or GS segments; #SS(0) for an illegal address in the SS segment; #PF (fault-code) for a page fault; #NM if either EM or TS in CR0 is set.

## Real Address Mode Exceptions

Interrupt 13 if any part of the operand would like outside the effective address space from 0 to 0FFFFH; Interrupt 7 if either EM or TS in CR0 is set

## Virtual 8086 Mode Exceptions

Same exceptions as in Real Address Mode; #PF (fault code) for a page fault.

## Notes

The source is loaded without rounding error. The sign of the source is preserved, including the case where the value is negative zero.

The packed decimal digits are assumed to be in the range 0-9. The instruction does not check for invalid digits (A-FH), and the result of attempting to load an invalid encoding is undefined.

ST(7) must be empty to avoid causing an invalid-operation exception.

# FBSTP — Store Binary Coded Decimal and Pop

| Opcode | Instruction | Clocks | Description |
|--------|-------------|--------|-------------|
| DF /6 | FBSTP m80dec | 512-534 | Store ST in m80dec and pop ST. |

## Operation

DEST ← ST(0);
pop ST F;

## Description

FBSTP converts the value in ST into a packed decimal integer, stores the result at the destination in memory, and pops ST. Non-integral values are first rounded according to the RC field of the control word.

## FPU Flags Affected

$C_1$ as described in Table 2-1; $C_0$, $C_2$, $C_3$ undefined

## Numeric Exceptions

P, I, IS

## Protected Mode Exceptions

#GP(0) if the destination is in a nonwritable segment; #GP(0) for an illegal memory operand effective address in the CS, DS, ES, FS, or GS segments; #SS(0) for an illegal address in the SS segment; #PF (fault-code) for a page fault; #NM if either EM or TS in CR0 is set.

## Real Address Mode Exceptions

Interrupt 13 if any part of the operand would like outside the effective address space from 0 to 0FFFFH; Interrupt 7 if either EM or TS in CR0 is set

## Virtual 8086 Mode Exceptions

Same exceptions as in Real Address Mode; #PF (fault code) for a page fault.

# FCHS — Change Sign

| Opcode | Instruction | Clocks | Description |
|--------|-------------|--------|-------------|
| D9 E0 | FCHS | 24-25 | Replace ST with a value of opposite sign. |

## Operation

sign bit of ST ← NOT (sign bit of ST)

## Description

The change sign instruction inverts the sign bit of ST. This operation replaces a positive value with a negative value of equal magnitude, or vice-versa.

## FPU Flags Affected

$C_1$ as described in Table 2-1; $C_0$, $C_2$, $C_3$ undefined

## Numeric Exceptions

IS

## Protected Mode Exceptions

#NM if either EM or TS in CR0 is set

## Real Address Mode Exceptions

Interrupt 7 if either EM or TS in CR0 is set

## Virtual 8086 Mode Exceptions

#NM if either EM or TS in CR0 is set

## Notes

The invalid-operation exception is raised only on stack underflow, even if the operand is a signalling NaN or is in an unsupported format.

**387™ DX INSTRUCTION SET**

# FCLEX/FNCLEX — Clear Exceptions

| Opcode | Instruction | Clocks | Description |
|--------|-------------|--------|-------------|
| 9B DB E2 | FCLEX | 11 + at least 6 for FWAIT | Clear floating-point exception flags after checking for floating-point error conditions. |
| DB E2 | FNCLEX | 11 | Clear floating-point exception flags without checking for floating-point error conditions. |

## Operation

SW[0..7] ← 0;
SW[15] ← 0;

## Description

FCLEX clears the exception flags, the exception status flag, and the busy flag of the FPU status word.

## FPU Flags Affected

$C_0$, $C_1$, $C_2$, $C_3$ undefined

## Numeric Exceptions

None

## Protected Mode Exceptions

#NM if either EM or TS in CR0 is set

## Real Address Mode Exceptions

Interrupt 7 if either EM or TS in CR0 is set

## Virtual 8086 Mode Exceptions

#NM if either EM or TS in CR0 is set

## Notes

FCLEX checks for unmasked floating-point error conditions before clearing the exception flags; FNCLEX does not.

# FCOM/FCOMP/FCOMPP — Compare Real

| Opcode | Instruction | Clocks | Description |
|--------|-------------|--------|-------------|
| D8 /2 | FCOM m32real | 26 | Compare ST with m32real. |
| DC /2 | FCOM m64real | 31 | Compare ST with m64real. |
| D8 D0+i | FCOM ST(i) | 24 | Compare ST with ST(i). |
| D8 D1 | FCOM | 24 | Compare ST with ST(1). |
| D8 /3 | FCOMP m32real | 26 | Compare ST with m32real and pop ST. |
| DC /3 | FCOMP m64real | 31 | Compare ST with m64real and pop ST. |
| D8 D8+i | FCOMP ST(i) | 26 | Compare ST with ST(i) and pop ST. |
| D8 D9 | FCOMP | 26 | Compare ST with ST(1) and pop ST. |
| DE D9 | FCOMPP | 26 | Compare ST with ST(1) and pop ST twice. |

## Operation

CASE (relation of operands) OF
　　　Not comparable:　C3, C2, C0 ← 111;
　　　ST > SRC:　　　　C3, C2, C0 ← 000;
　　　ST < SRC:　　　　C3, C2, C0 ← 001;
　　　ST = SRC:　　　　C3, C2, C0 ← 100;
IF instruction = FCOMP THEN pop ST; FI;
IF instruction = FCOMPP THEN pop ST; pop ST; FI;

## Description

The compare real instructions compare the stack top to the source, which can be a register or a single- or double-real memory operand. If no operand is encoded, ST is compared to ST(1). Following the instruction, the condition codes reflect the relation between ST and the source operand.

## FPU Flags Affected

$C_1$ as described in Table 2-1; $C_0$, $C_2$, $C_3$ as specified above

## Numeric Exceptions

D, I, IS

## Protected Mode Exceptions

#GP(0) for an illegal memory operand effective address in the CS, DS, ES, FS, or GS segments; #SS(0) for an illegal address in the SS segment; #PF (fault-code) for a page fault; #NM if either EM or TS in CR0 is set.

## Real Address Mode Exceptions

Interrupt 13 if any part of the operand would lie outside the effective address space from 0 to 0FFFFH; Interrupt 7 if either EM or TS in CR0 is set

## Virtual 8086 Mode Exceptions

Same exceptions as in Real Address Mode; #PF (fault code) for a page fault.

## Notes

If either operand is a NaN or is in an undefined format, or if a stack fault occurs, the invalid-operation exception is raised, and the condition bits are set to "unordered."

The sign of zero is ignored, so that $-0.0 = +0.0$.

# FCOS — Cosine

| Opcode | Instruction | Clocks | Description |
|--------|-------------|--------|-------------|
| D9 FF | FCOS | 123-772[1] | Replace ST with its cosine. |

**Note:** (1) For operands outside of the range $|x| < \pi/4$, up to 76 additional clocks may be needed to reduce the operand.

## Operation

```
IF operand is in range
THEN
     C2 ← 0;
     ST ← cos(ST);
ELSE
     C2 ← 1;
FI;
```

## Description

The cosine instruction replaces the contents of ST with cos(ST). ST, expressed in radians, must lie in the range $|\theta| < 2^{63}$.

## FPU Flags Affected

$C_1$ $C_2$, as described in Table 2-1; $C_0$, $C_3$ undefined

## Numeric Exceptions

P, U, D, I, IS

## Protected Mode Exceptions

#NM if either EM or TS in CR0 is set

## Real Address Mode Exceptions

Interrupt 7 if either EM or TS in CR0 is set

## Virtual 8086 Mode Exceptions

#NM if either EM or TS in CR0 is set

## Notes

If the operand is outside the acceptable range, the $C_2$ flag is set, and ST remains unchanged. It is the programmer's responsibility to reduce the operand to an absolute value smaller than $2^{63}$ by subtracting an appropriate integer multiple of $2\pi$.

# FDECSTP — Decrement Stack-Top Pointer

| Opcode | Instruction | Clocks | Description |
|--------|-------------|--------|-------------|
| D9 F6 | FDECSTP | 22 | Decrement top-of-stack pointer for 387 DX register stack. |

## Operation

IF TOP = 0
THEN TOP ← 7;
ELSE TOP ← TOP − 1;
FI;

## Description

FDECSTP subtracts one (without carry) from the three-bit TOP field of the 387 DX status word.

## FPU Flags Affected

$C_1$ as described in Table 2-1; $C_0$, $C_2$, $C_3$ undefined

## Numeric Exceptions

None

## Protected Mode Exceptions

#NM if either EM or TS in CR0 is set

## Real Address Mode Exceptions

Interrupt 7 if either EM or TS in CR0 is set

## Virtual 8086 Mode Exceptions

#NM if either EM or TS in CR0 is set

## Notes

The effect of FDECSTP is to rotate the stack. It does not alter register tags or contents, nor does it transfer data.

# FDIV/FDIVP/FIDIV — Divide

| Opcode | Instruction | Clocks | Description |
|--------|-------------|--------|-------------|
| D8 /6 | FDIV m32real | 89 | Divide ST by m32real. |
| DC /6 | FDIV m64real | 94 | Divide ST by m64real. |
| D8 F8+i | FDIV ST, ST(i) | 88[1] | Divide ST by ST(i). |
| DC F8+i | FDIV ST(i), ST | 88[1] | Replace ST(i) with ST ÷ ST(i). |
| DE F8+i | FDIVP ST(i), ST | 88[1] | Replace ST(i) with ST ÷ ST(i); pop ST. |
| DE F9 | FDIV | 88[1] | Replace ST(1) with ST ÷ ST(1); pop ST. |
| DA /6 | FIDIV m32int | 120-127[2] | Divide ST by m32int. |
| DE /6 | FIDIV m16int | 136-140[3] | Divide ST by m16int. |

**Note:** (1) Add 3 clocks to the range when d = 1
(2) Add 1 clock to the range when R = 1
(3) 135-141 when R = 1

## Operation

DEST ← ST ÷ Other Operand;
IF instruction = FDIVP THEN pop ST FI;

## Description

The division instructions divide the stack top by the other operand and return the quotient to the destination.

## FPU Flags Affected

$C_1$ as described in Table 2-1; $C_0$, $C_2$, $C_3$ undefined

## Numeric Exceptions

P, U, O, Z, D, I, IS

## Protected Mode Exceptions

#GP(0) for an illegal memory operand effective address in the CS, DS, ES, FS, or GS segments; #SS(0) for an illegal address in the SS segment; #PF(fault-code) for a page fault; #NM if either EM or TS in CR0 is set.

## Real Address Mode Exceptions

Interrupt 13 if any part of the operand would lie outside the effective address space from 0 to 0FFFFH; Interrupt 7 if either EM or TS in CR0 is set

## Virtual 8086 Mode Exceptions

Same exceptions as in Real Address Mode; #PF(fault code) for a page fault.

## Notes

If the source operand is in memory, it is automatically converted to the extended-real format.

The performance (clock counts) of the division instruction is independent of the PC field of the control word.

# FDIVR/FDIVPR/FIDIVR — Reverse Divide

| Opcode | Instruction | Clocks | Description |
|--------|-------------|--------|-------------|
| D8 /7 | FDIVR m32real | 89 | Replace ST with m32real ÷ ST. |
| DC /7 | FDIVR m64real | 94 | Replace ST with m64real ÷ ST. |
| D8 F0+i | FDIVR ST, ST(i) | 88[1] | Replace ST by ST(i) ÷ ST. |
| DC F0+i | FDIVR ST(i), ST | 88[1] | Divide ST(i) by ST. |
| DE F0+i | FDIVRP ST(i), ST | 88[1] | Divide ST(i) by ST and pop ST. |
| DE F1 | FDIVR | 88[1] | Divide ST(1) by ST and pop ST. |
| DA /7 | FIDIVR m32int | 120-127[2] | Replace ST with m32int ÷ ST. |
| DE /7 | FIDIVR m16int | 136-140 | Replace ST with m16int ÷ ST. |

**Note:** (1) Add 3 clocks to the range when d = 1
       (2) Add 1 clock tothe range when R = 1

## Operation

DEST ← Other Operand ÷ ST;
IF instruction = FDIVRP THEN pop ST FI;

## Description

The division instructions divide the other operand by the stack top and return the quotient to the destination.

## FPU Flags Affected

$C_1$ as described in Table 2-1; $C_0$, $C_2$, $C_3$ undefined

## Numeric Exceptions

P, U, O, Z, D, I, IS

## Protected Mode Exceptions

#GP(0) for an illegal memory operand effective address in the CS, DS, ES, FS, or GS segments; #SS(0) for an illegal address in the SS segment; #PF(fault-code) for a page fault; #NM if either EM or TS in CR0 is set.

## Real Address Mode Exceptions

Interrupt 13 if any part of the operand would lie outside the effective address space from 0 to 0FFFFH; Interrupt 7 if either EM or TS in CR0 is set

## Virtual 8086 Mode Exceptions

Same exceptions as in Real Address Mode; #PF(fault code) for a page fault.

## Notes

If the source operand is in memory, it is automatically converted to the extended-real format.

The performance (clock counts) of the reverse division instructions is independent of the PC field of the control word.

# FFREE — Free Floating-Point Register

| Opcode | Instruction | Clocks | Description |
|---|---|---|---|
| DD C0+i | FFREE ST(i) | 18 | Tag ST(i) as *empty*. |

## Operation

TAG(i) ← 11B;

## Description

FFREE tags the destination register as *empty*.

## FPU Flags Affected

$C_0$ $C_1$, $C_2$, $C_3$ undefined

## Numeric Exceptions

None

## Protected Mode Exceptions

#NM if either EM or TS in CR0 is set

## Real Address Mode Exceptions

Interrupt 7 if either EM or TS in CR0 is set

## Virtual 8086 Mode Exceptions

#NM if either EM or TS in CR0 is set

## Notes

FFREE does not affect the contents of the destination register. The floating-point stack-top pointer (TOP) is also unaffected.

# FICOM/FICOMP — Compare Integer

| Opcode | Instruction | Clocks | Description |
|--------|-------------|--------|-------------|
| DE /2 | FICOM *m16int* | 71-75 | Compare ST with *m16int*. |
| DA /2 | FICOM *m32int* | 56-63 | Compare ST with *m32int*. |
| DE /3 | FICOMP *m16int* | 71-75 | Compare ST with *m16int* and pop ST. |
| DA /3 | FICOMP *m32int* | 56-63 | Compare ST with *m32int* and pop ST. |

## Operation

CASE (relation of operands) OF  
　　Not comparable:　C3, C2, C0 ← 111;  
　　ST > SRC:　　　C3, C2, C0 ← 000;  
　　ST < SRC:　　　C3, C2, C0 ← 001;  
　　ST = SRC:　　　C3, C2, C0 ← 100;  
IF instruction = FICOMP THEN pop ST; FI;

## Description

The compare integer instructions compare the stack top to the source. Following the instruction, the condition codes reflect the relation between ST and the source operand.

## FPU Flags Affected

$C_1$ as described in Table 2-1; $C_0$, $C_2$, $C_3$ as specified above

## Numeric Exceptions

D, I, IS

## Protected Mode Exceptions

#GP(0) for an illegal memory operand effective address in the CS, DS, ES, FS, or GS segments; #SS(0) for an illegal address in the SS segment; #PF(fault-code) for a page fault; #NM if either EM or TS in CR0 is set.

## Real Address Mode Exceptions

Interupt 13 if any part of the operand would lie outside the effective address space from 0 to 0FFFFH; Interrupt 7 if either EM or TS in CR0 is set

## Virtual 8086 Mode Exceptions

Same exceptions as in Real Address Mode; #PF(fault code) for a page fault.

## Notes

The memory operand is converted to extended-real format before the comparison is performed.

If either operand is a NaN or is in an undefined format, or if a stack fault occurs, the invalid-operation exception is raised, and the condition bits are set to "unordered."

# FILD — Load Integer

| Opcode | Instruction | Clocks | Description |
|--------|-------------|--------|-------------|
| DF /0  | FILD[a] m16int | 61-65 | Push m16int onto the 387 DX stack. |
| DB /0  | FILD[a] m32int | 45-52 | Push m32int onto the 387 DX stack. |
| DF /5  | FILD[a] m64int | 56-67 | Push m64int onto the 387 DX stack. |

**Note:** a. When loading single- or double-precision zero from memory, add 5 clocks.

## Operation

Decrement NPX stack-top pointer;
ST(0) ← SRC;

## Description

FILD converts the source operand into extended-real format, and pushes it onto the NPX stack.

## FPU Flags Affected

$C_1$ as described in Table 2-1; $C_0$, $C_2$, $C_3$ undefined

## Numeric Exceptions

IS

## Protected Mode Exceptions

#GP(0) for an illegal memory operand effective address in the CS, DS, ES, FS, or GS segments; #SS(0) for an illegal address in the SS segment; #PF(fault-code) for a page fault; #NM if either EM or TS in CR0 is set.

## Real Address Mode Exceptions

Interrupt 13 if any part of the operand would lie outside the effective address space from 0 to 0FFFFH; Interrupt 7 if either EM or TS in CR0 is set

## Virtual 8086 Mode Exceptions

Same exceptions as in Real Address Mode; #PF(fault code) for a page fault.

## Notes

The source is loaded without rounding error.

ST(7) must be empty to avoid causing an invalid-operation exception.

## FINCSTP — Increment Stack-Top Pointer

| Opcode | Instruction | Clocks | Description |
|--------|-------------|--------|-------------|
| D9 F7 | FINCSTP | 21 | Increment top-of-stack pointer for 387 DX register stack. |

### Operation

IF TOP $= 7$
THEN TOP $\leftarrow$ 0;
ELSE TOP $\leftarrow$ TOP $+$ 1;
FI;

### Description

FINCSTP adds one (without carry) to the three-bit TOP field of the 387 DX status word.

### FPU Flags Affected

$C_1$ as described in Table 2-1; $C_0$, $C_2$, $C_3$ undefined

### Numeric Exceptions

None

### Protected Mode Exceptions

#NM if either EM or TS in CR0 is set

### Real Address Mode Exceptions

Interrupt 7 if either EM or TS in CR0 is set

### Virtual 8086 Mode Exceptions

#NM is either EM or TS in CR0 is set

### Notes

The effect of FINCSTP is to rotate the stack. It does not alter register tags or contents, nor does it transfer data. It is not equivalent to popping the stack, because it does not set the tag of the old stack-top to *empty*.

# FINIT/FNINIT — Initialize Floating-Point Unit

| Opcode | Instruction | Clocks | Description |
|---|---|---|---|
| 9B DB E3 | FINIT | 33 + at least 6 for FWAIT | Initialize 387 DX after checking for unmasked floating-point error condition. |
| DB E3 | FNINIT | 33 | Initialize 387 DX without checking for unmasked floating-point error condition. |

## Operation

CW ← 037FH;                    (* Control word *)
SW ← 0;                         (* Status word *)
TW ← FFFFH;                     (* Tag word *)
FEA ← 0; FDS ← 0;               (* Data pointer *)
FIP ← 0; FOP ← 0; FCS ← 0;      (* Instruction pointer *)

## Description

The initialization instructions set the 387 DX into a known state, unaffected by any previous activity.

The control word is set to 037FH (round to nearest, all exceptions masked, 64-bit precision). The status word is cleared (no exception flags set, stack register R0 = stack-top). The stack registers are all tagged as *empty*. The error pointers (both instruction and data) are cleared.

## FPU Flags Affected

$C_0$, $C_1$, $C_2$, $C_3$ cleared

## Numeric Exceptions

None

## Protected Mode Exceptions

#NM if either EM or TS in CR0 is set

## Real Address Mode Exceptions

Interrupt 7 if either EM or TS in CR0 is set

## Virtual 8086 Mode Exceptions

#NM if either EM or TS in CR0 is set

## Notes

FINIT checks for unmasked floating-point error conditions before performing the initialization; FNINIT does not.

FINIT and FNINIT leave the 387 DX in the same state as that which results from a hardware RESET signal with Built-In Self-Test.

# FIST/FISTP — Store Integer

| Opcode | Instruction | Clocks | Description |
|--------|-------------|--------|-------------|
| DF /2 | FIST m16int | 82-95 | Store ST in m16int. |
| DB /2 | FIST m32int | 79-93 | Store ST in m32int. |
| DF /3 | FISTP m16int | 82-95 | Store ST in m16int and pop ST. |
| DB /3 | FISTP m32int | 79-93 | Store ST in m32int and pop ST. |
| DF /7 | FISTP m64int | 80-97 | Store ST in m64int and pop ST. |

## Operation

DEST ← ST(0);
IF instruction = FISTP THEN pop ST FI;

## Description

FIST converts the value in ST into a signed integer according to the RC field of the control word and transfers the result to the destination. ST remains unchanged. FIST accepts word and short integer destinations; FISTP accepts these and long integers as well.

## FPU Flags Affected

$C_1$ as described in Table 2-1; $C_0$, $C_2$, $C_3$ undefined

## Numeric Exceptions

P, I, IS

## Protected Mode Exceptions

#GP(0) if the destination is in a nonwritable segment; #GP(0) for an illegal memory operand effective address in the CS, DS, ES, FS, or GS segments; #SS(0) for an illegal address in the SS segment; #PF(fault-code) for a page fault; #NM if either EM or TS in CR0 is set.

## Real Address Mode Exceptions

Interupt 13 if any part of the operand would lie outside the effective address space from 0 to 0FFFFH; Interrupt 7 if either EM or TS in CR0 is set

## Virtual 8086 Mode Exceptions

Same exceptions as in Real Address Mode; #PF(fault code) for a page fault.

## Notes

Negative zero is stored with the same encoding (00..00) as positive zero.

# FLD — Local Real

| Opcode | Instruction | Clocks | Description |
|--------|-------------|--------|-------------|
| D9 /0 | FLD[a] m32real | 20 | Push m32real onto the 387 DX stack. |
| DD /0 | FLD[a] m64real | 25 | Push m64real onto the 387 DX stack. |
| DB /5 | FLD[a] m80real | 44 | Push m80real onto the 387 DX stack. |
| D9 C0+i | FLD[a] ST(i) | 14 | Push ST(i) onto the 387 DX stack. |

**Note:** a. When loading single- or double-precision zero from memory, add 5 clocks.

## Operation

Decrement NPX stack-top pointer;
$ST(0) \leftarrow SRC$;

## Description

FLD pushes the source operand onto the 387 DX stack. If the source is a register, the register number used is that before the stack-top pointer is decremented. In particular, coding

FLD ST(0)

duplicates the stack top.

## FPU Flags Affected

$C_1$ as described in Table 2-1; $C_0$, $C_2$, $C_3$ undefined

## Numeric Exceptions

D, I, IS

## Protected Mode Exceptions

#GP(0) for an illegal memory operand effective address in the CS, DS, ES, FS, or GS segments; #SS(0) for an illegal address in the SS segment; #PF(fault-code) for a page fault; #NM if either EM or TS in CR0 is set.

## Real Address Mode Exceptions

Interrupt 13 if any part of the operand would lie outside the effective address space from 0 to 0FFFFH; Interrupt 7 if either EM or TS in CR0 is set

## Virtual 8086 Mode Exceptions

Same exceptions as in Real Address Mode; #PF(fault code) for a page fault.

## Notes

If the source operand is in single- or double-real format, it is automatically converted to the extended-real format. Loading an extended-real operand does not require conversion, so the I and D exceptions will not occur in this case.

ST(7) must be empty to avoid causing an invalid-operation exception.

# FLD1/FLDL2T/FLDL2E/ FLDPI/FLDLG2/FLDLN2/FLDZ — Load Constant

| Opcode | Instruction | Clocks | Description |
|--------|-------------|--------|-------------|
| D9 E8 | FLD1 | 24 | Push +1.0 onto the 387 DX Stack. |
| D9 E9 | FLDL2T | 40 | Push $\log_2 10$ onto the 387 DX Stack. |
| D9 EA | FLDL2E | 40 | Push $\log_2 e$ onto the 387 DX Stack. |
| D9 EB | FLDPI | 40 | Push $\pi$ onto the 387 DX Stack. |
| D9 EC | FLDLG2 | 41 | Push $\log_{10} 2$ onto the 387 DX Stack. |
| D9 ED | FLDLN2 | 41 | Push $\log_e 2$ onto the 387 DX Stack. |
| D9 EE | FLDZ | 20 | Push +0.0 onto the 387 DX Stack. |

## Operation

Decrement NPX stack-top pointer;
ST(0) ← CONSTANT;

## Description

Each of the constant instructions pushes a commonly-used constant (in extended-real format) onto the 387 DX stack.

## FPU Flags Affected

$C_1$ as described in Table 2-1; $C_0$, $C_2$, $C_3$ undefined

## Numeric Exceptions

IS

## Protected Mode Exceptions

#NM if either EM or TS in CR0 is set

## Real Address Mode Exceptions

Interrupt 7 if either EM or TS in CR0 is set

## Virtual 8086 Mode Exceptions

#NM if either EM or TS in CR0 is set

**Notes**

ST(7) must be empty to avoid an invalid exception.

Although the constant to be loaded is rounded to external-real format from a more precise internally-maintained value (as specified by the RC bit of the control word), the precision exception is not raised.

# FLDCW — Load Control Word

| Opcode | Instruction | Clocks | Description |
|--------|-------------|--------|-------------|
| D9 /5 | FNLDCW m2byte | 19 | Load control word from m2byte. |

## Operation

CW ← SRC;

## Description

FLDCW replaces the current value of the control word with the value contained in the specified memory word.

## FPU Flags Affected

$C_0$ $C_1$, $C_2$, $C_3$ undefined

## Numeric Exceptions

None, except for unmasking an existing exception

## Protected Mode Exceptions

#GP(0) for an illegal memory operand effective address in the CS, DS, ES, FS, or GS segments; #SS(0) for an illegal address in the SS segment; #PF(fault-code) for a page fault; #NM if either EM or TS in CR0 is set.

## Real Address Mode Exceptions

Interrupt 13 if any part of the operand would lie outside the effective address space from 0 to 0FFFFH; Interrupt 7 if either EM or TS in CR0 is set

## Virtual 8086 Mode Exceptions

Same exceptions as in Real Address Mode; #PF(fault code) for a page fault.

## Notes

FLDCW is typically used to establish or change the 387 DX's mode of operation.

In an exception bit in the status word is set, loading a new control word that unmasks that exception will result in a floating-point error condition. When changing modes, the recommended procedure is to clear any pending exceptions before loading the new control word.

# FLDENV—Load FPU Environment

| Opcode | Instruction | Clocks | Description |
|--------|-------------|--------|-------------|
| D9 /4 | FLDENV m14/28byte | 71 | Load NPX environment from *m14byte* or *m28byte*. |

## Operation

NPX environment ← SRC;

## Description

FLDENV reloads the NPX environment from the memory area defined by the source operand. This data should have been written by previous FSTENV or FNSTENV instruction.

The NPX environment consists of the control word, status word, tag word, and error pointers (both data and instruction). The environment layout in memory depends on both the operand size and the current operating mode of the processor. The USE attribute of the current code segment determines the operand size: the 14-byte operand applies to a USE16 segment, and the 28-byte operand applies to a USE32 segment. Figures 2-5 through 2-8 show the environment layouts for both operand sizes in both real mode and protected mode. (In virtual-8086 mode, the real mode layout is used.) FLDENV should be executed in the same operating mode as the corresponding FSTENV or FNSTENV.

## FPU Flags Affected

$C_0$, $C_1$, $C_2$, $C_3$ as loaded

## Numeric Exceptions

None, except for loading an unmasked exception

## Protected Mode Exceptions

#GP(0) for an illegal memory operand effective address in the CS, DS, ES, FS, or GS segments; #SS(0) for an illegal address in the SS segment; #PF(fault-code) for a page fault; #NM if either EM or TS in CR0 is set.

## Real Address Mode Exceptions

Interrupt 13 if any part of the operand would lie outside the effective address space from 0 to 0FFFFH; Interrupt 7 if either EM or TS in CR0 is set

## Virtual 8086 Mode Exceptions

Same exceptions as in Real Address Mode; #PF(fault code) for a page fault.

## Notes

If the environment image contains an unmasked exception, loading it will result in a floating-point error condition.

If the loaded data was not previously written by an FSTENV/FNSTENV instruction, the operand field may be invalid.

# FMUL/FMULP/FIMUL — Multiply

| Opcode | Instruction | Clocks | Description |
|---|---|---|---|
| D8 /1 | FMUL m32real | 27-35 | Multiply ST by m32real. |
| DC /1 | FMUL m64real | 32-57 | Multiply ST by m64real. |
| D8 C8+i | FMUL ST, ST(i) | 29-57[1] | Multiply ST by ST(i) |
| DC C8+i | FMUL ST(i), ST | 29-57[1] | Multiply ST(i) by ST. |
| DE C8+i | FMULP ST(i), ST | 29-57[1] | Multiply ST(i) by ST and pop ST. |
| DE C9 | FMUL | 29-57[1] | Multiply ST(1) by ST and pop ST. |
| DA /1 | FIMUL m32int | 61-82 | Multiply ST by m32int. |
| DE /1 | FIMUL m16int | 76-87 | Multiply ST by m16int. |

**Note:** (1) Typical = 52 (when d = 0, 46-54, typical = 49)

## Operation

DEST ← DEST x SRC;
IF instruction = FMULP THEN pop ST FI;

## Description

The multiplication instructions multiply the destination operand by the source operand and return the product to the destination.

## FPU Flags Affected

$C_1$ as described in Table 2-1; $C_0$, $C_2$, $C_3$ undefined

## Numeric Exceptions

P, U, O, D, I, I

## Protected Mode Exceptions

#GP(0) for an illegal memory operand effective address in the CS, DS, ES, FS, or GS segments; #SS(0) for an illegal address in the SS segment; #PF(fault-code) for a page fault; #NM if either EM or TS in CR0 is set.

## Real Address Mode Exceptions

Interrupt 13 if any part of the operand would lie outside the effective address space from 0 to 0FFFFH; Interrupt 7 if either EM or TS in CR0 is set

## Virtual 8086 Mode Exceptions

Same exceptions as in Real Address Mode; #PF(fault code) for a page fault.

## Notes

If the source operand is in memory, it is automatically converted to the extended-real format.

# FNOP — No Operation

| Opcode | Instruction | Clocks | Description |
|--------|-------------|--------|-------------|
| D9 D0 | FNOP | 12 | No operation is performed. |

## Description

FNOP performs no operation. It affects nothing except instruction pointers.

## FPU Flags Affected

$C_0$, $C_1$, $C_2$, $C_3$ undefined

## Numeric Exceptions

None

## Protected Mode Exceptions

#NM if either EM or TS in CR0 is set

## Real Address Mode Exceptions

Interrupt 7 if either EM or TS in CR0 is set

## Virtual 8086 Mode Exceptions

#NM if either EM or TS in CR0 is set

9
# FPATAN — Partial Arctangent

| Opcode | Instruction | Clocks | Description |
|--------|-------------|--------|-------------|
| D9 F3  | FPATAN      | 314-487 | Replace ST(1) with arctan(ST(1) ÷ ST) and pop ST. |

## Operation

ST(1) ← arctan(ST(1) ÷ ST);
pop ST;

## Description

The partial arctangent instruction computes the arctangent of ST(1) ÷ ST, and returns the computed value, expressed in radians, to ST(1). It then pops ST. The result has the same sign as the operand from ST(1), and a magnitude less than $\pi$.

## FPU Flags Affected

$C_1$ as described in Table 2-1; $C_0$, $C_2$, $C_3$ undefined

## Numeric Exceptions

P, U, D, I, IS

## Protected Mode Exceptions

#NM if either EM or TS in CR0 is set

## Real Address Mode Exceptions

Interrupt 7 if either EM or TS in CR0 is set

## Virtual 8086 Mode Exceptions

#NM if either EM or TS in CR0 is set

## Notes

There is no restriction on the range of arguments that FPATAN can accept.

The fact that FPATAN takes two arguments and computes the arctangent of their ratio simplifies the calculation of other trigonometric functions. For instance, arcsin(x) (which is the arctangent of $x \div \sqrt{(1-x^2)}$) can be computed using the following sequence of operations: Push x onto the FPU stack; compute $\sqrt{(1-x^2)}$ and push the resulting value onto the stack; execute FPATAN.

# FPREM — Partial Remainder

| Opcode | Instruction | Clocks | Description |
|--------|-------------|--------|-------------|
| D9 F8 | FPREM | 74-155 | Replace ST with the remainder obtained on dividing ST by ST(1). |

## Operation

EXPDIF ← exponent(ST) − exponent(ST(1));
IF EXPDIF < 64
THEN
    Q ← integer obtained by chopping ST ÷ ST(1) toward zero;
    ST ← ST − (ST(1) x Q);
    C2 ← 0;
    C0, C1, C3 ← three least-significant bits of Q; (* Q2, Q1, Q0 *)
ELSE
    C2 ← 1;
    N ← a number between 32 and 63;
    QQ ← integer obtained by chopping (ST ÷ ST(1)) ÷ $2^{EXPDIF-N}$
        toward zero;
    ST ← ST − (ST(1) x QQ x $2^{EXPDIF-N}$);
FI;

## Description

The partial remainder instruction computes the remainder obtained on dividing ST by ST(1), and leaves the result in ST. The sign of the remainder is the same as the sign of the original dividend in ST. The magnitude of the remainder is less than that of the modulus.

### FPU Flags Affected

$C_0$, $C_1$, $C_2$, $C_3$ as described in Table 2-1

### Numeric Exceptions

U, D, I, IS

### Protected Mode Exceptions

#NM if either EM or TS in CR0 is set

### Real Address Mode Exceptions

Interrupt 7 if either EM or TS in CR0 is set

## Virtual 8086 Mode Exceptions

#NM if either EM or TS in CR0 is set

## Notes

FPREM produces an exact result; the precision (inexact) exception does not occur and the rounding control has no effect.

The FPREM instruction is not the remainder operation specified in IEEE Std 754. To get that remainder, the FPREM1 instruction should be used. FPREM is supported for compatibility with the 8087 and 287 numeric coprocessors.

FPREM works by iterative subtraction, and can reduce the exponent of ST by no more than 63 in one execution. If FPREM succeeds in producing a remainder that is less than the modulus, the function is complete and the $C_2$ flag is cleared. Otherwise, $C_2$ is set, and the result in ST is called the *partial* remainder. The exponent of the partial remainder is less than the exponent of the original dividend by at least 32. Software can re-execute the instruction (using the partial remainder in ST as the dividend) until $C_2$ is cleared. A higher-priority interrupting routine that needs the 387 DX can force a context switch between the instructions in the remainder loop.

An important use of FPREM is to reduce the arguments of periodic functions. When reduction is complete, FPREM provides the three least-significant bits of the quotient in flags $C_3$, $C_1$, and $C_0$. This is important in argument reduction for the tangent function (using a modulus of $\pi/4$), because it locates the original angle in the correct one of eight sectors of the unit circle.

# FPREM1 — Partial Remainder

| Opcode | Instruction | Clocks | Description |
|--------|-------------|--------|-------------|
| D9 F5 | FPREM1 | 95-185 | Replace ST with the remainder obtained on dividing ST by ST(1). |

## Operation

EXPDIF ← exponent(ST) − exponent(ST(1));
IF EXPDIF < 64
THEN
    Q ← integer obtained by chopping ST ÷ ST(1);
    ST ← ST − (ST(1) x Q);
    C2 ← 0;
    C0, C1, C3 ← three least-significant bits of Q; (* Q2, Q1, Q0 *)
ELSE
    C2 ← 1;
    N ← a number between 32 and 63;
    QQ ← integer nearest to (ST ÷ ST(1)) ÷ $2^{EXPDIF-N}$;
    ST ← ST − (ST(1) x QQ x $2^{EXPDIF-N}$;
FI;

## Description

The partial remainder instruction computes the remainder obtained on dividing ST by ST(1), and leaves the result in ST. The magnitude of the remainder is less than half the magnitude of the modulus.

## FPU Flags Affected

$C_0$, $C_1$, $C_2$, $C_3$ as described in Table 2-1

## Numeric Exceptions

U, D, I, IS

## Protected Mode Exceptions

#NM if either EM or TS in CR0 is set

## Real Address Mode Exceptions

Interrupt 7 if either EM or TS in CR0 is set

## Virtual 8086 Mode Exceptions

#NM if either EM or TS in CR0 is set

## Notes

FPREM1 produces an exact result; the precision (inexact) exception does not occur and the rounding control has no effect.

The FPREM1 instruction is the remainder operation specified in IEEE Std 754. It differs from FPREM in the way it rounds the quotient of ST and ST(1).

FPREM1 works by iterative subtraction, and can reduce the exponent of ST by no more than 63 in one execution. If FPREM1 succeeds in producing a remainder that is less than one half the modulus, the function is complete and the $C_2$ flag is cleared. Otherwise, $C_2$ is set, and the result in ST is called the *partial* remainder. The exponent of the partial remainder is less than the exponent of the original dividend by at least 32. Software can re-execute the instruction (using the partial remainder in ST as the dividend) until $C_2$ is cleared. A higher-priority interrupting routine that needs the FPU can force a context switch between the instructions in the remainder loop.

An important use of FPREM1 is to reduce the arguments of periodic functions. When reduction is complete, FPREM1 provides the three least-significant bits of the quotient in flags $C_3$, $C_1$, and $C_0$. This is important in argument reduction for the tangent function (using a modulus of $\pi/4$), because it locates the original angle in the correct one of eight sectors of the unit circle.

# FPTAN — Partial Tangent

| Opcode | Instruction | Clocks | Description |
|--------|-------------|--------|-------------|
| D9 F2 | FPTAN | 191-497[1] | Replace ST with its tangent and push 1 onto the NPX stack. |

**Note:** (1) For operands outside of the range $|x| < \pi/4$, up to 76 additional clocks may be needed to reduce the operand.

## Operation

```
IF operand is in range
THEN
      C2 ← 0;
      ST ← tan(ST);
      Decrement stack-top pointer;
      ST ← 1.0;
ELSE
      C2 ← 1;
FI;
```

## Description

The partial tangent instruction replaces the contents of ST with tan(ST), and then pushes 1.0 onto the NPX stack. ST, expressed in radians, must lie in the range $|\theta| < 2^{63}$.

## FPU Flags Affected

$C_1$, $C_2$, as described in Table 2-1; $C_0$, $C_3$ undefined

## Numeric Exceptions

P, U, D, I, IS

## Protected Mode Exceptions

#NM if either EM or TS in CR0 is set

## Real Address Mode Exceptions

Interrupt 7 if either EM or TS in CR0 is set

## Virtual 8086 Mode Exceptions

#NM if either EM or TS in CR0 is set

## Notes

If the operand is outside the acceptable range, the $C_2$ flag is set, and ST remains unchanged. It is the programmer's responsibility to reduce the operand to an absolute value smaller than $2^{63}$ by subtracting an appropriate integer multiple of $2\pi$.

The fact that FPTAN pushes 1.0 onto the 387 DX stack after computing tan(ST) maintains compatibility with the 8087 and 80287 numeric coprocessors, and simplifies the calculation of other trigonometric functions. For instance, the cotangent (which is the reciprocal of the tangent) can be computed by executing FDIVR after FPTAN.

ST(7) must be empty to avoid an invalid-operation exception.

# FRNDINT — Round to Integer

| Opcode | Instruction | Clocks | Description |
|--------|-------------|--------|-------------|
| D9 FC | FRNDINT | 66-80 | Round ST to an integer. |

## Operation

ST ← rounded ST;

## Description

The round to integer instruction rounds the value in ST to an integer according to the RC field of the control word.

## FPU Flags Affected

$C_1$ as described in Table 2-1; $C_0$, $C_2$, $C_3$ undefined

## Numeric Exceptions

P, D, I, IS

## Protected Mode Exceptions

#NM if either EM or TS in CR0 is set

## Real Address Mode Exceptions

Interrupt 7 if either EM or TS in CR0 is set

## Virtual 8086 Mode Exceptions

#NM if either EM or TS in CR0 is set

# FRSTOR — Restore FPU State

| Opcode | Instruction | Clocks | Description |
|--------|-------------|--------|-------------|
| DB /4  | FRSTOR m94/108byte | 308 | Load 387 DX state from m94byte or m108byte. |

## Operation

NPX state ← SRC;

## Description

FRSTOR reloads the FPU state (environment and register stack) from the memory area defined by the source operand. This data should have been written by a previous FSAVE or FNSAVE instruction.

The 387 DX environment consists of the control word, status word, tag word, and error pointers (both data and instruction). The environment layout in memory depends on both the operand size and the current operating mode of the processor. The USE attribute of the current code segment determines the operand size: the 14-byte operand applies to a USE16 segment, and the 28-byte operand applies to a USE32 segment. Figures 2-5 through 2-8 show the environment layouts for both operand sizes in both real mode and protected mode. (In virtual-8086 mode, the real mode layout is used.) The stack registers, beginning with ST and ending with ST(7), are in the 80 bytes that immediately follow the environment image. FRSTOR should be executed in the same operating mode as the corresponding FSAVE or FNSAVE.

## FPU Flags Affected

$C_0$ $C_1$, $C_2$, $C_3$ as loaded

## Numeric Exceptions

None, except for loading an unmasked exception

## Protected Mode Exceptions

#GP(0) for an illegal memory operand effective address in the CS, DS, ES, FS, or GS segments; #SS(0) for an illegal address in the SS segment; #PF(fault-code) for a page fault; #NM if either EM or TS in CR0 is set.

## Real Address Mode Exceptions

Interrupt 13 if any part of the operand would lie outside the effective address space from 0 to 0FFFFH; Interrupt 7 if either EM or TS in CR0 is set

## Virtual 8086 Mode Exceptions

Same exceptions as in Real Address Mode; #PF(fault code) for a page fault.

## Notes

If the state image contains an unmasked exception, loading it will result in a floating-point error condition.

# FSAVE/FNSAVE — Store FPU State

| Opcode | Instruction | Clocks | Description |
|---|---|---|---|
| 9B DB /6 | FSAVE m94/108byte | 375-376<br>+ at least 6 for FWAIT | Store 387 DX state to m94byte or m108byte after checking for unmasked floating-point error condition. Then re-initialize the FPU. |
| DB /6 | FNSAVE m94/108byte | 375-376 | Store 387 DX environment to m94byte or m108byte without checking for unmasked floating-point error condition. Then re-initialize the FPU. |

## Operation

DEST ← NPX state;
initialize NPX; (* Equivalent to FNINIT *)

## Description

The save instructions write the current 387 DX state (environment and register stack) to the specified destination, and then re-initialize the 387 DX. The environment consists of the control word, status word, tag word, and error pointers (both data and instruction).

The state layout in memory depends on both the operand size and the current operating mode of the processor. The USE attribute of the current code segment determines the operand size: the 94-byte operand applies to a USE16 segment, and the 108-byte operand applies to a USE32 segment. Figures 2-5 through 2-8 show the environment layouts for both operand sizes in both real mode and protected mode. (In virtual-8086 mode, the real mode layout is used.) The stack registers, beginning with ST and ending with ST(7), are stored in the 80 bytes that immediately follow the environment image.

## FPU Flags Affected

$C_0$, $C_1$, $C_2$, $C_3$ cleared

## Numeric Exceptions

None

## Protected Mode Exceptions

#GP(0) if the destination is in a nonwritable segment; #GP(0) for an illegal memory operand effective address in the CS, DS, ES, FS, or GS segments; #SS(0) for an illegal address in the SS segment; #PF(fault-code) for a page fault; #NM if either EM or TS in CR0 is set.

## Real Address Mode Exceptions

Interrupt 13 if any part of the operand would lie outside the effective address space from 0 to 0FFFFH; Interrupt 7 if either EM or TS in CR0 is set

## Virtual 8086 Mode Exceptions

Same exceptions as in Real Address Mode; #PF(fault code) for a page fault.

## Notes

FSAVE and FNSAVE do not store the 387 DX state until all NPX activity is complete. Thus, the saved image reflects the state of the FPU after any previously decoded instruction has been executed.

If a program is to read from the memory image of the state following a save instruction, it must issue an FWAIT instruction to ensure that the storage is complete.

The save instructions are typically used when an operating system needs to perform a context switch, or an exception handler needs to use the NPX, or an application program wants to pass a "clean" NPX environment to a subroutine.

FSAVE checks for unmasked floating-point error conditions before storing the environment; FNSAVE does not.

# FSCALE — Scale

| Opcode | Instruction | Clocks | Description |
|--------|-------------|--------|-------------|
| D9 FD | FSCALE | 67-86 | Scale ST by ST(1). |

## Operation

$ST \leftarrow ST \times 2^{ST(1)};$

## Description

The scale instruction interprets the value in ST(1) as an integer, and adds this integer to the exponent of ST. Thus, FSCALE provides rapid multiplication or division by integral powers of 2.

## FPU Flags Affected

$C_1$ as described in Table 2-1; $C_0$, $C_2$, $C_3$ undefined

## Numeric Exceptions

P, U, O, D, I, IS

## Protected Mode Exceptions

#NM if either EM or TS in CR0 is set

## Real Address Mode Exceptions

Interrupt 7 if either EM or TS in CR0 is set

## Virtual 8086 Mode Exceptions

#NM if either EM or TS in CR0 is set

## Notes

FSCALE can be used as an inverse to FXTRACT. Since FSCALE does not pop the exponent part, however, FSCALE must be followed by FSTP ST(1) in order to completely undo the effect of a preceding FXTRACT.

There is no limit on the range of the scale factor in ST(1). If the value is not integral, FSCALE uses the nearest integer smaller in magnitude; i.e., it chops the value toward 0. If the resulting integer is zero, the value in ST is not changed.

# FSIN — Sine

| Opcode | Instruction | Clocks | Description |
|--------|-------------|--------|-------------|
| D9 FE | FSIN | 122-771[1] | Replace ST with its sine. |

**Note:** (1) For operands outside of the range $|x| < \pi/4$, up to 76 additional clocks may be needed to reduce the operand.

## Operation

```
IF operand is in range
THEN
      C2 ← 0;
      ST ← sin(ST);
ELSE
      C2 ← 1;
FI:
```

## Description

The sine instruction replaces the contents of ST with sin(ST). ST, expressed in radians, must lie in the range $| \theta | < 2^{63}$.

## FPU Flags Affected

$C_1$, $C_2$ as described in Table 2-1; $C_0$, $C_3$ undefined

## Numeric Exceptions

P, U, D, I, IS

## Protected Mode Exceptions

#NM if either EM or TS in CR0 is set

## Real Address Mode Exceptions

Interrupt 7 if either EM or TS in CR0 is set

## Virtual 8086 Mode Exceptions

#NM if either EM or TS in CR0 is set

## Notes

If the operand is outside the acceptable range, the $C_2$ flag is set, and ST remains unchanged. It is the programmer's responsibility to reduce the operand to an absolute value smaller than $2^{63}$ by subtracting an appropriate integer multiple of $2\pi$. See Chapter 3 for a discussion of the proper value to use for $\pi$ in performing such reductions.

# FSINCOS — Sine and Cosine

| Opcode | Instruction | Clocks | Description |
|--------|-------------|--------|-------------|
| D9 FB | FSINCOS | 194-809[1] | Compute the sine and cosine of ST; replace ST with the sine, and then push the cosine onto the 387 DX stack. |

**Note:** (1) Operands not in the range $|x| < \pi/4$, up to 76 additional clocks may be needed to reduce the operand.

## Operation

IF operand is in range
THEN
　　C2 ← 0;
　　TEMP ← cos(ST);
　　ST ← sin(ST);
　　Decrement NPX stack-top pointer;
　　ST ← TEMP;
ELSE
　　C2 ← 1;
FI:

## Description

FSINCOS computes both sin(ST) and cos(ST), replaces ST with the sine and then pushes the cosine onto the NPX stack. ST, expressed in radians, must lie in the range $|\theta| < 2^{63}$.

## FPU Flags Affected

$C_1$, $C_2$, as described in Table 2-1; $C_0$, $C_3$ undefined

## Numeric Exceptions

P, U, D, I, IS

## Protected Mode Exceptions

#NM if either EM or TS in CR0 is set

## Real Address Mode Exceptions

Interrupt 7 if either EM or TS in CR0 is set

## Virtual 8086 Mode Exceptions

#NM if either EM or TS in CR0 is set

## Notes

If the operand is outside the acceptable range, the $C_2$ flag is set, and ST remains unchanged. It is the programmer's responsibility to reduce the operand to an absolute value smaller than $2^{63}$ by subtracting an appropriate integer multiple of $2\pi$. See Chapter 3 for a discussion of the proper value to use for $\pi$ in performing such reductions.

It is faster to execute FSINCOS than to execute both FSIN and FCOS.

# FSQRT — Square Root

| Opcode | Instruction | Clocks | Description |
|--------|-------------|--------|-------------|
| D9 FA | FSQRT | 122-129 | Replace ST with its square root. |

## Operation

ST ← square root of ST;

## Description

The square root instruction replaces the value in ST with its square root.

## FPU Flags Affected

$C_1$ as described in Table 2-1; $C_0$, $C_2$, $C_3$ undefined

## Numeric Exceptions

P, D, I, IS

## Protected Mode Exceptions

#NM if either EM or TS in CR0 is set

## Real Address Mode Exceptions

Interrupt 7 if either EM or TS in CR0 is set

## Virtual 8086 Mode Exceptions

#NM if either EM or TS in CR0 is set

# FST/FSTP — Store Real

| Opcode | Instruction | Clocks | Description |
|---|---|---|---|
| D9 /2 | FST m32real | 44 | Copy ST to m32real. |
| DD /2 | FST m64real | 45 | Copy ST to m64real. |
| DD D0+i | FST ST(i) | 11 | Copy ST to ST(i). |
| D9 /3 | FSTP m32real | 44 | Copy ST to m32real and pop ST. |
| DD /3 | FSTP m64real | 45 | Copy ST to m64real and pop ST. |
| DB /7 | FSTP m80real | 53 | Copy ST to m80real and pop ST. |
| DD D8+i | FSTP ST(i) | 12 | Copy ST to ST(i) and pop ST. |

## Operation

DEST ← ST(0);
IF instruction = FSTP THEN pop ST FI;

## Description

FST copies the current value in the ST register to the destination, which can be another register or a single- or double-real memory operand. FSTP copies and then pops ST; it accepts extended-real memory operands as well as the types accepted by FST.

If the source is a register, the register number used is that before the stack is popped.

## FPU Flags Affected

$C_1$ as described in Table 2-1; $C_0$, $C_2$, $C_3$ undefined

## Numeric Exceptions

Register or extended-real destinations: IS
Single- or double-real destinations: P, U, O, D, I, IS

## Protected Mode Exceptions

#GP(0) if the destination is in a nonwritable segment; #GP(0) for an illegal memory operand effective address in the CS, DS, ES, FS, or GS segments; #SS(0) for an illegal address in the SS segment; #PF(fault-code) for a page fault; #NM if either EM or TS in CR0 is set.

## Real Address Mode Exceptions

Interrupt 13 if any part of the operand would lie outside the effective address space from 0 to 0FFFFH; Interrupt 7 if either EM or TS in CR0 is set

## Virtual 8086 Mode Exceptions

Same exceptions as in Real Address Mode; #PF(fault code) for a page fault.

## Notes

If the destination is single- or double-real, the significand is rounded to the width of the destination according to the RC field of the control word, and the exponent is converted to the width and bias of the destination format. The over/underflow condition is checked for as well.

If ST contains zero, $\pm\infty$, or a NaN, then the significand is not rounded, but chopped (on the right) to fit the destination. Nor is the exponent converted; it too is chopped on the right. These operations preserve the value's identity as $\infty$ or NaN (exponent all ones).

The invalid-operation exception is not raised when the destination is a nonempty stack element.

# FSTCW/FNSTCW — Store Control Word

| Opcode | Instruction | Clocks | Description |
|--------|-------------|--------|-------------|
| 9B D9 /7 | FSTCW m2byte | 15 + at least 6 for FWAIT | Store 387 DX control word to m2byte after checking for unmasked floating-point error condition. |
| D9 /7 | FNSTCW m2byte | 15 | Store 387 DX control word to m2byte without checking for unmasked floating-point error condition. |

## Operation

DEST ← CW;

## Description

FSTCW and FNSTCW write the current value of the 387 DX control word to the specified destination.

## FPU Flags Affected

$C_0$, $C_1$ $C_2$, $C_3$ undefined

## Numeric Exceptions

None

## Protected Mode Exceptions

#GP(0) if the destination is in a nonwritable segment; #GP(0) for an illegal memory operand effective address in the CS, DS, ES, FS, or GS segments; #SS(0) for an illegal address in the SS segment; #PF(fault-code) for a page fault; #NM if either EM or TS in CR0 is set.

## Real Address Mode Exceptions

Interrupt 13 if any part of the operand would lie outside the effective address space from 0 to 0FFFFH; Interrupt 7 if either EM or TS in CR0 is set

## Virtual 8086 Mode Exceptions

Same exceptions as in Real Address Mode; #PF(fault code) for a page fault.

## Notes

FSTCW checks for unmasked floating-point error conditions before storing the control word; FNSTCW does not.

# FSTENV/FNSTENV — Store FPU Environment

| Opcode | Instruction | Clocks | Description |
|---|---|---|---|
| 9B D9 /6 | FSTENV m14/28byte | 103-104<br>+ at least 6 for FWAIT | Store 387 DX environment to m14byte or m28byte after checking for unmasked floating-point error condition. Then mask all floating-point exceptions. |
| D9 /6 | FNSTENV m14/28byte | 103-104 | Store 387 DX environment to m14byte or m28byte without checking for unmasked floating-point error condition. Then mask all floating-point exceptions. |

## Operation

DEST ← NPX environment;
CW[0..5] ← 111111B;

## Description

The store environment instructions write the current environment to the specified destination, and then mask all floating-point exceptions. The environment consists of the control word, status word, tag word, and error pointer (both data and instruction).

The environment layout in memory depends on both the operand size and the current operating mode of the processor. The USE attribute of the current code segment determines the operand size: the 14-byte operand applies to a USE16 segment, and the 28-byte operand applies to a USE32 segment. Figures 2-5 through 2-8 show the environment layouts for both operand sizes in both real mode and protected mode. (In virtual-8086 mode, the real mode layout is used.)

## FPU Flags Affected

$C_0$, $C_1$, $C_2$, $C_3$ undefined

## Numeric Exceptions

None

## Protected Mode Exceptions

#GP(0) if the destination is in a nonwritable segment; #GP(0) for an illegal memory operand effective address in the CS, DS, ES, FS, or GS segments; #SS(0) for an illegal address in the SS segment; #PF(fault-code) for a page fault; #NM if either EM or TS in CR0 is set.

## Real Address Mode Exceptions

Interrupt 13 if any part of the operand would lie outside the effective address space from 0 to 0FFFFH; Interrupt 7 if either EM or TS in CR0 is set

## Virtual 8086 Mode Exceptions

Same exceptions as in Real Address Mode; #PF(fault code) for a page fault.

## Notes

FSTENV and FNSTENV do not store the environment until all 387 DX activity is complete. Thus, the saved environment reflects the state of the 387 DX after any previously decoded instruction has been executed.

The store environment instructions are often used by exception handlers because they provide access to the 387 DX error pointers. The instructions are also used by operating systems to save the numeric state before a task switch. The environment is typically saved onto the memory stack. After saving the environment, FSTENV and FNSTENV sets all the exception masks in the 387 DX control word. This prevents floating-point errors from interrupting the exception handler.

FSTENV checks for unmasked floating-point error conditions before storing the 387 DX environment; FNSTENV does not.

# FSTSW/FNSTSW — Store Status Word

| Opcode | Instruction | Clocks | Description |
|--------|-------------|--------|-------------|
| 9B DF /7 | FSTSW m2byte | 15 + at least 6 for FWAIT | Store 387 DX status word to m2byte after checking for unmasked floating-point error condition. |
| 9B DF E0 | FSTSW AX | 13 + at least 6 for FWAIT | Store 387 DX status word to AX register after checking for unmasked floating-point error condition. |
| DF /7 | FNSTSW m2byte | 15 | Store 387 DX status word to m2byte without checking for unmasked floating-point error condition. |
| DF E0 | FNSTSW AX | 13 | Store 387 DX status word to AX register without checking for unmasked floating-point error condition. |

## Operation

DEST ← SW;

## Description

FSTSW and FNSTSW write the current value of the 387 DX status word to the specified destination, which can be either a two-byte location in memory or the AX register.

## FPU Flags Affected

$C_0$, $C_1$, $C_2$, $C_3$ undefined

## Numeric Exceptions

None

## Protected Mode Exceptions

#GP(0) if the destination is in a nonwritable segment; #GP(0) for an illegal memory operand effective address in the CS, DS, ES, FS, or GS segments; #SS(0) for an illegal address in the SS segment; #PF(fault-code) for a page fault; #NM if either EM or TS in CR0 is set.

## Real Address Mode Exceptions

Interrupt 13 if any part of the operand would lie outside the effective address space from 0 to 0FFFFH; Interrupt 7 if either EM or TS in CR0 is set

## Virtual 8086 Mode Exceptions

Same exceptions as in Real Address Mode; #PF(fault code) for a page fault.

## Notes

FSTSW checks for unmasked floating-point error conditions before storing the status word; FNSTSW does not.

FSTSW and FNSTSW are used primarily in conditional branching (after a comparison, FPREM, FPREM1, or FXAM instruction). They can also be used to invoke exception handlers (by polling the exception bits) in environments that do not use interrupts.

When FNSTSW AX is executed, the AX register is updated before the CPU processor executes any further instructions. The status stored is that from the completion of the prior ESC instruction.

# FSUB/FSUBP/FISUB — Subtract

| Opcode | Instruction | Clocks | Description |
|--------|-------------|--------|-------------|
| D8 /4 | FSUB m32real | 24-32 | Subtract m32real from ST. |
| DC /4 | FSUB m64real | 28-36 | Subtract m64real from ST. |
| D8 E8+i | FSUB ST, ST(i) | 26-34[1] | Subtract ST(i) from ST. |
| DC E8+i | FSUB ST(i), ST | 26-34[1] | Replace ST(i) with ST − ST(i). |
| DE E8+i | FSUBP ST(i), ST | 26-34[1] | Replace ST(i) with ST − ST(i); pop ST. |
| DE E9 | FSUB | 26-34[1] | Replace ST(1) with ST − ST(1); pop ST. |
| DA /4 | FISUB m32int | 57-82 | Subtract m32int from ST. |
| DE /4 | FISUB m16int | 71-83[2] | Subtract m16int from ST. |

**Note:** (1) Add 1 clock to each range when R = 1.
(2) Add 3 clocks to the range when d = 0.

## Operation

DEST ← ST − Other Operand;
IF instruction = FSUBP THEN pop ST FI;

## Description

The subtraction instructions subtract the other operand from the stack top and return the difference to the destination.

## FPU Flags Affected

$C_1$ as described in Table 2-1; $C_0$, $C_2$, $C_3$ undefined

## Numeric Exceptions

P, U, O, D, I, IS

## Protected Mode Exceptions

#GP(0) for an illegal memory operand effective address in the CS, DS, ES, FS, or GS segments; #SS(0) for an illegal address in the SS segment; #PF(fault-code) for a page fault; #NM if either EM or TS in CR0 is set.

## Real Address Mode Exceptions

Interrupt 13 if any part of the operand would lie outside the effective address space from 0 to 0FFFFH; Interrupt 7 if either EM or TS in CR0 is set

## Virtual 8086 Mode Exceptions

Same exceptions as in Real Address Mode; #PF(fault code) for a page fault.

## Notes

If the source operand is in memory, it is automatically converted to the extended-real format.

# FSUBR/FSUBPR/FISUBR – Reverse Subtract

| Opcode | Instruction | Clocks | Description |
|--------|-------------|--------|-------------|
| D8 /5 | FSUBR m32real | 24-32 | Replace ST with m32real − ST. |
| DC /5 | FSUBR m64real | 28-36 | Replace ST with m64real − ST. |
| D8 E0+i | FSUBR ST, ST(i) | 26-34[1] | Replace ST with ST(i) − ST. |
| DC E0+i | FSUBR ST(i), ST | 26-34[1] | Subtract ST from ST(i). |
| DE E0+i | FSUBRP ST(i), ST | 26-34[1] | Subtract ST from ST(i) and pop ST. |
| DE E1 | FSUBR | 26-34[1] | Subtract ST from ST(1) and pop ST. |
| DA /5 | FISUBR m32int | 57-82 | Replace ST with m32int − ST. |
| DE /5 | FISUBR m16int | 71-83[2] | Replace ST with m16int − ST. |

**Note:** (1) Add 1 clock to each range when R = 0.
(2) Add 3 clocks to the range when d = 0.

## Operation

DEST ← Other Operand − ST;
IF instruction = FSUBRP THEN pop ST FI;

## Description

The reverse subtraction instructions subtract the stack top from the other operand and return the difference to the destination.

## FPU Flags Affected

$C_1$ as described in Table 2-1; $C_0$, $C_2$, $C_3$ undefined

## Numeric Exceptions

P, U, O, D, I, IS

## Protected Mode Exceptions

#GP(0) for an illegal memory operand effective address in the CS, DS, ES, FS, or GS segments; #SS(0) for an illegal address in the SS segment; #PF(fault-code) for a page fault; #NM if either EM or TS in CR0 is set.

## Real Address Mode Exceptions

Interrupt 13 if any part of the operand would lie outside the effective address space from 0 to 0FFFFH; Interrupt 7 if either EM or TS in CR0 is set

## Virtual 8086 Mode Exceptions

Same exceptions as in Real Address Mode; #PF(fault code) for a page fault.

## Notes

If the source operand is in memory, it is automatically converted to the extended-real format.

# FTST — TEST

| Opcode | Instruction | Clocks | Description |
|--------|-------------|--------|-------------|
| D9 E4 | FTST | 28 | Compare ST with 0.0. |

## Operation

CASE (relation of operands) OF
    Not comparable:   C3, C2, C0 ← 111;
    ST > 0.0:         C3, C2, C0 ← 000;
    ST < 0.0:         C3, C2, C0 ← 001;
    ST = 0.0:         C3, C2, C0 ← 100;

## Description

The test instruction compares the stack top to 0.0. Following the instruction, the condition codes reflect the result of the comparison.

## FPU Flags Affected

$C_1$ as described in Table 2-1; $C_0$, $C_2$, $C_3$ as specified above

## Numeric Exceptions

D, I, IS

## Protected Mode Exceptions

#NM if either EM or TS in CR0 is set

## Real Address Mode Exceptions

Interrupt 7 if either EM or TS in CR0 is set

## Virtual 8086 Mode Exceptions

#NM if either EM or TS in CR0 is set

## Notes

If ST contains a NaN or an object of undefined format, or if a stack fault occurs, the invalid-operation exception is raised, and the condition bits are set to "unordered."

The sign of zero is ignored, so that $-0.0 = -+0.0$.

# FUCOM/FUCOMP/FUCOMPP — Unordered Compare Real

| Opcode | Instruction | Clocks | Description |
|--------|-------------|--------|-------------|
| DD E0+i | FUCOM ST(i) | 24 | Compare ST with ST(i). |
| DD E1 | FUCOM | 24 | Compare ST with ST(1). |
| DD E8+i | FUCOMP ST(i) | 26 | Compare ST with ST(i) and pop ST. |
| DD E9 | FUCOMP | 26 | Compare ST with ST(1) and pop ST. |
| DA E9 | FUCOMPP | 26 | Compare ST with ST(1) and pop ST twice. |

## Operation

```
CASE (relation of operands) OF
    Not comparable:   C3, C2, C0 ← 111;
    ST > SRC:         C3, C2, C0 ← 000;
    ST < SRC:         C3, C2, C0 ← 001;
    ST = SRC:         C3, C2, C0 ← 100;
IF instruction = FUCOMP THEN pop ST; FI;
IF instruction = FUCOMPP THEN pop ST; pop ST; FI;
```

## Description

The unordered compare real instructions compare the stack top to the source, which must be a register. If no operand is encoded, ST is compared to ST(1). Following the instruction, the condition codes reflect the relation between ST and the source operand.

## FPU Flags Affected

$C_1$ as described in Table 2-1; $C_0$, $C_2$, $C_3$ as specified above

## Numeric Exceptions

D, I, IS

## Protected Mode Exceptions

#NM if either EM or TS in CR0 is set

## Real Address Mode Exceptions

Interrupt 7 if either EM or TS in CR0 is set

## Virtual 8086 Mode Exceptions

#NM if either EM or TS in CR0 is set

## Notes

If either operand is an SNaN or is in an undefined format, or if a stack fault occurs, the invalid-operation exception is raised, and the condition bits are set to "unordered."

If either operand is a QNaN, the condition bits are set to "unordered." Unlike the ordinary compare instructions (FCOM, etc.), the unordered compare instructions do not raise the invalid-operation exception on account of a QNaN operand.

The sign of zero is ignored, so that $-0.0 = - +0.0$.

# FWAIT — Wait

| Opcode | Instruction | Clocks | Description |
|--------|-------------|--------|-------------|
| 9B | FWAIT | 6 | Alias for WAIT. |

## Description

FWAIT causes the processor to check for pending unmasked numeric exceptions before proceding.

## FPU Flags Affected

$C_0$, $C_1$, $C_2$, $C_3$ undefined

## Numeric Exceptions

None

## Protected Mode Exceptions

#NM if both MP and TS in CR0 are set

## Real Address Mode Exceptions

Interrupt 7 if both MP and TS in CR0 are set

## Virtual 8086 Mode Exceptions

#NM if both MP and TS in CR0 are set

## Notes

As its opcode shows, FWAIT is not actually an ESC instruction, but an alternate mnemonic for WAIT.

Coding FWAIT after an ESC instruction ensures that any unmasked floating-point exceptions the instruction may cause are handled before the processor has a chance to modify the instruction's results.

# FXAM — Examine

| Opcode | Instruction | Clocks | Description |
|--------|-------------|--------|-------------|
| D9 E5 | · FXAM | 30-38 | Report the type of object in the ST register. |

## Operation

C1 ← sign bit of ST; (* 0 for positive, 1 for negative *)

CASE (type of object in ST) OF
| | | |
|---|---|---|
| Unsupported: | C3, C2, C0 ← 000; |
| NaN: | C3, C2, C0 ← 001; |
| Normal: | C3, C2, C0 ← 010; |
| Infinity: | C3, C2, C0 ← 011; |
| Zero: | C3, C2, C0 ← 100; |
| Empty: | C3, C2, C0 ← 101; |
| Denormal: | C3, C2, C0 ← 110; |

## Description

The examine instruction reports the type of object contained in the ST register by setting the 387 DX Flags.

## FPU Flags Affected

$C_0$, $C_1$, $C_2$, $C_3$ as shown above.

## Numeric Exceptions

None

## Protected Mode Exceptions

#NM if either EM or TS in CR0 is set

## Real Address Mode Exceptions

Interrupt 7 if either EM or TS in CR0 is set

## Virtual 8086 Mode Exceptions

#NM if either EM or TS in CR0 is set

# FXCH — Exchange Register Contents

| Opcode | Instruction | Clocks | Description |
|--------|-------------|--------|-------------|
| D9 C8+i | FXCH ST(i) | 18 | Exchange thecontents of ST and ST(i). |
| D9 C9 | FXCH | 18 | Exchange the contents of ST and ST(1). |

## Operation

TEMP ← ST;
ST ← DEST;
DEST ← TEMP;

## Description

FXCH swaps the contents of the destination and stack-top registers. If the destination is not coded explicitly, ST(1) is used.

## FPU Flags Affected

$C_1$ as described in Table 2-1; $C_0$, $C_2$, $C_3$ undefined

## Numeric Exceptions

IS

## Protected Mode Exceptions

#NM if either EM or TS in CR0 is set

## Real Address Mode Exceptions

Interrupt 7 if either EM or TS in CR0 is set

## Virtual 8086 Mode Exceptions

#NM if either EM or TS in CR0 is set

## Notes

Many numeric instructions operate only on the stack top; FXCH provides a simple means for using these instructions on lower stack elements. For example, the following sequence takes the square root of the third register form the top (assuming that ST is nonempty):

FXCH ST(3)
FSQRT
FXCH ST(3)

# FXTRACT — Extract Exponent and Significand

| Opcode | Instruction | Clocks | Description |
|--------|-------------|--------|-------------|
| D9 F4 | FXTRACT | 70-76 | Separate ST into its exponent and significand; replace ST with the exponent and then push the significand onto the 387 DX stack. |

## Operation

TEMP ← significand of ST;
ST ← exponent of ST;
Decrement NPX stack-top pointer;
ST ← TEMP;

## Description

FXTRACT splits the value in ST into its exponent and significand. The exponent replaces the original operand on the stack and the significand is pushed onto the stack. Following execution of FXTRACT, ST (the new stack top) contains the value of the original significand expressed as a real number: its sign is the same as the operand's, its exponent is 0 true (16,383 or 3FFFH biased), and its significand is identical to the original operand's. ST(1) contains the value of the original operand's true (unbiased) exponent expressed as a real number.

To illustrate the operation of FXTRACT, assume that ST contains a number whose true exponent is $+4$ (i.e., its exponent field contains 4003H). After executing FXTRACT, ST(1) will contain the real number $+4.0$; its sign will be positive, its exponent field will contain 4001H ($+2$ true) and its significand field will contain $1_\Delta 00...00$B. In other words, the value in ST(1) will be $1.0 \times 2^2 = 4$. If ST contains an operand whose true exponent is $-7$ (i.e., its exponent field contains 3FF8H), then FXTRACT will return an "exponent" of $-7.0$; after the instruction executes, ST(1)'s sign and exponent fields will contain C001H (negative sign, true exponent of 2), and its significand will be $1_\Delta 1100...00$B. In other words, the value in ST(1) will be $-1.75 \times 2^2 = -7.0$. In both cases, following FXTRACT, ST's sign and significand fields will be the same as the original operand's, and its exponent field will contain 3FFFH (0 true).

## FPU Flags Affected

$C_1$ as described in Table 2-1; $C_0$, $C_2$, $C_3$ undefined

## Numeric Exceptions

Z, D, I, IS

## Protected Mode Exceptions

#NM if either EM or TS in CR0 is set

## Real Address Mode Exceptions

Interrupt 7 if either EM or TS in CR0 is set

## Virtual 8086 Mode Exceptions

#NM if either EM or TS in CR0 is set

## Notes

FXTRACT (extract exponent and significand) performs a superset of the IEEE-recommended **logb(x)** function.

If the original operand is zero, FXTRACT leaves $-\infty$ in ST(1) (the exponent) while ST is assigned the value zero with a sign equal to that of the original operand. The zero-divide exception is raised in this case, as well.

ST(7) must be empty to avoid the invalid-operation exception.

FXTRACT is useful for power and range scaling operations. Both FXTRACT and the base 2 exponential instruction F2XM1 are needed to perform a general power operation. Converting numbers in extended-real format to decimal representations (e.g., for printing or displaying) requires not only FBSTP but also FXTRACT to allow scaling that does not overflow the range of the extended format. FXTRACT can also be useful for debugging, because it allows the exponent and significand parts of a real number to be examined separately.

# FYL2X — Compute y × log₂x

| Opcode | Instruction | Clocks | Description |
|--------|-------------|--------|-------------|
| D9 F1 | FYL2X | 120-538 | Replace ST(1) with ST(1) × log$_2$ST and pop ST. |

ST(1) ← ST(1) × log$_2$ST;
pop ST;

## Description

FYL2X computes the base-2 logarithm of ST, multiplies the logarithm by ST(1), and returns the resulting value to ST(1). It then pops ST. The operand in ST cannot be negative.

## FPU Flags Affected

C1 as described in Table 2-1; $C_0$, $C_2$, $C_3$ undefined

## Numeric Exceptions

P, U, O, Z, D, I, IS

## Protected Mode Exceptions

#NM if either EM or TS in CR0 is set

## Real Address Mode Exceptions

Interrupt 7 if either EM or TS in CR0 is set

## Virtual 8086 Mode Exceptions

#NM if either EM or TS in CR0 is set

## Notes

If the operand in ST is negative, the invalid-operation exception is raised.

The FYL2X instruction is designed with a built-in multiplication to optimize the calculation of logarithms with arbitrary positive base:

$\log_b x = (\log_2 b)^{-1} \times \log_2 x$

The instructions FLDL2T and FLDL2E load the constants $\log_2 10$ and $\log_2 e$, respectively.

# FYL2XP1 — Compute y × log₂(x + 1)

| Opcode | Instruction | Clocks | Description |
|--------|-------------|--------|-------------|
| D9 F9 | FYL2XP1 | 257-547 | Replace ST(1) with ST(1) × log₂(ST + 1.0) and pop ST. |

## Operation

$ST(1) \leftarrow ST(1) \times \log_2(ST + 1.0)$;
pop ST;

## Description

FYL2XP1 computes the base-2 logarithm of (ST + 1.0), multiplies the logarithm by ST(1), and returns the resulting value to ST(1). It then pops ST. The operand in ST must be in the range

$$-(1 - (\sqrt{2/2})) \leq ST \leq \sqrt{2} - 1$$

## FPU Flags Affected

$C_1$ as described in Table 2-1; $C_0$, $C_2$, $C_3$ undefined

## Numeric Exceptions

P, U, D, I, IS

## Protected Mode Exceptions

#NM if either EM or TS in CR0 is set

## Real Address Mode Exceptions

Interrupt 7 if either EM or TS in CR0 is set

## Virtual 8086 Mode Exceptions

#NM if either EM or TS in CR0 is set

## Notes

If the operand in ST is outside the acceptable range, the result of FYL2XP1 is undefined.

The FYL2XP1 instruction provides improved accuracy over FYL2X when computing the logarithms of numbers very close to 1. When $\varepsilon$ is small, more significant digits can be retained by providing $\varepsilon$ as an argument to FYL2XP1 than by providing $1 + \varepsilon$ as an argument to FYL2X.

# Programming Numeric Applications

5

# CHAPTER 5
# PROGRAMMING NUMERIC APPLICATIONS

## 5.1 PROGRAMMING FACILITIES

As described previously, the 387™ DX NPX is programmed simply as an extension of the 386™ DX CPU. This section describes how programmers in ASM386 and in a variety of higher-level languages can work with the 387 DX.

The level of detail in this section is intended to give programmers a basic understanding of the software tools that can be used with the 387 DX, but this information does not document the full capabilities of these facilities. Complete documentation is available with each program development product.

### 5.1.1 High-Level Languages

For programmers using high-level languages, the programming and operation of the NPX is handled automatically by the compiler. A variety of Intel high-level languages are available that automatically make use of the 387 DX NPX when appropriate. These languages include C-386 and PL/M-386. In addition many high-level language compilers are available from independent software vendors.

Each of these high-level languages has special numeric libraries allowing programs to take advantage of the capabilities of the 387 DX NPX. No special programming conventions are necessary to make use of the 387 DX NPX when programming numeric applications in any of these languages.

Programmers in PL/M-386 and ASM386 can also make use of many of these library routines by using routines contained in the 387 DX Support Library. These libraries implement many of the functions provided by higher-level languages, including exception handlers, ASCII-to-floating-point conversions, and a more complete set of transcendental functions than that provided by the 387 DX instruction set.

### 5.1.2 C Programs

C programmers automatically cause the C compiler to generate 387 DX instructions when they use the **double** and **float** data types. The **float** type corresponds to the 387 DX's single real format; the **double** type corresponds to the 387 DX's double real format. The statement **#include <math.h>** causes mathematical functions such as **sin** and **sqrt** to return values of type **double**. Figure 5-1 illustrates the ease with which C programs interface with the 387 DX.

```
XENIX286 C386 COMPILER, VØ.2 COMPILATION OF MODULE SAMPLE
OBJECT MODULE PLACED IN sample.obj
COMPILER INVOKED BY:  c386 sample.c

stmt level

   1      /*****************************************
   2      *                                       *
   3      *            SAMPLE C PROGRAM            *
   4      *                                       *
   5      *****************************************/
   6
   7      /** Include /usr/include/stdio.h if necessary **/
   8      /** Include math declarations for transcendentals and others **/
   9
  10      #include </usr/include/math.h>
  36      #define PI 3.1415926535897932
  37
  38      main()
  39      {
  40  1   double    sin_result, cos_result;
  41  1   double    angle_deg = Ø.Ø, angle_rad;
  42  1   int       i, no_of_trial = 4;
  43  1
  44  1      for( i= 1; i <= no_of_trial; i++){
  45  2          angle_rad = PI/(18Ø.Ø/angle_deg);
  46  2          sin_result = sin (angle_rad);
  47  2          cos_result = cos (angle_rad);
  48  2          printf("sine of %f degrees equals %f\n", angle_deg, sin_result);
  49  2          printf("cosine of %f degrees equals %f\n\n", angle_deg, cos_result);
  50  2          angle_deg = angle_deg + 3Ø.Ø;
  51  2          {
  52  1      /** etc. **/
  53  1      {

C386 COMPLIATION COMPLETE. Ø WARNINGS, Ø ERRORS
```

**Figure 5-1. Sample C-386 Program**

## 5.1.3 PL/M-386

Programmers in PL/M-386 can access a very useful subset of the 387 DX's numeric capabilities. The PL/M-386 REAL data type corresponds to the NPX's single real (32-bit) format. This data type provides a range of about $8.43 \times 10^{-37} \leq |X| \leq 3.38 \times 10^{38}$, with about seven significant decimal digits. This representation is adequate for the data manipulated by many microcomputer applications.

The utility of the REAL data type is extended by the PL/M-386 compiler's practice of holding intermediate results in the 387 DX's extended real format. This means that the full range and precision of the processor are utilized for intermediate results. Underflow, overflow, and rounding exceptions are most likely to occur during intermediate computations rather than during calculation of an expression's final result. Holding intermediate results in extended-precision real format greatly reduces the likelihood of overflow and underflow and eliminates roundoff as a serious source of error until the final assignment of the result is performed.

The compiler generates 387 DX code to evaluate expressions that contain REAL data types, whether variables or constants or both. This means that addition, subtraction, multiplication, division, comparison, and assignment of REALs will be performed by the NPX. INTEGER expressions, on the other hand, are evaluated on the CPU.

Five built-in procedures (Table 5-1) give the PL/M-386 programmer access to 387 DX functions manipulated by the processor control instructions. Prior to any arithmetic operations, a typical PL/M-386 program will set up the NPX using the INIT$REAL$MATH$UNIT procedure and then issue SET$REAL$MODE to configure the NPX. SET$REAL$MODE loads the 387 DX control word, and its 16-bit parameter has the format shown for the control word in Chapter 1. The recommended value of this parameter is 033EH (round to nearest, 64-bit precision, all exceptions masked except invalid operation). Other settings may be used at the programmer's discretion.

**Table 5-1. PL/M-386 Built-in Procedures**

| Procedure | 387™ DX Instruction | Description |
|---|---|---|
| INIT$REAL$MATH$UNIT[1] | FINIT | Initialize processor. |
| SET$REAL$MODE | FLDCW | Set exception masks, rounding precision, and infinity controls. |
| GET$REAL$ERROR[2] | FNSTSW & FNCLEX | Store, then clear, exception flags. |
| SAVE$REAL$STATUS | FNSAVE | Save processor state. |
| RESTORE$REAL$STATUS | FRSTOR | Restore processor state. |

If any exceptions are unmasked, an exception handler must be provided in the form of an interrupt procedure that is designated to be invoked via CPU interrupt vector number 16. The exception handler can use the GET$REAL$ERROR procedure to obtain the low-order byte of the 387 DX status word and to then clear the exception flags. The byte returned by GET$REAL$ERROR contains the exception flags; these can be examined to determine the source of the exception.

The SAVE$REAL$STATUS and RESTORE$REAL$STATUS procedures are provided for multitasking environments where a running task that uses the 387 DX may be preempted by another task that also uses the 387 DX. It is the responsibility of the operating system to issue SAVE$REAL$STATUS before it executes any statements that affect the 387 DX; these include the INIT$REAL$MATH$UNIT and SET$REAL$MODE procedures as well as arithmetic expressions. SAVE$REAL $STATUS saves the 387 DX state (registers, status, and control words, etc.) on the

CPU's stack. RESTORE$REAL$STATUS reloads the state information; the preempting task must invoke this procedure before terminating in order to restore the 387 DX to its state at the time the running task was preempted. This enables the preempted task to resume execution from the point of its preemption.

## 5.1.4 ASM386

The ASM386 assembly language provides programmers with complete access to all of the facilities of the 386 DX and 387 DX processors.

The programmer's view of the 386 DX/387 DX hardware is a single machine with these resources:

- 160 instructions
- 12 data types
- 8 general registers
- 6 segment registers
- 8 floating-point registers, organized as a stack

### 5.1.4.1 DEFINING DATA

The ASM386 directives shown in Table 5-2 allocate storage for 387 DX variables and constants. As with other storage allocation directives, the assembler associates a type with any variable defined with these directives. The type value is equal to the length of the storage unit in bytes (10 for DT, 8 for DQ, etc.). The assembler checks the type of any variable coded in an instruction to be certain that it is compatible with the instruction. For example, the coding FIADD ALPHA will be flagged as an error if ALPHA's type is not 2 or 4, because integer addition is only available for word and short integer (doubleword) data types. The operand's type also tells the assembler which machine instruction to produce; although to the programmer there is only an FIADD instruction, a different machine instruction is required for each operand type.

**Table 5-2. ASM386 Storage Allocation Directives**

| Directive | Interpretation | Data Types |
|-----------|----------------|------------|
| DW | Define Word | Word integer |
| DD | Define Doubleword | Short integer, short real |
| DQ | Dfine Quadword | Long integer, long real |
| DT | Define Tenbyte | Packed decimal, temporary real |

On occasion it is desirable to use an instruction with an operand that has no declared type. For example, if register BX points to a short integer variable, a programmer may want to code FIADD [BX]. This can be done by informing the assembler of the operand's type in the instruction, coding FIADD DWORD PTR [BX]. The corresponding overrides for the other storage allocations are WORD PTR, QWORD PTR, and TBYTE PTR.

The assembler does not, however, check the types of operands used in processor control instructions. Coding FRSTOR [BP] implies that the programmer has set up register BP to point to the location (probably in the stack) where the processor's 94-byte state record has been previously saved.

The initial values for 387 DX constants may be coded in several different ways. Binary integer constants may be specified as bit strings, decimal integers, octal integers, or hexadecimal strings. Packed decimal values are normally written as decimal integers, although the assembler will accept and convert other representations of integers. Real values may be written as ordinary decimal real numbers (decimal point required), as decimal numbers in scientific notation, or as hexadecimal strings. Using hexadecimal strings is primarily intended for defining special values such as infinities, NaNs, and denormalized numbers. Most programmers will find that ordinary decimal and scientific decimal provide the simplest way to initialize 387 DX constants. Figure 5-2 compares several ways of setting the various 387 DX data types to the same initial value.

Note that preceding 387 DX variables and constants with the ASM386 EVEN directive ensures that the operands will be word-aligned in memory. The best performance is obtained when data transfers are double-word aligned. All 387 DX data types occupy integral numbers of words so that no storage is "wasted" if blocks of variables are defined together and preceded by a single EVEN declarative.

## 5.1.4.2 RECORDS AND STRUCTURES

The ASM386 RECORD and STRUC (structure) declaratives can be very useful in NPX programming. The record facility can be used to define the bit fields of the control, status, and tag words. Figure 5-3 shows one definition of the status word and how it might be used in a routine that polls the 387 DX until it has completed an instruction.

```
; THE FOLLOWING ALL ALLOCATE THE CONSTANT: -126
; NOTE TWO'S COMPLETE STORAGE OF NEGATIVE BINARY INTEGERS.
;
; EVEN                                    ; FORCE WORD ALIGNMENT
WORD_INTEGER     DW   1111111110000010B   ; BIT STRING
SHORT_INTEGER    DD   0FFFFFF82H          ; HEX STRING MUST START
                                          ; WITH DIGIT
LON_INTEGER      DQ   -126                ; ORDINARY DECIMAL
SINGLE_REAL      DD   -126.0              ; NOTE PRESENCE OF '.'
DOUBLE_REAL      DD   -1.26E2             ; "SCIENTIFIC"
PACKED_DECIMAL   DT   -126                ; ORDINARY DECIMAL INTEGER
;
;  IN THE FOLLOWING, SIGN AND EXPONENT IS 'C005'
;    SIGNIFICAND IS '7E00...00', 'R' INFORMS ASSEMBLER THAT
;    THE STRING REPRESENTS A REAL DATA TYPE.
;
EXTENDED_REAL    DT   0C0057E0000000000000000R  ; HEX STRING
```

**Figure 5-2. Sample 387™ DX Constants**

```
; RESERVE SPACE FOR STATUS WORD
STATUS_WORD
; LAY OUT STATUS WORD FIELDS
STATUS RECORD
    ⌐   BUSY:           1,
    ⌐   COND_CODE3:     1,
    ⌐   STACK_TOP:      3,
    ⌐   COND_CODE2:     1,
    ⌐   COND_CODE1:     1,
    ⌐   COND_CODE0:     1,
    ⌐   INT_REQ:        1,
    ⌐   S_FLAG:         1,
    ⌐   P_FLAG:         1,
    ⌐   U_FLAG:         1,
    ⌐   O_FLAG:         1,
    ⌐   Z_FLAG:         1,
    ⌐   D_FLAG:         1,
    ⌐   I_FLAG:         1
; REDUCE UNTIL COMPLETE
REDUCE: FPREM1
        FNSTSW    STATUS_WORD
        TEST      STATUS_WORD, MASK_COND_CODE2
        JNZ       REDUCE
```

**Figure 5-3. Status Word Record Definition**

Because structures allow different but related data types to be grouped together, they often provide a natural way to represent "real world" data organizations. The fact that the structure template may be "moved" about in memory adds to its flexibility. Figure 5-4 shows a simple structure that might be used to represent data consisting of a series of test score samples. A structure could also be used to define the organization of the information stored and loaded by the FSTENV and FLDENV instructions.

```
SAMPLE      STRUC
    N_OBS   DD  ?   ; SHORT INTEGER
    MEAN    DQ  ?   ; DOUBLE REAL
    MODE    DW  ?   ; WORD INTEGER
    STD_DEV DQ  ?   ; DOUBLE REAL
    ; ARRAY OF OBSERVATIONS -- WORD INTEGER
    TEST_SCORES DW 1000 DUP (?)
SAMPLE      ENDS
```

**Figure 5-4. Structure Definition**

### 5.1.4.3 ADDRESSING METHODS

387 DX memory data can be accessed with any of the memory addressing methods provided by the ModR/M byte and (optionally) the SIB byte. This means that 387 DX data types can be incorporated in data aggregates ranging from simple to complex according to the needs of the application. The addressing methods and the ASM386 notation used to specify them in instructions make the accessing of structures, arrays, arrays of structures, and other organizations direct and straightforward. Table 5-3 gives several examples of 387 DX instructions coded with operands that illustrate different addressing methods.

**Table 5-3. Addressing Method Examples**

| Coding | Interpretation |
|---|---|
| FIADD ALPHA | ALPHA is a simple scalar (mode is direct). |
| FDIVR ALPHA.BETA | BETA is a field in a structure that is "overlaid" on ALPHA (mode is direct). |
| FMUL QWORD PTR [BX] | BX contains the address of a long real variable (mode is register indirect). |
| FSUB ALPHA [SI] | ALPHA is an array and SI contains the offset of an array element from the start of the array (mode is indexed). |
| FILD [BP].BETA | BP contains the address of a structure on the CPU stack and BETA is a field in the structure (mode is based). |
| FBLD TBYTE PTR [BX] [DI] | BX contains the address of a packed decimal array and DI contains the offset of an array element (mode is based indexed). |

## 5.1.5 Comparative Programming Example

Figures 5-5 and 5-6 show the PL/M-386 and ASM386 code for a simple 387 DX program, called ARRSUM. The program references an array (X$ARRAY), which contains 0–100 single real values; the integer variable N$OF$X indicates the number of array elements the program is to consider. ARRSUM steps through X$ARRAY accumulating three sums:

- SUM$X, the sum of the array values

- SUM$INDEXES, the sum of each array value times its index, where the index of the first element is 1, the second is 2, etc.

- SUM$SQUARES, the sum of each array element squared

(A true program, of course, would go beyond these steps to store and use the results of these calculations.) The control word is set with the recommended values: round to nearest, 64-bit precision, interrupts enabled, and all exceptions masked except invalid operation. It is assumed that an exception handler has been written to field the invalid operation if it occurs, and that it is invoked by interrupt pointer 16. Either version of the program will run on an actual or an emulated 387 DX without altering the code shown.

```
XENIX286 PL/M-386 DEBUG X291a COMPILATION OF MODULE ARRAYSUM
OBJECT MODULE PLACED IN arraysum.obj
COMPILER INVOKED BY:  plm386 arraysum.plm



          /************************************************************
          *                                                          *
          *                  ARRAYSUM  MODDULE                       *
          *                                                          *
          ************************************************************/
    1      array$sum:     do;

    2   1      declare (sum$x, sum$indexes, sum$squares) real;
    3   1      declare x$array(100) real;
    4   1      declare (n$of$x, i) integer;
    5   1      declare control$387 literally '033eh';

              /*  Assume x$array and n$of$x are initialized */
    6   1      call init$real$math$unit;
    7   1      call set$real$mode(control$387);

              /* Clear sums */
    8   1      sum$x, sum$indexes, sum$squares = 0.0;

              /* Loop through array, accumulating sums */
    9   1      do i = 0 to n$of$x - 1;
   10   2          sum$x = sum$x + x$array(i);
   11   2          sum$indexes = sum$indexes + (x$array(i)*float(i+1));
   12   2          sum$squares = sum$squares + (x$array(i)*x$array(i));
   13   2      end;

              /* etc. */

   14   1      end array$sum;




MODULE INFORMATION:

    CODE AREA SIZE     = 000000A0H      160D
    CONSTANT AREA SIZE = 00000004H        4D
    VARIABLE AREA SIZE = 000001A4H      420D
    MAXIMUM STACK SIZE = 00000004H        4D
    32 LINES READ
    0 PROGRAM WARNINGS
    0 PROGRAM ERRORS

DICTIONARY SUMMARY:

    8KB MEMORY USED
    0KB DISK SPACE USED

END OF PL/M-386 COMPILATION
```

**Figure 5-5. Sample PL/M-386 Program**

The PL/M-386 version of ARRSUM (Figure 5-5) is very straightforward and illustrates how easily the 387 DX can be used in this language. After declaring variables, the program calls built-in procedures to initialize the processor (or its emulator) and to load to the control word. The program clears the sum variables and then steps through X$ARRAY with a DO-loop. The loop control takes into account PL/M-386's practice of considering the index of the first element of an array to be 0. In the computation of

```
XENIX286 80386 MACRO ASSEMBLER V1.0, ASSEMBLY OF MODULE ARRAYSUM
OBJECT MODULE PLACED IN arraysum.obj
ASSEMBLER INVOKED BY: asm386 arraysum.asm

LOC       OBJ                  LINE    SOURCE

                                 1     name       arraysum
                                 2
                                 3     ; Define initialization routine
                                 4
                                 5     extrn      init387:far
                                 6
                                 7     ; Allocate space for data
                                 8
--------                         9     data       segment rw public
00000000  3E03                  10     control_387        dw 033eh
00000002  ????????              11     n_of_x             dd ?
00000006  (100                  12     x_array            dd 100 dup (?)
          ????????
          )
00000196  ????????              13     sum_squares        dd ?
0000019A  ????????              14     sum_indexes        dd ?
0000019E  ????????              15     sum_x              dd ?
--------                        16     data       ends
                                17
                                18     ; Allocate CPU stack space
                                19
--------                        20     stack      stackseg   400
                                21
                                22     ; Begin code
                                23
--------                        24     code       segment er public
                                25
                                26     assume  ds:data, ss:stack
                                27
00000000                        28     start:
00000000  66B8----          R   29             mov    ax, data
00000004  8ED8                  30             mov    ds, ax
00000006  66B8----          R   31             mov    ax, stack
0000000A  B800000000            32             mov    eax, 0h
0000000F  8ED0                  33             mov    ss, ax
00000011  BC00000000        R   34             mov    esp, stackstart stack
                                35
                                36     ; Assume x_array and n_of_x have
                                37     ; been initialized
                                38
                                39     ; Prepare the 80387 or its emulator
                                40
00000016  9A00000000----    E   41             call   init387
0000001D  D92D00000000      R   42             fldcw  control_387
                                43
                                44     ; Clear three registers to hold
                                45     ; running sums
                                46
00000023  D9EE                  47             fldz
00000025  D9EE                  48             fldz
00000027  D9EE                  49             fldz
```

**Figure 5-6. Sample ASM386 Program**

SUM$INDEXES, the built-in procedure FLOAT converts $I+1$ from integer to real because the language does not support "mixed mode" arithmetic. One of the strengths of the NPX, of course, is that it *does* support arithmetic on mixed data types (because all values are converted internally to the 80-bit extended-precision real format).

The ASM386 version (Figure 5-6) defines the external procedure INIT387, which makes the different initialization requirements of the processor and its emulator transparent to

```
LOC        OBJ                         LINE    SOURCE

                                        50
                                        51    ; Setup ECX as loop counter and ESI
                                        52    ; as index into x_array
                                        53
00000029 8B0D02000000        R          54        mov      ecx, n_of_x
0000002F F7E9                           55        imul     ecx
00000031 8BF0                           56        mov      esi, eax
                                        57
                                        58    ; ESI now contains index of last
                                        59    ; element + 1
                                        60    ; Loop through x_array and
                                        61    ; accumulate sum
                                        62
00000033                                63    sum_next:
                                        64    ; backup one element and push on
                                        65    ; the stack
                                        66
00000033 83EE04                         67        sub      esi, type x_array
00000036 D98606000000        R          68        fld      x_array[esi]
                                        69
                                        70    ; add to the sum and duplicate x
                                        71    ; on the stack
                                        72
0000003C DCC3                           73        fadd     st(3), st
0000003E D9C0                           74        fld      st
                                        75
                                        76    ; square it and add into the sum of
                                        77    ; (index+1) and discard
                                        78
00000040 DCC8                           79        fmul     st, st
00000042 DEC2                           80        faddp    st(2), st
                                        81
                                        82    ; reduce index for next iteration
                                        83
00000044 FF0D02000000        R          84        dec      n_of_x
0000004A E2E7                           85        loop     sum_next
                                        86
                                        87    ; Pop sums into memory
                                        88
0000004C                                89    pop_results:
0000004C D91D96010000        R          90        fstp     sum_squares
00000052 D91D9A010000        R          91        fstp     sum_indexes
00000058 D91D9E010000        R          92        fstp     sum_x
0000005E 9B                             93        fwait
                                        94
                                        95    ;
                                        96    ; Etc.
                                        97    ;
........                                98    code     ends
                                        99    end      start, ds:data, ss:stack

    ASSEMBLY COMPLETE,   NO WARNINGS,   NO ERRORS.
```

**Figure 5-6. Sample ASM386 Program (Cont'd.)**

the source code. After defining the data and setting up the segment registers and stack pointer, the program calls INIT387 and loads the control word. The computation begins with the next three instructions, which clear three registers by loading (pushing) zeros onto the stack. As shown in Figure 5-7, these registers remain at the bottom of the stack throughout the computation while temporary values are pushed on and popped off the stack above them.

The program uses the CPU LOOP instruction to control its iteration through X_ARRAY; register ECX, which LOOP automatically decrements, is loaded with N_OF_X, the number of array elements to be summed. Register ESI is used to select

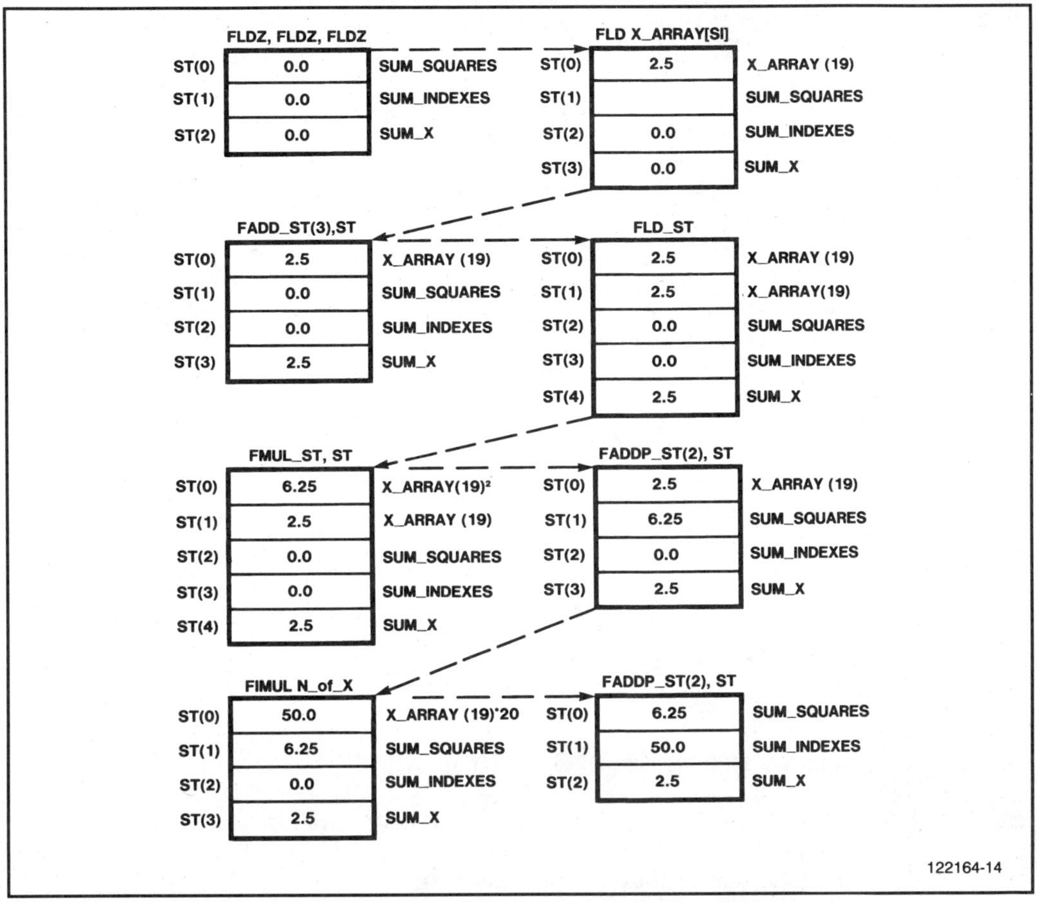

**FLDZ, FLDZ, FLDZ**

| ST(0) | 0.0 | SUM_SQUARES |
| ST(1) | 0.0 | SUM_INDEXES |
| ST(2) | 0.0 | SUM_X |

**FLD X_ARRAY[SI]**

| ST(0) | 2.5 | X_ARRAY (19) |
| ST(1) |     | SUM_SQUARES |
| ST(2) | 0.0 | SUM_INDEXES |
| ST(3) | 0.0 | SUM_X |

**FADD_ST(3),ST**

| ST(0) | 2.5 | X_ARRAY (19) |
| ST(1) | 0.0 | SUM_SQUARES |
| ST(2) | 0.0 | SUM_INDEXES |
| ST(3) | 2.5 | SUM_X |

**FLD_ST**

| ST(0) | 2.5 | X_ARRAY (19) |
| ST(1) | 2.5 | X_ARRAY(19) |
| ST(2) | 0.0 | SUM_SQUARES |
| ST(3) | 0.0 | SUM_INDEXES |
| ST(4) | 2.5 | SUM_X |

**FMUL_ST, ST**

| ST(0) | 6.25 | X_ARRAY(19)$^2$ |
| ST(1) | 2.5 | X_ARRAY (19) |
| ST(2) | 0.0 | SUM_SQUARES |
| ST(3) | 0.0 | SUM_INDEXES |
| ST(4) | 2.5 | SUM_X |

**FADDP_ST(2), ST**

| ST(0) | 2.5 | X_ARRAY (19) |
| ST(1) | 6.25 | SUM_SQUARES |
| ST(2) | 0.0 | SUM_INDEXES |
| ST(3) | 2.5 | SUM_X |

**FIMUL N_of_X**

| ST(0) | 50.0 | X_ARRAY (19)*20 |
| ST(1) | 6.25 | SUM_SQUARES |
| ST(2) | 0.0 | SUM_INDEXES |
| ST(3) | 2.5 | SUM_X |

**FADDP_ST(2), ST**

| ST(0) | 6.25 | SUM_SQUARES |
| ST(1) | 50.0 | SUM_INDEXES |
| ST(2) | 2.5 | SUM_X |

122164-14

**Figure 5-7. Instructions and Register Stack**

(index) the array elements. The program steps through X_ARRAY from back to front, so ESI is initialized to point at the element just beyond the first element to be processed. The ASM386 TYPE operator is used to determine the number of bytes in each array element. This permits changing X_ARRAY to a double-precision real array by simply changing its definition (DD to DQ) and reassembling.

Figure 5-7 shows the effect of the instructions in the program loop on the NPX register stack. The figure assumes that the program is in its first iteration, that N_OF_X is 20, and that X_ARRAY(19) (the 20th element) contains the value 2.5. When the loop terminates, the three sums are left as the top stack elements so that the program ends by simply popping them into memory variables.

## 5.1.6 387™ DX Emulation

The programming of applications to execute on both 386 DX with an 387 DX and 386 DX systems without an 387 DX is made much easier by the existence of an 387 DX emulator for 386 DX systems. The Intel EMUL387 emulator offers a complete software counterpart to the 387 DX hardware; NPX instructions can be simply emulated in software rather than being executed in hardware. With software emulation, the distinction between 386 DX systems with or without an 387 DX is reduced to a simple performance differential. Identical numeric programs will simply execute more slowly (using software emulation of NPX instructions) on 386 DX systems without an 387 DX than on an 386 DX/387 DX system executing NPX instructions directly.

When incorporated into the systems software, the emulation of NPX instructions on the 386 DX systems is completely transparent to the applications programmer. Applications software needs no special libraries, linking, or other activity to allow it to run on an 386 DX with 387 DX emulation.

To the applications programmer, the development of programs for 386 DX systems is the same whether the 387 DX NPX hardware is available or not. The full 387 DX instruction set is available for use, with NPX instructions being either emulated or executed directly. Applications programmers need not be concerned with the hardware configuration of the computer systems on which their applications will eventually run.

For systems programmers, details relating to 387 DX emulators are described in Chapter 6.

The EMUL387 software emulator for 386 DX systems is available from Intel as a separate program product.

## 5.2 CONCURRENT PROCESSING WITH THE 387™ DX

Because the 386 DX CPU and the 387 DX NPX have separate execution units, it is possible for the NPX to execute numeric instructions in parallel with instructions executed by the CPU. This simultaneous execution of different instructions is called concurrency.

No special programming techniques are required to gain the advantages of concurrent execution; numeric instructions for the NPX are simply placed in line with the instructions for the CPU. CPU and numeric instructions are initiated in the same order as they are encountered by the CPU in its instruction stream. However, because numeric operations performed by the NPX generally require more time than operations performed by the CPU, the CPU can often execute several of its instructions before the NPX completes a numeric instruction previously initiated.

This concurrency offers obvious advantages in terms of execution performance, but concurrency also imposes several rules that must be observed in order to assure proper synchronization of the 386 DX CPU and 387 DX NPX.

All Intel high-level languages automatically provide for and manage concurrency in the NPX. Assembly-language programmers, however, must understand and manage some areas of concurrency in exchange for the flexibility and performance of programming in assembly language. This section is for the assembly-language programmer or well-informed high-level-language programmer.

## 5.2.1 Managing Concurrency

Concurrent execution of the host and 387 DX is easy to establish and maintain. The activities of numeric programs can be split into two major areas: program control and arithmetic. The program control part performs activities such as deciding what functions to perform, calculating addresses of numeric operands, and loop control. The arithmetic part simply adds, subtracts, multiplies, and performs other operations on the numeric operands. The NPX and host are designed to handle these two parts separately and efficiently.

Concurrency management is required to check for an exception before letting the 386 DX change a value just used by the 387 DX. Almost any numeric instruction can, under the wrong circumstances, produce a numeric exception. For programmers in higher-level languages, all required synchronization is automatically provided by the appropriate compiler. For assembly-language programmers exception synchronization remains the responsibility of the assembly-language programmer.

A complication is that a programmer may not expect his numeric program to cause numeric exceptions, but in some systems, they may regularly happen. To better understand these points, consider what can happen when the NPX detects an exception.

Depending on options determined by the software system designer, the NPX can perform one of two things when a numeric exception occurs:

- The NPX can provide a default fix-up for selected numeric exceptions. Programs can mask individual exception types to indicate that the NPX should generate a safe, reasonable result whenever that exception occurs. The default exception fix-up activity is treated by the NPX as part of the instruction causing the exception; no external indication of the exception is given. When exceptions are detected, a flag is set in the numeric status register, but no information regarding where or when is available. If the NPX performs its default action for all exceptions, then the need for exception synchronization is not manifest. However, as will be shown later, this is not sufficient reason to ignore exception synchronization when designing programs that use the 387 DX.

- As an alternative to the NPX default fix-up of numeric exceptions, the 386 DX CPU can be notified whenever an exception occurs. When a numeric exception is unmasked and the exception occurs, the NPX stops further execution of the numeric instruction and signals this event to the CPU. On the next occurrence of an ESC or WAIT instruction, the CPU traps to a software exception handler. The exception handler can then implement any sort of recovery procedures desired for any numeric exception detectable by the NPX. Some ESC instructions do not check for exceptions. These are the nonwaiting forms FNINIT, FNSTENV, FNSAVE, FNSTSW, FNSTCW, and FNCLEX.

When the NPX signals an unmasked exception condition, it is requesting help. The fact that the exception was unmasked indicates that further numeric program execution under the arithmetic and programming rules of the NPX is unreasonable.

If concurrent execution is allowed, the state of the CPU when it recognizes the exception is undefined. The CPU may have changed many of its internal registers and be executing a totally different program by the time the exception occurs. To handle this situation, the NPX has special registers updated at the start of each numeric instruction to describe the state of the numeric program when the failed instruction was attempted.

Exception synchronization ensures that the NPX is in a well-defined state after an unmasked numeric exception occurs. Without a well-defined state, it would be impossible for exception recovery routines to determine why the numeric exception occurred, or to recover successfully from the exception.

The following two sections illustrate the need to always consider exception synchronization when writing 387 DX code, even when the code is initially intended for execution with exceptions masked. If the code is later moved to an environment where exceptions are unmasked, the same code may not work correctly. An example of how some instructions written without exception synchronization will work initially, but fail when moved into a new environment is shown in Figure 5-8.

### 5.2.1.1 INCORRECT EXCEPTION SYNCHRONIZATION

In Figure 5-8, three instructions are shown to load an integer, calculate its square root, then increment the integer. The 386 DX-to-387 DX interface and synchronous execution of the NPX emulator will allow this program to execute correctly when no exceptions occur on the FILD instruction.

This situation changes if the 387 DX numeric register stack is extended to memory. To extend the NPX stack to memory, the invalid exception is unmasked. A push to a full register or pop from an empty register sets SF and causes an invalid exception.

```
                    INCORRECT ERROR SYNCHRONIZATION

    FILD    COUNT       ; NPX instruction
    INC     COUNT       ; CPU instruction alters operand
    FSQRT   COUNT       ; subsequent NPX instruction -- error from
                        ;    previous NPX instruction detected here

                     PROPER ERROR SYNCHRONIZATION

    FILD    COUNT       ; NPX instruction
    FSQRT               ; subsequent NPX instruction -- error from
                        ;    previous NPX instruction detected here
    INC     COUNT       ; CPU instruction alters operand
```

**Figure 5-8. Exception Synchronization Examples**

The recovery routine for the exception must recognize this situation, fix up the stack, then perform the original operation. The recovery routine will not work correctly in the first example shown in the figure. The problem is that the value of COUNT is incremented before the NPX can signal the exception to the CPU. Because COUNT is incremented before the exception handler is invoked, the recovery routine will load an incorrect value of COUNT, causing the program to fail or behave unreliably.

## 5.2.1.2 PROPER EXCEPTION SYNCHRONIZATION

Exception synchronization relies on the WAIT instruction and the BUSY# and ERROR# signals of the 387 DX. When an unmasked exception occurs in the 387 DX, it asserts the ERROR# signal, signaling to the CPU that a numeric exception has occurred. The next time the CPU encounters a WAIT instruction or an exception-checking ESC instruction, the CPU acknowledges the ERROR# signal by trapping automatically to Interrupt #16, the processor-extension exception vector. If the following ESC or WAIT instruction is properly placed, the CPU will not yet have disturbed any information vital to recovery from the exception.

# System-Level Numeric Programming

6

# CHAPTER 6
# SYSTEM-LEVEL NUMERIC PROGRAMMING

System programming for 387™ DX systems requires a more detailed understanding of the 387 DX NPX than does application programming. Such things as emulation, initialization, exception handling, and data and error synchronization are all the responsibility of the systems programmer. These topics are covered in detail in the sections that follow.

## 6.1 386™ DX/387™ DX ARCHITECTURE

On a software level, the 387 DX NPX appears as an extension of the 386™ DX CPU. On the hardware level, however, the mechanisms by which the 386 DX and 387 DX interact are more complex. This section describes how the 387 DX NPX and 386 DX CPU interact and points out features of this interaction that are of interest to systems programmers.

### 6.1.1 Instruction and Operand Transfer

All transfers of instructions and operands between the 387 DX and system memory are performed by the 386 DX using I/O bus cycles. The 387 DX appears to the CPU as a special peripheral device. It is special in two respects: the CPU initiates I/O automatically when it encounters ESC instructions, and the CPU uses reserved I/O addresses to communicate with the 387 DX. These I/O operations are completely transparent to software.

Because the 386 DX actually performs all transfers between the 387 DX and memory, no additional bus drivers, controllers, or other components are necessary to interface the 387 DX NPX to the local bus. The 387 DX can utilize instructions and operands located in any memory accessible to the 386 DX CPU.

### 6.1.2 Independent of CPU Addressing Modes

Unlike the 80287, the 387 DX is not sensitive to the addressing and memory management of the CPU. The 387 DX operates the same regardless of whether the 386 DX CPU is operating in real-address mode, in protected mode, or in virtual 8086 mode.

The instruction FSETPM that was necessary in 80286/80287 systems to set the 80287 into protected mode is not needed for the 387 DX. The 387 DX treats this instruction as a no-op.

Because the 386 DX actually performs all transfers between the 387 DX and memory, 387 DX instructions can utilize any memory location accessible by the task currently executing on the 386 DX. When operating in protected mode, all references to memory operands are automatically verified by the 386 DX's memory management and protection mechanisms as for any other memory references by the currently-executing task. Protection violations associated with NPX instructions automatically cause the 386 DX to trap to an appropriate exception handler.

To the numerics programmer, the operating modes of the 386 DX affect only the manner in which the NPX instruction and data pointers are represented in memory following an FSAVE or FSTENV instruction. Each of these instructions produces one of four formats depending on both the operating mode and on the operand-size attribute in effect for the instruction. The differences are detailed in the discussion of the FSAVE and FSTENV instructions in Chapter 4.

### 6.1.3 Dedicated I/O Locations

The 387 DX NPX does not require that any memory addresses be set aside for special purposes. The 387 DX does make use of I/O port addresses, but these are 32-bit addresses with the high-order bit set (i.e. > 80000000H); therefore, these I/O operations are completely transparent to the 386 DX software. Because these addresses are beyond the 64 Kbyte I/O addressing limit of I/O instructions, 386 DX programs cannot reference these reserved I/O addresses directly.

## 6.2 PROCESSOR INITIALIZATION AND CONTROL

One of the principal responsibilities of systems software is the initialization, monitoring, and control of the hardware and software resources of the system, including the 387 DX NPX. In this section, issues related to system initialization and control are described, including recognition of the NPX, emulation of the 387 DX NPX in software if the hardware is not available, and the handling of exceptions that may occur during the execution of the 387 DX.

### 6.2.1 System Initialization

During initialization of an 386 DX system, systems software must

• Recognize the presence or absence of the NPX.

• Set flags in the 386 DX MSW to reflect the state of the numeric environment.

If an 387 DX NPX is present in the system, the NPX must be initialized. All of these activities can be quickly and easily performed as part of the overall system initialization.

### 6.2.2 Hardware Recognition of the NPX

The 386 DX identifies the type of its coprocessor (80287 or 387 DX) by sampling its ERROR# input some time after the falling edge of RESET and before executing the first ESC instruction. The 80287 keeps its ERROR# output in inactive state after hardware reset; the 387 DX keeps its ERROR# output in active state after hardware reset. The 386 DX may record this difference in the ET bit of control register zero (CR0). But, because this bit is a reserved bit in the 386 DX, it is unreliable for coprocessor identification.

## 6.2.3 Software Recognition of the NPX

Figure 6-1 shows an example of a recognition routine that determines whether an NPX is present, and distinguishes between the 387 DX and the 8087/80287. This routine can be executed on any 386 DX, 80286, or 8086 hardware configuration that has an NPX socket.

```
8086/87/88/186 MACRO ASSEMBLER    Test for presence of a Numerics Chip, Revision 1.0                    PAGE    1


DOS 3.20 (033-N) 8086/87/88/186 MACRO ASSEMBLER V2.0 ASSEMBLY OF MODULE TEST_NPX
OBJECT MODULE PLACED IN FINDNPX.OBJ



LOC  OBJ               LINE      SOURCE

                       1 +1  $title('Test for presence of a Numerics Chip, Revision 1.0')
                       2
                       3          name    Test_NPX
                       4
----                   5  stack   segment stack 'stack'
0000 (100              6          dw      100 dup (?)
     ????
     )
00C8 ????              7  sst     dw              ?
----                   8  stack   ends
                       9
----                   10 data    segment public 'data'
0000 0000              11 temp    dw      0h
----                   12 data    ends
                       13
                       14 dgroup  group   data, stack
                       15 cgroup  group   code
                       16
----                   17 code    segment public 'code'
                       18         assume  cs:cgroup, ds:dgroup
                       19
0000                   20 start:
                       21 ;
                       22 ;       Look for an 8087, 80287, or 80387 NPX.
                       23 ;       Note that we cannot execute WAIT on 8086/88 if no 8087 is present.
                       24 ;
0000                   25 test_npx:
0000 90DBE3            26         fninit                          ; Must use non-wait form
0003 BE0000      R     27         mov     si,offset dgroup:temp
0006 C7045A5A          28         mov     word ptr [si],5A5AH ; Initialize temp to non-zero value
000A 90DD3C            29         fnstsw  [si]                    ; Must use non-wait form of fstsw
                       30                                         ; It is not necessary to use a WAIT instruction
                       31                                         ; after fnstsw or fnstcw. Do not use one here.
000D 803C00            32         cmp     byte ptr [si],0 ; See if correct status with zeroes was read
0010 752A              33         jne     no_npx          ; Jump if not a valid status word, meaning no NPX
                       34 ;
                       35 ;       Now see if ones can be correctly written from the control word.
                       36 ;
0012 90D93C            37         fnstcw  [si]                    ; Look at the control word; do not use WAIT form
                       38                                         ; Do not use a WAIT instruction here!
0015 8B04              39         mov     ax,[si]         ; See if ones can be written by NPX
0017 253F10            40         and     ax,103fh        ; See if selected parts of control word look OK
001A 3D3F00            41         cmp     ax,3fh          ; Check that ones and zeroes were correctly read
001D 751D              42         jne     no_npx          ; Jump if no NPX is installed
                       43 ;
                       44 ;       Some numerics chip is installed. NPX instructions and WAIT are now safe.
                       45 ;       See if the NPX is an 8087, 80287, or 80387.
                       46 ;       This code is necessary if a denormal exception handler is used or the
                       47 ;       new 80387 instructions will be used.
                       48 ;
```

**Figure 6-1. Software Routine to Recognize the 80287**

```
8086/87/88/186 MACRO ASSEMBLER    Test for presence of a Numerics Chip, Revision 1.0                    PAGE    2

LOC  OBJ              LINE    SOURCE

001F 9BD9E8            49            fld1                       ; Must use default control word from FNINIT
0022 9BD9EE            50            fldz                       ; Form infinity
0025 9BDEF9            51            fdiv                       ; 8087/287 says +inf = -inf
0028 9BD9C0            52            fld      st                ; Form negative infinity
002B 9BD9E0            53            fchs                       ; 80387 says +inf <> -inf
002E 9BDED9            54            fcompp                     ; See if they are the same and remove them
0031 9BDD3C            55            fstsw    [si]              ; Look at status from FCOMPP
0034 8B04              56            mov      ax,[si]
0036 9E                57            sahf                       ; See if the infinities matched
0037 7406              58            je       found_87_287      ; Jump if 8087/287 is present
                       59    ;
                       60    ;       An 80387 is present.  If denormal exceptions are used for an 8087/287,
                       61    ;       they must be masked.  The 80387 will automatically normalize denormal
                       62    ;       operands faster than an exception handler can.
                       63    ;
0039 EB0790            64            jmp      found_387
003C                   65    no_npx:
                       66    ;       set up for no NPX
                       67    ;          ...
                       68    ;
003C EB0490            69            jmp exit
003F                   70    found_87_287:
                       71    ;       set up for 87/287
                       72    ;          ...
                       73    ;
003F EB0190            74            jmp exit
0042                   75    found_387:
                       76    ;       set up for 387
                       77    ;          ...
                       78    ;
0042                   79    exit:
----                   80    code     ends
                       81            end      start,ds:dgroup,ss:dgroup:sst

ASSEMBLY COMPLETE, NO ERRORS FOUND
```

**Figure 6-1. Software Routine to Recognize the 80287 (Cont'd.)**

The example guards against the possibility of accidentally reading an expected value from a floating data bus when no NPX is present. Data read from a floating bus is undefined. By expecting to read a specific bit pattern from the NPX, the routine protects itself from the indeterminate state of the bus. The example also avoids depending on any values in reserved bits, thereby maintaining compatibility with future numerics coprocessors.

## 6.2.4 Configuring the Numerics Environment

Once the 386 DX CPU has determined the presence or absence of the 387 DX or 80287 NPX, the 386 DX must set either the MP or the EM bit in its own control register zero (CR0) accordingly. The initialization routine can either:

- Set the MP bit in CR0 to allow numeric instructions to be executed directly by the NPX.

- Set the EM bit in the CR0 to permit software emulation of the numeric instructions.

The MP (monitor coprocessor) flag of CR0 indicates to the 386 DX whether an NPX is physically available in the system. The MP flag controls the function of the WAIT instruction. When executing a WAIT instruction, the 386 DX tests the task switched (TS) bit only if MP is set; if it finds TS set under these conditions, the CPU traps to exception #7.

The Emulation Mode (EM) bit of CR0 indicates to the 386 DX whether NPX functions are to be emulated. If the CPU finds EM set when it executes an ESC instruction, program control is automatically trapped to exception #7, giving the exception handler the opportunity to emulate the functions of an 387 DX.

For correct 386 DX operation, the EM bit must never be set concurrently with MP. The EM and MP bits of the 386 DX are described in more detail in the *386™ DX Programmer's Reference Manual*. More information on software emulation for the 387 DX NPX is described in the "387 DX Emulation" section later in this chapter. In any case, if ESC instructions are to be executed, either the MP or EM bit must be set, but not both.

## 6.2.5 Initializing the 387™ DX

Initializing the 387 DX NPX simply means placing the NPX in a known state unaffected by any activity performed earlier. A single FNINIT instruction performs this initialization. All the error masks are set, all registers are tagged empty, TOP is set to zero, and default rounding and precision controls are set. Table 6-1 shows the state of the 387 DX NPX following FINIT or FNINIT. This state is compatible with that of the 80287 after FINIT or after hardware RESET.

**Table 6-1. NPX Processor State Following Initialization**

| Field | Value | Interpretation |
|---|---|---|
| Control Word | | |
|   (Infinity Control)* | 0 | Affine |
|   Rounding Control | 00 | Round to nearest |
|   Precision Control | 11 | 64 bits |
|   Exception Masks | 111111 | All exceptions masked |
| Status Word | | |
|   (Busy) | 0 | — |
|   Condition Code | 0000 | — |
|   Stack Top | 000 | Register 0 is stack top |
|   Exception Summary | 0 | No exceptions |
|   Stack Flag | 0 | — |
|   Exception Flags | 000000 | No exceptions |
| Tag Word | | |
|   Tags | 11 | Empty |
| Registers | N.C. | Not changed |
| Exception Pointers | | |
|   Instruction Code | N.C. | Not changed |
|   Instruction Address | N.C. | Not changed |
|   Operand Address | N.C. | Not changed |

*The 387 DX does not have infinity control. This value is listed to emphasize that programs written for the 80287 may not behave the same on the 387 DX if they depend on this bit.

The FNINIT instruction *does not* leave the 387 DX in the same state as that which results from the hardware RESET signal. Following a hardware RESET signal, such as after initial power-up, the state of the 387 DX differs in the following respects:

1. The mask bit for the invalid-operation exception is reset.

2. The invalid-operation exception flag is set.

3. The exception-summary bit is set (along with its mirror image, the B-bit).

These settings cause assertion of the ERROR# signal as described previously. The FNINIT instruction must be used to change the 387 DX state to one compatible with the 80287.

## 6.2.6 387™ DX Emulation

If it is determined that no 387 DX NPX is available in the system, systems software may decide to emulate ESC instructions in software. This emulation is easily supported by the 386 DX hardware, because the 386 DX can be configured to trap to a software emulation routine whenever it encounters an ESC instruction in its instruction stream.

Whenever the 386 DX CPU encounters an ESC instruction, and its MP and EM status bits are set appropriately (MP=0, EM=1), the 386 DX automatically traps to interrupt #7, the "processor extension not available" exception. The return link stored on the stack points to the first byte of the ESC instruction, including the prefix byte(s), if any. The exception handler can use this return link to examine the ESC instruction and proceed to emulate the numeric instruction in software.

The emulator must step the return pointer so that, upon return from the exception handler, execution can resume at the first instruction following the ESC instruction.

To an application program, execution on an 386 DX system with 387 DX emulation is almost indistinguishable from execution on a system with an 387 DX, except for the difference in execution speeds.

There are several important considerations when using emulation on an 386 DX system:

- When operating in protected mode, numeric applications using the emulator must be executed in execute-readable code segments. Numeric software cannot be emulated if it is executed in execute-only code segments. This is because the emulator must be able to examine the particular numeric instruction that caused the emulation trap.

- Only privileged tasks can place the 386 DX in emulation mode. The instructions necessary to place the 386 DX in emulation mode are privileged instructions, and are not typically accessible to an application.

An emulator package (EMUL387) that runs on 386 DX systems is available from Intel. This emulation package operates in both real and protected mode as well as in virtual 8086 mode, providing a complete functional equivalent for the 387 DX emulated in software.

When using the EMUL387 emulator, writers of numeric exception handlers should be aware of one slight difference between the emulated 387 DX and the 387 DX hardware:

- On the 387 DX hardware, exception handlers are invoked by the 386 DX at the first WAIT or ESC instruction following the instruction causing the exception. The return link, stored on the 386 DX stack, points to this second WAIT or ESC instruction where execution will resume following a return from the exception handler.

- Using the EMUL387 emulator, numeric exception handlers are invoked from within the emulator itself. The return link stored on the stack when the exception handler is invoked will therefore point back to the EMUL387 emulator, rather than to the program code actually being executed (emulated). An IRET return from the exception handler returns to the emulator, which then returns immediately to the emulated program. This added layer of indirection should not cause confusion, however, because the instruction causing the exception can always be identified from the 387 DX's instruction and data pointers.

## 6.2.7 Handling Numerics Exceptions

Once the 387 DX has been initialized and normal execution of applications has been commenced, the 387 DX NPX may occasionally require attention in order to recover from numeric processing exceptions. This section provides details for writing software exception handlers for numeric exceptions. Numeric processing exceptions have already been introduced in Chapter 3.

The 387 DX NPX can take one of two actions when it recognizes a numeric exception:

- If the exception is masked, the NPX will automatically perform its own masked exception response, correcting the exception condition according to fixed rules, and then continuing with its instruction execution.

- If the exception is unmasked, the NPX signals the exception to the 386 DX CPU using the ERROR# status line between the two processors. Each time the 386 DX encounters an ESC or WAIT instruction in its instruction stream, the CPU checks the condition of this ERROR# status line. If ERROR# is active, the CPU automatically traps to Interrupt vector #16, the Processor Extension Error trap.

Interrupt vector #16 typically points to a software exception handler, which may or may not be a part of systems software. This exception handler takes the form of an 386 DX interrupt procedure.

When handling numeric errors, the CPU has two responsibilities:

- The CPU must not disturb the numeric context when an error is detected.
- The CPU must clear the error and attempt recovery from the error.

Although the manner in which programmers may treat these responsibilities varies from one implementation to the next, most exception handlers will include these basic steps:

- Store the NPX environment (control, status, and tag words, operand and instruction pointers) as it existed at the time of the exception.
- Clear the exception bits in the status word.
- Enable interrupts on the CPU.

- Identify the exception by examining the status and control words in the saved environment.
- Take some system-dependent action to rectify the exception.
- Return to the interrupted program and resume normal execution.

### 6.2.8 Simultaneous Exception Response

In cases where multiple exceptions arise simultaneously, the 387 DX signals one exception according to the precedence shown at the end of Chapter 3. This means, for example, that an SNaN divided by zero results in an invalid operation, not in a zero divide exception.

### 6.2.9 Exception Recovery Examples

Recovery routines for NPX exceptions can take a variety of forms. They can change the arithmetic and programming rules of the NPX. These changes may redefine the default fix-up for an error, change the appearance of the NPX to the programmer, or change how arithmetic is defined on the NPX.

A change to an exception response might be to automatically normalize all denormals loaded from memory. A change in appearance might be extending the register stack into memory to provide an "infinite" number of numeric registers. The arithmetic of the NPX can be changed to automatically extend the precision and range of variables when exceeded. All these functions can be implemented on the NPX via numeric exceptions and associated recovery routines in a manner transparent to the application programmer.

Some other possible application-dependent actions might include:

- Incrementing an exception counter for later display or printing
- Printing or displaying diagnostic information (e.g., the 387 DX environment and registers)
- Aborting further execution
- Storing a diagnostic value (a NaN) in the result and continuing with the computation

Notice that an exception may or may not constitute an error, depending on the application. Once the exception handler corrects the condition causing the exception, the floating-point instruction that caused the exception can be restarted, if appropriate. This cannot be accomplished using the IRET instruction, however, because the trap occurs at the ESC or WAIT instruction following the offending ESC instruction. The exception handler must obtain (using FSAVE or FSTENV) the address of the offending instruction in the task that initiated it, make a copy of it, execute the copy in the context of the offending task, and then return via IRET to the current CPU instruction stream.

In order to correct the condition causing the numeric exception, exception handlers must recognize the precise state of the NPX at the time the exception handler was invoked, and be able to reconstruct the state of the NPX when the exception initially occurred. To reconstruct the state of the NPX, programmers must understand when, during the execution of an NPX instruction, exceptions are actually recognized.

Invalid operation, zero divide, and denormalized exceptions are detected before an operation begins, whereas overflow, underflow, and precision exceptions are not raised until a true result has been computed. When a *before* exception is detected, the NPX register stack and memory have not yet been updated, and appear as if the offending instructions has not been executed.

When an *after* exception is detected, the register stack and memory appear as if the instruction has run to completion; i.e., they may be updated. (However, in a store or store-and-pop operation, unmasked over/underflow is handled like a *before* exception; memory is not updated and the stack is not popped.) The programming examples contained in Chapter 7 include an outline of several exception handlers to process numeric exceptions for the 387 DX.

# Numeric Programming Examples

7

# CHAPTER 7
# NUMERIC PROGRAMMING EXAMPLES

The following sections contain examples of numeric programs for the 387 DX NPX written in ASM386. These examples are intended to illustrate some of the techniques for programming the 386 DX/387 DX computing system for numeric applications.

## 7.1 CONDITIONAL BRANCHING EXAMPLE

As discussed in Chapter 2, several numeric instructions post their results to the condition code bits of the 387 DX status word. Although there are many ways to implement conditional branching following a comparison, the basic approach is as follows:

- Execute the comparison.
- Store the status word. (387 DX allows storing status directly into AX register.)
- Inspect the condition code bits.
- Jump on the result.

Figure 7-1 is a code fragment that illustrates how two memory-resident double-format real numbers might be compared (similar code could be used with the FTST instruction). The numbers are called A and B, and the comparison is A to B.

The comparison itself requires loading A onto the top of the 387 DX register stack and then comparing it to B, while popping the stack with the same instruction. The status word is then written into the 386 DX AX register.

A and B have four possible orderings, and bits C3, C2, and C0 of the condition code indicate which ordering holds. These bits are positioned in the upper byte of the NPX status word so as to correspond to the CPU's zero, parity, and carry flags (ZF, PF, and CF), when the byte is written into the flags. The code fragment sets ZF, PF, and CF of the CPU status word to the values of C3, C2, and C0 of the NPX status word, and then uses the CPU conditional jump instructions to test the flags. The resulting code is extremely compact, requiring only seven instructions.

The FXAM instruction updates all four condition code bits. Figure 7-2 shows how a jump table can be used to determine the characteristics of the value examined. The jump table (FXAM_TBL) is initialized to contain the 32-bit displacement of 16 labels, one for each possible condition code setting. Note that four of the table entries contain the same value, "EMPTY." The first two condition code settings correspond to "EMPTY." The two other table entries that contain "EMPTY" will never be used on the 387 DX, but may be used if the code is executed with an 80287.

The program fragment performs the FXAM and stores the status word. It then manipulates the condition code bits to finally produce a number in register AX that equals the condition code times 2. This involves zeroing the unused bits in the byte that contains the code, shifting C3 to the right so that it is adjacent to C2, and then shifting the code to multiply it by 2. The resulting value is used as an index that selects one of the displacements from FXAM_TBL (the multiplication of the condition code is required

```
                .
                .
                .
 A      DQ    ?
 B      DQ    ?
                .
                .
                .
        FLD        A  ; LOAD A ONTO TOP OF FPU STACK
        FCOMP      B  ; COMPARE A:B, POP A
        FSTSW      AX ; STORE RESULT TO AX REGISTER
 ;
 ; CPU AX REGISTER CONTAINS CONDITION CODES
 ;    (RESULTS OF COMPARE)
 ; LOAD CONDITION CODES INTO FLAGS
 ;
        SAHF
 ;
 ; USE CONDITIONAL JUMPS TO DETERMINE ORDERING OF A TO B
 ;
        JP A_B_UNORDERED            ; TEST C2 (PF)
        JB A_LESS          ; TEST C0 (CF)
        JE A_EQUAL         ; TEST C3 (ZF)
 A_GREATER:                ; C0 (CF) = 0, C3 (ZF) = 0
        .
        .
 A_EQUAL:                  ; C0 (CF) = 0, C3 (ZF) = 1
        .
        .
 A_LESS:                   ; C0 (CF) = 1, C3 (ZF) = 0
        .
        .
 A_B_UNORDERED:            ; C2 (PF) = 1
        .
        .
```

**Figure 7-1. Conditional Branching for Compares**

because of the 2-byte length of each value in FXAM_TBL). The unconditional JMP instruction effectively vectors through the jump table to the labeled routine that contains code (not shown in the example) to process each possible result of the FXAM instruction.

## 7.2 EXCEPTION HANDLING EXAMPLES

There are many approaches to writing exception handlers. One useful technique is to consider the exception handler procedure as consisting of "prologue," "body," and "epilogue" sections of code. This procedure is invoked via interrupt number 16.

At the beginning of the prologue, CPU interrupts have been disabled. The prologue performs all functions that must be protected from possible interruption by higher-priority sources. Typically, this involves saving CPU registers and transferring diagnostic information from the 387 DX to memory. When the critical processing has been completed, the prologue may enable CPU interrupts to allow higher-priority interrupt handlers to preempt the exception handler.

```
; JUMP TABLE FOR EXAMINE ROUTINE
;
FXAM_TBL   DD POS_UNNORM, POS NAN, NEG_UNNORM, NEG_NAN,
&          POS_NORM, POS_INFINITY, NEG_NORM,
&          NEG_INFINITY, POS_ZERO, EMPTY, NEG_ZERO,
&          EMPTY, POS_DENORM, EMPTY, NEG_DENORM, EMPTY

     .

; EXAMINE ST AND STORE RESULT (CONDITION CODES)

     FXAM
     XOR EAX,EAX  ; CLEAR EAX
     FSTSW AX

; CALCULATE OFFSET INTO JUMP TABLE

     AND AX,0100011100000000B ; CLEAR ALL BITS EXCEPT C3, C2-C0
     SHR EAX,6   ;  SHIFT C2-C0 INTO PLACE   (000XXX00)
     SAL AH,5    ;  POSITION C3              (00X00000)
     OR  AL,AH   ;  DROP C3 IN ADJACENT TO C2 (00XXXX00)
     XOR AH,AH   ;  CLEAR OUT THE OLD COPY OF C3

; JUMP TO THE ROUTINE 'ADDRESSED' BY CONDITION CODE

     JMP FXAM_TBL[EAX]

; HERE ARE THE JUMP TARGETS, ONE TO HANDLE
;     EACH POSSIBLE RESULT OF FXAM

POS_UNNORM:
     .
POS_NAN:
     .
NEG_UNNORM:
     .
NEG_NAN:
     .
POS_NORM:
     .
POS_INFINITY:
     .
NEG_NORM:
     .
NEG_INFINITY:
     .
POS_ZERO:
     .
EMPTY:
     .
NEG_ZERO:
     .
POS_DENORM:
     .
NEG_DENORM:
```

**Figure 7-2. Conditional Branching for FXAM**

The body of the exception handler examines the diagnostic information and makes a response that is necessarily application-dependent. This response may range from halting execution, to displaying a message, to attempting to repair the problem and proceed with normal execution.

The epilogue essentially reverses the actions of the prologue, restoring the CPU and the NPX so that normal execution can be resumed. The epilogue must *not* load an unmasked exception flag into the 387 DX or another exception will be requested immediately.

Figures 7-3 through 7-5 show the ASM386 coding of three skeleton exception handlers. They show how prologues and epilogues can be written for various situations, but provide comments indicating only where the application dependent exception handling body should be placed.

Figures 7-3 and 7-4 are very similar; their only substantial difference is their choice of instructions to save and restore the 387 DX. The tradeoff here is between the increased diagnostic information provided by FNSAVE and the faster execution of FNSTENV. For applications that are sensitive to interrupt latency or that do not need to examine register contents, FNSTENV reduces the duration of the "critical region," during which the CPU does not recognize another interrupt request.

```
SAVE_ALL          PROC
;
; SAVE REGISTERS, ALLOCATE STACK SPACE
; FOR FPU STATE IMAGE
    PUSH EBP
    MOV  EBP,ESP
    SUB  ESP,108
; SAVE FULL FPU STATE, ENABLE INTERRUPTS
    FNSAVE [EBP-108]
    STI
;
; APPLICATION-DEPENDENT EXCEPTION HANDLING
; CODE GOES HERE
;
; CLEAR EXCEPTION FLAGS IN STATUS WORD
;   (WHICH IS IN MEMORY)
; RESTORE MODIFIED STATE IMAGE
    MOV BYTE PTR [EBP-104], 0H
    FRSTOR  [EBP-108]
; DEALLOCATE STACK SPACE, RESTORE REGISTERS
    MOVE ESP,EBP
        .
        .
        .
    POP EBP
;
; RETURN TO INTERRUPTED CALCULATION
    IRET
SAVE_ALL          ENDP
```

**Figure 7-3. Full-State Exception Handler**

```
SAVE_ENVIRONMENT PROC
;
; SAVE REGISTERS, ALLOCATE STACK SPACE
; FOR FPU ENVIRONMENT
     PUSH     EBP

     MOV      EBP,ESP
     SUB      ESP,28
; SAVE ENVIRONMENT, ENABLE INTERRUPTS
     FNSTENV [EBP-28]
     STI

;
; APPLICATION EXCEPTION-HANDLING CODE GOES HERE

;
; CLEAR EXCEPTION FLAGS IN STATUS WORD
;  (WHICH IS IN MEMORY)
; RESTORE MODIFIED ENVIRONMENT IMAGE
     MOV      BYTE PTR [EBP-24], 0H
     FLDENV [EBP-28]
; DE-ALLOCATE STACK SPACE, RESTORE REGISTERS
     MOV      ESP,EBP
     POP      EBP

;
; RETURN TO INTERRUPTED CALCULATION
     IRET
SAVE_ENVIRONMENT ENDP
```

**Figure 7-4. Reduced-Latency Exception Handler**

After the exception handler body, the epilogues prepare the CPU and the NPX to resume execution from the point of interruption (i.e., the instruction following the one that generated the unmasked exception). Notice that the exception flags in the memory image that is loaded into the 387 DX are cleared to zero prior to reloading (in fact, in these examples, the entire status word image is cleared).

The examples in Figures 7-3 and 7-4 assume that the exception handler itself will not cause an unmasked exception. Where this is a possibility, the general approach shown in Figure 7-5 can be employed. The basic technique is to save the full 387 DX state and then to load a new control word in the prologue. Note that considerable care should be taken when designing an exception handler of this type to prevent the handler from being reentered endlessly.

## 7.3 FLOATING-POINT TO ASCII CONVERSION EXAMPLES

Numeric programs must typically format their results at some point for presentation and inspection by the program user. In many cases, numeric results are formatted as ASCII strings for printing or display. This example shows how floating-point values can be converted to decimal ASCII character strings. The function shown in Figure 7-6 can be invoked from PL/M-386, Pascal-386, FORTRAN-386, or ASM386 routines.

Shortness, speed, and accuracy were chosen rather than providing the maximum number of significant digits possible. An attempt is made to keep integers in their own domain to avoid unnecessary conversion errors.

```
            .
            .
            .
        LOCAL CONTROL  DW  ?  ; ASSUME INITIALIZED
            .
            .
            .
REENTRANT               PROC
;
; SAVE REGISTERS, ALLOCATE STACK SPACE FOR
; FPU STATE IMAGE
    PUSH    EBP
            .
            .
            .
    MOV     EBP,ESP
    SUB     ESP,108
; SAVE STATE, LOAD NEW CONTROL WORD,
; ENABLE INTERRUPTS
    FNSAVE  [EBP-108]
    FLDCW   LOCAL_CONTROL
    STI
            .
            .
            .
; APPLICATION EXCEPTION HANDLING CODE GOES HERE.
; AN UNMASKED EXCEPTION GENERATED HERE WILL
; CAUSE THE EXCEPTION HANDLER TO BE REENTERED.
; IF LOCAL STORAGE IS NEEDED, IT MUST BE
; ALLOCATED ON THE STACK.
            .
            .
            .
; CLEAR EXCEPTION FLAGS IN STATUS WORD
; (WHICH IS IN MEMORY)
; RESTORE MODIFIED STATE IMAGE
    MOV     BYTE PTR [EBP-104], 0H
    FRSTOR  [EBP-108]
; DE-ALLOCATE STACK SPACE, RESTORE REGISTERS
    MOV     ESP,EBP
            .
            .
            .
    POP     EBP
; RETURN TO POINT OF INTERRUPTION
    IRET
REENTRANT               ENDP
```

**Figure 7-5. Reentrant Exception Handler**

Using the extended precision real number format, this routine achieves a worst case accuracy of three units in the 16th decimal position for a noninteger value or integers greater than $10^{18}$. This is double precision accuracy. With values having decimal exponents less than 100 in magnitude, the accuracy is one unit in the 17th decimal position.

```
         XENIX286 80386 MACRO ASSEMBLER V1.0, ASSEMBLY OF MODULE FLOATING_TO_ASCII
         OBJECT MODULE PLACED IN fpasc.obj
         ASSEMBLER INVOKED BY: asm386 fpasc.asm

    LOC      OBJ            LINE    SOURCE

                              1  +1 $title('Convert a floating point number to ASCII')
                              2
                              3                name   floating_to_ascii
                              4
    00000000                  5                public floating_to_ascii
                              6                extrn  get_power_10:near,tos_status:near
                              7  ;
                              8  ; This subroutine will convert the floating point
                              9  ; number in the top of the NPX stack to an ASCII
                             10  ; string and separate power of 10 scaling value
                             11  ; (in binary).  The maximum width of the ASCII string
                             12  ; formed is controlled by a parameter which must be
                             13  ; > 1.  Unnormal values, denormal values, and psuedo
                             14  ; zeroes will be correctly converted. However, unnormals
                             15  ; and pseudo zeros are no longer supported formats on the
                             16  ; 80387( in conformance with the IEEE floating point
                             17  ; standard) and hence not generated internally. A
                             18  ; returned value will indicate how many binary bits
                             19  ; of precision were lost in an unnormal or denormal
                             20  ; value.  The magnitude (in terms of binary power)
                             21  ; of a pseudo zero will also be indicated. Integers
                             22  ; less than 10**18 in magnitude are accurately converted
                             23  ; if the destination ASCII string field is wide enough
                             24  ; to hold all the digits. Otherwise the value is converted
                             25  ; to scientific notation.
                             26  ;
                             27  ; The status of the conversion is identified by the
                             28  ; return value, it can be:
                             29  ;
                             30  ;      0        conversion complete, string_size is defined
                             31  ;      1        invalid arguments
                             32  ;      2        exact integer conversion, string_size is defined
                             33  ;      3        indefinite
                             34  ;      4        + NAN (Not A Number)
                             35  ;      5        - NAN
                             36  ;      6        + Infinity
                             37  ;      7        - Infinity
                             38  ;      8        pseudo zero found, string_size is defined
                             39  ;
                             40  ;        The PLM/386 calling convention is:
                             41  ;
                             42  ; floating_to_ascii:
                             43  ;        procedure (number,denormal_ptr,string_ptr,size_ptr,
                             44  ;        field_size, power_ptr) word external;
                             45  ;        declare (denormal_ptr,string_ptr,power_ptr,size_ptr)
                             46  ;        pointer;
                             47  ;        declare field_size word,
                             48  ;        string_size based size_ptr word;
                             49  ;        declare number real;
                             50  ;        declare denormal integer based denormal_ptr;
```

**Figure 7-6. Floating-Point to ASCII Conversion Routine**

Higher precision can be achieved with greater care in programming, larger program size, and lower performance.

## 7.3.1 Function Partitioning

Three separate modules implement the conversion. Most of the work of the conversion is done in the module FLOATING_TO_ASCII. The other modules are provided separately, because they have a more general use. One of them, GET_POWER_10, is also

```
LOC       OBJ              LINE   SOURCE

                           51    ;        declare power integer based power_ptr;
                           52    ;        end floating_to_ascii;
                           53    ;
                           54    ;        The floating point value is expected to be
                           55    ; on the top of the NPX stack.  This subroutine
                           56    ; expects 3 free entries on the NPX stack and
                           57    ; will pop the passed value off when done.  The
                           58    ; generated ASCII string will have a leading
                           59    ; character either '-' or '+' indicating the sign
                           60    ; of the value.  The ASCII decimal digits will
                           61    ; immediately follow. The numeric value of the
                           62    ; ASCII string is (ASCII STRING.)*10**POWER. If
                           63    ; the given number was zero, the ASCII string will
                           64    ; contain a sign and a single zero chacter.  The
                           65    ; value string_size indicates the total length of
                           66    ; the ASCII string including the sign character.
                           67    ; String(0) will always hold the sign.  It is
                           68    ; possible for string_size to be less than
                           69    ; field_size. This occurs for zeroes or integer
                           70    ; values.  A pseudo zero will return a special
                           71    ; return code.  The denormal count will indicate
                           72    ;     the power of two originally associated with the
                           73    ; value.  The power of ten and ASCII string will
                           74    ; be as if the value was an ordinary zero.
                           75    ;
                           76    ; This subroutine is accurate up to a maximum of
                           77    ; 18 decimal digits for integers.  Integer values
                           78    ; will have a decimal power of zero associated
                           79    ; with them.  For non integers, the result will be
                           80    ; accurate to within 2 decimal digits of the 16th
                           81    ; decimal place(double precision).  The exponentiate
                           82    ; instruction is also used for scaling the value into
                           83    ; the range acceptable for the BCD data  type.  The
                           84    ; rounding mode in effect on entry to the
                           85    ; subroutine is used for the conversion.
                           86    ;
                           87    ;        The following registers are not transparent:
                           88    ;
                           89    ;             eax ebx ecx edx esi edi eflags
                           90    ;
                           91    ;
                           92    ;        Define the stack layout.
                           93    ;
00000000 []                94    ebp_save         equ      dword ptr [ebp]
00000004 []                95    es_save          equ      ebp_save + size ebp_save
00000008 []                96    return_ptr       equ      es_save + size es_save
0000000C []                97    power_ptr        equ      return_ptr + size return_ptr
00000010 []                98    field_size       equ      power_ptr + size power_ptr
00000014 []                99    size_ptr         equ      field_size + size field_size
00000018 []               100    string_ptr       equ      size_ptr + size size_ptr
0000001C []               101    denormal_ptr     equ      string_ptr + size string_ptr
                          102
0014                      103    parms_size       equ      size power_ptr + size field_size +
                          104    &                         size size_ptr + size string_ptr +
                          105    &                         size denormal_ptr
```

**Figure 7-6. Floating-Point to ASCII Conversion Routine (Cont'd.)**

used by the ASCII to floating-point conversion routine. The other small module, TOS_STATUS, identifies what, if anything, is in the top of the numeric register stack.

## 7.3.2 Exception Considerations

Care is taken inside the function to avoid generating exceptions. Any possible numeric value is accepted. The only possible exception is insufficient space on the numeric register stack.

```
    LOC      OBJ                    LINE    SOURCE

                                    106     ;
                                    107     ;          Define constants used
                                    108     ;
    0012                            109     BCD_DIGITS    equ    18        ; Number of digits in bcd_value
    0004                            110     WORD_SIZE     equ    4
    000A                            111     BCD_SIZE      equ    10
    0001                            112     MINUS         equ    1         ; Define return values
    0004                            113     NAN           equ    4         ; The exact values chosen
    0006                            114     INFINITY      equ    6         ; here are important.  They must
    0003                            115     INDEFINITE    equ    3         ; correspond to the possible return
    0008                            116     PSEUDO_ZERO   equ    8         ; values and be in the same numeric
   -0002                            117     INVALID       equ    -2        ; order as tested by the program.
   -0004                            118     ZERO          equ    -4
   -0006                            119     DENORMAL      equ    -6
   -0008                            120     UNNORMAL      equ    -8
    0000                            121     NORMAL        equ    0
    0002                            122     EXACT         equ    2
                                    123     ;
                                    124     ;          Define layout of temporary storage area.
                                    125     ;
    FFFFFFFC[]                      126     power_two     equ    word ptr [ebp - WORD_SIZE]
    FFFFFFF2[]                      127     bcd_value     equ    tbyte ptr power_two - BCD_SIZE
    FFFFFFF7[]                      128     bcd_byte      equ    byte ptr bcd_value
    FFFFFFF2[]                      129     fraction      equ    bcd_value
                                    130
    000C                            131     local_size    equ    size power_two + size bcd_value
                                    132     ;
                                    133     ;          Allocate stack space for the temporaries so
                                    134     ;      the stack will be big enough
                                    135     ;
    ........                        136     stack  stackseg (local_size+6) ; Allocate stack
                                    137                                    ; space for locals
                                    138  +1 $eject
```

**Figure 7-6. Floating-Point to ASCII Conversion Routine (Cont'd.)**

The value passed in the numeric stack is checked for existence, type (NaN or infinity), and status (denormal, zero, sign). The string size is tested for a minimum and maximum value. If the top of the register stack is empty, or the string size is too small, the function returns with an error code.

Overflow and underflow is avoided inside the function for very large or very small numbers.

## 7.3.3 Special Instructions

The functions demonstrate the operation of several numeric instructions, different data types, and precision control. Shown are instructions for automatic conversion to BCD, calculating the value of 10 raised to an integer value, establishing and maintaining concurrency, data synchronization, and use of directed rounding on the NPX.

Without the extended precision data type and built-in exponential function, the double precision accuracy of this function could not be attained with the size and speed of the shown example.

The function relies on the numeric BCD data type for conversion from binary floating-point to decimal. It is not difficult to unpack the BCD digits into separate ASCII decimal digits. The major work involves scaling the floating-point value to the comparatively limited range of BCD values. To print a 9-digit result requires accurately scaling the

```
LOC      OBJ                          LINE    SOURCE

                                      139     code         segment public er
                                      140                  extrn   power_table:qword
                                      141     ;
                                      142     ;            Constants used by this function.
                                      143     ;
                                      144                  even                    ; Optimize for 16 bits
00000000 0A00                         145     const10      dw      10              ; Adjustment value for
                                      146     ;                    ; too big BCD
                                      147     ;
                                      148     ; Convert the C3,C2,C1,C0 encoding from tos_status
                                      149     ; into meaningful bit flags and values.
                                      150     ;
00000002 F8                           151     status_table db      UNNORMAL, NAN, UNNORMAL + MINUS,
00000003 04                           152     &            NAN + MINUS, NORMAL, INFINITY,
00000004 F9                           153     &            NORMAL + MINUS, INFINITY + MINUS,
00000005 05                           154     &            ZERO, INVALID, ZERO + MINUS, INVALID,
00000006 00                           155     &            DENORMAL, INVALID, DENORMAL + MINUS, INVALID
00000007 06
00000008 01
00000009 07
0000000A FC
0000000B FE
0000000C FD
0000000D FE
0000000E FA
0000000F FE
00000010 FB
00000011 FE
                                      156
00000012                              157     floating_to_ascii proc
                                      158
00000012 E800000000         E         159          call    tos_status      ; Look at status of ST(0)
                                      160
                                      161     ; Get descriptor from table
00000017 2E0FB68002000000   R         162          movzx   eax, status_table[eax]
0000001F 3CFE                         163          cmp     al,INVALID              ; Look for empty ST(0)
00000021 7527                         164          jne     not_empty
                                      165     ;
                                      166     ;    ST(0) is empty!  Return the status value.
                                      167     ;
00000023 C21400                       168          ret     parms_size
                                      169     ;
                                      170     ;    Remove infinity from stack and exit.
                                      171     ;
00000026                              172     found_infinity:
00000026 DDD8                         173          fstp    st(0)           ; OK to leave fstp running
00000028 EB02                         174          jmp     short exit_proc
                                      175     ;
                                      176     ;       String space is too small!
                                      177     ;    Return invalid code.
                                      178     ;
0000002A                              179     small_string:
0000002A B0FE                         180          mov     al,INVALID
0000002C                              181     exit_proc:
0000002C C9                           182          leave           ; Restore stack setup
```

**Figure 7-6. Floating-Point to ASCII Conversion Routine (Cont'd.)**

given value to an integer between $10^8$ and $10^9$. For example, the number $+0.123456789$ requires a scaling factor of $10^9$ to produce the value $+123456789.0$, which can be stored in 9 BCD digits. The scale factor must be an exact power of 10 to avoid changing any of the printed digit values.

```
    LOC      OBJ                        LINE    SOURCE

 0000002D 07                            183           pop      es
 0000002E C21400                        184           ret      parms_size
                                        185     ;
                                        186     ; ST(0) is NAN or indefinite.  Store the
                                        187     ; value in memory and look at the fraction
                                        188     ; field to separate indefinite from an ordinary NAN.
                                        189     ;
 00000031                               190     NAN_or_indefinite:
 00000031 DB7DF2                        191           fstp     fraction        ; Remove value from stack
                                        192                                    ; for examination
 00000034 A801                          193           test     al,MINUS        ; Look at sign bit
 00000036 9B                            194           fwait                    ; Insure store is done
 00000037 74F3                          195           jz       exit_proc       ; Can't be indefinite if
                                        196                                    ; positive
                                        197
 00000039 BB000000C0                    198           mov      ebx,0C0000000H  ; Match against upper 32
                                        199                                    ;bits of fraction
                                        200
                                        201     ; Compare bits 63-32
 0000003E 2B5DF6                        202           sub      ebx, dword ptr fraction + 4
                                        203
                                        204     ; Bits 31-0 must be zero
 00000041 0B5DF2                        205           or       ebx, dword ptr fraction
 00000044 75E6                          206           jnz      exit_proc
                                        207
                                        208     ; Set return value for indefinite value
 00000046 B003                          209           mov al,INDEFINITE
 00000048 EBE2                          210           jmp      exit_proc
                                        211     ;
                                        212     ;       Allocate stack space for local variables
                                        213     ;    and establish parameter addressibility.
                                        214     ;
 0000004A                               215     not_empty:
 0000004A 06                            216           push     es              ; Save working register
 0000004B C80C0000                      217           enter local_size, 0      ; Setup stack addressing
                                        218
                                        219
                                        220     ; Check for enough string space
 0000004F 8B4D10                        221           mov      ecx,field_size
 00000052 83F902                        222           cmp      ecx,2
 00000055 7CD3                          223           jl       small_string
                                        224
 00000057 49                            225           dec      ecx             ; Adjust for sign character
                                        226
                                        227     ; See if string is too large for BCD
 00000058 83F912                        228           cmp      ecx,BCD_DIGITS
 0000005B 7605                          229           jbe      size_ok
                                        230
                                        231     ; Else set maximum string size
 0000005D B912000000                    232           mov      ecx,BCD_DIGITS
 00000062                               233     size_ok:
 00000062 3C06                          234           cmp      al,INFINITY     ; Look for infinity
                                        235
                                        236     ; Return status value for + or - inf
 00000064 7DC0                          237           jge      found_infinity
```

**Figure 7-6. Floating-Point to ASCII Conversion Routine (Cont'd.)**

These routines should exactly convert all values exactly representable in decimal in the field size given. Integer values that fit in the given string size are not be scaled, but directly stored into the BCD form. Noninteger values exactly representable in decimal within the string size limits are also exactly converted. For example, 0.125 is exactly representable in binary or decimal. To convert this floating-point value to decimal, the scaling factor is 1000, resulting in 125. When scaling a value, the function must keep track of where the decimal point lies in the final decimal value.

```
   LOC      OBJ                     LINE    SOURCE

                                    238
   00000066 3C04                    239           cmp      al,NAN          ; Look for NAN or INDEFINITE
   00000068 7DC7                    240           jge      NAN_or_indefinite
                                    241     ;
                                    242     ; Set default return values and check that
                                    243     ; the number is normalized.
                                    244     ;
   0000006A D9E1                    245           fabs     ; Use positive value only
                                    246                    ; sign bit in al has true sign of value
   0000006C 31D2                    247           xor      edx,edx              ; Form 0 constant
   0000006E 8B7D1C                  248           mov      edi,denormal_ptr; Zero denormal count
   00000071 668917                  249           mov      [edi], dx
   00000074 8B5D0C                  250           mov      ebx,power_ptr   ; Zero power of ten value
   00000077 668913                  251           mov      [ebx], dx
   0000007A 88C2                    252           mov dl, al
   0000007C 80E201                  253           and dl, 1
   0000007F 80C202                  254           add dl, EXACT
   00000082 3CFC                    255           cmp      al,ZERO              ; Test for zero
   00000084 0F83BC000000            256           jae      convert_integer ; Skip power code if value
                                    257                                   ; is zero
   0000008A DB7DF2                  258           fstp     fraction
   0000008D 9B                      259           fwait
   0000008E 8A45F9                  260           mov      al, bcd_byte + 7
   00000091 804DF980                261           or       byte ptr bcd_byte + 7, 80h
   00000095 DB6DF2                  262           fld      fraction
   00000098 D9F4                    263           fxtract
   0000009A A880                    264           test     al, 80h
   0000009C 7524                    265           jnz      normal_value
                                    266
   0000009E D9E8                    267           fld1
   000000A0 DEE9                    268           fsub
   000000A2 D9E4                    269           ftst
   000000A4 9BDFE0                  270           fstsw    ax
   000000A7 9E                      271           sahf
   000000A8 7510                    272           jnz      set_unnormal_count
                                    273     ;
                                    274     ; Found a pseudo zero
                                    275     ;
   000000AA D9EC                    276           fldlg2              ; Develop power of ten estimate
   000000AC 80C206                  277           add      dl, PSEUDO_ZERO - EXACT
   000000AF DECA                    278           fmulp    st(2), st
   000000B1 D9C9                    279           fxch
   000000B3 DF1B                    280           fistp word ptr [ebx] ; Set power of ten
   000000B5 E98C000000              281           jmp      convert_integer
                                    282
   000000BA                         283     set_unnormal_count:
   000000BA D9F4                    284           fxtract             ; Get original fraction,
                                    285                               ; now normalized
   000000BC D9C9                    286           fxch                ; Get unnormal count
   000000BE D9E0                    287           fchs
   000000C0 DF1F                    288           fistp word ptr [edi] ; Set unnormal count
                                    289
                                    290
                                    291     ; Calculate the decimal magnitude associated
                                    292     ; with this number to within one order.  This
```

**Figure 7-6. Floating-Point to ASCII Conversion Routine (Cont'd.)**

## 7.3.4 Description of Operation

Converting a floating-point number to decimal ASCII takes three major steps: identifying the magnitude of the number, scaling it for the BCD data type, and converting the BCD data type to a decimal ASCII string.

Identifying the magnitude of the result requires finding the value X such that the number is represented by $I \times 10^X$, where $1.0 \le I < 10.0$. Scaling the number requires

```
  LOC     OBJ                    LINE    SOURCE

                                 293     ; error will always be inevitable due to
                                 294     ; rounding and lost precision. As a result,
                                 295     ; we will deliberately  fail to consider the
                                 296     ; LOG10 of the fraction value in calculating
                                 297     ; the order. Since the fraction will always
                                 298     ; be 1 <= F < 2, its  LOG10 will not change
                                 299     ; the basic accuracy of the function.  To
                                 300     ; get the decimal order of magnitude, simply
                                 301     ; multiply the power of two by LOG10(2) and
                                 302     ; truncate the result to an integer.
                                 303     ;
  000000C2                       304     normal_value:
  000000C2 DB7DF2                305             fstp    fraction        ; Save the fraction field
                                 306                                     ; for later use
  000000C5 DF55FC                307             fist    power_two       ; Save power of two
  000000C8 D9EC                  308             fldlg2                  ; Get LOG10(2)
                                 309                                     ; Power_two is now safe to use
  000000CA DEC9                  310             fmul                    ; Form LOG10(of exponent of number)
  000000CC DF1B                  311             fistp   word ptr [ebx]  ; Any rounding mode
                                 312                                                    ; will work here
                                 313     ;
                                 314     ;       Check if the magnitude of the number rules
                                 315     ;   out treating it as an integer.
                                 316     ;
                                 317     ;       CX has the maximum number of decimal digits
                                 318     ;   allowed.
                                 319     ;
  000000CE 9B                    320             fwait                   ; Wait for power_ten to be valid
                                 321
                                 322     ; Get power of ten of value
  000000CF 668B33                323             movsx si, word ptr [ebx]
  000000D2 29CE                  324             sub     esi,ecx                 ; Form scaling factor
                                 325                                     ; necessary in ax
  000000D4 771C                  326             ja      adjust_result   ; Jump if number will not fit
                                 327     ;
                                 328     ;       The number is between 1 and 10**(field_size).
                                 329     ;   Test if it is an integer.
                                 330     ;
  000000D6 DF45FC                331             fild    power_two       ; Restore original number
  000000D9 80EAFE                332             sub     dl,NORMAL-EXACT ; Convert to exact return
                                 333                                     ; value
  000000DC DB6DF2                334             fld     fraction
  000000DF D9FD                  335             fscale                  ; Form full value, this
                                 336                                     ; is safe here
  000000E1 DDD1                  337             fst     st(1)           ; Copy value for compare
  000000E3 D9FC                  338             frndint                 ; Test if its an integer
  000000E5 DBD9                  339             fcomp                   ; Compare values
  000000E7 9BDFE0                340             fstsw   ax              ; Save status
  000000EA 9E                    341             sahf                    ; C3=1 implies it was
                                 342                                     ; an integer
  000000EB 7559                  343             jnz     convert_integer
                                 344
  000000ED DDD8                  345             fstp    st(0)           ; Remove non integer value
  000000EF 80C2FE                346             add     dl,NORMAL-EXACT ; Restore original return value
                                 347     ;
```

**Figure 7-6. Floating-Point to ASCII Conversion Routine (Cont'd.)**

multiplying it by a scaling factor $10^S$, so that the result is an integer requiring no more decimal digits than provided for in the ASCII string.

Once scaled, the numeric rounding modes and BCD conversion put the number in a form easy to convert to decimal ASCII by host software.

Implementing each of these three steps requires attention to detail. To begin with, not all floating-point values have a numeric meaning. Values such as infinity, indefinite, or

```
   LOC      OBJ                      LINE    SOURCE

                                     348     ;       Scale the number to within the range allowed
                                     349     ;    by the BCD format.The scaling operation should
                                     350     ;    produce a number within one decimal order of
                                     351     ;    magnitude of the largest decimal number
                                     352     ;    representable within the given string width.
                                     353     ;
                                     354     ;       The scaling power of ten value is in si.
                                     355     ;
   000000F2                          356     adjust_result:
   000000F2 8BC6                     357          mov     eax,esi             ; Setup for pow10
   000000F4 668903                   358          mov     word ptr [ebx],ax   ; Set initial power
                                     359                                      ; of ten return value
   000000F7 F7D8                     360          neg     eax                 ; Subtract one for each order of
                                     361                                      ; magnitude the value is scaled by
   000000F9 E800000000         E     362          call    get_power_10        ; Scaling factor is
                                     363                                      ; returned as
                                     364                                      ; exponent and fraction
   000000FE DB6DF2                   365          fld     fraction                 ; Get fraction
   00000101 DEC9                     366          fmul                             ; Combine fractions
   00000103 8BF1                     367          mov     esi,ecx             ; Form power of ten of
                                     368                                      ; the maximum
   00000105 C1E603                   369          shl     esi,3                    ; BCD value to fit in
                                     370                                      ; the string
   00000108 DF45FC                   371          fild    power_two           ; Combine powers of two
   0000010B DEC2                     372          faddp   st(2),st
   0000010D D9FD                     373          fscale                           ; Form full value,
                                     374                                      ; exponent was safe
   0000010F DDD9                     375          fstp    st(1)               ; Remove exponent
                                     376     ;
                                     377     ;       Test the adjusted value against a table
                                     378     ;    of exact powers of ten. The combined errors
                                     379     ;    of the magnitude estimate and power function
                                     380     ;    can result in a value one order of magnitude
                                     381     ;    too small or too large to fit correctly in
                                     382     ;    the BCD field. To handle this problem, pretest
                                     383     ;    the adjusted value, if it is too small or
                                     384     ;    large, then adjust it by ten and adjust the
                                     385     ;    power of ten value.
                                     386     ;
   00000111                          387     test_power:
                                     388
                                     389     ; Compare against exact power entry. Use the next
                                     390     ; entry since cx has been decremented by one
   00000111 2EDC9608000000     E     391          fcom    power_table[esi]+type power_table
   00000118 9BDFE0                   392          fstsw   ax                  ; No wait is necessary
   0000011B 9E                       393          sahf                        ; If C3 = C0 = 0 then
   0000011C 720F                     394          jb      test_for_small  ; too big
                                     395
   0000011E 2EDE3500000000     R     396          fidiv   const10             ; Else adjust value
   00000125 80E2FD                   397          and     dl,not EXACT        ; Remove exact flag
   00000128 66FF03                   398          inc     word ptr [ebx]  ; Adjust power of ten value
   0000012B EB17                     399          jmp     short in_range  ; Convert the value to a BCD
                                     400                                      ; integer
   0000012D                          401     test_for_small:
   0000012D 2EDC9600000000     E     402          fcom    power_table[esi]       ; Test relative size
```

**Figure 7-6. Floating-Point to ASCII Conversion Routine (Cont'd.)**

NaN may be encountered by the conversion routine. The conversion routine should recognize these values and identify them uniquely.

Special cases of numeric values also exist. Denormals have numeric values, but should be recognized because they indicate that precision was lost during some earlier calculations.

Once it has been determined that the number has a numeric value, and it is normalized (setting appropriate denormal flags, if necessary, to indicate this to the calling program), the value must be scaled to the BCD range.

```
OC      OBJ                    LINE    SOURCE

 0000134 9BDFE0                403        fstsw    ax                                        ; No wait is necess
                                      ary
 0000137 9E                    404        sahf                                              ; If C0 = 0 then
                               405                                         ; st(0) >= lower bound
 0000138 720A                  406        jc       in_range                                 ; Convert the value
                                      to a
                               407                                         ; BCD integer
                               408
 000013A 2EDE0D00000000    R   409        fimul    const10       ; Adjust value into range
 0000141 66FF0B                410        dec      word ptr [ebx]  ; Adjust power of ten value
 0000144                       411    in_range:
 0000144 D9FC                  412        frndint                          ; Form integer value
                               413    ;
                               414    ;        Assert: 0 <= TOS <= 999,999,999,999,999,999
                               415    ;        The TOS number will be exactly representable
                               416    ;    in 18 digit BCD format.
                               417    ;
 0000146                       418    convert_integer:
 0000146 DF75F2                419        fbstp    bcd_value       ; Store as BCD format number
                               420    ;
                               421    ;        While the store BCD runs, setup registers
                               422    ;    for the conversion to ASCII.
                               423    ;
 0000149 BE08000000            424        mov      esi,BCD_SIZE-2 ; Initial BCD index value
 000014E 66B9040F              425        mov      cx,0f04h      ; Set shift count and mask
 0000152 BB01000000            426        mov      ebx,1         ; Set initial size of ASCII
                               427                               ; field for sign
 0000157 8B7D18                428        mov      edi,string_ptr ; Get address of start of
                               429                               ; ASCII string
 000015A 8CD8                  430        mov      ax,ds                   ; Copy ds to es
 000015C 8EC0                  431        mov      es,ax
 000015E FC                    432        cld                                      ; Set autoincrement mode
 000015F B02B                  433        mov      al,'+'                  ; Clear sign field
 0000161 F6C201                434        test     dl,MINUS        ; Look for negative value
 0000164 7402                  435        jz       positive_result
                               436
 0000166 B02D                  437        mov      al,'-'
 0000168                       438    positive_result:
 0000168 AA                    439        stosb                            ; Bump string pointer
                               440                                 ; past sign
 0000169 80E2FE                441        and      dl,not MINUS   ; Turn off sign bit
 000016C 9B                    442        fwait                            ; Wait for fbstp to finish
                               443    ;
                               444    ;        Register usage:
                               445    ;                          ah:    BCD byte value in use
                               446    ;                          al:    ASCII character value
                               447    ;                          dx:    Return value
                               448    ;                          ch:    BCD mask = 0fh
                               449    ;                          cl:    BCD shift count = 4
                               450    ;                          bx:    ASCII string field width
                               451    ;                          esi:   BCD field index
                               452    ;                          di:    ASCII string field pointer
                               453    ;                          ds,es: ASCII string segment base
                               454    ;
                               455    ;        Remove leading zeroes from the number.
```

**Figure 7-6. Floating-Point to ASCII Conversion Routine (Cont'd.)**

## 7.3.5 Scaling the Value

To scale the number, its magnitude must be determined. It is sufficient to calculate the magnitude to an accuracy of 1 unit, or within a factor of 10 of the required value. After scaling the number, a check is made to see if the result falls in the range expected. If not, the result can be adjusted one decimal order of magnitude up or down. The adjustment test after the scaling is necessary due to inevitable inaccuracies in the scaling value.

```
LOC        OBJ                      LINE    SOURCE

                                    456   ;
0000016D                           457   skip_leading_zeroes:
0000016D 8A6435F2                  458          mov      ah,bcd_byte[esi]                ; Get BCD byte
00000171 88E0                      459          mov      al,ah                   ; Copy value
00000173 D2E8                      460          shr      al,cl                   ; Get high order digit
00000175 240F                      461          and      al,0fh                  ; Set zero flag
00000177 7517                      462          jnz      enter_odd               ; Exit loop if leading
                                    463                         ; non zero found
                                    464
00000179 88E0                      465          mov      al,ah                   ; Get BCD byte again
0000017B 240F                      466          and      al,0fh                  ; Get low order digit
0000017D 7519                      467          jnz      enter_even              ; Exit loop if non zero
                                    468                       ; digit found
                                    469
0000017F 4E                        470          dec      esi                             ; Decrement BCD index
00000180 79EB                      471          jns      skip_leading_zeroes
                                    472   ;
                                    473   ;       The significand was all zeroes.
                                    474   ;
00000182 B030                      475          mov      al,'0'                  ; Set initial zero
00000184 AA                        476          stosb
00000185 43                        477          inc      ebx                             ; Bump string length
00000186 EB17                      478          jmp      short exit_with_value
                                    479   ;
                                    480   ;       Now expand the BCD string into digit
                                    481   ;    per byte values 0-9.
                                    482   ;
00000188                           483   digit_loop:
00000188 8A6435F2                  484          mov      ah,bcd_byte[esi]        ; Get BCD byte
0000018C 88E0                      485          mov      al,ah
0000018E D2E8                      486          shr      al,cl                   ; Get high order digit
00000190                           487   enter_odd:
00000190 0430                      488          add      al,'0'                  ; Convert to ASCII
00000192 AA                        489          stosb                           ; Put digit into ASCII
                                    490                         ; string area
00000193 88E0                      491          mov      al,ah                   ; Get low order digit
00000195 240F                      492          and      al,0fh
00000197 43                        493          inc      ebx                     ; Bump field size counter
00000198                           494   enter_even:
00000198 0430                      495          add      al,'0'          ; Convert to ASCII
0000019A AA                        496          stosb                   ; Put digit into ASCII area
0000019B 43                        497          inc      ebx                     ; Bump field size counter
0000019C 4E                        498          dec      esi                     ; Go to next BCD byte
0000019D 79E9                      499          jns      digit_loop
                                    500   ;
                                    501   ;       Conversion complete.  Set the string
                                    502   ;    size and remainder.
                                    503   ;
0000019F                           504   exit_with_value:
0000019F 8B7D14                    505          mov      edi,size_ptr
000001A2 66891F                    506          mov      word ptr [edi],bx
000001A5 8BC2                      507          mov      eax,edx                 ; Set return value
000001A7 E980FEFFFF                508          jmp      exit_proc
                                    509
000001AC                           510   floating_to_ascii        endp
                                    511
........                            512   code                     ends
                                    513                            end

ASSEMBLY COMPLETE,   NO WARNINGS,   NO ERRORS.
```

**Figure 7-6. Floating-Point to ASCII Conversion Routine (Cont'd.)**

Because the magnitude estimate for the scale factor need only be close, a fast technique is used. The magnitude is estimated by multiplying the power of 2, the unbiased floating-point exponent, associated with the number by $\log_{10}2$. Rounding the result to an integer produces an estimate of sufficient accuracy. Ignoring the fraction value can introduce a maximum error of 0.32 in the result.

```
XENIX286 80386 MACRO ASSEMBLER V1.0, ASSEMBLY OF MODULE GET_POWER_10
OBJECT MODULE PLACED IN power10.obj
ASSEMBLER INVOKED BY: asm386 power10.asm


LOC       OBJ                     LINE    SOURCE

                                  1  +1  $title(Calculate the value of 10**ax)
                                  2      ;
                                  3      ;        This subroutine will calculate the
                                  4      ;        value of 10**eax. For values of
                                  5      ;        0 <= eax < 19, the result will exact.
                                  6      ;        All 80386 registers are transparent
                                  7      ;        and the value is returned on the TOS
                                  8      ;        as two numbers, exponent in ST(1) and
                                  9      ;        fraction in ST(0). The exponent value
                                  10     ;        can be larger than the largest
                                  11     ;        exponent of an extended real format
                                  12     ;        number.  Three stack entries are used.
                                  13     ;

                                  14                name      get_power_10
00000000                          15                public    get_power_10,power_table
                                  16
........                          17     stack         stackseg    8
                                  18
........                          19     code          segment public er
                                  20     ;
                                  21     ;        Use exact values from 1.0 to 1e18.
                                  22     ;
                                  23                even              ; Optimize 16 bit access
00000000 000000000000F03F         24     power_table   dq      1.0,1e1,1e2,1e3
00000008 0000000000002440
00000010 0000000000005940
00000018 000000000408F40
00000020 00000000088C340         25                   dq      1e4,1e5,1e6,1e7
00000028 00000000006AF840
00000030 0000000080842E41
00000038 00000000D0126341
00000040 0000000084D79741         26                  dq      1e8,1e9,1e10,1e11
00000048 0000000065CDCD41
00000050 000000205FA00242
00000058 000000E876483742
00000060 000000A2941A6D42         27                  dq      1e12,1e13,1e14,1e15
00000063 000040E59C30A242
00000070 0000901EC4BCD642
00000078 00003426F56B0C43
00000080 0080E03779C34143         28                  dq      1e16,1e17,1e18
00000088 00A0D88557347643
00000090 00C84E676DC1AB43
                                  29
00000098                          30     get_power_10     proc
                                  31
00000098 3D12000000               32            cmp      eax,18        ; Test for 0 <= ax < 19
0000009D 770B                     33            ja       out_of_range
                                  34
0000009F 2EDD04C500000000   R     35            fld      power_table[eax*8]; Get exact value
000000A7 D9F4                     36            fxtract                ; Separate power
```

**Figure 7-6. Floating-Point to ASCII Conversion Routine (Cont'd.)**

Using the magnitude of the value and size of the number string, the scaling factor can be calculated. Calculating the scaling factor is the most inaccurate operation of the conversion process. The relation $10^X = 2^{(X*\log_2 10)}$ is used for this function. The exponentiate instruction F2XM1 is used.

Due to restrictions on the range of values allowed by the F2XM1 instruction, the power of 2 value is split into integer and fraction components. The relation $2^{(I + F)} = 2^I \times 2^F$ allows using the FSCALE instruction to recombine the $2^F$ value, calculated through F2XM1, and the $2^I$ part.

```
    LOC      OBJ                   LINE    SOURCE

                                    37                              ; and fraction
    000000A9 C3                     38          ret                 ; OK to leave fxtract running
                                    39    ;
                                    40    ;         Calculate the value using the
                                    41    ;         exponentiate instruction. The following
                                    42    ;         relations are used:
                                    43    ;               10**x = 2**(log2(10)*x)
                                    44    ;               2**(I+F) = 2**I * 2**F
                                    45    ;               if st(1) = I and st(0) = 2**F then
                                    46    ;               fscale produces 2**(I+F)
                                    47    ;
    000000AA                        48    out_of_range:
                                    49
    000000AA D9E9                   50              fldl2t                  ; TOS = LOG2(10)
    000000AC C8040000               51              enter   4,0
                                    52
                                    53          ; save power of 10 value, P
    000000B0 8945FC                 54          mov     [ebp-4],eax
                                    55
                                    56          ; TOS,X = LOG2(10)*P = LOG2(10**P)
    000000B3 DA4DFC                 57              fimul   dword ptr [ebp-4]
    000000B6 D9E8                   58              fld1            ; Set TOS = -1.0
    000000B8 D9E0                   59              fchs
    000000BA D9C1                   60              fld     st(1)   ; Copy power value
                                    61                              ; in base two
    000000BC D9FC                   62              frndint         ; TOS = I: -inf < I <= X
                                    63                              ; where I is an integer
                                    64                              ; Rounding mode does
                                    65                              ; not matter
    000000BE D9CA                   66              fxch    st(2)   ; TOS = X, ST(1) = -1.0
                                    67                              ; ST(2) = I
    000000C0 D8E2                   68              fsub    st,st(2) ; TOS,F = X-I:
                                    69                              ; -1.0 < TOS <= 1.0
                                    70
                                    71          ; Restore orignal rounding control
    000000C2 58                     72              pop     eax
    000000C3 D9F0                   73              f2xm1                   ; TOS = 2**(F) - 1.0
    000000C5 C9                     74              leave                   ; Restore stack
    000000C6 DEE1                   75              fsubr                   ; Form 2**(F)
    000000C8 C3                     76              ret                     ; OK to leave fsubr running
                                    77
    000000C9                        78    get_power_10    endp
                                    79
    . . . . . . . .                 80    code            ends
                                    81                    end

    ASSEMBLY COMPLETE,   NO WARNINGS,   NO ERRORS.
```

**Figure 7-6. Floating-Point to ASCII Conversion Routine (Cont'd.)**

## 7.3.5.1 INACCURACY IN SCALING

The inaccuracy in calculating the scale factor arises because of the trailing zeros placed into the fraction value of the power of two when stripping off the integer valued bits. For each integer valued bit in the power of 2 value separated from the fraction bits, one bit of precision is lost in the fraction field due to the zero fill occurring in the least significant bits.

Up to 14 bits may be lost in the fraction because the largest allowed floating point exponent value is $2^{14} - 1$. These bits directly reduce the accuracy of the calculated scale factor, thereby reducing the accuracy of the scaled value. For numbers in the range of $10^{\pm 30}$, a maximum of 8 bits of precision are lost in the scaling process.

### 7.3.5.2 AVOIDING UNDERFLOW AND OVERFLOW

The fraction and exponent fields of the number are separated to avoid underflow and overflow in calculating the scaling values. For example, to scale $10^{-4932}$ to $10^8$ requires a scaling factor of $10^{4950}$, which cannot be represented by the NPX.

By separating the exponent and fraction, the scaling operation involves adding the exponents separate from multiplying the fractions. The exponent arithmetic involves small integers, all easily represented by the NPX.

### 7.3.5.3 FINAL ADJUSTMENTS

It is possible that the power function (Get_Power_10) could produce a scaling value such that it forms a scaled result larger than the ASCII field could allow. For example, scaling $9.9999999999999999 \times 10^{4900}$ by $1.0000000000000010 \times 10^{-4883}$ produces $1.0000000000000009 \times 10^{18}$. The scale factor is within the accuracy of the NPX and the result is within the conversion accuracy, but it cannot be represented in BCD format. This is why there is a post-scaling test on the magnitude of the result. The result can be multiplied or divided by 10, depending on whether the result was too small or too large, respectively.

## 7.3.6 Output Format

For maximum flexibility in output formats, the position of the decimal point is indicated by a binary integer called the power value. If the power value is zero, then the decimal point is assumed to be at the right of the rightmost digit. Power values greater than zero indicate how many trailing zeros are not shown. For each unit below zero, move the decimal point to the left in the string.

The last step of the conversion is storing the result in BCD and indicating where the decimal point lies. The BCD string is then unpacked into ASCII decimal characters. The ASCII sign is set corresponding to the sign of the original value.

## 7.4 TRIGONOMETRIC CALCULATION EXAMPLES

In this example, the kinematics of a robot arm is modeled with the $4 \times 4$ homogeneous transformation matrices proposed by Denavit and Hartenberg[1,2]. The translational and rotational relationships between adjacent links are described with these matrices using the D-H matrix method. For each link, there is a $4 \times 4$ homogeneous transformation matrix that represents the link's coordinate system ($L_i$) at the joint ($J_i$) with respect to the previous link's coordinate system ($J_{i-1}$, $L_{i-1}$). The following four geometric quantities completely describe the motion of any rigid joint/link pair ($J_i$, $L_i$), as Figure 7-7 illustrates.

$\theta_i$ = The angular displacement of the $x_i$ axis from the $x_{i-1}$ axis by rotating around the $z_{i-1}$ axis (anticlockwise).

$d_i$ = The distance from the origin of the $(i-1)^{th}$ coordinate system along the $z_{i-1}$ axis to the $x_i$ axis.

$a_i$ = The distance of the origin of the $i^{th}$ coordinate system from the $z_{i-1}$ axis along the $-x_i$ axis.

$\alpha_i$ = The angular displacement of the $z_i$ axis from the $z_{i-1}$ about the $x_i$ axis (anticlockwise).

The D-H transformation matrix $A_{i-1}$ for adjacent coordinate frames (from joint$_{i-1}$ to joint$_i$ is calculated as follows:

$$A_{i-1} = T_{z,d} \times T_{z,\theta} \times T_{x,a} \times T_{x,\alpha}$$

...where...

$T_{z,d}$   represents a translation along the $z_{i-1}$ axis

$T_{z,\theta}$   represents a rotation of angle $\theta$ about the $z_{i-1}$ axis

$T_{x,a}$   represents a translation along the $x_i$ axis

$T_{x,\alpha}$   represents a rotation of angle $\alpha$ about the $x_i$ axis

$$A_{i-1}^{i} = \begin{vmatrix} COS\ \theta_1 & -COS\ \alpha_i\ SIN\ \theta_i & SIN\ \alpha_i\ COS\ \theta_i & COS\ \theta_i \\ SIN\ \theta_i & COS\ \alpha_i\ COS\ \theta & -SIN\ \alpha_i\ COS\ \theta_i & SIN\ \theta_i \\ 0 & SIN\ \alpha_i & COS\ \alpha_i & d_i \\ 0 & 0 & 0 & 1 \end{vmatrix}$$

1. J. Denavit and R.S. Hartenberg, "A Kinematic Notation for Lower-Pair Mechanisms Based on Matrices," *J. Applied Mechanics,* June 1955, pp. 215-221.

2. C.S. George Lee, "Robot Arm Kinematics, Dynamics, and Control," *IEEE Computer,* Dec. 1982.

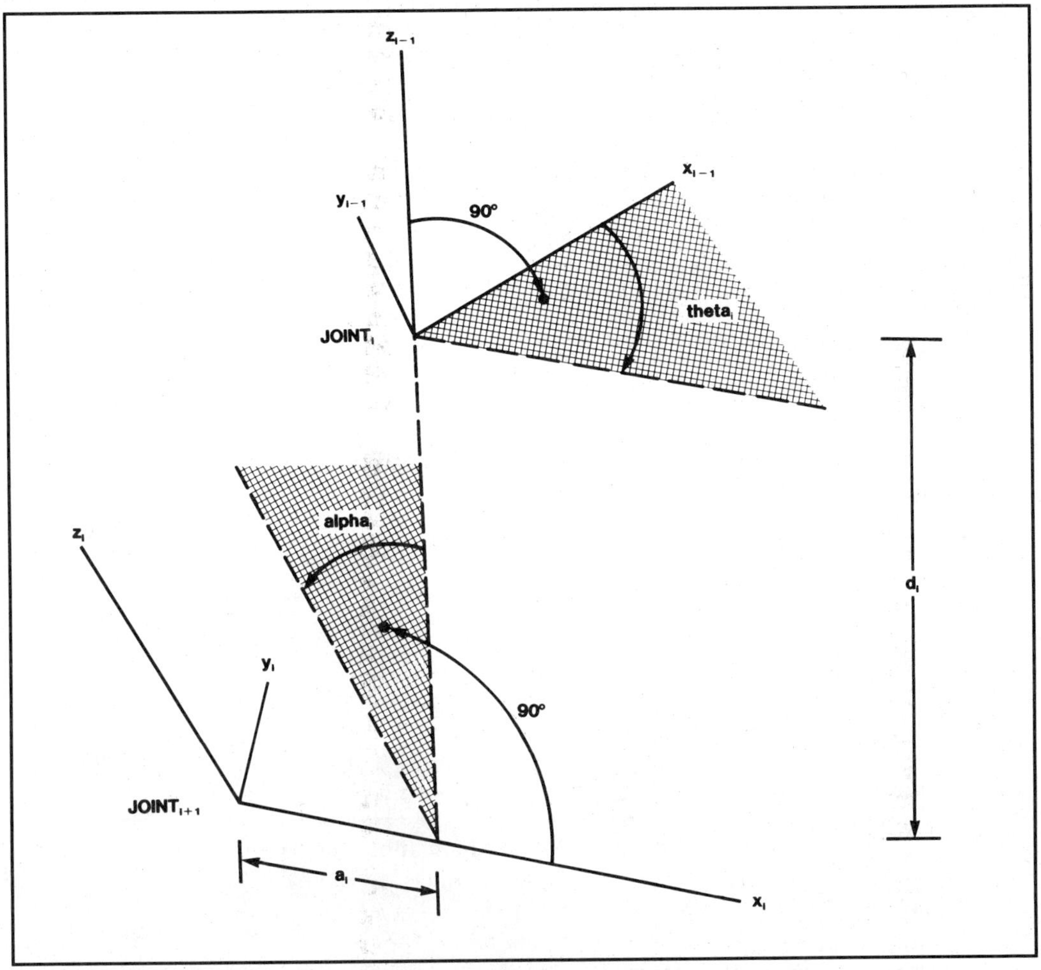

**Figure 7-7. Relationships between Adjacent Joints**

The composite homogeneous matrix **T** which represents the position and orientation of the joint/link pair with respect to the base system is obtained by successively multiplying the D-H transformation matrices for adjacent coordinate frames.

$$T_0^i = A_0^1 \times A_1^2 \times ... \times A_{i-1}^i$$

This example in Figure 7-8 illustrates how the transformation process can be accomplished using the 387 DX. The program consists of two major procedures. The first procedure TRANS PROC is used to calculate the elements in each D-H matrix, $A_{i-1}^i$. The second procedure MATRIXMUL PROC finds the product of two successive D-H matrices.

```
XENIX286 80386 MACRO ASSEMBLER V1.0, ASSEMBLY OF MODULE TOS_STATUS
OBJECT MODULE PLACED IN tos.obj
ASSEMBLER INVOKED BY: asm386 tos.asm


LOC        OBJ                    LINE      SOURCE

                                   1   +1 $title(Determine TOS register contents)
                                   2   ;
                                   3   ;          This subroutine will return a value
                                   4   ;      from 0-15 in eax corresponding
                                   5   ;          to the contents of NPX TOS.  All
                                   6   ;      registers are transparent and no
                                   7   ;          errors are possible.  The return
                                   8   ;      value corresponds to c3,c2,c1,c0
                                   9   ;          of FXAM instruction.
                                  10   ;

                                  11          name    tos_status
00000000                          12          public  tos_status
                                  13
........                          14   stack          stackseg    6
                                  15
........                          16   code           segment public er
                                  17
00000000                          18   tos_status     proc
                                  19
00000000 D9E5                     20          fxam                      ; Get status of TOS register
00000002 9BDFE0                   21          fstsw  ax        ; Get current status
00000005 88E0                     22          mov    al,ah      ; Put bit 10-8 into bits 2-0
00000007 2507400000               23          and    eax,4007h  ; Mask out bits c3,c2,c1,c0
0000000C C0EC03                   24          shr    ah, 3      ; Put bit c3 into bit 11
0000000F 08E0                     25          or     al,ah      ; Put c3 into bit 3
00000011 B400                     26          mov    ah,0       ; Clear return value
00000013 C3                       27          ret
                                  28
00000014                          29   tos_status     endp
                                  30
........                          31   code           ends
                                  32                 end

ASSEMBLY COMPLETE,   NO WARNINGS,   NO ERRORS.
```

**Figure 7-8. Robot Arm Kinematics Example**

```
XENIX286 80386 MACRO ASSEMBLER V1.0, ASSEMBLY OF MODULE ROT_MATRIX_CAL
OBJECT MODULE PLACED IN transx.obj
ASSEMBLER INVOKED BY: asm386 transx.asm


LOC       OBJ                    LINE     SOURCE

                                 1        Name ROT_MATRIX_CAL
                                 2
                                 3
                                 4
                                 5        ; This example illustrates the use
                                 6        ; of the 80387 floating point
                                 7        ; instructions, in particular, the
                                 8        ; FSINCOS function which gives both
                                 9        ; the SIN and COS values.
                                 10       ; The program calculates the
                                 11       ; composite matrix for base to end-
                                 12       ; effector transformation.
                                 13       ;
                                 14       ; Only the kinematics is considered in
                                 15       ; this example.
                                 16       ;
                                 17       ; If the composite matrix mentioned above
                                 18       ; is given by:
                                 19       ; T1n = A1 x A2 x ... x An
                                 20       ; T1n is found by successively calling
                                 21       ; trans_proc and matrixmul_pro until
                                 22       ; all matrices have been exhausted.
                                 23       ;
                                 24       ; trans_proc calculates entries in each
                                 25       ; A(A1,...,An) while matrixmul_proc
                                 26       ; performs the matrix multiplication for
                                 27       ; Ai and Ai+1. matrixmul_proc in turn
                                 28       ; calls matrix_row and matrix_elem to
                                 29       ; do the multiplication.
                                 30
                                 31
                                 32       ; Define stack space
                                 33
--------                         34       trans_stack stackseg 400
                                 35
                                 36       ; Define the matrix structure for
                                 37       ; 4X4 transformational matrices
                                 38
--------                         39          a_matrix struc
00000000                         40               a11      dq      ?
00000008                         41               a12      dq      ?
00000010                         42               a13      dq      ?
00000018                         43               a14      dq      ?
00000020                         44               a21      dq      ?
00000028                         45               a22      dq      ?
00000030                         46               a23      dq      ?
00000038                         47               a24      dq      ?
00000040                         48               a31      dq      0h
00000048                         49               a32      dq      ?
00000050                         50               a33      dq      ?
00000058                         51               a34      dq      ?
00000060                         52               a41      dq      0h
00000068                         53               a42      dq      0h
00000070                         54               a43      dq      0h
00000078                         55               a44      dq      1h
--------                         56          a_matrix ends
                                 57
```

**Figure 7-8. Robot Arm Kinematics Example (Cont'd.)**

```
                                     58      ; Assume One joint in the storage
                                     59      ; allocation and hence for
                                     60      ; two sets of parameters; however,
                                     61      ; more joints are possible
                                     62      ;
--------                             63      alp_deg struc
00000000                             64              alpha_deg1 dd  ?
00000004                             65              alpha_deg2 dd  ?
--------                             66      alp_deg ends
                                     67
--------                             68      tht_deg struc
00000000                             69              theta_deg1 dd  ?
00000004                             70              theta_deg2 dd  ?
--------                             71      tht_deg ends
                                     72
--------                             73      A_array struc
00000000                             74              A1          dq  ?
00000008                             75              A2          dq  ?
--------                             76      A_array ends
                                     77
--------                             78      D_array struc
00000000                             79              D1          dq  ?
00000008                             80              D2          dq  ?
--------                             81      D_array ends
                                     82
                                     83      ; trans_data is the data segment
                                     84      ;
                                     85
--------                             86      trans_data      segment rw public
                                     87
00000000 ????????????????           88          Amx         a_matrix<>
00000008 ????????????????
00000010 ????????????????
00000018 ????????????????
00000020 ????????????????
00000028 ????????????????
00000030 ????????????????
00000038 ????????????????
00000040 0000000000000000
00000048 ????????????????
00000050 ????????????????
00000058 ????????????????
00000060 0000000000000000
00000068 0000000000000000
00000070 0000000000000000
00000078 0100000000000000
00000080 ????????????????           89          Bmx         a_matrix<>
00000088 ????????????????
00000090 ????????????????
00000098 ????????????????
000000A0 ????????????????
000000A8 ????????????????
000000B0 ????????????????
000000B8 ????????????????
000000C0 0000000000000000
000000C8 ????????????????
000000D0 ????????????????
000000D8 ????????????????
000000E0 0000000000000000
000000E8 0000000000000000
000000F0 0000000000000000
000000F8 0100000000000000
```

**Figure 7-8. Robot Arm Kinematics Example (Cont'd.)**

```
00000100 ????????????????    90          Tmx         a_matrix<>
00000108 ????????????????
00000110 ????????????????
00000118 ????????????????
00000120 ????????????????
00000128 ????????????????
00000130 ????????????????
00000138 ????????????????
00000140 0000000000000000
00000148 ????????????????
00000150 ????????????????
00000158 ????????????????
00000160 0000000000000000
00000168 0000000000000000
00000170 0000000000000000
00000178 0100000000000000
00000180 ????????            91          ALPHA_DEG   alp_deg<>
00000184 ????????
00000188 ????????            92          THETA_DEG   tht_deg<>
0000018C ????????
00000190 ????????????????    93          A_VECTOR    A_array<>
00000198 ????????????????
000001A0 ????????????????    94          D_VECTOR    D_array<>
000001A8 ????????????????
000001B0 00000000            95          ZERO        dd          0
000001B4 B4000000            96          d180        dd          180
     0001                    97          NUM_JOINT   equ         1
     0004                    98          NUM_ROW     equ         4
     0004                    99          NUM_COL     equ         4
000001B8 01                 100          REVERSE     db          1h
--------                    101     trans_data ends
                            102
                            103     assume    ds:trans_data, es:trans_data
                            104
                            105
                            106     ; trans_code contains the procedures
                            107     ; for calculating matrix elements and
                            108     ; matrix multiplications
                            109
--------                    110     trans_code    segment    er public
                            111
                            112     ; create mnemonics for fsincos which is not
                            113     ; yet available from ASM386 as of now
                            114
   C MACRO                  115     codemacro fsincos
      #                     116     dw 0fbd9h
      #                     117     endm
                            118
00000000                    119     trans_proc proc far
                            120
                            121
                            122         ; Calculate alpha and theta in radians
                            123         ; from their values in degrees
                            124
00000000 D9EB               125         fldpi
00000002 D835B4010000    R  126         fdiv     d180
                            127
                            128     ; Duplicate pi/180
00000008 D9C0               129         fld      st
                            130
0000000A DC0CCD80010000  R  131         fmul     qword ptr ALPHA_DEG[ecx*8]
00000011 D9C9               132         fxch     st(1)
00000013 DC0CCD88010000  R  133         fmul     qword ptr THETA_DEG[ecx*8]
                            134
```

**Figure 7-8. Robot Arm Kinematics Example (Cont'd.)**

```
                                           135        ; theta(radians) in ST and
                                           136        ; alpha(radians) in ST(1)
                                           137
                                           138        ; Calculate matrix elements
                                           139        ; a11 = cos theta
                                           140        ; a12 = - cos alpha * sin thet
                                           141        ; a13 = sin alpha * sin theta
                                           142        ; a14 = A * cos theta
                                           143        ; a21 = sin theta
                                           144        ; a22 = cos alpha * cos theta
                                           145        ; a23 = -sin alpha * cos theta
                                           146        ; a24 = A * sin theta
                                           147        ; a32 = sin alpha
                                           148        ; a33 = cos alpha
                                           149        ; a34 = D
                                           150        ; a31 = a41 = a42 = a43 = 0.0
                                           151        ; a44 =1
                                           152
                                           153        ; ebx contains the offset for the matrix
                                           154
0000001A D9FB                              155        fsincos          ;cos theta in ST
                                           156                         ;sin theta in ST(1)
0000001C D9C0                              157        fld     st        ;duplicate cos theta
0000001E DD13                              158        fst     [ebx].a11 ;cos theta in a11
00000020 DC0CCD90010000         R          159        fmul    qword ptr A_VECTOR[ecx*8]
00000027 DD5818                            160        fstp    [ebx].a14 ;A * cos thetain a14
0000002A D9C9                              161        fxch    st(1)     ;sin theta in ST
0000002C DD5320                            162        fst     [ebx].a21 ;sin theta in a21
0000002F D9C0                              163        fld     st        ;duplicate sin theta
00000031 DC0CCD90010000         R          164        fmul    qword ptr A_VECTOR[ecx*8]
00000038 DD5B38                            165        fstp    [ebx].a24 ;A * sin theta in a24
0000003B D9C2                              166        fld     st(2)     ;alpha in ST
0000003D D9FB                              167        fsincos          ;cos alpha in ST
                                           168                         ;sin alpha in ST(1)
                                           169                         ;sin theta in ST(2)
                                           170                         ;cos theta in ST(3)
0000003F DD5350                            171        fst     [ebx].a33 ;cos alpha in a33
00000042 D9C9                              172        fxch    st(1)     ;sin alpha in ST
00000044 DD5348                            173        fst     [ebx].a32 ;sin alpha in a32
00000047 D9C2                              174        fld     ST(2)     ;sin theta in ST
                                           175                         ;sin alpha in ST(1)
00000049 D8C9                              176        fmul    st,st(1)  ;sin alpha * sin theta
0000004B DD5B10                            177        fstp    [ebx].a13 ;stored in a13
0000004E D8CB                              178        fmul    st,st(3)  ;cos theta * sin alpha
00000050 D9E0                              179        fchs             ;-cos theta * sin alpha
00000052 DD5B30                            180        fstp    [ebx].a23 ;stored in a23
00000055 D9C2                              181        fld     st(2)     ;cos theta in ST
                                           182                         ;cos alpha in ST(1)
                                           183                         ;sin theta in ST(2)
                                           184                         ;cos theta in ST(3)
00000057 D8C9                              185        fmul    st,st(1)  ;cos theta * cos alpha
00000059 DD5B28                            186        fstp    [ebx].a22 ;stored in a22
0000005C D8C9                              187        fmul    st,st(1)  ;cos alpha * sin theta
                                           188        ;
                                           189        ; To take advantage of parallel operations
                                           190        ; between the CPU and NPX
                                           191        ;
0000005E 50                               192        push    eax  ; save eax
                                           193        ;
                                           194        ; also move D into a34 in a faster way
0000005F 8B04CDA0010000         R          195        mov     eax, dword ptr D_VECTOR[ecx*8]
00000066 894358                            196        mov     dword ptr [ebx + 88], eax
```

**Figure 7-8. Robot Arm Kinematics Example (Cont'd.)**

```
00000069 8B04CDA4010000    R    197        mov     eax, dword ptr D_VECTOR[ecx*8 + 4]
00000070 89435C                 198        mov     dword ptr [ebx + 92], eax
00000073 58                     199        pop     eax  ; restore eax
00000074 D9E0                   200        fchs               ;-cos alpha * sin theta
00000076 DD5B08                 201        fstp    [ebx].a12 ;stored in a12
                                202                          ;and all nonzero elements
                                203                          ;have been calculated
00000079 CB                     204        ret
                                205
0000007A                       206    trans_proc endp
                                207
                                208
0000007A                       209    matrix_elem proc far
                                210
                                211        ; This procedure calculate the dot product
                                212        ; of the ith row of the first matrix and
                                213        ; the jth column of the second matrix:
                                214        ;
                                215        ; Tij where Tij = sum of Aik x Bkj over k
                                216        ;
                                217        ; parameters passed from the calling routine,
                                218        ; matrix_row:
                                219        ; ESI = (i-1)*8
                                220        ; EDI = (j-1)*8
                                221        ; local register, EBP = (k-1)*8
                                222        ;
0000007A 55                     223        push    ebp    ; save ebp
0000007B 51                     224        push    ecx    ; ecx to be used as a tmp reg
0000007C 8BCE                   225        mov     ecx, esi; save it for later indexing
                                226
                                227        ; locating the element in the first matrix, A
0000007E 6BC904                 228        imul    ecx, NUM_COL    ; ecx contains offset due
                                229                                ; to preceding rows; the
                                230                                ; offset is from the
                                231                                ; beginning of the matrix
                                232
00000081 31ED                   233        xor     ebp, ebp; clear ebp, which will be
                                234                                ; used a temp reg to index( k)
                                235                                ; across the ith row of the first
                                236                                ; matrix as well as down the jth
                                237                                ; column of the second matrix
                                238
                                239        ; clear Tij for accumulating Aik*Bkj
00000083 892C39                 240        mov     dword ptr [ecx][edi],ebp
00000086 896C3904               241        mov     dword ptr [ecx][edi+4], ebp
                                242
0000008A 51                     243        push    ecx    ; save on stack: esi * num_col =
                                244                                ; the offset of the beginnging
                                245                                ; of the ith row from the
                                246                                ; beginning of the A matrix
                                247
0000008B                       248    NXT_k:
0000008B 01E9                   249        add     ecx, ebp ; get to the kth column entry
                                250                                ; of the ith row of the A matrix
                                251
                                252        ; load Aik into 80387
0000008D DD0408                 253        fld     qword ptr [eax][ecx]
                                254
                                255        ; locating  Bkj
00000090 8BCD                   256        mov     ecx, ebp
00000092 6BC904                 257        imul    ecx, NUM_ROW ; ecx contains the offset
                                258                                ; of the beginning of the
                                259                                ; kth row from the
```

**Figure 7-8. Robot Arm Kinematics Example (Cont'd.)**

```
                                            260                                                ; beginning of the B matrix
00000095 01F9                               261                    add        ecx, edi         ; get to the jth column
entry
                                            262                                                ; of the kth row of the B
                                            263                                                ; matrix
00000097 DC0C0B                             264                    fmul       qword ptr [ebx][ecx]; Aik * Bkj
0000009A 59                                 265                    pop        ecx              ; esi * num_col
                                            266                                                ; in ecx again
0000009B 51                                 267                    push       ecx              ; also at top of program
                                            268                                                ; stack
                                            269
                                            270              ; add to the result in the output matrix,Tij
0000009C 01F9                               271                    add        ecx, edi
                                            272
                                            273              ; accumulating the sum of Aik * Bkj
0000009E DC040A                             274                    fadd       qword ptr [edx][ecx]
000000A1 DD1C0A                             275                    fstp       qword ptr [edx][ecx]
                                            276              ; increment k by 1, i.e., ebp by 8
000000A4 83C508                             277                    add        ebp, 8
                                            278
                                            279              ; Has k reached the width of the matrix yet?
000000A7 83FD20                             280                    cmp        ebp, NUM_COL*8
000000AA 7CDF                               281                    jl         NXT_k
                                            282
                                            283              ; Restore registers
000000AC 59                                 284                    pop        ecx              ; clear esi*num_col from stack
000000AD 59                                 285                    pop        ecx              ; restore ecx
000000AE 5D                                 286                    pop        ebp              ; restore ebp
000000AF CB                                 287                    ret
                                            288
000000B0                                    289       matrix_elem endp
                                            290
                                            291
000000B0                                    292       matrix_row proc far
                                            293
000000B0 31FF                               294                    xor        edi, edi
                                            295              ; scan across a row
                                            296
000000B2                                    297       NXT_COL:
000000B2 9A7A000000----         R           298                    call       matrix_elem
000000B9 83C708                             299                    add        edi, 8
000000BC 83FF20                             300                    cmp        edi, NUM_COL*8
000000BF 7CF1                               301                    jl         NXT_COL
000000C1 CB                                 302                    ret
                                            303
000000C2                                    304       matrix_row endp
                                            305
                                            306
000000C2                                    307       matrixmul_proc proc far
                                            308
                                            309              ; This procedure does the matrix
                                            310              ; multiplication by calling matrix_row
                                            311              ; to calculate entries in each row
                                            312              ;
                                            313              ; The matrix multiplication is
                                            314              ; performed in the following manner,
                                            315              ;    Tij = Aik x Bkj
                                            316              ; where i and j denote the row and column
                                            317              ; respectively and k is the index for
                                            318              ; scanning across the ith row of the
                                            319              ; first matrix and the jth column of the
                                            320              ; second matrix.
```

**Figure 7-8. Robot Arm Kinematics Example (Cont'd.)**

```
                                          mov ebp, esp; use base pointer for indexing
000000C2 5A                    321           mov edx, dword ptr [ebp+4] ; offset Tmx in edx
000000C3 5B                    322           mov ebx, dword ptr [ebp + 8] ; offset Bmx in edx
000000C4 58                    323           move eax, dword ptr [ebp + 12] ; offset Amx in eax
                               324
                               325        ; setup esi and edi
                               326        ; edi points to the column
                               327        ; esi points to the row
                               328
000000C5 31F6                  329           xor     esi, esi ; clear esi
                               330
000000C7                       331    NXT_ROW:
000000C7 9AB0000000----   R    332           call    matrix_row
000000CE 83C608                333           add     esi, 8
000000D1 83FE20                334           cmp     esi, NUM_ROW*8
000000D4 7CF1                  335           jl      NXT_ROW
000000D6 CB                    336           ret     12 ; pop off matrix pointers
                               337
000000D7                       338    matrixmul_proc endp
                               339
                               340
.........                      341    trans_code ends
                               342
                               343    ;****************************************
                               344    ;                                      ;
                               345    ;                                      ;
                               346    ;                                      ;
                               347    ;              Main program            ;
                               348    ;                                      ;
                               349    ;                                      ;
                               350    ;                                      ;
                               351    ;****************************************
                               352
.........                      353    main_code segment er
                               354
00000000                       355    START:
                               356
00000000 BC00000000       R    357           mov esp,  stackstart trans_stack
                               358        ; save all registers
                               359
00000005 60                    360           pushad
                               361
                               362        ; ECX denotes the number of joints
                               363        ; where no of matrices = NUM_JOINT + 1
                               364        ; Find the first matrix( from the base
                               365        ; of the system to the first joint)
                               366        ; and call it Bmx
00000006 31C9                  367           xor ecx, ecx            ; 1st matrix
00000008 BB80000000       R    368           mov ebx, offset Bmx  ;
0000000D 9A00000000----   R    369           call trans_proc        ; is Bmx
00000014 41                    370           inc ecx
                               371
00000015                       372    NXT_MATRIX:
                               373        ; From the 2nd matrix and on, it
                               374        ; will be stored in Amx.
                               375        ; The result from the first matrix mult.
                               376        ; is stored in Tmx but will be accessed
                               377        ; as Bmx in the next multiplication.
                               378        ; As a matter of fact, the roles of Bmx
                               379        ; and Tmx alternate in successive
                               380        ; multiplications. This is achieved by
                               381        ; reversing the order of the Bmx and Tmx
                               382        ; pointers being passed onto the program
```

**Figure 7-8. Robot Arm Kinematics Example (Cont'd.)**

```
                                           383       ; stack. Thus, this is invisible to the
                                           384       ; matrix multiplication procedure.
                                           385       ; REVERSE serves as the indicator;
                                           386       ; REVERSE = 0 means that the result
                                           387       ;            is to placed in Tmx.
                                           388
00000015 BB00000000        R               389           mov     ebx, offset Amx   ;find Amx
0000001A 9A00000000----    R               390           call    trans_proc
00000021 41                                391           inc     ecx
00000022 8035B801000001    R               392           xor     REVERSE, 1h
00000029 7511                              393           jnz     Bmx_as_Tmx
                                           394
                                           395       ; no reversing.  Bmx as the second input
                                           396       ; matrix while Tmx as the output matrix.
0000002B 6800000000        R               397           push    offset Amx
00000030 6880000000        R               398           push    offset Bmx
00000035 6800010000        R               399           push    offset Tmx
0000003A EB0F                              400           jmp     CONTINUE
                                           401
                                           402       ; reversing. Tmx as the second input
                                           403       ; matrix while Bmx as the output matrix.
0000003C                                   404       Bmx_as_Tmx:
0000003C 6800000000        R               405           push    offset Amx
00000041 6800010000        R               406           push    offset Tmx  ;reversing the
00000046 6880000000        R               407           push    offset Bmx  ;pointers passed
                                           408
0000004B                                   409       CONTINUE:
0000004B 9AC2000000----    R               410           call    matrixmul_proc
00000052 83F901                            411           cmp     ecx, NUM_JOINT
00000055 7EBE                              412           jle     NXT_MATRIX
                                           413
                                           414       ; if REVERSE = 1 then the final answer
                                           415       ; will be in Bmx otherwise, in Tmx.
                                           416
00000057 61                                417           popad
                                           418
--------                                   419       main_code  ends
                                           420
                                           421       end START, ds:trans_data, ss:trans_stack

ASSEMBLY COMPLETE,   NO WARNINGS,   NO ERRORS.
```

**Figure 7-8. Robot Arm Kinematics Example (Cont'd.)**

# Machine Instruction
# Encoding and Decoding

A

# APPENDIX A
# MACHINE INSTRUCTION ENCODING AND DECODING

| 1st Byte | | 2nd Byte | Bytes 3-7 | ASM386 Instruction Format | |
|---|---|---|---|---|---|
| Hex | Binary | | | | |
| D8 | 1101 1000 | MOD 000 R/M | SIB, displ | FADD | single-real |
| D8 | 1101 1000 | MOD 001 R/M | SIB, displ | FMUL | single-real |
| D8 | 1101 1000 | MOD 010 R/M | SIB, displ | FCOM | single-real |
| D8 | 1101 1000 | MOD 011 R/M | SIB, displ | FCOMP | single-real |
| D8 | 1101 1000 | MOD 100 R/M | SIB, displ | FSUB | single-real |
| D8 | 1101 1000 | MOD 101 R/M | SIB, displ | FSUBR | single-real |
| D8 | 1101 1000 | MOD 110 R/M | SIB, displ | FDIV | single-real |
| D8 | 1101 1000 | MOD 111 R/M | SIB, displ | FDIVR | single-real |
| D8 | 1101 1000 | 1100 0 REG | | FADD | ST,ST(i) |
| D8 | 1101 1000 | 1100 1 REG | | FMUL | ST,ST(i) |
| D8 | 1101 1000 | 1101 0 REG | | FCOM | ST(i) |
| D8 | 1101 1000 | 1101 1 REG | | FCOMP | ST(i) |
| D8 | 1101 1000 | 1110 0 REG | | FSUB | ST,ST(i) |
| D8 | 1101 1000 | 1110 1 REG | | FSUBR | ST,ST(i) |
| D8 | 1101 1000 | 1111 0 REG | | FDIV | ST,ST(i) |
| D8 | 1101 1000 | 1111 1 REG | | FDIVR | ST,ST(i) |
| D9 | 1101 1001 | MOD 000 R/M | SIB, displ | FLD | single-real |
| D9 | 1101 1001 | MOD 001 R/M | | reserved | |
| D9 | 1101 1001 | MOD 010 R/M | SIB, displ | FST | single-real |
| D9 | 1101 1001 | MOD 011 R/M | SIB, displ | FSTP | single-real |
| D9 | 1101 1001 | MOD 100 R/M | SIB, displ | FLDENV | 14 or 28 bytes*** |
| D9 | 1101 1001 | MOD 101 R/M | SIB, displ | FLDCW | 2 bytes |
| D9 | 1101 1001 | MOD 110 R/M | SIB, displ | FSTENV | 14 or 28 bytes*** |
| D9 | 1101 1001 | MOD 111 R/M | SIB, displ | FSTCW | 2 bytes |
| D9 | 1101 1001 | 1100 0 REG | | FLD | ST(i) |
| D9 | 1101 1001 | 1100 1 REG | | FXCH | ST(i) |
| D9 | 1101 1001 | 1101 0000 | | FNOP | |
| D9 | 1101 1001 | 1101 0001 | | reserved | |
| D9 | 1101 1001 | 1101 001– | | reserved | |
| D9 | 1101 1001 | 1101 01– – | | reserved | |
| D9 | 1101 1001 | 1101 1 REG | | reserved | |
| D9 | 1101 1001 | 1110 0000 | | FCHS | |
| D9 | 1101 1001 | 1110 0001 | | FABS | |
| D9 | 1101 1001 | 1110 001– | | reserved | |
| D9 | 1101 1001 | 1110 0100 | | FTST | |
| D9 | 1101 1001 | 1110 0101 | | FXAM | |
| D9 | 1101 1001 | 1110 011– | | reserved | |
| D9 | 1101 1001 | 1110 1000 | | FLD1 | |
| D9 | 1101 1001 | 1110 1001 | | FLDL2T | |
| D9 | 1101 1001 | 1110 1010 | | FLDL2E | |
| D9 | 1101 1001 | 1110 1011 | | FLDPI | |
| D9 | 1101 1001 | 1110 1100 | | FLDLG2 | |
| D9 | 1101 1001 | 1110 1101 | | FLDLN2 | |
| D9 | 1101 1001 | 1110 1110 | | FLDZ | |
| D9 | 1101 1001 | 1110 1111 | | reserved | |

| 1st Byte | | 2nd Byte | Bytes 3-7 | ASM386 Instruction Format | |
|---|---|---|---|---|---|
| Hex | Binary | | | | |
| D9 | 1101 1001 | 1111 0000 | | F2XM1 | |
| D9 | 1101 1001 | 1111 0001 | | FYL2X | |
| D9 | 1101 1001 | 1111 0010 | | FPTAN | |
| D9 | 1101 1001 | 1111 0011 | | FPATAN | |
| D9 | 1101 1001 | 1111 0100 | | FXTRACT | |
| D9 | 1101 1001 | 1111 0101 | | FPREM1 | |
| D9 | 1101 1001 | 1111 0110 | | FDECSTP | |
| D9 | 1101 1001 | 1111 0111 | | FINCSTP | |
| D9 | 1101 1001 | 1111 1000 | | FPREM | |
| D9 | 1101 1001 | 1111 1001 | | FYL2XP1 | |
| D9 | 1101 1001 | 1111 1010 | | FSQRT | |
| D9 | 1101 1001 | 1111 1011 | | FSINCOS | |
| D9 | 1101 1001 | 1111 1100 | | FRNDINT | |
| D9 | 1101 1001 | 1111 1101 | | FSCALE | |
| D9 | 1101 1001 | 1111 1110 | | FSIN | |
| D9 | 1101 1001 | 1111 1111 | | FCOS | |
| DA | 1101 1010 | MOD 000 R/M | SIB, displ | FIADD | short-integer |
| DA | 1101 1010 | MOD 001 R/M | SIB, displ | FIMUL | short-integer |
| DA | 1101 1010 | MOD 010 R/M | SIB, displ | FICOM | short-integer |
| DA | 1101 1010 | MOD 011 R/M | SIB, displ | FICOMP | short-integer |
| DA | 1101 1010 | MOD 100 R/M | SIB, displ | FISUB | short-integer |
| DA | 1101 1010 | MOD 101 R/M | SIB, displ | FISUBR | short-integer |
| DA | 1101 1010 | MOD 110 R/M | SIB, displ | FIDIV | short-integer |
| DA | 1101 1010 | MOD 111 R/M | SIB, displ | FIDIVR | short-integer |
| DA | 1101 1010 | 110– – – – – | | reserved | |
| DA | 1101 1010 | 1110 0– – – | | reserved | |
| DA | 1101 1010 | 1110 1000 | | reserved | |
| DA | 1010 1010 | 1110 1001 | | FUCOMPP | |
| DA | 1101 1010 | 1110 101– | | reserved | |
| DA | 1101 1010 | 1110 11– – | | reserved | |
| DA | 1101 1010 | 1111 – – – – | | reserved | |
| DB | 1101 1011 | MOD 000 R/M | SIB, displ | FILD | short-integer |
| DB | 1101 1011 | MOD 001 R/M | SIB, displ | reserved | |
| DB | 1101 1011 | MOD 010 R/M | SIB, displ | FIST | short-integer |
| DB | 1101 1011 | MOD 011 R/M | SIB, displ | FISTP | short-integer |
| DB | 1101 1011 | MOD 100 R/M | SIB, displ | reserved | |
| DB | 1101 1011 | MOD 101 R/M | SIB, displ | FLD | extended-real |
| DB | 1101 1011 | MOD 110 R/M | SIB, displ | reserved | |
| DB | 1101 1011 | MOD 111 R/M | SIB, displ | FSTP | extended-real |
| DB | 1101 1011 | 110– – – – – | | reserved | |
| DB | 1101 1011 | 1110 0000 | | **(1) | |
| DB | 1101 1011 | 1110 0001 | | **(2) | |
| DB | 1101 1011 | 1110 0010 | | FCLEX | |
| DB | 1101 1011 | 1110 0011 | | FINIT | |
| DB | 1101 1011 | 1110 0100 | | **(3) | |
| DB | 1101 1011 | 1110 0101 | | reserved | |
| DB | 1101 1011 | 1110 011– | | reserved | |
| DB | 1101 1011 | 1110 1– – – | | reserved | |
| DB | 1101 1011 | 1111 – – – – | | reserved | |

| 1st Byte | | 2nd Byte | Bytes 3-7 | ASM386 Instruction Format | |
|---|---|---|---|---|---|
| Hex | Binary | | | | |
| DC | 1101 1100 | MOD 000 R/M | SIB, displ | FADD | double-real |
| DC | 1101 1100 | MOD 001 R/M | SIB, displ | FMUL | double-real |
| DC | 1101 1100 | MOD 010 R/M | SIB, displ | FCOM | double-real |
| DC | 1101 1100 | MOD 011 R/M | SIB, displ | FCOMP | double-real |
| DC | 1101 1100 | MOD 100 R/M | SIB, displ | FSUB | double-real |
| DC | 1101 1100 | MOD 101 R/M | SIB, displ | FSUBR | double-real |
| DC | 1101 1100 | MOD 110 R/M | SIB, displ | FDIV | double-real |
| DC | 1101 1100 | MOD 111 R/M | SIB, displ | FDIVR | double-real |
| DC | 1101 1100 | 1100 0 REG | | FADD | ST(i),ST |
| DC | 1101 1100 | 1100 1 REG | | FMUL | ST(i),ST |
| DC | 1101 1100 | 1101 0 REG | | reserved | |
| DC | 1101 100 | 1101 1 REG | | reserved | |
| DC | 1101 1100 | 1110 0 REG | | FSUBR | ST(i),ST |
| DC | 1101 1100 | 1110 1 REG | | FSUB | ST(i),ST |
| DC | 1101 1100 | 1111 0 REG | | FDIVR | ST(i),ST |
| DC | 1101 1100 | 1111 1 REG | | FDIV | ST(i),ST |
| DD | 1101 1101 | MOD 000 R/M | SIB, displ | FLD | double-real |
| DD | 1101 1101 | MOD 001 R/M | | reserved | |
| DD | 1101 1101 | MOD 010 R/M | SIB, displ | FST | double-real |
| DD | 1101 1101 | MOD 011 R/M | SIB, displ | FSTP | double-real |
| DD | 1101 1101 | MOD 100 R/M | SIB, displ | FRSTOR | 94 or 108 bytes*** |
| DD | 1101 1101 | MOD 101 R/M | SIB, displ | reserved | |
| DD | 1101 1101 | MOD 110 R/M | SIB, displ | FSAVE | 94 or 108 bytes*** |
| DD | 1101 1101 | MOD 111 R/M | SIB, displ | FSTSW | 2 bytes |
| DD | 1101 1101 | 1100 0 REG | | FFREE | ST(i) |
| DD | 1101 1101 | 1100 1 REG | | reserved | |
| DD | 1101 1101 | 1101 0 REG | | FST | ST(i) |
| DD | 1101 1101 | 1101 1 REG | | FSTP | ST(i) |
| DD | 1101 1101 | 1110 0 REG | | FUCOM | ST(i) |
| DD | 1101 1101 | 1110 1 REG | | FUCOMP | ST(i) |
| DD | 1101 1101 | 1111 – – – – | | reserved | |
| DE | 1101 1110 | MOD 000 R/M | SIB, displ | FIADD | word-integer |
| DE | 1101 1110 | MOD 001 R/M | SIB, displ | FIMUL | word-integer |
| DE | 1101 1110 | MOD 010 R/M | SIB, displ | FICOM | word-integer |
| DE | 1101 1110 | MOD 011 R/M | SIB, displ | FICOMP | word-integer |
| DE | 1101 1110 | MOD 100 R/M | SIB, displ | FISUB | word-integer |
| DE | 1101 1110 | MOD 101 R/M | SIB, displ | FISUBR | word-integer |
| DE | 1101 1110 | MOD 110 R/M | SIB, displ | FIDIV | word-integer |
| DE | 1101 1110 | MOD 111 R/M | SIB, displ | FIDIVR | word-integer |
| DE | 1101 1110 | 1100 0 REG | | FADDP | ST(i),ST |
| DE | 1101 1110 | 1100 1 REG | | FMULP | ST(i),ST |
| DE | 1101 1110 | 1101 0– – – | | reserved | |
| DE | 1101 1110 | 1101 1000 | | reserved | |
| DE | 1101 1110 | 1101 1001 | | FCOMPP | |
| DE | 1101 1110 | 1101 101– | | reserved | |
| DE | 1101 1110 | 1101 11– – | | reserved | |
| DE | 1101 1110 | 1110 0 REG | | FSUBRP | ST(i),ST |
| DE | 1101 1110 | 1110 1 REG | | FSUBP | ST(i),ST |
| DE | 1101 1110 | 1111 0 REG | | FDIVRP | ST(i),ST |

| 1st Byte | | 2nd Byte | Bytes 3-7 | ASM386 Instruction Format | |
|---|---|---|---|---|---|
| Hex | Binary | | | | |
| DE | 1101 1110 | 1111 1 REG | | FDIVP | ST(i),ST |
| DF | 1101 1111 | MOD 000 R/M | SIB, displ | FILD | word-integer |
| DF | 1101 1111 | MOD 001 R/M | SIB, displ | reserved | |
| DF | 1101 1111 | MOD 010 R/M | SIB, displ | FIST | word-integer |
| DF | 1101 1111 | MOD 011 R/M | SIB, displ | FISTP | word-integer |
| DF | 1101 1111 | MOD 100 R/M | SIB, displ | FBLD | packed-decimal |
| DF | 1101 1111 | MOD 101 R/M | SIB, displ | FILD | long-integer |
| DF | 1101 1111 | MOD 110 R/M | SIB, displ | FBSTP | packed-decimal |
| DF | 1101 1111 | MOD 111 R/M | SIB, displ | FISTP | long-integer |
| DF | 1101 1111 | 1100 0 REG | | reserved | |
| DF | 1101 1111 | 1100 1 REG | | reserved | |
| DF | 1101 1111 | 1101 0 REG | | reserved | |
| DF | 1101 1111 | 1101 1 REG | | reserved | |
| DF | 1101 1111 | 1110 0000 | | FSTSW AX | |
| DF | 1101 1111 | 1110 0001 | | reserved | |
| DF | 1101 1111 | 1110 001– | | reserved | |
| DF | 1101 1111 | 1110 01– – | | reserved | |
| DF | 1101 1111 | 1110 1– – – | | reserved | |
| DF | 1101 1111 | 1111 – – – – | | reserved | |

**The marked encodings can be generated by the language translators; however, the 387™ DX treats them as FNOP. They correspond to the following 8087 or 80287 instructions.

(1) FENI
(2) FDISI
(3) FSETPM

***The size of operand transferred depends on the 386 DX operand-size attribute in effect for the instruction.

# Exception Summary

B

# APPENDIX B
# EXCEPTION SUMMARY

The following table lists the instruction mnemonics in alphabetical order. For each mnemonic, it summarizes the exceptions that the instruction may cause. When writing programs that may be used in an environment that employs numerics exception handlers, assembly-language programmers should be aware of the possible exceptions for each instruction in order to determine the need for exception synchronization. Chapter 4 explains the need for exception synchronization.

| Mnemonic | Instruction | IS | I | D | Z | O | U | P |
|---|---|---|---|---|---|---|---|---|
| F2XM1 | $2^x - 1$ | Y | Y | Y | | | Y | Y |
| FABS | Absolute value | Y | | | | | | |
| FADD(P) | Add real | Y | Y | Y | | Y | Y | Y |
| FBLD | BCD load | Y | | | | | | |
| FBSTP | BCD store and pop | Y | Y | | | | | Y |
| FCHS | Change sign | Y | | | | | | |
| FCLEX | Clear exceptions | | | | | | | |
| FCOM(P)(P) | Compare real | Y | Y | Y | | | | |
| FCOS | Cosine | Y | Y | Y | | | Y | Y |
| FDECSTP | Decrement stack pointer | | | | | | | |
| FDIV(R)(P) | Divide real | Y | Y | Y | Y | Y | Y | Y |
| FFREE | Free register | | | | | | | |
| FIADD | Integer add | Y | Y | Y | | Y | Y | Y |
| FICOM(P) | Integer compare | Y | Y | Y | | | | |
| FIDIV | Integer divide | Y | Y | Y | Y | | Y | Y |
| FIDIVR | Integer divide reversed | Y | Y | Y | Y | Y | Y | Y |
| FILD | Integer load | Y | | | | | | |
| FIMUL | Integer multiply | Y | Y | Y | | Y | Y | Y |
| FINCSTP | Increment stack pointer | | | | | | | |
| FINIT | Initialize processor | | | | | | | |
| FIST(P) | Integer store | Y | Y | | | | | Y |
| FISUB(R) | Integer subtract | Y | Y | Y | | | Y | Y |
| FLD extended or stack | Load real | Y | | | | | | |
| FLD single or double | Load real | Y | Y | Y | | | | |
| FLD1 | Load + 1.0 | Y | | | | | | |
| FLDCW | Load Control word | Y | Y | Y | Y | Y | Y | Y |
| FLDENV | Load environment | Y | Y | Y | Y | Y | Y | Y |
| FLDL2E | Load $\log_2 e$ | Y | | | | | | |
| FLDL2T | Load $\log_2 10$ | Y | | | | | | |
| FLDLG2 | Load $\log_{10} 2$ | Y | | | | | | |
| FLDLN2 | Load $\log_e 2$ | Y | | | | | | |
| FLDPI | Load $\pi$ | Y | | | | | | |

IS — Invalid operand due to stack overflow/underflow
I — Invalid operand due to other cause
D — Denormal operand
Z — Zero-divide
O — Overflow
U — Underflow
P — Inexact result (precision)

| Mnemonic | Instruction | IS | I | D | Z | O | U | P |
|---|---|---|---|---|---|---|---|---|
| FLDZ | Load + 0.0 | Y | | | | | | |
| FMUL(P) | Multiply real | Y | Y | Y | | Y | Y | Y |
| FNOP | No operation | | | | | | | |
| FPATAN | Partial arctangent | Y | Y | Y | | | Y | Y |
| FPREM | Partial remainder | Y | Y | Y | | | Y | |
| FPREM1 | IEEE partial remainder | Y | Y | Y | | | Y | |
| FPTAN | Partial tangent | Y | Y | Y | | | Y | Y |
| FRNDINT | Round to integer | Y | Y | Y | | | | Y |
| FRSTOR | Restore state | Y | Y | Y | Y | Y | Y | Y |
| FSAVE | Save state | | | | | | | |
| FSCALE | Scale | Y | Y | Y | | Y | Y | Y |
| FSIN | Sine | Y | Y | Y | | | Y | Y |
| FSINCOS | Sine and cosine | Y | Y | Y | | | Y | Y |
| FSQRT | Square root | Y | Y | Y | | | | Y |
| FST(P) stack or extended | Store real | Y | | | | | | |
| FST(P) single or double | Store real | Y | Y | Y | | Y | Y | Y |
| FSTCW | Store control word | | | | | | | |
| FSTENV | Store environment | | | | | | | |
| FSTSW (AX) | Store status word | | | | | | | |
| FSUB(R)(P) | Subtract real | Y | Y | Y | | Y | Y | Y |
| FTST | Test | Y | Y | Y | | | | |
| FUCOM(P)(P) | Unordered compare real | Y | Y | Y | | | | |
| FWAIT | CPU Wait | | | | | | | |
| FXAM | Examine | | | | | | | |
| FXCH | Exchange registers | Y | | | | | | |
| FXTRACT | Extract | Y | Y | Y | Y | | | |
| FYL2X | $Y \cdot \log_2 X$ | Y | Y | Y | Y | Y | Y | Y |
| FYL2XP1 | $Y \cdot \log_2(X + 1)$ | Y | Y | Y | | | Y | Y |

IS — Invalid operand due to stack overflow/underflow
I — Invalid operand due to other cause
D — Denormal operand
Z — Zero-divide
O — Overflow
U — Underflow
P — Inexact result (precision)

# Compatibility Between the 387™ DX and the 80287/8087   C

# APPENDIX C
# COMPATIBILITY BETWEEN THE 387™ DX
# AND THE 80287/8087

This appendix summarizes the differences between the 387™ DX and its predecessors the 80287 and the 8087, and analyzes the impact of these differences on software that must be transported from the 80287 or 8087 to the 387 DX. Any migration from the 8087 directly to the 387 DX must also take into account the additional differences between the 8087 and the 387 DX as listed in Appendix D of this manual.

## C.1 INITIALIZATION SEQUENCE

| Issue | Difference Description | | Impact on Software | Reason for the Difference |
|-------|------------------------|---|--------------------|---------------------------|
|       | 387™ DX Behavior | 8087/80287 Behavior | | |
| RESET, FINIT, and ERROR# PIN | After a hardware RESET, the ERROR# output is asserted to indicate that an 387 DX is present. To accomplish this, the IE and ES bits of the status word are set, and the IM bit in the control word is reset. After FINIT, the status word and the control word have the same values as in an 80287/8087 after RESET. | No difference between RESET and FINIT. | 387 DX initialization software must execute an FNINIT instruction to clear ERROR#. The FNINIT is not required for 80287/8087 software, though Intel documentation recommends its use (refer to the Numerics Supplement to the *iAPX 286 Programmer's Reference Manual*). | Permits the 386 DX to differentiate between the 80287 and the 387 DX. |

## C.2 DATA TYPES AND EXCEPTION HANDLING

| Issue | Difference Description | | Impact on Software | Reason for the Difference |
|-------|------------------------|---|--------------------|---------------------------|
|       | 387™ DX Behavior | 8087/80287 Behavior | | |
| NaN | The 387 DX distinguishes between signaling NaNs and quiet NaNs. The 387 DX only generates quiet NaNs. An invalid-operation exception is raised only upon encountering a signaling NaN (except for FCOM, FIST, and FBSTP which also raise IE for quiet NaNs). | The 80287/8087 only generates one kind of NaN (the equivalent of a quiet NaN) but raises an invalid-operation exception upon encountering any kind of NaN. | Uninitialized memory locations that contain QNaNs should be changed to SNaNs to cause the 387 DX to fault when uninitialized memory locations are referenced. | IEEE Standard 754 compatibility. |
| Pseudozero, Pseudo-NaN, Pseudoinfinity, and Unnormal Formats | The 387 DX neither generates not supports these formats; it raises an invalid-operation exception whenever it encounters them in an arithmetic operation. | The 80287/8087 defines and supports special handling for these formats. | None. The 387 DX does not generate these formats, and therefore will not encounter them unless a programmer deliberately enters them. | IEEE Standard 754 compatibility. |

| Issue | Difference Description | | Impact on Software | Reason for the Difference |
|---|---|---|---|---|
| | 387™ DX Behavior | 8087/80287 Behavior | | |
| Tag Word Bits for Unsupported Data Formats | The encoding in the tag word for the unsupported data formats mentioned in Section C.2.2 is "special data" (type 10). | The encoding for pseudo-zero and unnormal is "valid" (type 00); the others are "special data" (type 10). | The exception handler may need to be changed if programmers use such data types. | IEEE Standard 754 compatibility. |
| Invalid-Operation Exception | No invalid-operation exception is raised upon encountering a denormal in FSQRT, FDIV, or FPREM or upon conversion to BCD or to integer. The operation proceeds by first normalizing the value. | Upon encountering a denormal in FSQRT, FDIV, or FPREM or upon conversion to BCD or to integer, the invalid-operation exception is raised. | None. Software on the 387 DX will continue to execute in cases where the 80287/8087 would trap. | Upgrade, to eliminate exception. |
| Denormal Exception | The denormal exception is raised in transcendental instructions and FXTRACT. | The denormal exception is not raised in transcendental instructions and FXTRACT. | The exception handler needs to be changed only if it gives special treatment to different opcodes. | Performance enhancement for normal case. |
| Overflow Exception | Overflow exception masked.<br><br>If the rounding mode is set to chop (toward zero), the result is the most positive or most negative number. | Overflow exception masked.<br><br>The 80287/8087 does not signal the overflow exception when the masked response is not infinity; i.e., it signals overflow only when the rounding control is not set to round to zero. If rounding is set to chop (toward zero), the result is positive or negative infinity. | Overflow exception masked.<br><br>Under the most common rounding modes, no impact. If rounding is toward zero (chop), a program on the 387 DX produces under overflow conditions a result that is different in the least significant bit of the significand, compared to the result on the 80287. | IEEE Standard 754 compatibility. |
| | Overflow exception not masked.<br><br>The precision exception is flagged. When the result is stored in the stack, the significand is rounded according to the precision control (PC) bit of the control word or according to the opcode. | Overflow exception not masked.<br><br>The precision exception is not flagged and the significand is not rounded. | Overflow exception not masked.<br><br>If the result is stored on the stack, a program on the 387 DX produces a different result under overflow conditions than on the 80287/8087. The difference is apparent only to the exception handler. | |

| Issue | Difference Description | | Impact on Software | Reason for the Difference |
|---|---|---|---|---|
| | **387™ DX Behavior** | **8087/80287 Behavior** | | |
| Underflow Exception<br><br>Two related events contribute to underflow:<br><br>1. The creation *tiny* result. A tiny number, because it is so small, may cause some other exception later (such as overflow upon division).<br><br>2. Loss of accuracy during the denormalization of a tiny number.<br><br>Which of these events triggers the underflow exception depends on whether the underflow exception is masked. | Conditions for underflow.<br><br>When the underflow exception is masked, the underflow exception is signaled when both the result is tiny and denormalization results in a loss of accuracy.<br><br>Response to underflow.<br><br>When the underflow exception is unmasked and the instruction is supposed to store the result on the stack, the significand is rounded to the appropriate precision (according to the precision control (PC) bit of the control word, for those instructions controlled by PC, otherwise to extended precision). | Conditions for underflow.<br><br>When the underflow exception is masked and rounding is toward zero, the underflow exception flag is raised on tininess, regardless of loss of accuracy.<br><br>Response to underflow.<br><br>When the underflow exception is not masked and the destination is the stack, the significand is not rounded but rather is left as is. | Underflow exception masked.<br><br>No impact. The underflow exception occurs less often when rounding is toward zero.<br><br>Underflow exception not masked.<br><br>A program on the 387 DX produces a different result during underflow conditions than on the 80287/8087 if the result is stored on the stack. The difference is only in the least significant bit of the significand and is apparent only to the exception handler. | IEEE Standard 754 compatibility. |
| Exception Precedence | There is no difference in the precedence of the denormal exception, whether it be masked or not. | When the denormal exception is not masked, it takes precedence over all other exceptions. | None, but some unneeded normalization of denormal operands is prevented on the 387 DX. | Operational improvement. |

## C.3 TAG, STATUS, AND CONTROL WORDS

| Issue | Difference Description | | Impact on Software | Reason for the Difference |
|---|---|---|---|---|
| | **387™ DX Behavior** | **8087/80287 Behavior** | | |
| Bits C3-C0 of Status Word | After FINIT, incomplete FPREM, and hardware reset, the 387 DX sets these bits to zero. | After FINIT, incomplete FPREM, and hardware reset, the 80287/8087 leaves these bits intact (they contain the prior value). | None. | Upgrade, to provide consistent state after reset. |

| Issue | Difference Description | | Impact on Software | Reason for the Difference |
|---|---|---|---|---|
| | 387™ DX Behavior | 8087/80287 Behavior | | |
| Bit C2 of Status Word | Bit 10 (C2) serves as an incomplete bit for FPTAN. | This bit is undefined for FPTAN. | None. Programs don't check C2 after FPTAN. | Upgrade to allow fast checking of operand range. |
| Infinity Control | Only affine closure is supported. Bit 12 remains programmable but has no effect on 387 DX operation. | Both affine and projective closures are supported. After RESET, the default value in the control word is projective. | Software that requires projective infinity arithmetic may give different results. | IEEE Standard 754 compatibility. |
| Status Word Bit 6 for Stack Fault | When an invalid-operation exception occurs due to stack overflow or underflow, not only is bit 0 (IE) of the status word set, but also bit 6 is set to indicate a stack fault and bit 9 (C1) specifies overflow or underflow. Bit 6 is called SF and serves to distinguish invalid exceptions caused by stack overflow/underflow from those caused by numeric operations. | When an invalid-operation exception occurs due to stack overflow or underflow, only bit 0 (IE) of the status word is set. Bit 6 is RESERVED. | None. Existing exception handlers need not change, but may be upgraded to take advantage of the additional information. Newly written handlers will be more effective. | Upgrade and performance improvement. |
| Tag Word | When loading the tag word with an FLDENV or FRSTOR instruction, the only interpretations of tag values used by the 387 DX are *empty* (value 11) and *nonempty* (values 00, 01, and 10). Subsequent operations on a nonempty register always examine the value in the register, not the value in its tag. The FSTENV and FSAVE instructions examine the nonempty registers and put the correct values in the tags before storing the tag word. | The corresponding tag is checked before each register access to determine the class of operand in the register; the tag is updated after every change to a register so that the tag always reflects the most recent status of the register. Programmers can load a tag with a value that disagrees with the contents of a register (for example, the register contains valid contents, but the tag says *special*; the 80287/8087, in this case, honors the tag and does not examine the register). | Software may not operate correctly if it uses FLDENV or FRSTOR to change tags to values (other than empty) that are different from actual register contents. | Performance improvement. |

## C.4 INSTRUCTION SET

| Issue | Difference Description | | Impact on Software | Reason for the Difference |
|---|---|---|---|---|
| | 387™ DX Behavior | 8087/80287 Behavior | | |
| FBSTP, FDIV, FIST(P), FPREM, FSQRT | Operation on denormal operand is supported. An underflow exception can occur. | Operation on denormal operand raises invalid-operation exception. Underflow is not possible. | The exception handler for underflow may require change only if it gives different treatment to different opcodes. Possibly fewer invalid-operation exceptions will occur. | IEEE Standard 754 compatibility. |
| FSCALE | The range of the scaling operand is not restricted. If $0 < |ST(1)| < 1$, the scaling factor is zero; therefore, ST(0) remains unchanged. If the rounded result is not exact or if there was a loss of accuracy (masked underflow), the precision exception is signaled. | The range of the scaling operand is retricted. If $0 < |ST(1)| < 1$, the result is undefined and no exception is signaled. | Different result when $0 < |ST(1)| < 1$. | Upgrade. |
| FPREM1 | Performs partial remainder according to IEEE Standard 754 standard. | Does not exist. | None. | IEEE Standard 754 compatibility and upgrade. |
| FPREM | Bits C0, C3, C1 of the status word, correctly reflect the three low-order bits of the quotient. | The quotient bits are incorrect when performing a reduction of $64^N + M$ when $N \geq 1$ and $M = 1$ or $M = 2$. | None. Software that works around the bug should not be affected. | Upgrade. |
| FUCOM, FUCOMP, FUCOMPP | Perform unordered compare according to IEEE Standard 754 standard. | Do not exist. | None. | IEEE Standard 754 compatibility. |
| FPTAN | Range of operand is much less restricted ($|ST(0)| < 2^{63}$); reduces operand internally using an internal $\pi/4$ constant that is more accurate.<br><br>After a stack overflow when the invalid-operation exception is masked, both ST and ST(1) contain quiet NaNs. | Range of operand is restricted ($|ST(0)| < \pi/4$); operand must be reduced to range using FPREM.<br><br>After a stack overflow when the invalid-operation exception is masked, the original operand remains unchanged, but is pushed to ST(1). | None. | Upgrade.<br><br><br><br><br>IEEE Standard 754 compatibility. |
| FSIN, FCOS, FSINCOS | Perform three common trigonometric functions. | Do not exist. | None. | Upgrade. |
| FPATAN | Range of operands is unrestricted. | $|ST(0)|$ must be smaller than $|ST(1)|$. | None. | Upgrade. |
| F2XM1 | Wider range of operand ($-1 \leq ST(0) \leq +1$). | The supported operand range is $0 \leq ST(0) \leq 0.5$. | None. | Upgrade. |

| Issue | Difference Description | | Impact on Software | Reason for the Difference |
|---|---|---|---|---|
| | 387™ DX Behavior | 8087/80287 Behavior | | |
| FLD extended-real | Does not report denormal exception because the instruction is not arithmetic. | Reports denormal exception. | None. | Upgrade. |
| FXTRACT | If the operand is zero, the zero-divide exception is reported and ST(1) is −∞. If the operand is +∞, no exception is reported. | If the operand is zero, ST(1) is zero and no exception is reported. If the operand is +∞, the invalid-operation exception is reported. | None. Software usually bypasses zero and ∞. | IEEE 754 recommendation to fully support the logb function. |
| FLD constant | Rounding control is in effect. | Rounding control is not in effect. | Results are the same as for the 8087/80287 when rounding control is set to round to zero, round to −∞, and (in the case of FLDL2T) round to nearest. Results are different by one in the least significant bit of the significand in round to +∞ and round to nearest (excluding FLDL2T). FLD1 and FLDZ are always the same. | IEEE 754 recommendation. |
| FLD single/ double precision | Loading a denormal causes the number to be converted to extended precision (because it is put on the stack). | Loading a denormal causes the number to be converted to an unnormal. | If the next instruction is FXTRACT or FXAM, the 387 DX will give a different result than the 80287/8087. | IEEE Standard 754 compatibility. |
| FLD single/ double precision | When loading a signaling NaN, raises invalid exception. | Does not raise an exception when loading a signaling NaN. | The exception handler need to be updated to handle this condition. | IEEE Standard 754 compatibility. |
| FSETPM | Treated as FNOP (no operation). | Informs the 80287 that the system is in protected mode. | None. | The 386 DX handles all addressing and exception-pointer information, whether in protected mode or not. |
| FXAM | When encountering an empty register, the 387 DX will not generate combinations of C3-C0 equal to 1101 or 1111. | May generate these combinations, among others. | None. | Upgrade, to provide repeatable results. |
| All Transcendental Instructions | May generate different results in round-up bit of status word. | Round-up bit of status word is undefined for these instructions. | None. | Upgrade, to signal rounding status. |

# Compatibility Between 387™ DX and the 808

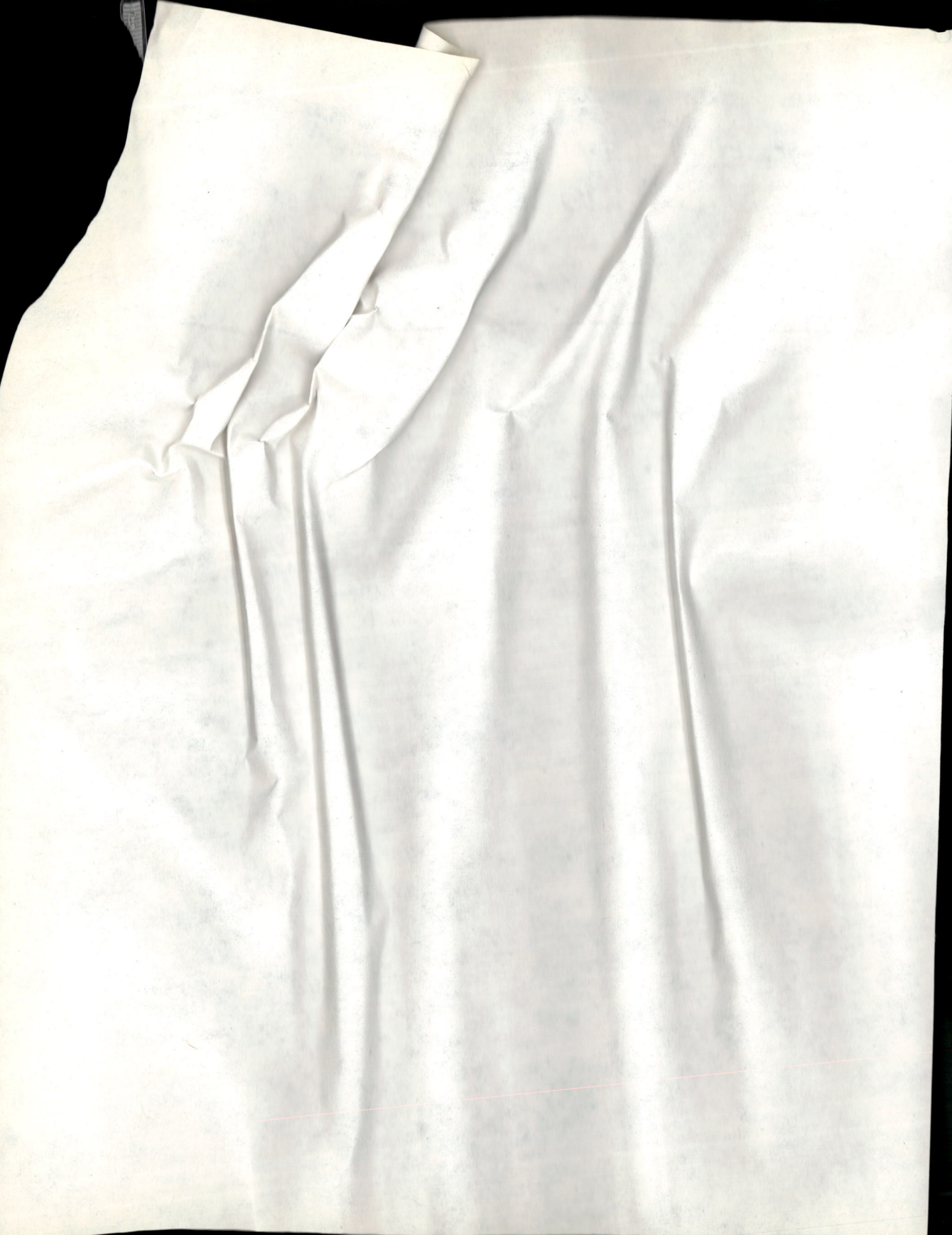

# APPENDIX D
# COMPATIBILITY BETWEEN THE
# 387™ DX AND THE 8087

The 386™ DX/387™ DX operating in real-address mode will execute 8087 programs without major modification. However, because of differences in the handling of numeric exceptions between the 387 DX NPX and the 8087 NPX, exception-handling routines *may* need to be changed.

This appendix summarizes the additional differences between the 387 DX NPX and the 8087 NPX (other than those already included in Appendix B), and provides details showing how 8087 programs can be ported to the 387 DX.

1. The 387 DX signals exceptions through a dedicated ERROR# line to the 386 DX; no interrupt controller is needed for this purpose. The 8087 requires an interrupt controller (8259A) to interrupt the CPU when an unmasked exception occurs. Therefore, any interrupt-controller-oriented instructions in numeric exception handlers for the 8087 should be deleted.

2. The 8087 instructions FENI/FNENI and FDISI/FNDISI perform no useful function in the 387 DX. If the 387 DX encounters one of these opcodes in its instruction stream, the instruction will effectively be ignored—none of the 387 DX internal states will be updated. While 8087 code containing these instructions may be executed on the 387 DX, it is unlikely that the exception-handling routines containing these instructions will be completely portable to the 387 DX.

3. In real mode and protected mode (not including virtual 8086 mode), interrupt vector 16 must point to the numeric exception handling routine. In virtual 8086 mode, the V86 monitor can be programmed to accommodate a different location of the interrupt vector for numeric exceptions.

4. The ESC instruction address saved in the 386 DX/387 DX or 386 DX/80287 includes any leading prefixes before the ESC opcode. The corresponding address saved in the 8086/8087 does not include leading prefixes.

5. In protected mode (not including virtual 8086 mode), the format of the 387 DX's saved instruction and address pointers is different than for the 8087. The instruction opcode is not saved in protected mode—exception handlers will have to retrieve the opcode from memory if needed.

6. Interrupt 7 will occur in the 386 DX when executing ESC instructions with either TS (task switched) or EM (emulation) of the 386 DX MSW set (TS = 1 or EM = 1). If TS is set, then a WAIT instruction will also cause interrupt 7. An exception handler should be included in 387 DX code to handle these situations.

7. Interrupt 9 will occur if the second or subsequent words of a floating-point operand fall outside a segment's size. Interrupt 13 will occur if the starting address of a numeric operand falls outside a segment's size. An exception handler should be included to report these programming errors.

8. Except for the processor control instructions, all of the 387 DX numeric instructions are automatically synchronized by the 386 DX CPU—the 386 DX automatically waits until all operands have been transferred between the 386 DX and the 387 DX before executing the next ESC instruction. No explicit WAIT instructions are required to assure this synchronization. For the 8087 used with 8086 and 8088 processors, explicit WAITs are required before each numeric instruction to ensure synchronization. Although 8087 programs having explicit WAIT instructions will execute perfectly on the 387 DX without reassembly, these WAIT instructions are unnecessary.

9. Since the 387 DX does not require WAIT instructions before each numeric instruction, the ASM386 assembler does not automatically generate these WAIT instructions. The ASM86 assembler, however, automatically precedes every ESC instruction with a WAIT instruction. Although numeric routines generated using the ASM86 assembler will generally execute correctly on the 386 DX/20, reassembly using ASM386 may result in a more compact code image and faster execution.

   The processor control instructions for the 387 DX may be coded using either a WAIT or No-WAIT form of mnemonic. The WAIT forms of these instructions cause ASM386 to precede the ESC instruction with a CPU WAIT instruction, in the identical manner as does ASM86.

10. The address of a memory operand stored by FSAVE or FSTENV is undefined if the previous ESC instruction did not refer to memory.

11. Because the 387 DX automatically normalizes denormal numbers when possible, an 8087 program that uses the denormal exception solely to normalize denormal operands can run on an 387 DX by masking the denormal exception. The 8087 denormal exception handler would not be used by the 387 DX in this case. A numerics program runs faster when the 387 DX performs normalization of denormal operands. A program can detect at run-time whether it is running on an 387 DX or 8087/80287 and disable the denormal exception when an 387 DX is used.

# 387™ DX Math Coprocessor

E

This appendix is a copy of the 387™ DX Data Sheet, which is also available separately. (The AC and DC specifications have been deliberately left out.) The specifications in data sheets are subject to change; *consult the most recent data sheet for design-in information.*

# 387™ DX
# MATH COPROCESSOR

- **High Performance 80-Bit Internal Architecture**
- **Implements ANSI/IEEE Standard 754-1985 for Binary Floating-Point Arithmetic**
- **Six to Eleven Times 8087/80287 Performance**
- **Expands 386™ DX CPU Data Types to Include 32-, 64-, 80-Bit Floating Point, 32-, 64-Bit Integers and 18-Digit BCD Operands**
- **Directly Extends 386™ DX CPU Instruction Set to Include Trigonometric, Logarithmic, Exponential and Arithmetic Instructions for All Data Types**

- **Upward Object-Code Compatible from 8087 and 80287**
- **Full-Range Transcendental Operations for SINE, COSINE, TANGENT, ARCTANGENT and LOGARITHM**
- **Built-In Exception Handling**
- **Operates Independently of Real, Protected and Virtual-8086 Modes of the 386™ DX Microprocessor**
- **Eight 80-Bit Numeric Registers, Usable as Individually Addressable General Registers or as a Register Stack**
- **Available in 68-Pin PGA Package**
  (See Packaging Spec: Order # 231369)

The Intel 387™ DX Math CoProcessor is an extension to the Intel 386™ microprocessor architecture. The combination of the 387 DX with the 386™ DX Microprocessor dramatically increases the processing speed of computer application software which utilize mathmatical operations. This makes an ideal computer workstation platform for applications such as financial modeling and spreadsheets, CAD/CAM, or graphics.

The 387 DX Math CoProcessor adds over seventy mnemonics to the 386 DX Microprocessor instruction set. Specific 387 DX math operations include logarithmic, arithmetic, exponentional, and triginometric functions. The 387 DX supports integer, extended integer, floating point and BCD data formats, and fully conforms to the ANSI/IEEE floating point standard.

The 387 DX Math CoProcessor is object code compatible with the 80387SX, and upward object code compatible from the 80287 and 8087 math coprocessors. Object code for 386 DX/387 DX is also compatible with the Intel 486™ microprocessor. The 387 DX is manufactured on 1 micron, CHMOS IV technology and packaged in a 68-pin PGA package.

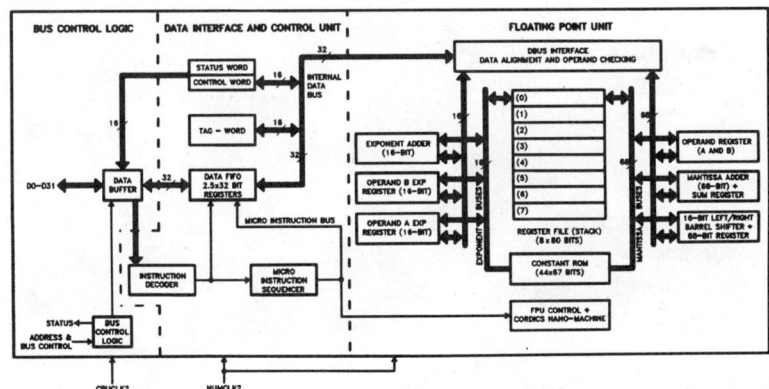

**Figure 0.1. 387™ DX Math Coprocessor Block Diagram**

240448–1

# CONTENTS PAGE

# CONTENTS

# FIGURES

# FIGURES

PAGE

# TABLES

PAGE

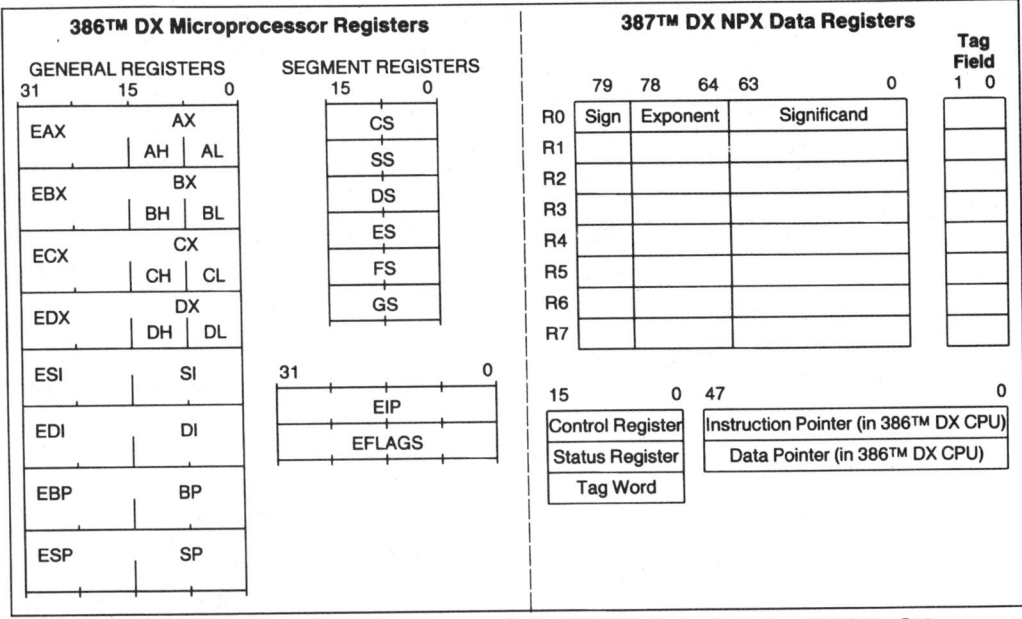

**Figure 1.1. 386™ DX Microprocessor and 387™ DX Math Coprocessor Register Set**

## 1.0 FUNCTIONAL DESCRIPTION

The 387™ DX Math Coprocessor provides arithmetic instructions for a variety of numeric data types in 386™ DX Microprocessor and 387 DX Math Coprocessor systems. It also executes numerous built-in transcendental functions (e.g. tangent, sine, cosine, and log functions). The 387 DX Math Coprocessor effectively extends the register and instruction set of a 386 DX Microprocessor system for existing data types and adds several new data types as well. Figure 1.1 shows the model of registers visible to 386 DX Microprocessor and 387 DX Math Coprocessor programs. Essentially, the 387 DX Math Coprocessor can be treated as an additional resource or an extension to the 386 DX Microprocessor. The 386 DX Microprocessor together with a 387 DX Math Coprocessor can be used as a single unified system, the 386 DX Microprocessor and 387 DX Math Coprocessor.

The 387 DX Math Coprocessor works the same whether the 386 DX Microprocessor is executing in real-address mode, protected mode, or virtual-8086 mode. All memory access is handled by the 386 DX Microprocessor; the 387 DX Math Coprocessor merely operates on instructions and values passed to it by the 386 DX Microprocessor. Therefore, the 387 DX Math Coprocessor is not sensitive to the processing mode of the 386 DX Microprocessor.

In real-address mode and virtual-8086 mode, the 386 DX Microprocessor and 387 DX Math Coprocessor are completely upward compatible with software for 8086/8087, 80286/80287 real-address mode, and 386 DX Microprocessor and 80287 Coprocessor real-address mode systems.

In protected mode, the 386 DX Microprocessor and 387 DX Math Coprocessor are completely upward compatible with software for 80286/80287 protected mode, and 386 DX Microprocessor and 80287 Coprocessor protected mode systems.

The only differences of operation that may appear when 8086/8087 programs are ported to a protected-mode 386 DX Microprocessor and 387 DX Math Coprocessor system (*not* using virtual-8086 mode), is in the format of operands for the administrative instructions FLDENV, FSTENV, FRSTOR and FSAVE. These instructions are normally used only by exception handlers and operating systems, not by applications programs.

The 387 DX Math Coprocessor contains three functional units that can operate in parallel to increase system performance. The 386 DX Microprocessor can be transferring commands and data to the NPX *bus control logic* for the next instruction while the NPX *floating-point unit* is performing the current numeric instruction.

## 2.0 PROGRAMMING INTERFACE

The NPX adds to the 386 DX Microprocessor system additional data types, registers, instructions, and interrupts specifically designed to facilitate high-speed numerics processing. To use the NPX requires no special programming tools, because all new instructions and data types are directly supported by the 386 DX CPU assembler and compilers for high-level languages. All 8086/8088 development tools that support the 8087 can also be used to develop software for the 386 DX Microprocessor and 387 DX Math Coprocessor in real-address mode or virtual-8086 mode. All 80286 development tools that support the 80287 can also be used to develop software for the 386 DX Microprocessor and 387 DX Math Coprocessor.

All communication between the 386 DX Microprocessor and the NPX is transparent to applications software. The CPU automatically controls the NPX whenever a numerics instruction is executed. All physical memory and virtual memory of the CPU are available for storage of the instructions and operands of programs that use the NPX. All memory addressing modes, including use of displacement, base register, index register, and scaling, are available for addressing numerics operands.

Section 6 at the end of this data sheet lists by class the instructions that the NPX adds to the instruction set of the 386 DX Microprocessor system.

## 2.1 Data Types

Table 2.1 lists the seven data types that the 387 DX NPX supports and presents the format for each type. Operands are stored in memory with the least significant digit at the lowest memory address. Programs retrieve these values by generating the lowest address. For maximum system performance, all operands should start at physical-memory addresses evenly divisible by four (doubleword boundaries); operands may begin at any other addresses, but will require extra memory cycles to access the entire operand.

Internally, the 387 DX NPX holds all numbers in the extended-precision real format. Instructions that load operands from memory automatically convert operands represented in memory as 16-, 32-, or 64-bit integers, 32- or 64-bit floating-point numbers, or 18-digit packed BCD numbers into extended-precision real format. Instructions that store operands in memory perform the inverse type conversion.

## 2.2 Numeric Operands

A typical NPX instruction accepts one or two operands and produces a single result. In two-operand instructions, one operand is the contents of an NPX register, while the other may be a memory location. The operands of some instructions are predefined; for example FSQRT always takes the square root of the number in the top stack element.

**Table 2.1. 387™ DX NPX Data Type Representation in Memory**

| Data Formats | Range | Precision | Most Significant Byte = Highest Addressed Byte |
|---|---|---|---|
| Word Integer | $\pm 10^4$ | 16 Bits | (TWO'S COMPLEMENT) — 15...0 |
| Short Integer | $\pm 10^9$ | 32 Bits | (TWO'S COMPLEMENT) — 31...0 |
| Long Integer | $\pm 10^{18}$ | 64 Bits | (TWO'S COMPLEMENT) — 63...0 |
| Packed BCD | $\pm 10^{\pm 18}$ | 18 Digits | S X MAGNITUDE $d_{17}\,d_{16}\,d_{15}\,d_{14}\,d_{13}\,d_{12}\,d_{11}\,d_{10}\,d_9\,d_8\,d_7\,d_6\,d_5\,d_4\,d_3\,d_2\,d_1\,d_0$ — 79 72...0 |
| Single Precision | $\pm 10^{\pm 38}$ | 24 Bits | S BIASED EXPONENT SIGNIFICAND — 31 23...0 |
| Double Precision | $\pm 10^{\pm 308}$ | 53 Bits | S BIASED EXPONENT SIGNIFICAND — 63 52...0 |
| Extended Precision | $\pm 10^{\pm 4932}$ | 64 Bits | S BIASED EXPONENT I SIGNIFICAND — 79 64 63...0 |

240448-2

**NOTES:**

(1) S = Sign bit (0 = positive, 1 = negative)
(2) $d_n$ = Decimal digit (two per byte)
(3) X = Bits have no significance, 387™ DX NPX ignores when loading, zeros when storing
(4) ▲ = Position of implicit binary point
(5) I = Integer bit of significand; stored in temporary real, implicit in single and double precision
(6) Exponent Bias (normalized values):
   Single: 127 (7FH)
   Double: 1023 (3FFH)
   Extended Real: 16383 (3FFFH)
(7) Packed BCD: $(-1)^S (D_{17}...D_0)$
(8) Real: $(-1)^S (2^{E-BIAS}) (F_0 F_1...)$

```
15                                                                    0
┌─────────┬─────────┬─────────┬─────────┬─────────┬─────────┬─────────┬─────────┐
│ TAG (7) │ TAG (6) │ TAG (5) │ TAG (4) │ TAG (3) │ TAG (2) │ TAG (1) │ TAG (0) │
└─────────┴─────────┴─────────┴─────────┴─────────┴─────────┴─────────┴─────────┘
```

**NOTE:**
The index i of tag(i) is **not** top-relative. A program typically uses the "top" field of Status Word to determine which tag(i) field refers to logical top of stack.
TAG VALUES:
  00 = Valid
  01 = Zero
  10 = QNaN, SNaN, Infinity, Denormal and Unsupported Formats
  11 = Empty

**Figure 2.1. 387™ DX NPX Tag Word**

## 2.3 Register Set

Figure 1.1 shows the 387 DX NPX register set. When an NPX is present in a system, programmers may use these registers in addition to the registers normally available on the 386 DX CPU.

### 2.3.1 DATA REGISTERS

387 DX NPX computations use the NPX's data registers. These eight 80-bit registers provide the equivalent capacity of twenty 32-bit registers. Each of the eight data registers in the NPX is 80 bits wide and is divided into "fields" corresponding to the NPXs extended-precision real data type.

The 387 DX NPX register set can be accessed either as a stack, with instructions operating on the top one or two stack elements, or as a fixed register set, with instructions operating on explicitly designated registers. The TOP field in the status word identifies the current top-of-stack register. A "push" operation decrements TOP by one and loads a value into the new top register. A "pop" operation stores the value from the current top register and then increments

TOP by one. Like the 386 DX Microprocessor stacks in memory, the NPX register stack grows "down" toward lower-addressed registers.

Instructions may address the data registers either implicitly or explicitly. Many instructions operate on the register at the TOP of the stack. These instructions implicitly address the register at which TOP points. Other instructions allow the programmer to explicitly specify which register to user. This explicit register addressing is also relative to TOP.

### 2.3.2 TAG WORD

The tag word marks the content of each numeric data register, as Figure 2.1 shows. Each two-bit tag represents one of the eight numerics registers. The principal function of the tag word is to optimize the NPXs performance and stack handling by making it possible to distinguish between empty and nonempty register locations. It also enables exception handlers to check the contents of a stack location without the need to perform complex decoding of the actual data.

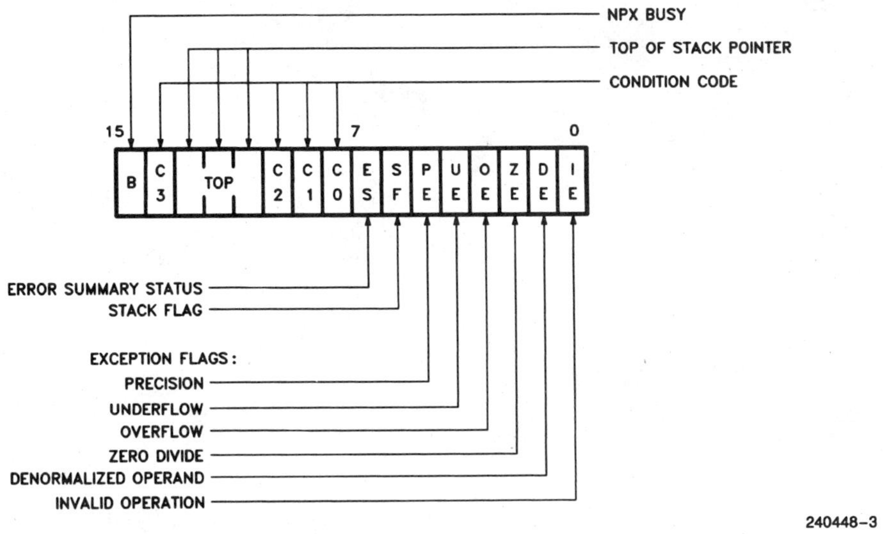

ES is set if any unmasked exception bit is set; cleared otherwise.
See Table 2.2 for interpretation of condition code.
TOP values:
    000 = Register 0 is Top of Stack
    001 = Register 1 is Top of Stack
        •
        •
        •
    111 = Register 7 is Top of Stack
For definitions of exceptions, refer to the section entitled
"Exception Handling"

240448-3

**Figure 2.2. NPX Status Word**

### 2.3.3 STATUS WORD

The 16-bit status word (in the status register) shown in Figure 2.2 reflects the overall state of the NPX. It may be read and inspected by CPU code.

Bit 15, the B-bit (busy bit) is included for 8087 compatibility only. It reflects the contents of the ES bit (bit 7 of the status word), not the status of the BUSY# output of the 387 DX NPX.

Bits 13–11 (TOP) point to the 387 DX NPX register that is the current top-of-stack.

The four numeric condition code bits ($C_3$–$C_0$) are similar to the flags in a CPU; instructions that perform arithmetic operations update these bits to reflect the outcome. The effects of these instructions on the condition code are summarized in Tables 2.2 through 2.5.

Bit 7 is the error summary (ES) status bit. This bit is set if any unmasked exception bit is set; it is clear otherwise. If this bit is set, the ERROR# signal is asserted.

Bit 6 is the stack flag (SF). This bit is used to distinguish invalid operations due to stack overflow or underflow from other kinds of invalid operations. When SF is set, bit 9 ($C_1$) distinguishes between stack overflow ($C_1 = 1$) and underflow ($C_1 = 0$).

Figure 2.2 shows the six exception flags in bits 5–0 of the status word. Bits 5–0 are set to indicate that the NPX has detected an exception while executing an instruction. A later section entitled "Exception Handling" explains how they are set and used.

Note that when a new value is loaded into the status word by the FLDENV or FRSTOR instruction, the value of ES (bit 7) and its reflection in the B-bit (bit 15) are not derived from the values loaded from memory but rather are dependent upon the values of the exception flags (bits 5–0) in the status word and their corresponding masks in the control word. If ES is set in such a case, the ERROR# output of the NPX is activated immediately.

**Table 2.2. Condition Code Interpretation**

| Instruction | C0 (S) | C3 (Z) | C1 (A) | C2 (C) |
|---|---|---|---|---|
| FPREM, FPREM1 (see Table 2.3) | Three least significant bits of quotient Q2 | Q0 | Q1 or O/U# | Reduction 0 = complete 1 = incomplete |
| FCOM, FCOMP, FCOMPP, FTST, FUCOM, FUCOMP, FUCOMPP, FICOM, FICOMP | Result of comparison (see Table 2.4) | | Zero or O/U# | Operand is not comparable (Table 2.4) |
| FXAM | Operand class (see Table 2.5) | | Sign or O/U# | Operand class (Table 2.5) |
| FCHS, FABS, FXCH, FINCSTP, FDECSTP, Constant loads, FXTRACT, FLD, FILD, FBLD, FSTP (ext real) | UNDEFINED | | Zero or O/U# | UNDEFINED |
| FIST, FBSTP, FRNDINT, FST, FSTP, FADD, FMUL, FDIV, FDIVR, FSUB, FSUBR, FSCALE, FSQRT, FPATAN, F2XM1, FYL2X, FYL2XP1 | UNDEFINED | | Roundup or O/U# | UNDEFINED |
| FPTAN, FSIN FCOS, FSINCOS | UNDEFINED | | Roundup or O/U#, undefined if C2 = 1 | Reduction 0 = complete 1 = incomplete |
| FLDENV, FRSTOR | Each bit loaded from memory | | | |
| FLDCW, FSTENV, FSTCW, FSTSW, FCLEX, FINIT, FSAVE | UNDEFINED | | | |

| | |
|---|---|
| O/U# | When both IE and SF bits of status word are set, indicating a stack exception, this bit distinguishes between stack overflow (C1 = 1) and underflow (C1 = 0). |
| Reduction | If FPREM or FPREM1 produces a remainder that is less than the modulus, reduction is complete. When reduction is incomplete the value at the top of the stack is a partial remainder, which can be used as input to further reduction. For FPTAN, FSIN, FCOS, and FSINCOS, the reduction bit is set if the operand at the top of the stack is too large. In this case the original operand remains at the top of the stack. |
| Roundup | When the PE bit of the status word is set, this bit indicates whether the last rounding in the instruction was upward. |
| UNDEFINED | Do not rely on finding any specific value in these bits. |

**Table 2.3. Condition Code Interpretation after FPREM and FPREM1 Instructions**

| Condition Code | | | | Interpretation after FPREM and FPREM1 |
|---|---|---|---|---|
| C2 | C3 | C1 | C0 | |
| 1 | X | X | X | Incomplete Reduction: further interation required for complete reduction |
| | Q1 | Q0 | Q2 | Q MOD8 | |
| 0 | 0 | 0 | 0 | 0 | Complete Reduction: C0, C3, C1 contain three least significant bits of quotient |
| | 0 | 1 | 0 | 1 | |
| | 1 | 0 | 0 | 2 | |
| | 1 | 1 | 0 | 3 | |
| | 0 | 0 | 1 | 4 | |
| | 0 | 1 | 1 | 5 | |
| | 1 | 0 | 1 | 6 | |
| | 1 | 1 | 1 | 7 | |

**Table 2.4. Condition Code Resulting from Comparison**

| Order | C3 | C2 | C0 |
|---|---|---|---|
| TOP > Operand | 0 | 0 | 0 |
| TOP < Operand | 0 | 0 | 1 |
| TOP = Operand | 1 | 0 | 0 |
| Unordered | 1 | 1 | 1 |

**Table 2.5. Condition Code Defining Operand Class**

| C3 | C2 | C1 | C0 | Value at TOP |
|---|---|---|---|---|
| 0 | 0 | 0 | 0 | + Unsupported |
| 0 | 0 | 0 | 1 | + NaN |
| 0 | 0 | 1 | 0 | − Unsupported |
| 0 | 0 | 1 | 1 | − NaN |
| 0 | 1 | 0 | 0 | + Normal |
| 0 | 1 | 0 | 1 | + Infinity |
| 0 | 1 | 1 | 0 | − Normal |
| 0 | 1 | 1 | 1 | − Infinity |
| 1 | 0 | 0 | 0 | + 0 |
| 1 | 0 | 0 | 1 | + Empty |
| 1 | 0 | 1 | 0 | − 0 |
| 1 | 0 | 1 | 1 | − Empty |
| 1 | 1 | 0 | 0 | + Denormal |
| 1 | 1 | 1 | 0 | − Denormal |

### 2.3.4 INSTRUCTION AND DATA POINTERS

Because the NPX operates in parallel with the CPU, any errors detected by the NPX may be reported after the CPU has executed the ESC instruction which caused it. To allow identification of the failing numeric instruction, the 386 DX Microprocessor and 387 DX Math Coprocessor contains two pointer registers that supply the address of the failing numeric instruction and the address of its numeric memory operand (if appropriate).

The instruction and data pointers are provided for user-written error handlers. These registers are actually located in the 386 DX CPU, but appear to be located in the NPX because they are accessed by the ESC instructions FLDENV, FSTENV, FSAVE, and FRSTOR. (In the 8086/8087 and 80286/80287, these registers are located in the NPX.) Whenever

the 386 DX CPU decodes a new ESC instruction, it saves the address of the instruction (including any prefixes that may be present), the address of the operand (if present), and the opcode.

The instruction and data pointers appear in one of four formats depending on the operating mode of the 386 DX Microprocessor (protected mode or real-address mode) and depending on the operand-size attribute in effect (32-bit operand or 16-bit operand). When the 386 DX Microprocessor is in virtual-8086 mode, the real-address mode formats are used. (See Figures 2.3 through 2.6.) The ESC instructions FLDENV, FSTENV, FSAVE, and FRSTOR are used to transfer these values between the 386 DX Microprocessor registers and memory. Note that the value of the data pointer is *undefined* if the prior ESC instruction did not have a memory operand.

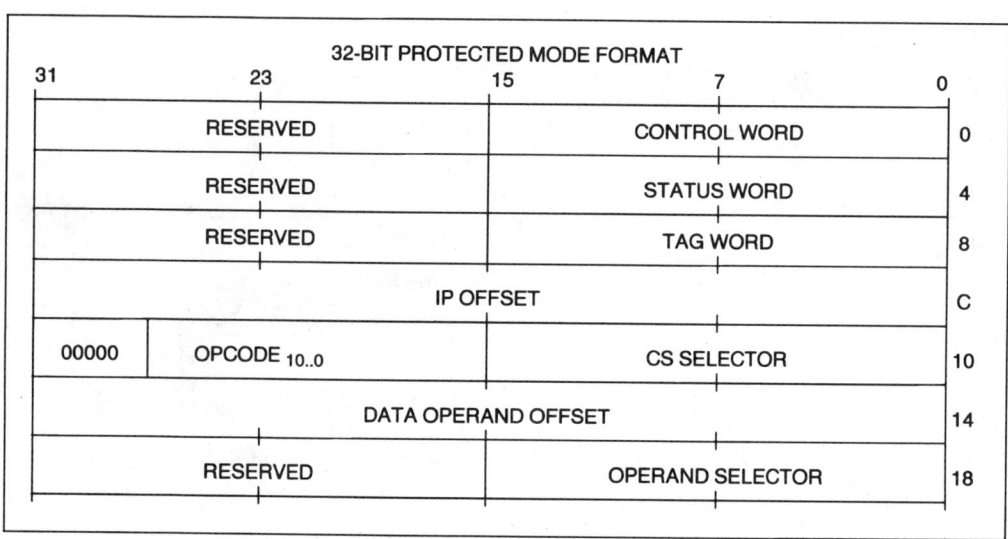

**Figure 2.3. Protected Mode 387™ DX NPX Instruction and Data Pointer Image in Memory, 32-Bit Format**

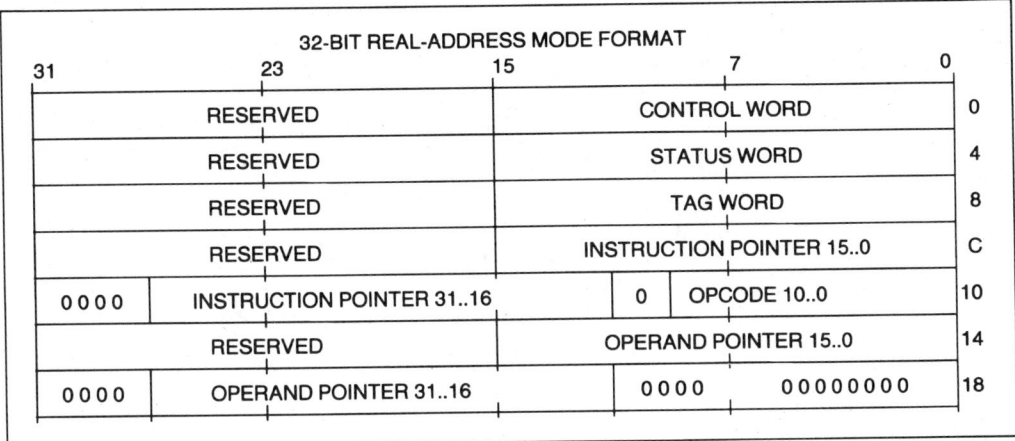

**Figure 2.4. Real Mode 387™ DX NPX Instruction and Data Pointer Image in Memory, 32-Bit Format**

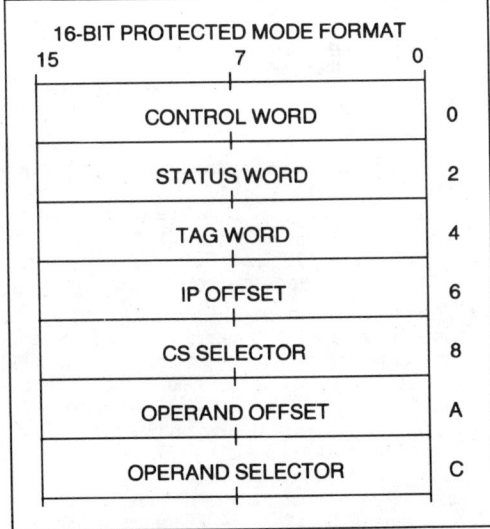

**Figure 2.5. Protected Mode 387™ DX NPX Instruction and Data Pointer Image in Memory, 16-Bit Format**

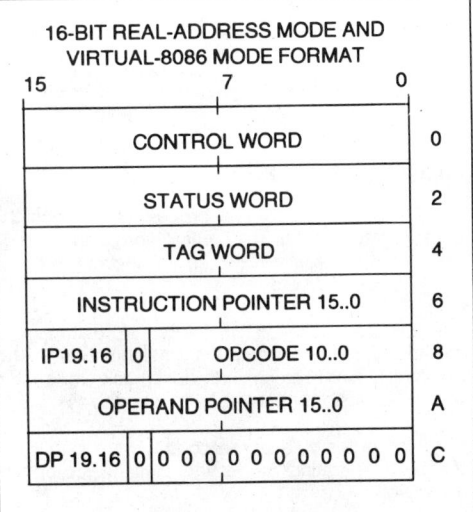

**Figure 2.6. Real Mode 387™ DX NPX Instruction and Data Pointer Image in Memory, 16-Bit Format**

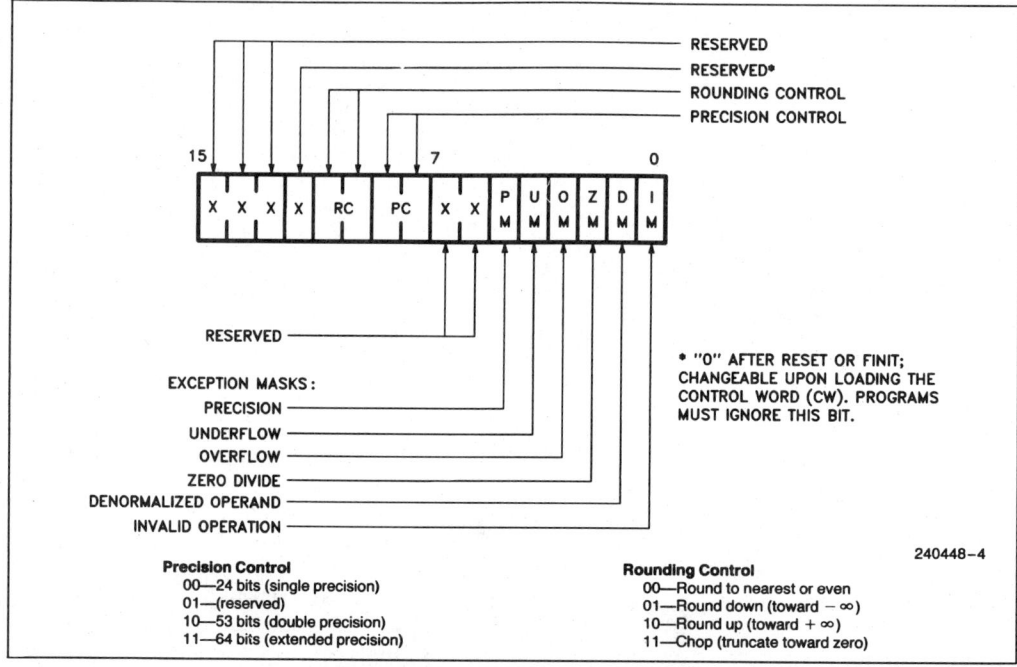

**Figure 2.7. 387™ DX NPX Control Word**

### 2.3.5 CONTROL WORD

The NPX provides several processing options that are selected by loading a control word from memory into the control register. Figure 2.7 shows the format and encoding of fields in the control word.

The low-order byte of this control word configures the NPX error and exception masking. Bits 5–0 of the control word contain individual masks for each of the six exceptions that the NPX recognizes.

The high-order byte of the control word configures the NPX operating mode, including precision and rounding.

- Bit 12 no longer defines infinity control and is a reserved bit. Only affine closure is supported for infinity arithmetic. The bit is initialized to zero after RESET or FINIT and is changeable upon loading the CW. Programs must ignore this bit.

- The rounding control (RC) bits (bits 11–10) provide for directed rounding and true chop, as well as the unbiased round to nearest even mode specified in the IEEE standard. Rounding control affects only those instructions that perform rounding at the end of the operation (and thus can generate a precision exception); namely, FST, FSTP, FIST, all arithmetic instructions (except FPREM, FPREM1, FXTRACT, FABS, and FCHS), and all transcendental instructions.

- The precision control (PC) bits (bits 9–8) can be used to set the NPX internal operating precision of the significand at less than the default of 64 bits (extended precision). This can be useful in providing compatibility with early generation arithmetic processors of smaller precision. PC affects only the instructions ADD, SUB, DIV, MUL, and SQRT. For all other instructions, either the precision is determined by the opcode or extended precision is used.

## 2.4 Interrupt Description

Several interrupts of the 386 DX CPU are used to report exceptional conditions while executing numeric programs in either real or protected mode. Table 2.6 shows these interrupts and their causes.

**Table 2.6. 386™ DX Microprocessor Interrupt Vectors Reserved for NPX**

| Interrupt Number | Cause of Interrupt |
|---|---|
| 7 | An ESC instruction was encountered when EM or TS of the 386™ DX CPU control register zero (CR0) was set. EM = 1 indicates that software emulation of the instruction is required. When TS is set, either an ESC or WAIT instruction causes interrupt 7. This indicates that the current NPX context may not belong to the current task. |
| 9 | An operand of a coprocessor instruction wrapped around an addressing limit (0FFFFH for small segments, 0FFFFFFFFH for big segments, zero for expand-down segments) and spanned inaccessible addresses[a]. The failing numerics instruction is not restartable. The address of the failing numerics instruction and data operand may be lost; an FSTENV does not return reliable addresses. As with the 80286/80287, the segment overrun exception should be handled by executing an FNINIT instruction (i.e. an FINIT without a preceding WAIT). The return address on the stack does not necessarily point to the failing instruction nor to the following instruction. The interrupt can be avoided by never allowing numeric data to start within 108 bytes of the end of a segment. |
| 13 | The first word or doubleword of a numeric operand is not entirely within the limit of its segment. The return address pushed onto the stack of the exception handler points at the ESC instruction that caused the exception, including any prefixes. The 387™ DX NPX has not executed this instruction; the instruction pointer and data pointer register refer to a previous, correctly executed instruction. |
| 16 | The previous numerics instruction caused an unmasked exception. The address of the faulty instruction and the address of its operand are stored in the instruction pointer and data pointer registers. Only ESC and WAIT instructions can cause this interrupt. The 386™ DX CPU return address pushed onto the stack of the exception handler points to a WAIT or ESC instruction (including prefixes). This instruction can be restarted after clearing the exception condition in the NPX. FNINIT, FNCLEX, FNSTSW, FNSTENV, and FNSAVE cannot cause this interrupt. |

a. An operand may wrap around an addressing limit when the segment limit is near an addressing limit and the operand is near the largest valid address in the segment. Because of the wrap-around, the beginning and ending addresses of such an operand will be at opposite ends of the segment. There are two ways that such an operand may also span inaccessible addresses: 1) if the segment limit is not equal to the addressing limit (e.g. addressing limit is FFFFH and segment limit is FFFDH) the operand will span addresses that are not within the segment (e.g. an 8-byte operand that starts at valid offset FFFC will span addresses FFFC–FFFF and 0000-0003; however addresses FFFE and FFFF are not valid, because they exceed the limit); 2) if the operand begins and ends in present and accessible pages but intermediate bytes of the operand fall in a not-present page or a page to which the procedure does not have access rights.

## 2.5 Exception Handling

The 387 DX NPX detects six different exception conditions that can occur during instruction execution. Table 2.7 lists the exception conditions in order of precedence, showing for each the cause and the default action taken by the NPX if the exception is masked by its corresponding mask bit in the control word.

Any exception that is not masked by the control word sets the corresponding exception flag of the status word, sets the ES bit of the status word, and asserts the ERROR# signal. When the CPU attempts to execute another ESC instruction or WAIT, exception 7 occurs. The exception condition must be resolved via an interrupt service routine. The 386 DX Microprocessor and 387 DX Math Coprocessor save the address of the floating-point instruction that caused the exception and the address of any memory operand required by that instruction.

## 2.6 Initialization

387 DX NPX initialization software must execute an FNINIT instruction (i.e. an FINIT without a preceding WAIT) to clear ERROR#. After a hardware RESET, the ERROR# output is asserted to indicate that a 387 DX NPX is present. To accomplish this, the IE and ES bits of the status word are set, and the IM bit in the control word is reset. After FNINIT, the status word and the control word have the same values as in an 80287 after RESET.

## 2.7 8087 and 80287 Compatibility

This section summarizes the differences between the 387 DX NPX and the 80287. Any migration from the 8087 directly to the 387 DX NPX must also take into account the differences between the 8087 and the 80287 as listed in Appendix A.

Many changes have been designed into the 387 DX NPX to directly support the IEEE standard in hardware. These changes result in increased performance by eliminating the need for software that supports the standard.

### 2.7.1 GENERAL DIFFERENCES

The 387 DX NPX supports only affine closure for infinity arithmetic, not projective closure. Bit 12 of the Control Word (CW) no longer defines infinity control. It is a reserved bit; but it is initialized to zero after RESET or FINIT and is changeable upon loading the CW. Programs must ignore this bit.

Operands for FSCALE and FPATAN are no longer restricted in range (except for $\pm \infty$); F2XM1 and FPTAN accept a wider range of operands.

The results of transcendental operations may be slightly different from those computed by 80287.

In the case of FPTAN, the 387 DX NPX supplies a true tangent result in ST(1), and (always) a floating point 1 in ST.

Rounding control is in effect for FLD *constant*.

Software cannot change entries of the tag word to values (other than empty) that do not reflect the actual register contents.

After reset, FINIT, and incomplete FPREM, the 387 DX NPX resets to zero the condition code bits $C_3$–$C_0$ of the status word.

In conformance with the IEEE standard, the 387 DX NPX does not support the special data formats: pseudozero, pseudo-NaN, pseudoinfinity, and unnormal.

**Table 2.7. Exceptions**

| Exception | Cause | Default Action (if exception is masked) |
|---|---|---|
| Invalid Operation | Operation on a signaling NaN, unsupported format, indeterminate form ($0^* \infty$, $0/0$, $(+\infty) + (-\infty)$, etc.), or stack overflow/underflow (SF is also set). | Result is a quiet NaN, integer indefinite, or BCD indefinite |
| Denormalized Operand | At least one of the operands is denormalized, i.e. it has the smallest exponent but a nonzero significand. | Normal processing continues |
| Zero Divisor | The divisor is zero while the dividend is a noninfinite, nonzero number. | Result is $\infty$ |
| Overflow | The result is too large in magnitude to fit in the specified format. | Result is largest finite value or $\infty$ |
| Underflow | The true result is nonzero but too small to be represented in the specified format, and, if underflow exception is masked, denormalization causes loss of accuracy. | Result is denormalized or zero |
| Inexact Result (Precision) | The true result is not exactly representable in the specified format (e.g. 1/3); the result is rounded according to the rounding mode. | Normal processing continues |

### 2.7.2 EXCEPTIONS

A number of differences exist due to changes in the IEEE standard and to functional improvements to the architecture of the 387 DX NPX:

1. When the overflow or underflow exception is masked, the 387 DX NPX differs from the 80287 in rounding when overflow or underflow occurs. The 387 DX NPX produces results that are consistent with the rounding mode.

2. When the underflow exception is masked, the 387 DX NPX sets its underflow flag only if there is also a loss of accuracy during denormalization.

3. Fewer invalid-operation exceptions due to denormal operands, because the instructions FSQRT, FDIV, FPREM, and conversions to BCD or to integer normalize denormal operands before proceeding.

4. The FSQRT, FBSTP, and FPREM instructions may cause underflow, because they support denormal operands.

5. The denormal exception can occur during the transcendental instructions and the FXTRACT instruction.

6. The denormal exception no longer takes precedence over all other exceptions.

7. When the denormal exception is masked, the 387 DX NPX automatically normalizes denormal operands. The 8087/80287 performs unnormal arithmetic, which might produce an unnormal result.

8. When the operand is zero, the FXTRACT instruction reports a zero-divide exception and leaves $-\infty$ in ST(1).

9. The status word has a new bit (SF) that signals when invalid-operation exceptions are due to stack underflow or overflow.

10. FLD *extended precision* no longer reports denormal exceptions, because the instruction is not numeric.

11. FLD *single/double precision* when the operand is denormal converts the number to extended precision and signals the denormalized operand exception. When loading a signaling NaN, FLD *single/double precision* signals an invalid-operand exception.

12. The 387 DX NPX only generates quiet NaNs (as on the 80287); however, the 387 DX NPX distinguishes between quiet NaNs and signaling NaNs. Signaling NaNs trigger exceptions when they are used as operands; quiet NaNs do not (except for FCOM, FIST, and FBSTP which also raise IE for quiet NaNs).

13. When stack overflow occurs during FPTAN and overflow is masked, both ST(0) and ST(1) contain quiet NaNs. The 80287/8087 leaves the original operand in ST(1) intact.

14. When the scaling factor is $\pm\infty$, the FSCALE (ST(0), ST(1)) instruction behaves as follows (ST(0) and ST(1) contain the scaled and scaling operands respectively):

   - FSCALE(0,$\infty$) generates the invalid operation exception.
   - FSCALE(finite, $-\infty$) generates zero with the same sign as the scaled operand.
   - FSCALE(finite, $+\infty$) generates $\infty$ with the same sign as the scaled operand.

   The 8087/80287 returns zero in the first case and raises the invalid-operation exception in the other cases.

15. The 387 DX NPX returns signed infinity/zero as the unmasked response to massive overflow/underflow. The 8087 and 80287 support a limited range for the scaling factor; within this range either massive overflow/underflow do not occur or undefined results are produced.

## 3.0 HARDWARE INTERFACE

In the following description of hardware interface, the # symbol at the end of a signal name indicates that the active or asserted state occurs when the signal is at a low voltage. When no # is present after the signal name, the signal is asserted when at the high voltage level.

### 3.1 Signal Description

In the following signal descriptions, the 387 DX Math Coprocessor pins are grouped by function as follows:

1. Execution control—CPUCLK2, NUMCLK2, CKM, RESETIN
2. NPX handshake—PEREQ, BUSY#, ERROR#
3. Bus interface pins—D31–D0, W/R#, ADS#, READY#, READYO#
4. Chip/Port Select—STEN, NPS1#, NPS2, CMD0#
5. Power supplies—V$_{CC}$, V$_{SS}$

Table 3.1 lists every pin by its identifier, gives a brief description of its function, and lists some of its characteristics. All output signals are tristate; they leave floating state only when STEN is active. The output buffers of the bidirectional data pins D31–D0 are also tristate; they leave floating state only in read cycles when the NPX is selected (i.e. when STEN, NPS1#, and NPS2 are all active).

Figure 3.1 and Table 3.2 together show the location of every pin in the pin grid array.

## Table 3.1. 387™ DX NPX Pin Summary

| Pin Name | Function | Active State | Input/Output | Referenced To |
|---|---|---|---|---|
| CPUCLK2 | 386™ DX CPU CLocK 2 | | I | |
| NUMCLK2 | 387™ DX NPX CLocK 2 | | I | |
| CKM | 387™ DX NPX CLocKing Mode | | I | |
| RESETIN | System reset | High | I | CPUCLK2 |
| PEREQ | Processor Extension REQuest | High | O | CPUCLK2/STEN |
| BUSY# | Busy status | Low | O | CPUCLK2/STEN |
| ERROR# | Error status | Low | O | NUMCLK2/STEN |
| D31–D0 | Data pins | High | I/O | CPUCLK2 |
| W/R# | Write/Read bus cycle | Hi/Lo | I | CPUCLK2 |
| ADS# | ADdress Strobe | Low | I | CPUCLK2 |
| READY# | Bus ready input | Low | I | CPUCLK2 |
| READYO# | Ready output | Low | O | CPUCLK2/STEN |
| STEN | STatus ENable | High | I | CPUCLK2 |
| NPS1# | NPX select #1 | Low | I | CPUCLK2 |
| NPS2 | NPX select #2 | High | I | CPUCLK2 |
| CMD0# | CoMmanD | Low | I | CPUCLK2 |
| VCC | | | I | |
| VSS | | | I | |

NOTE:
STEN is referenced to only when getting the output pins into or out of tristate mode.

## Table 3.2. 387™ DX NPX Pin Cross-Reference

| | | | | | | | | | |
|---|---|---|---|---|---|---|---|---|---|
| ADS# | — | K7 | D18 | — | A8 | STEN | — | L4 | |
| BUSY# | — | K2 | D19 | — | B9 | W/R# | — | K4 | |
| CKM | — | J11 | D20 | — | B10 | | | | |
| CPUCLK24 | — | K10 | D21 | — | A10 | VCC | — | A6, A9, B4, |
| CMD0# | — | L8 | D22 | — | B11 | | | E1, F1, F10, |
| D0 | — | H2 | D23 | — | C10 | | | J2, K3, K5, |
| D1 | — | H1 | D24 | — | D10 | | | L7, L9 |
| D2 | — | G2 | D25 | — | D11 | | | |
| D3 | — | G1 | D26 | — | E10 | VSS | — | B2, B7, C11, |
| D4 | — | D2 | D27 | — | E11 | | | E2, F2, F11, |
| D5 | — | D1 | D28 | — | G10 | | | J1, J10, L5 |
| D6 | — | C2 | D29 | — | G11 | | | |
| D7 | — | C1 | D30 | — | H10 | NO CONNECT | — | K9 |
| D8 | — | B1 | D31 | — | H11 | | | |
| D9 | — | A2 | ERROR# | — | L2 | | | |
| D10 | — | B3 | NPS1# | — | L6 | | | |
| D11 | — | A3 | NPS2 | — | K6 | | | |
| D12 | — | A4 | NUMCLK2 | — | K11 | | | |
| D13 | — | B5 | PEREQ | — | K1 | | | |
| D14 | — | A5 | READY# | — | K8 | | | |
| D15 | — | B6 | READYO# | — | L3 | | | |
| D16 | — | A7 | RESETIN | — | L10 | | | |
| D17 | — | B8 | | | | | | |

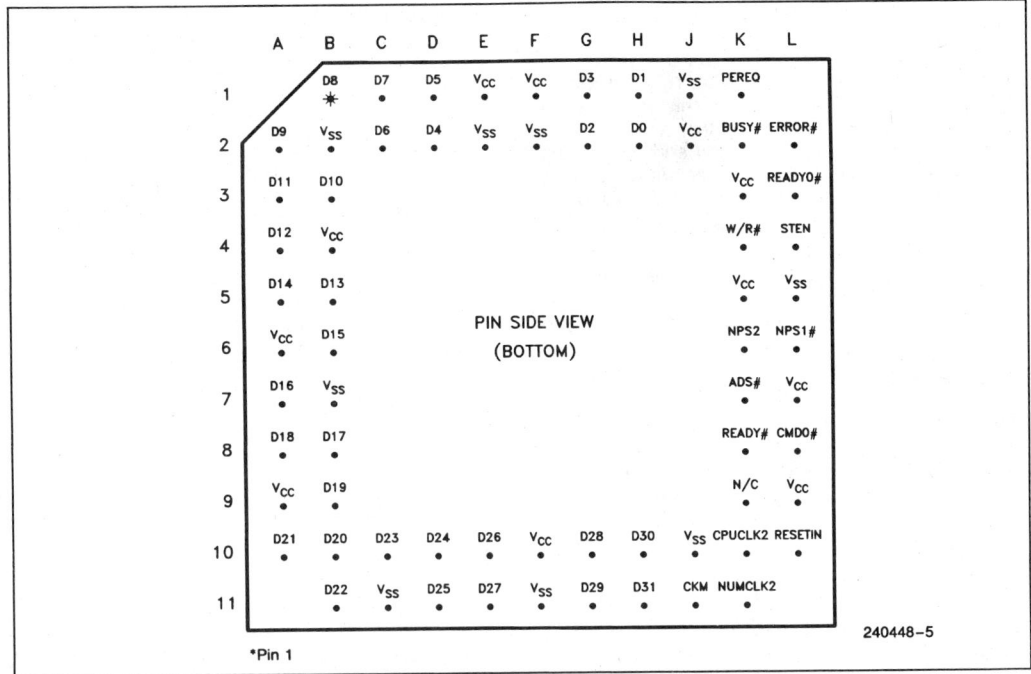

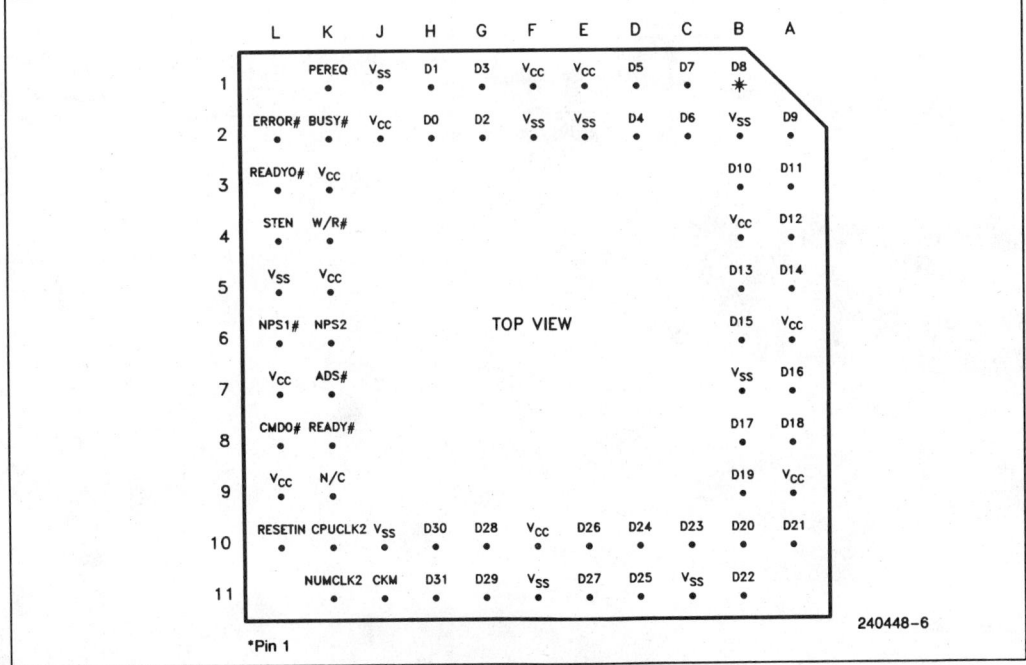

**Figure 3.1. 387™ DX NPX Pin Configuration**

### 3.1.1 386™ DX CPU CLOCK 2 (CPUCLK2)

This input uses the 386 DX CPU CLK2 signal to time the bus control logic. Several other NPX signals are referenced to the rising edge of this signal. When CKM = 1 (synchronous mode) this pin also clocks the data interface and control unit and the floating-point unit of the NPX. This pin requires MOS-level input. The signal on this pin is divided by two to produce the internal clock signal CLK.

### 3.1.2 387™ DX NPX CLOCK 2 (NUMCLK2)

When CKM = 0 (asynchronous mode) this pin provides the clock for the data interface and control unit and the floating-point unit of the NPX. In this case, the ratio of the frequency of NUMCLK2 to the fre-

quency of CPUCLK2 must lie within the range 10:16 to 14:10. When CKM = 1 (synchronous mode) this pin is ignored; CPUCLK2 is used instead for the data interface and control unit and the floating-point unit. This pin requires TTL-level input.

### 3.1.3 387™ DX NPX CLOCKING MODE (CKM)

This pin is a strapping option. When it is strapped to $V_{CC}$, the NPX operates in synchronous mode; when strapped to $V_{SS}$, the NPX operates in asynchronous mode. These modes relate to clocking of the data interface and control unit and the floating-point unit only; the bus control logic always operates synchronously with respect to the 386 DX Microprocessor.

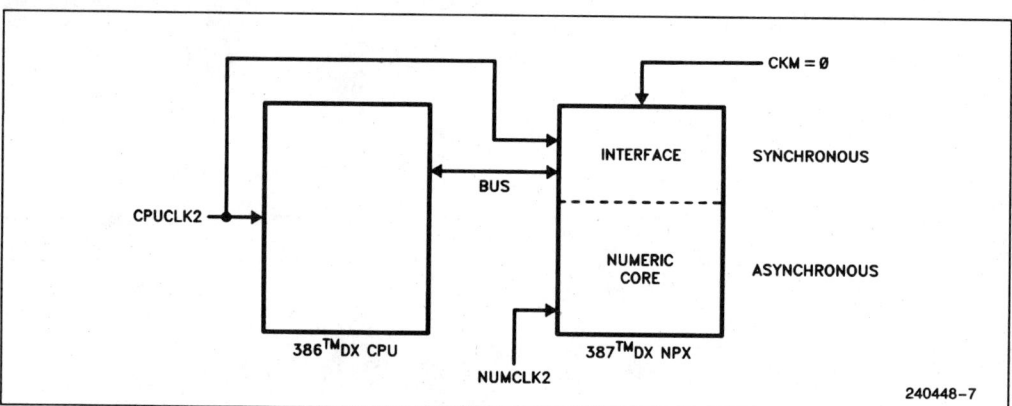

**Figure 3.2. Asynchronous Operation**

### 3.1.4 SYSTEM RESET (RESETIN)

A LOW to HIGH transition on this pin causes the NPX to terminate its present activity and to enter a dormant state. RESETIN must remain HIGH for at least 40 NUMCLK2 periods. The HIGH to LOW transitions of RESETIN must be synchronous with CPUCLK2, so that the phase of the internal clock of the bus control logic (which is the CPUCLK2 divided by 2) is the same as the phase of the internal clock of the 386 DX CPU. After RESETIN goes LOW, at least 50 NUMCLK2 periods must pass before the first NPX instruction is written into the 387 DX NPX. This pin should be connected to the 386 DX CPU RESET pin. Table 3.3 shows the status of other pins after a reset.

**Table 3.3. Output Pin Status During Reset**

| Pin Value | Pin Name |
|---|---|
| HIGH | READYO#, BUSY# |
| LOW | PEREQ, ERROR# |
| Tri-State OFF | D31–D0 |

### 3.1.5 PROCESSOR EXTENSION REQUEST (PEREQ)

When active, this pin signals to the 386 DX CPU that the NPX is ready for data transfer to/from its data FIFO. When all data is written to or read from the data FIFO, PEREQ is deactivated. This signal always goes inactive before BUSY# goes inactive. This signal is referenced to CPUCLK2. It should be connected to the 386 DX CPU PEREQ input. Refer to Figure 3.8 for the timing relationships between this and the BUSY# and ERROR# pins.

### 3.1.6 BUSY STATUS (BUSY#)

When active, this pin signals to the 386 DX CPU that the NPX is currently executing an instruction. This signal is referenced to CPUCLK2. It should be connected to the 386 DX CPU BUSY# pin. Refer to Figure 3.8 for the timing relationships between this and the PEREQ and ERROR# pins.

### 3.1.7 ERROR STATUS (ERROR#)

This pin reflects the ES bits of the status register. When active, it indicates that an unmasked exception has occurred (except that, immediately after a reset, it indicates to the 386 DX Microprocessor that a 387 DX NPX is present in the system). This signal can be changed to inactive state only by the following instructions (without a preceding WAIT): FNINIT, FNCLEX, FNSTENV, and FNSAVE. This signal is referenced to NUMCLK2. It should be connected to the 386 DX CPU ERROR# pin. Refer to Figure 3.8 for the timing relationships between this and the PEREQ and BUSY# pins.

### 3.1.8 DATA PINS (D31–D0)

These bidirectional pins are used to transfer data and opcodes between the 386 DX CPU and 387 DX NPX. They are normally connected directly to the corresponding 386 DX CPU data pins. HIGH state indicates a value of one. D0 is the least significant data bit. Timings are referenced to CPUCLK2.

### 3.1.9 WRITE/READ BUS CYCLE (W/R#)

This signal indicates to the NPX whether the 386 DX CPU bus cycle in progress is a read or a write cycle. This pin should be connected directly to the 386 DX CPU W/R# pin. HIGH indicates a write cycle; LOW, a read cycle. This input is ignored if any of the signals STEN, NPS1#, or NPS2 is inactive. Setup and hold times are referenced to CPUCLK2.

### 3.1.10 ADDRESS STROBE (ADS#)

This input, in conjunction with the READY# input indicates when the NPX bus-control logic may sample W/R# and the chip-select signals. Setup and hold times are referenced to CPUCLK2. This pin should be connected to the 386 DX CPU ADS# pin.

### 3.1.11 BUS READY INPUT (READY#)

This input indicates to the NPX when a 386 DX CPU bus cycle is to be terminated. It is used by the bus-control logic to trace bus activities. Bus cycles can be extended indefinitely until terminated by READY#. This input should be connected to the same signal that drives the 386 DX CPU READY# input. Setup and hold times are referenced to CPUCLK2.

### 3.1.12 READY OUTPUT (READYO#)

This pin is activated at such a time that write cycles are terminated after two clocks (except FLDENV and FRSTOR) and read cycles after three clocks. In configurations where no extra wait states are required, this pin must directly or indirectly drive the 386 DX CPU READY# input. Refer to section 3.4 "Bus Operation" for details. This pin is activated only during bus cycles that select the NPX. This signal is referenced to CPUCLK2.

### 3.1.13 STATUS ENABLE (STEN)

This pin serves as a chip select for the NPX. When inactive, this pin forces BUSY#, PEREQ, ERROR#, and READYO# outputs into floating state. D31–D0 are normally floating and leave floating state only if STEN is active and additional conditions are met. STEN also causes the chip to recognize its other chip-select inputs. STEN makes it easier to do on-board testing (using the overdrive method) of other chips in systems containing the NPX. STEN should be pulled up with a resistor so that it can be pulled down when testing. In boards that do not use on-board testing, STEN should be connected to V$_{CC}$. Setup and hold times are relative to CPUCLK2. Note that STEN must maintain the same setup and hold times as NPS1#, NPS2, and CMD0# (i.e. if STEN changes state during a 387 DX NPX bus cycle, it should change state during the same CLK period as the NPS1#, NPS2, and CMD0# signals).

### 3.1.14 NPX Select #1 (NPS1#)

When active (along with STEN and NPS2) in the first period of a 386 DX CPU bus cycle, this signal indicates that the purpose of the bus cycle is to commu-

nicate with the NPX. This pin should be connected directly to the 386 DX CPU M/IO# pin, so that the NPX is selected only when the 386 DX CPU performs I/O cycles. Setup and hold times are referenced to CPUCLK2.

### 3.1.15 NPX SELECT #2 (NPS2)

When active (along with STEN and NPS1#) in the first period of an 386 DX CPU bus cycle, this signal indicates that the purpose of the bus cycle is to communicate with the NPX. This pin should be connected directly to the 386 DX CPU A31 pin, so that the NPX is selected only when the 386 DX CPU uses one of the I/O addresses reserved for the NPX (800000F8 or 800000FC). Setup and hold times are referenced to CPUCLK2.

### 3.1.16 COMMAND (CMD0#)

During a write cycle, this signal indicates whether an opcode (CMD0# active) or data (CMD0# inactive) is being sent to the NPX. During a read cycle, it indicates whether the control or status register (CMD0# active) or a data register (CMD0# inactive) is being read. CMD0# should be connected directly to the A2 output of the 386 DX Microprocessor. Setup and hold times are referenced to CPUCLK2.

## 3.2 Processor Architecture

As shown by the block diagram on the front page, the NPX is internally divided into three sections: the bus control logic (BCL), the data interface and control unit, and the floating point unit (FPU). The FPU (with the support of the control unit which contains the sequencer and other support units) executes all numerics instructions. The data interface and control unit is responsible for the data flow to and from the FPU and the control registers, for receiving the instructions, decoding them, and sequencing the microinstructions, and for handling some of the administrative instructions. The BCL is responsible for the 386 DX CPU bus tracking and interface. The BCL is the only unit in the 387 DX NPX that must run synchronously with the 386 DX CPU; the rest of the NPX can run asynchronously with respect to the 386 DX Microprocessor.

### 3.2.1 BUS CONTROL LOGIC

The BCL communicates solely with the CPU using I/O bus cycles. The BCL appears to the CPU as a special peripheral device. It is special in two respects: the CPU initiates I/O automatically when it encounters ESC instructions, and the CPU uses reserved I/O addresses to communicate with the BCL. The BCL does not communicate directly with memory. The CPU performs all memory access, transferring input operands from memory to the NPX and transferring outputs from the NPX to memory.

### 3.2.2 DATA INTERFACE AND CONTROL UNIT

The data interface and control unit latches the data and, subject to BCL control, directs the data to the FIFO or the instruction decoder. The instruction decoder decodes the ESC instructions sent to it by the CPU and generates controls that direct the data flow in the FIFO. It also triggers the microinstruction sequencer that controls execution of each instruction. If the ESC instruction is FINIT, FCLEX, FSTSW, FSTSW AX, or FSTCW, the control executes it independently of the FPU and the sequencer. The data interface and control unit is the one that generates the BUSY#, PEREQ and ERROR# signals that synchronize 387 DX NPX activities with the 386 DX CPU. It also supports the FPU in all operations that it cannot perform alone (e.g. exceptions handling, transcendental operations, etc.).

### 3.2.3 FLOATING POINT UNIT

The FPU executes all instructions that involve the register stack, including arithmetic, logical, transcendental, constant, and data transfer instructions. The data path in the FPU is 84 bits wide (68 significant bits, 15 exponent bits, and a sign bit) which allows internal operand transfers to be performed at very high speeds.

## 3.3 System Configuration

As an extension to the 386 DX Microprocessor, the 387 DX Math Coprocessor can be connected to the CPU as shown by Figure 3.3. A dedicated communi-

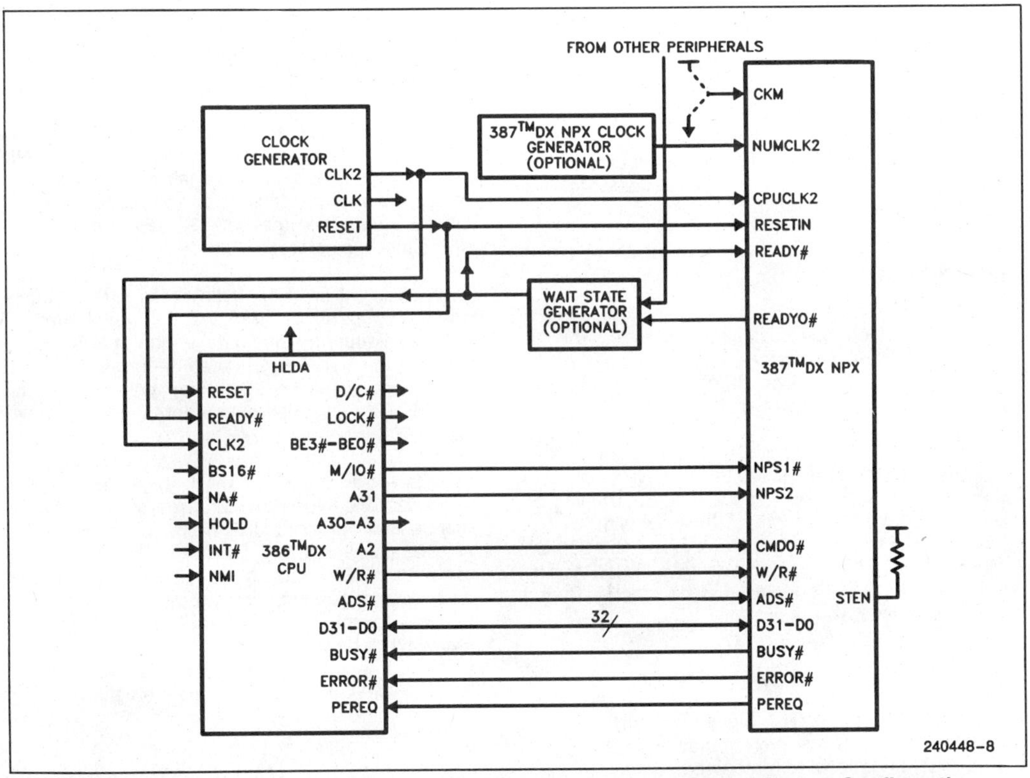

Figure 3.3. 386™ DX Microprocessor and 387™ DX Math Coprocessor System Configuration

**Table 3.4. Bus Cycles Definition**

| STEN | NPS1# | NPS2 | CMD0# | W/R# | Bus Cycle Type |
|------|-------|------|-------|------|----------------|
| 0 | x | x | x | x | NPX not selected and all outputs in floating state |
| 1 | 1 | x | x | x | NPX not selected |
| 1 | x | 0 | x | x | NPX not selected |
| 1 | 0 | 1 | 0 | 0 | CW or SW read from NPX |
| 1 | 0 | 1 | 0 | 1 | Opcode write to NPX |
| 1 | 0 | 1 | 1 | 0 | Data read from NPX |
| 1 | 0 | 1 | 1 | 1 | Data write to NPX |

cation protocol makes possible high-speed transfer of opcodes and operands between the 386 DX CPU and 387 DX NPX. The 387 DX NPX is designed so that no additional components are required for interface with the 386 DX CPU. The 387 DX NPX shares the 32-bit wide local bus of the 386 DX CPU and most control pins of the 387 DX NPX are connected directly to pins of the 386 DX Microprocessor.

### 3.3.1 BUS CYCLE TRACKING

The ADS# and READY# signals allow the NPX to track the beginning and end of the 386 DX CPU bus cycles, respectively. When ADS# is asserted at the same time as the NPX chip-select inputs, the bus cycle is intended for the NPX. To signal the end of a bus cycle for the NPX, READY# may be asserted directly or indirectly by the NPX or by other bus-control logic. Refer to Table 3.4 for definition of the types of NPX bus cycles.

### 3.3.2 NPX ADDRESSING

The NPS1#, NPS2 and STEN signals allow the NPX to identify which bus cycles are intended for the NPX. The NPX responds only to I/O cycles when bit 31 of the I/O address is set. In other words, the NPX acts as an I/O device in a reserved I/O address space.

Because $A_{31}$ is used to select the NPX for data transfers, it is not possible for a program running on the 386 DX CPU to address the NPX with an I/O instruction. Only ESC instructions cause the 386 DX Microprocessor to communicate with the NPX. The 386 DX CPU BS16# input must be inactive during I/O cycles when $A_{31}$ is active.

### 3.3.3 FUNCTION SELECT

The CMD0# and W/R# signals identify the four kinds of bus cycle: control or status register read, data read, opcode write, data write.

### 3.3.4 CPU/NPX Synchronization

The pin pairs BUSY#, PEREQ, and ERROR# are used for various aspects of synchronization between the CPU and the NPX.

BUSY# is used to synchronize instruction transfer from the 386 DX CPU to the NPX. When the NPX recognizes an ESC instruction, it asserts BUSY#. For most ESC instructions, the 386 DX CPU waits for the NPX to deassert BUSY# before sending the new opcode.

The NPX uses the PEREQ pin of the 386 DX CPU to signal that the NPX is ready for data transfer to or from its data FIFO. The NPX does not directly access memory; rather, the 386 DX Microprocessor provides memory access services for the NPX. Thus, memory access on behalf of the NPX always obeys the rules applicable to the mode of the 386 DX CPU, whether the 386 DX CPU be in real-address mode or protected mode.

Once the 386 DX CPU initiates an NPX instruction that has operands, the 386 DX CPU waits for PEREQ signals that indicate when the NPX is ready for operand transfer. Once all operands have been transferred (or if the instruction has no operands) the 386 DX CPU continues program execution while the NPX executes the ESC instruction.

In 8086/8087 systems, WAIT instructions may be required to achieve synchronization of both commands and operands. In 80286/80287, 386 DX Microprocessor and 387 DX Math Coprocessor systems, WAIT instructions are required only for operand synchronization; namely, after NPX stores to memory (except FSTSW and FSTCW) or loads from memory. Used this way, WAIT ensures that the value has already been written or read by the NPX before the CPU reads or changes the value.

Once it has started to execute a numerics instruction and has transferred the operands from the 386 DX CPU, the NPX can process the instruction in parallel with and independent of the host CPU. When the NPX detects an exception, it asserts the ERROR# signal, which causes a 386 DX CPU interrupt.

### 3.3.5 SYNCHRONOUS OR ASYNCHRONOUS MODES

The internal logic of the 387 DX NPX (the FPU) can either operate directly from the CPU clock (synchronous mode) or from a separate clock (asynchronous mode). The two configurations are distinguished by the CKM pin. In either case, the bus control logic (BCL) of the NPX is synchronized with the CPU clock. Use of asynchronous mode allows the 386 DX CPU and the FPU section of the NPX to run at different speeds. In this case, the ratio of the frequency of NUMCLK2 to the frequency of CPUCLK2 must lie within the range 10:16 to 14:10. Use of synchronous mode eliminates one clock generator from the board design.

### 3.3.6 AUTOMATIC BUS CYCLE TERMINATION

In configurations where no extra wait states are required, READYO# can be used to drive the 386 DX CPU READY# input. If this pin is used, it should be connected to the logic that ORs all READY outputs from peripherals on the 386 DX CPU bus. READYO# is asserted by the NPX only during I/O cycles that select the NPX. Refer to section 3.4 "Bus Operation" for details.

## 3.4 Bus Operation

With respect to the bus interface, the 387 DX NPX is fully synchronous with the 386 DX Microprocessor. Both operate at the same rate, because each generates its internal CLK signal by dividing CPUCLK2 by two.

The 386 DX CPU initiates a new bus cycle by activating ADS#. The NPX recognizes a bus cycle, if, during the cycle in which ADS# is activated, STEN, NPS1#, and NPS2 are all activated. Proper operation is achieved if NPS1# is connected to the M/IO# output of the 386 DX CPU, and NPS2 to the A31 output. The 386 DX CPU's A31 output is guaranteed to be inactive in all bus cycles that do not address the NPX (i.e. I/O cycles to other devices, interrupt acknowledge, and reserved types of bus cycles). System logic must not signal a 16-bit bus cycle via the 386 DX CPU BS16# input during I/O cycles when A31 is active.

During the CLK period in which ADS# is activated, the NPX also examines the W/R# input signal to determine whether the cycle is a read or a write cycle and examines the CMD0# input to determine whether an opcode, operand, or control/status register transfer is to occur.

The 387 DX NPX supports both pipelined and nonpipelined bus cycles. A nonpipelined cycle is one for which the 386 DX CPU asserts ADS# when no other NPX bus cycle is in progress. A pipelined bus cycle is one for which the 386 DX CPU asserts ADS# and provides valid next-address and control signals as soon as in the second CLK period after the ADS# assertion for the previous 386 DX CPU bus cycle. Pipelining increases the availability of the bus by at least one CLK period. The NPX supports pipelined bus cycles in order to optimize address pipelining by the 386 DX CPU for memory cycles.

Bus operation is described in terms of an abstract *state machine*. Figure 3.4 illustrates the states and state transitions for NPX bus cycles:

- $T_I$ is the idle state. This is the state of the bus logic after RESET, the state to which bus logic returns after evey nonpipelined bus cycle, and the state to which bus logic returns after a series of pipelined cycles.

- $T_{RS}$ is the READY# sensitive state. Different types of bus cycle may require a minimum of one or two successive $T_{RS}$ states. The bus logic remains in $T_{RS}$ state until READY# is sensed, at which point the bus cycle terminates. Any number of wait states may be implemented by delaying READY#, thereby causing additional successive $T_{RS}$ states.

- $T_P$ is the first state for every pipelined bus cycle.

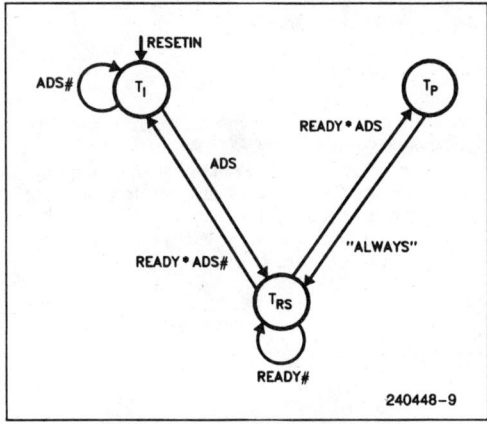

**Figure 3.4. Bus State Diagram**

The READYO# output of the 387 DX NPX indicates when a bus cycle for the NPX may be terminated if no extra wait states are required. For all write cycles (except those for the instructions FLDENV and FRSTOR), READYO# is always asserted in the first $T_{RS}$ state, regardless of the number of wait states. For all read cycles and write cycles for FLDENV and FRSTOR, READYO# is always asserted in the second $T_{RS}$ state, regardless of the number of wait states. These rules apply to both pipelined and non-pipelined cycles. Systems designers must use READYO# in one of the following ways:

1. Connect it (directly or through logic that ORs READY signals from other devices) to the READY# inputs of the 386 DX CPU and 387 DX NPX.

2. Use it as one input to a wait-state generator.

The following sections illustrate different types of NPX bus cycles.

Because different instructions have different amounts of overhead before, between, and after operand transfer cycles, it is not possible to represent in a few diagrams all of the combinations of successive operand transfer cycles. The following bus-cycle diagrams show memory cycles between NPX operand-transfer cycles. Note however that, during the instructions FLDENV, FSTENV, FSAVE, and FRSTOR, some consecutive accesses to the NPX do not have intervening memory accesses. For the timing relationship between operand transfer cycles and opcode write or other overhead activities, see Figure 3.8.

### 3.4.1 NONPIPELINED BUS CYCLES

Figure 3.5 illustrates bus activity for consecutive nonpipelined bus cycles.

#### 3.4.1.1 Write Cycle

At the second clock of the bus cycle, the 387 DX NPX enters the $T_{RS}$ (READY#-sensitive) state. During this state, the 387 DX NPX samples the READY# input and stays in this state as long as READY# is inactive.

In write cycles, the NPX drives the READYO# signal for one CLK period beginning with the second CLK of the bus cycle; therefore, the fastest write cycle takes two CLK cycles (see cycle 2 of Figure 3.5). For the instructions FLDENV and FRSTOR, however, the NPX forces a wait state by delaying the activation of READYO# to the second $T_{RS}$ cycle (not shown in Figure 3.5).

When READY# is asserted the NPX returns to the idle state, in which ADS# could be asserted again by the 386 DX Microprocessor for the next cycle.

#### 3.4.1.2 Read Cycle

At the second clock of the bus cycle, the NPX enters the $T_{RS}$ state. See Figure 3.5. In this state, the NPX samples the READY# input and stays in this state as long as READY# is inactive.

At the rising edge of CLK in the second clock period of the cycle, the NPX starts to drive the D31–D0 outputs and continues to drive them as long as it stays in $T_{RS}$ state.

In read cycles that address the NPX, at least one wait state must be inserted to insure that the 386 DX CPU latches the correct data. Since the NPX starts driving the system data bus only at the rising edge of CLK in the second clock period of the bus cycle, not enough time is left for the data signals to propagate and be latched by the 386 DX CPU at the falling edge of the same clock period. The NPX drives the READYO# signal for one CLK period in the third CLK of the bus cycle. Therefore, if the READYO# output is used to drive the 386 DX CPU READY# input, one wait state is inserted automatically.

Because one wait state is required for NPX reads, the minimum is three CLK cycles per read, as cycle 3 of Figure 3.5 shows.

When READY# is asserted the NPX returns to the idle state, in which ADS# could be asserted again by the 386 DX CPU for the next cycle. The transition from $T_{RS}$ state to idle state causes the NPX to put the tristate D31–D0 outputs into the floating state, allowing another device to drive the system data bus.

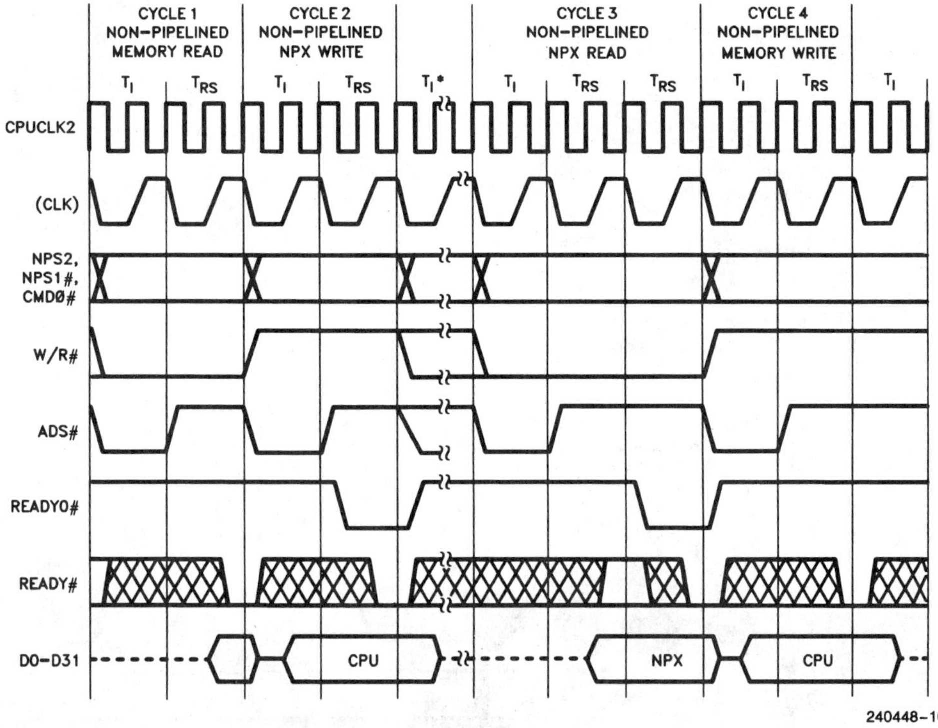

Cycles 1 & 2 represent part of the operand transfer cycle for instructions involving either 4-byte or 8-byte operand loads.
Cycles 3 & 4 represent part of the operand transfer cycle for a store operation.
*Cycles 1 & 2 could repeat here or T$_I$ states for various non-operand transfer cycles and overhead.

**Figure 3.5. Nonpipelined Read and Write Cycles**

### 3.4.2 PIPELINED BUS CYCLES

Because all the activities of the 387 DX NPX bus interface occur either during the T$_{RS}$ state or during the transitions to or from that state, the only difference between a pipelined and a nonpipelined cycle is the manner of changing from one state to another. The exact activities in each state are detailed in the previous section "Nonpipelined Bus Cycles".

When the 386 DX CPU asserts ADS# before the end of a bus cycle, both ADS# and READY# are active during a T$_{RS}$ state. This condition causes the NPX to change to a different state named T$_P$. The NPX activities in the transition from a T$_{RS}$ state to a T$_P$ state are exactly the same as those in the transition from a T$_{RS}$ state to a T$_I$ state in nonpipelined cycles.

T$_P$ state is metastable; therefore, one clock period later the NPX returns to T$_{RS}$ state. In consecutive pipelined cycles, the NPX bus logic uses only T$_{RS}$ and T$_P$ states.

Figure 3.6 shows the fastest transition into and out of the pipelined bus cycles. Cycle 1 in this figure represents a nonpipelined cycle. (Nonpipelined write cycles with only one T$_{RS}$ state (i.e. no wait states) are always followed by another nonpipelined cycle, because READY# is asserted before the earliest possible assertion of ADS# for the next cycle.)

Figure 3.7 shows the pipelined write and read cycles with one additional T$_{RS}$ states beyond the minimum required. To delay the assertion of READY# requires external logic.

### 3.4.3 BUS CYCLES OF MIXED TYPE

When the 387 DX NPX bus logic is in the $T_{RS}$ state, it distinguishes between nonpipelined and pipelined cycles according to the behavior of ADS# and READY#. In a nonpipelined cycle, only READY# is activated, and the transition is from $T_{RS}$ to idle state. In a pipelined cycle, both READY# and ADS# are active and the transition is first from $T_{RS}$ state to $T_P$ state then, after one clock period, back to $T_{RS}$ state.

### 3.4.4 BUSY# AND PEREQ TIMING RELATIONSHIP

Figure 3.8 shows the activation of BUSY# at the beginning of instruction execution and its deactiva-

tion after execution of the instruction is complete. When possible, the 387 DX NPX may deactivate BUSY# prior to the completion of the current instruction allowing the CPU to transfer the next instruction's opcode and operands. PEREQ is activated in this interval. If ERROR# (not shown in the diagram) is ever asserted, it would occur at least six CPUCLK2 periods after the deactivation of PEREQ and at least six CPUCLK2 periods before the deactivation of BUSY#. Figure 3.8 shows also that STEN is activated at the beginning of a bus cycle.

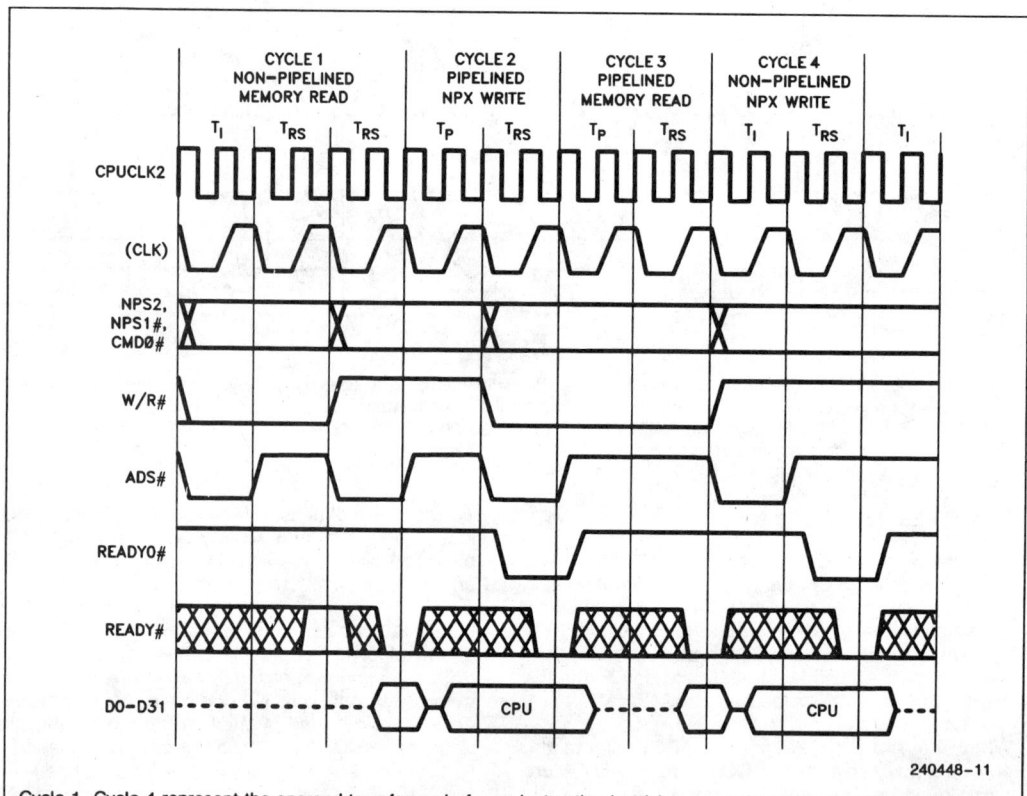

Cycle 1–Cycle 4 represent the operand transfer cycle for an instruction involving a transfer of two 32-bit loads in total. The opcode write cycles and other overhead are not shown.
Note that the next cycle will be a pipelined cycle if both READY# and ADS# are sampled active at the end of a $T_{RS}$ state of the current cycle.

**Figure 3.6. Fastest Transitions to and from Pipelined Cycles**

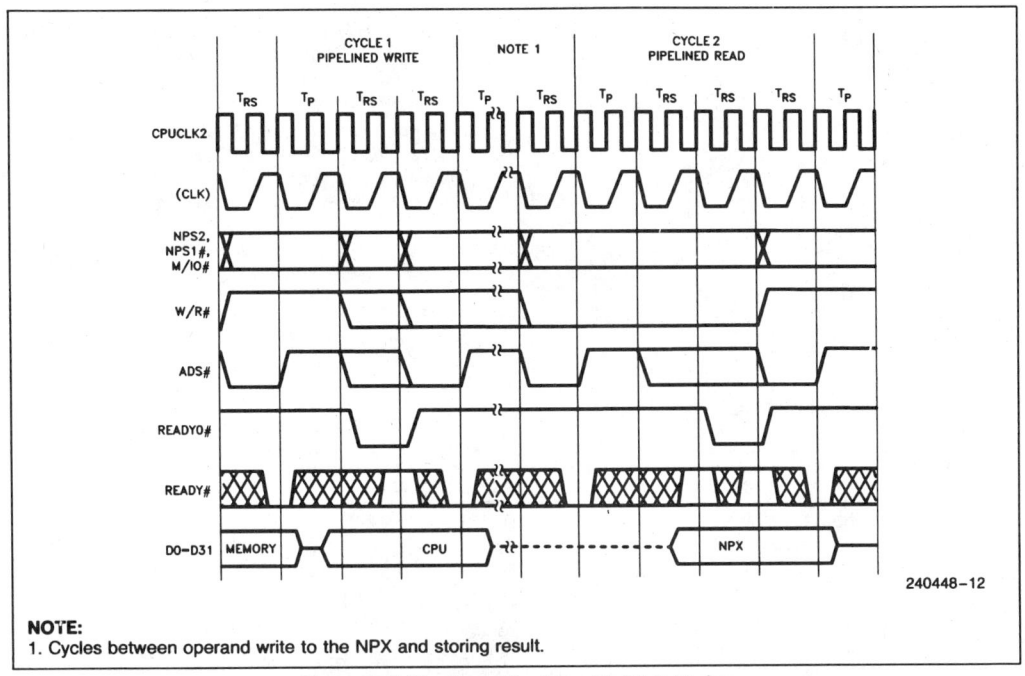

**NOTE:**
1. Cycles between operand write to the NPX and storing result.

**Figure 3.7. Pipelined Cycles with Wait States**

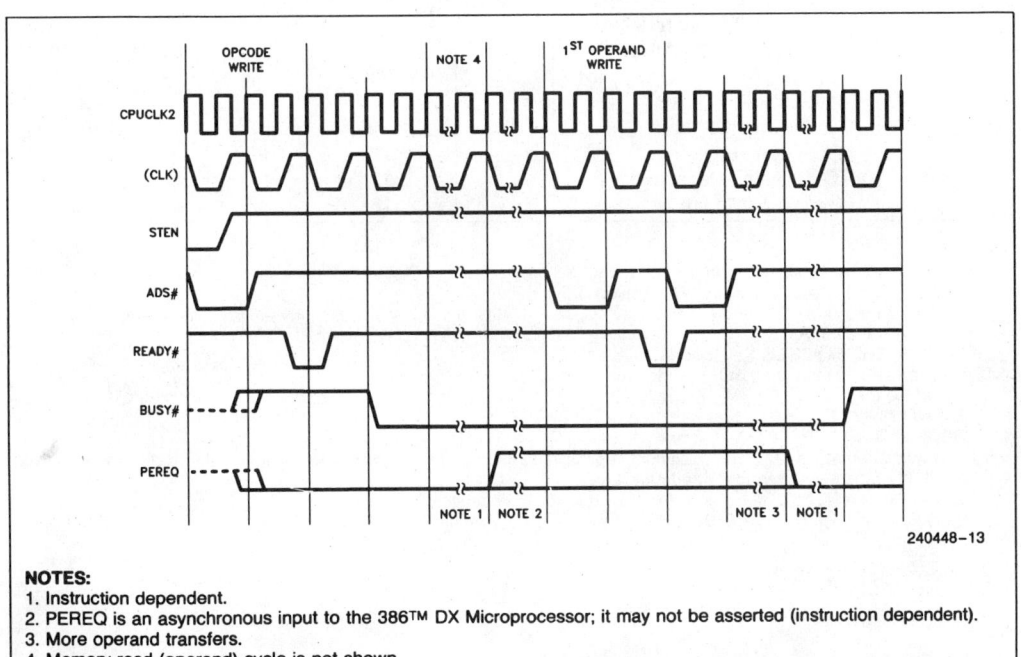

**NOTES:**
1. Instruction dependent.
2. PEREQ is an asynchronous input to the 386™ DX Microprocessor; it may not be asserted (instruction dependent).
3. More operand transfers.
4. Memory read (operand) cycle is not shown.

**Figure 3.8. STEN, BUSY # and PEREQ Timing Relationship**

## 4.0 ELECTRICAL DATA

### 4.1 Absolute Maximum Ratings*

Case Temperature $T_C$
Under Bias . . . . . . . . . . . . . . . . $-65°C$ to $+110°C$
Storage Temperature . . . . . . . . . . $-65°C$ to $+150°C$
Voltage on Any Pin with
Respect to Ground . . . . . . . . . $-0.5$ to $V_{CC} +0.5V$
Power Dissipation . . . . . . . . . . . . . . . . . . . . . . . . 1.5W

*Notice: Stresses above those listed under "Absolute Maximum Ratings" may cause permanent damage to the device. This is a stress rating only and functional operation of the device at these or any other conditions above those indicated in the operational sections of this specification is not implied. Exposure to absolute maximum rating conditions for extended periods may affect device reliability.*

*NOTICE: Specifications contained within the following tables are subject to change.*

### 4.2 D.C. Characteristics

**Table 5.1. DC Specifications** $T_C = 0°$ to $85°C$, $V_{CC} = 5V \pm 5\%$

| Symbol | Parameter | Min | Max | Units | Test Conditions |
|--------|-----------|-----|-----|-------|-----------------|
| $V_{IL}$ | Input LO Voltage | $-0.3$ | $+0.8$ | V | (Note 1) |
| $V_{IH}$ | Input HI Voltage | 2.0 | $V_{CC} + 0.3$ | V | (Note 1) |
| $V_{CL}$ | CPUCLK2 Input LO Voltage | $-0.3$ | $+0.8$ | V | |
| $V_{CH}$ | CPUCLK2 Input HI Voltage | 3.7 | $V_{CC} +0.3$ | V | |
| $V_{OL}$ | Output LO Voltage | | 0.45 | V | (Note 2) |
| $V_{OH}$ | Output HI Voltage | 2.4 | | V | (Note 3) |
| $I_{CC}$ | Supply Current | | | | |
| | NUMCLK2 = 32 MHz[4,6] | | 250 | mA | $I_{CC}$ typ. = 150 mA |
| | NUMCLK2 = 40 MHz[4,6] | | 310 | mA | $I_{CC}$ typ. = 190 mA |
| | NUMCLK2 = 50 MHz[4,6] | | 390 | mA | $I_{CC}$ typ. = 250 mA |
| | NUMCLK2 = 66.6 MHz[4,5] | | 250 | mA | $I_{CC}$ typ. = 150 mA |
| $I_{LI}$ | Input Leakage Current | | $\pm 15$ | $\mu$A | $0V \leq V_{IN} \leq V_{CC}$ |
| $I_{LO}$ | I/O Leakage Current | | $\pm 15$ | $\mu$A | $0.45V \leq V_O \leq V_{CC}$ |
| $C_{IN}$ | Input Capacitance | | 10 | pF | fc = 1 MHz |
| $C_O$ | I/O or Output Capacitance | | 12 | pF | fc = 1 MHz |
| $C_{CLK}$ | Clock Capacitance | | 15 | pF | fc = 1 MHz |

**NOTES:**
1. This parameter is for all inputs, including NUMCLK2 but excluding CPUCLK2.
2. This parameter is measured at $I_{OL}$ as follows:
   data = 4.0 mA
   READYO# = 2.5 mA
   ERROR#, BUSY#, PEREQ = 2.5 mA
3. This parameter is measured at $I_{OH}$ as follows:
   data = 1.0 mA
   READYO# = 0.6 mA
   ERROR#, BUSY#, PEREQ = 0.6 mA
4. $I_{CC}$ is measured at steady state, maximum capacitive loading on the outputs, and worst-case DC level at the inputs; CPUCLK2 at the same frequency as NUMCLK2.
5. $I_{CC}$ specification for 387 DX-33 only (low power CHMOS IV process).
6. $I_{CC}$ specification for 387 DX-16, 20, 25 at corresponding maximum NUMCLK2 FREQ.

## 4.3 A.C. Characteristics

### Table 4.2a. Combinations of Bus Interface and Execution Speeds

| Functional Block | 80387-16 | 80387-20 | 80387-25 | 80387DX-33 |
|---|---|---|---|---|
| Bus Interface Unit (MHz) | 16 | 20 | 25 | 33 |
| Execution Unit (MHz) | 16 | 20 | 25 | 33 |

### Table 4.2b. Timing Requirements of the Execution Unit
$T_C = 0°C$ to $+85°C$, $V_{CC} = 5V \pm 5\%$

| Pin | Symbol | Parameter | 16 MHz | | 20 MHz | | 25 MHz | | 33 MHz | | Test | Figure |
|---|---|---|---|---|---|---|---|---|---|---|---|---|
| | | | Min (ns) | Max (ns) | Min (ns) | Max (ns) | Min (ns) | Max (ns) | Min (ns) | Max (ns) | Conditions | Reference |
| NUMCLK2 | t1 | Period | 31.25 | 125 | 25 | 125 | 20 | 125 | 15 | 125 | 2.0V | 4.1 |
| NUMCLK2 | t2a | High Time | 9 | | 8 | | 7 | | 6.25 | | 2.0V | |
| NUMCLK2 | t2b | High Time | 5 | | 5 | | 4 | | 4.5 | | 3.7V | |
| NUMCLK2 | t3a | Low Time | 9 | | 8 | | 7 | | 6.25 | | 2.0V | |
| NUMCLK2 | t3b | Low Time | 7 | | 6 | | 5 | | 4.5 | | 0.8V | |
| NUMCLK2 | t4 | Fall Time | | 8 | | 8 | | 7 | | 6 | 3.7V to 0.8V | |
| NUMCLK2 | t5 | Rise Time | | 8 | | 8 | | 7 | | 6 | 0.8V to 8.7V | |

### Table 4.2c. Timing Requirements of the Bus Interface Unit
$T_C = 0°C$ to $+85°C$, $V_{CC} = 5V \pm 5\%$
(All measurements made at 1.5V and $C_L = 50$ pF unless otherwise specified)

| Pin | Symbol | Parameter | 16 MHz | | 20 MHz | | 25 MHz | | 33 MHz | | Test | Figure |
|---|---|---|---|---|---|---|---|---|---|---|---|---|
| | | | Min (ns) | Max (ns) | Min (ns) | Max (ns) | Min (ns) | Max (ns) | Min (ns) | Max (ns) | Conditions | Reference |
| CPUCLK2 | t1 | Period | 31.25 | 125 | 25 | 125 | 20 | 125 | 15 | 125 | 2.0V | 4.1 |
| CPUCLK2 | t2a | High Time | 9 | | 8 | | 7 | | 6.25 | | 2.0V | |
| CPUCLK2 | t2b | High Time | 5 | | 5 | | 4 | | 4.5 | | 3.7V | |
| CPUCLK2 | t3a | Low Time | 9 | | 8 | | 7 | | 6.25 | | 2.0V | |
| CPUCLK2 | t3b | Low Time | 7 | | 6 | | 5 | | 4.5 | | 0.8V | |
| CPUCLK2 | t4 | Fall Time | | 8 | | 8 | | 7 | | 4 | 3.7V to 0.8V | |
| CPUCLK2 | t5 | Rise Time | . | 8 | | 8 | | 7 | | 4 | 0.8V to 3.7V | |
| CPUCLK2/ NUMCLK2 | | Ratio | 10/16 | 14/10 | 10/16 | 14/10 | 10/16 | 14/10 | 10/16 | 14/10 | | |
| READYO# | t7 | Out Delay | 3 | 34 | 3 | 31 | 3 | 24 | 3 | 17 | $C_L = 75$ pF† | 4.2 |
| READYO# [2] | t7 | Out Delay | 4 | 31 | 3 | 27 | 3 | 21 | 3 | 15 | $C_L = 25$ pF†† | |
| PEREQ [1] | t7 | Out Delay | 5 | 34 | 5 | 34 | 4 | 33 | 4 | 25 | $C_L = 75$ pF† | |
| BUSY# [1] | t7 | Out Delay | 5 | 34 | 5 | 29 | 4 | 29 | 4 | 21 | $C_L = 75$ pF† | |
| BUSY# [1, 2] | t7 | Out Delay | N/A | N/A | N/A | N/A | 4 | 27 | 4 | 19 | $C_L = 25$ pF†† | |
| ERROR# [1] | t7 | Out Delay | 5 | 34 | 5 | 34 | 4 | 33 | 4 | 25 | $C_L = 75$ pF† | |
| D31–D0 | t8 | Out Delay | 1 | 54 | 1 | 54 | 0 | 40 | 0 | 37 | $C_L = 120$ pF† | 4.3 |
| D31–D0 | t10 | Setup Time | 11 | | 11 | | 11 | | 8 | | | |
| D31–D0 | t11 | Hold Time | 11 | | 11 | | 11 | | 8 | | | |
| D31–D0 [3] | t12* | Float Time | 6 | 33 | 6 | 27 | 5 | 24 | 3 | 19 | $C_L = 120$ pF† | |
| PEREQ [3] | t13* | Float Time | 1 | 60 | 1 | 50 | 1 | 40 | 1 | 30 | $C_L = 75$ pF† | 4.5 |
| BUSY# [3] | t13* | Float Time | 1 | 60 | 1 | 50 | 1 | 40 | 1 | 30 | $C_L = 75$ pF† | |
| ERROR# [3] | t13* | Float Time | 1 | 60 | 1 | 50 | 1 | 40 | 1 | 30 | $C_L = 75$ pF† | |
| READYO# [3] | t13* | Float Time | 1 | 60 | 1 | 50 | 1 | 40 | 1 | 30 | $C_L = 75$ pF† | |

*Float condition occurs when maximum output current becomes less than $I_{LO}$ in magnitude. Float delay is not tested.
†For 25 MHz and 33 MHz, $C_L = 50$ pF
††For 33 MHz, $C_L = 50$ pF

**Table 4.2c. Timing Requirements of the Bus Interface Unit** (Continued)
$T_C = 0°C$ to $+85°C$, $V_{CC} = 5V \pm 5\%$
(All measurements made at 1.5V and $C_L = 50$ pF unless otherwise specified)

| Pin | Symbol | Parameter | 16 MHz | | 20 MHz | | 25 MHz | | 33 MHz | | Figure |
|-----|--------|-----------|--------|--------|--------|--------|--------|--------|--------|--------|--------|
| | | | Min (ns) | Max (ns) | Min (ns) | Max (ns) | Min (ns) | Max (ns) | Max (ns) | Min (ns) | Reference |
| ADS# | t14 | Setup Time | 25 | | 20 | | 15 | | 13 | | 4.3 |
| ADS# | t15 | Hold Time | 5 | | 5 | | 4 | | 4 | | |
| W/R# | t14 | Setup Time | 25 | | 20 | | 15 | | 13 | | |
| W/R# | t15 | Hold Time | 5 | | 5 | | 4 | | 4 | | |
| READY# | t16 | Setup Time | 20 | | 11 | | 8 | | 7 | | |
| READY# | t17 | Hold Time | 4 | | 4 | | 4 | | 4 | | |
| CMD0# | t16 | Setup Time | 20 | | 18 | | 15 | | 13 | | |
| CMD0# | t17 | Hold Time | 2 | | 2 | | 4 | | 4 | | |
| NPS1# NPS2 | t16 | Setup Time | 20 | | 18 | | 15 | | 13 | | |
| NPS1# NPS2 | t17 | Hold Time | 2 | | 2 | | 4 | | 4 | | |
| STEN | t16 | Setup Time | 20 | | 20 | | 14 | | 13 | | |
| STEN | t17 | Hold Time | 2 | | 2 | | 2 | | 2 | | |
| RESETIN | t18 | Setup Time | 13 | | 12 | | 10 | | 5 | | 4.4 |
| RESETIN | t19 | Hold Time | 4 | | 4 | | 3 | | 3 | | |

**NOTES:**
1.  PEREQ, BUSY#, ERROR#
    Out Delay          4  @ $T_C = 0°C$
                       4  @ $T_C = 85°C$
2. Not tested at 25 pF.
3. Float delay is not tested. Float condition occurs when maximum output current becomes less than $I_{LO}$ in magnitude.

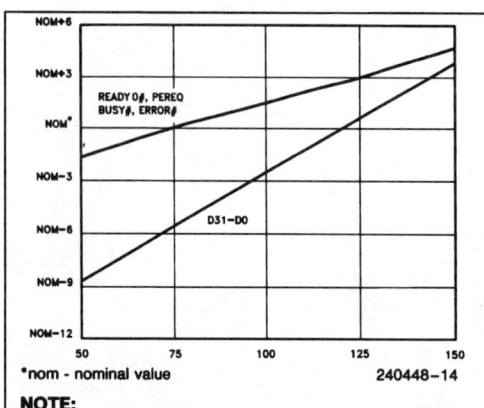

**NOTE:**
This graph will not be linear outside of the $C_L$ range shown.

**Figure 4.0a. Typical Output Valid Delay vs Load Capacitance at Max Operating Temperature**

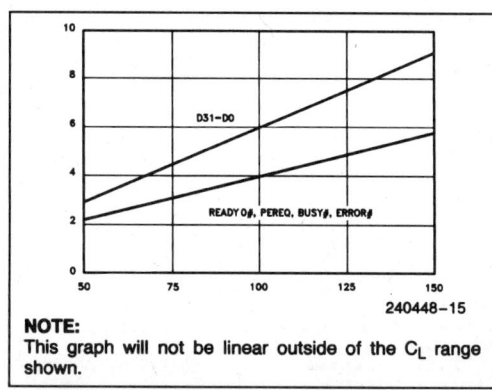

240448–15

**NOTE:**
This graph will not be linear outside of the $C_L$ range shown.

**Figure 4.0b. Typical Output Rise Time vs Load Capacitance at Max Operating Temperature**

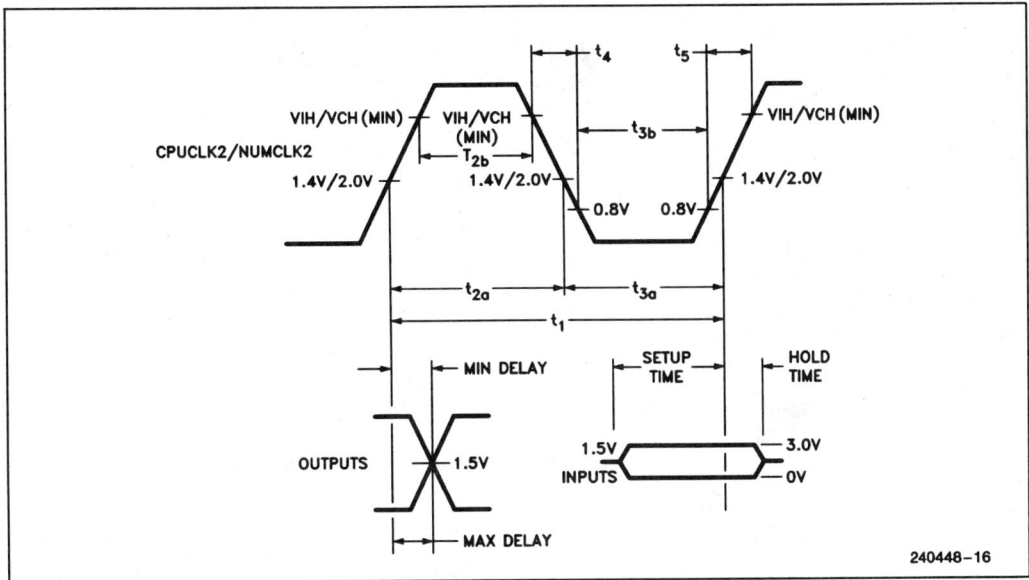

**Figure 4.1. CPUCLK2/NUMCLK2 Waveform and Measurement Points for Input/Output A.C. Specifications**

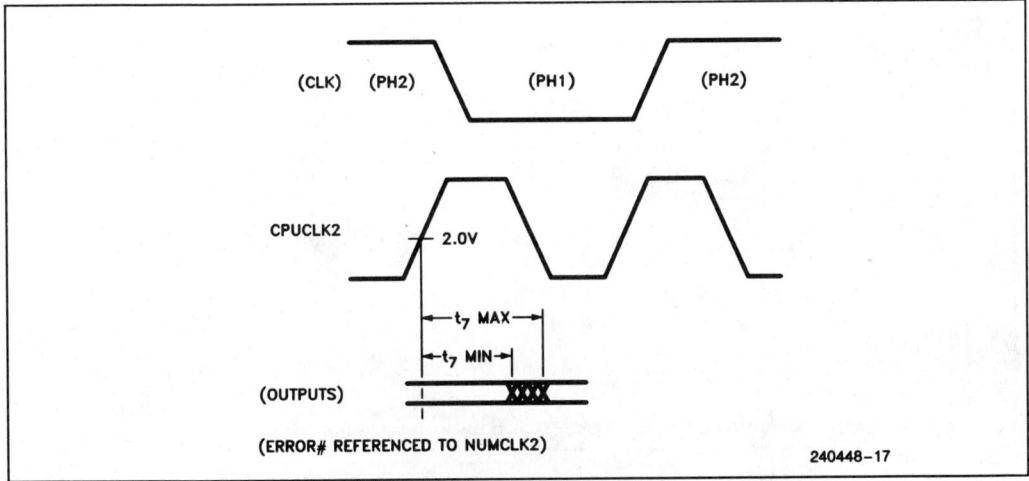

**Figure 4.2. Output Signals**

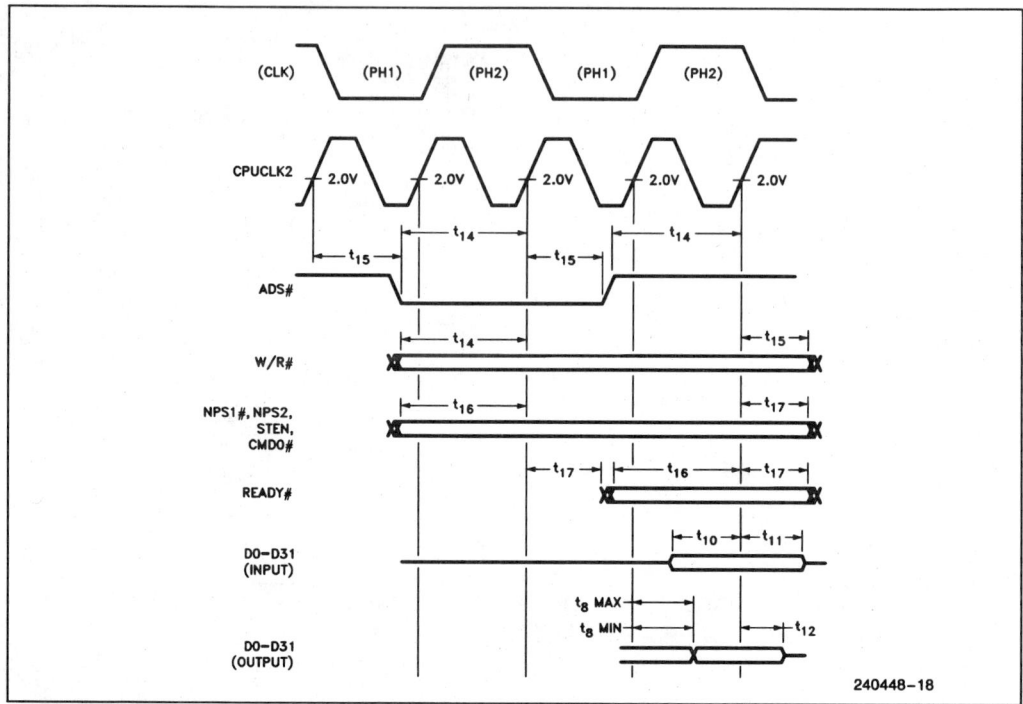

**Figure 4.3. Input and I/O Signals**

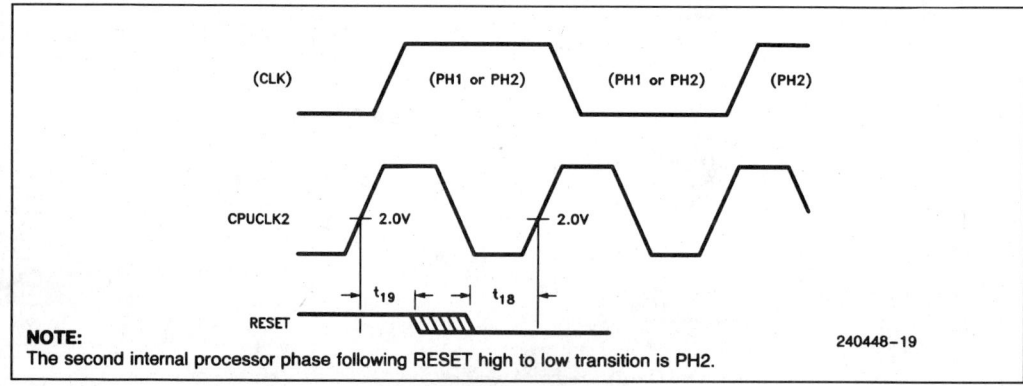

**NOTE:**
The second internal processor phase following RESET high to low transition is PH2.

**Figure 4.4. RESET Signal**

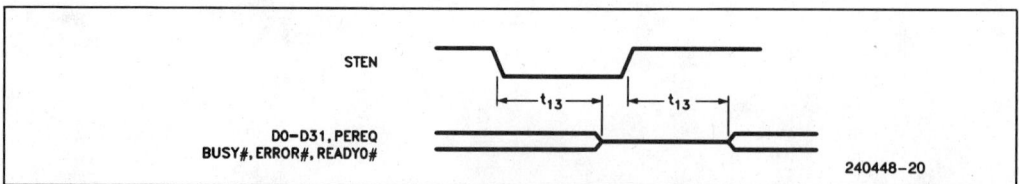

**Figure 4.5. Float from STEN**

**Table 4.3. Other Parameters**

| Pin | Symbol | Parameter | Min | Max | Units |
|---|---|---|---|---|---|
| RESETIN | t30 | Duration | 40 | | NUMCLK2 |
| RESETIN | t31 | RESETIN Inactive to 1st Opcode Write | 50 | | NUMCLK2 |
| BUSY# | t32 | Duration | 6 | | CPUCLK2 |
| BUSY#, ERROR# | t33 | ERROR# (In) Active to BUSY# Inactive | 6 | | CPUCLK2 |
| PEREQ, ERROR# | t34 | PEREQ Inactive to ERROR# Active | 6 | | CPUCLK2 |
| READY#, BUSY# | t35 | READY# Active to BUSY# Active | 4 | 4 | CPUCLK2 |
| READY# | t36 | Minimum Time from Opcode Write to Opcode/Operand Write | 6 | | CPUCLK2 |
| READY# | t37 | Minimum Time from Operand Write to Operand Write | 8 | | CPUCLK2 |

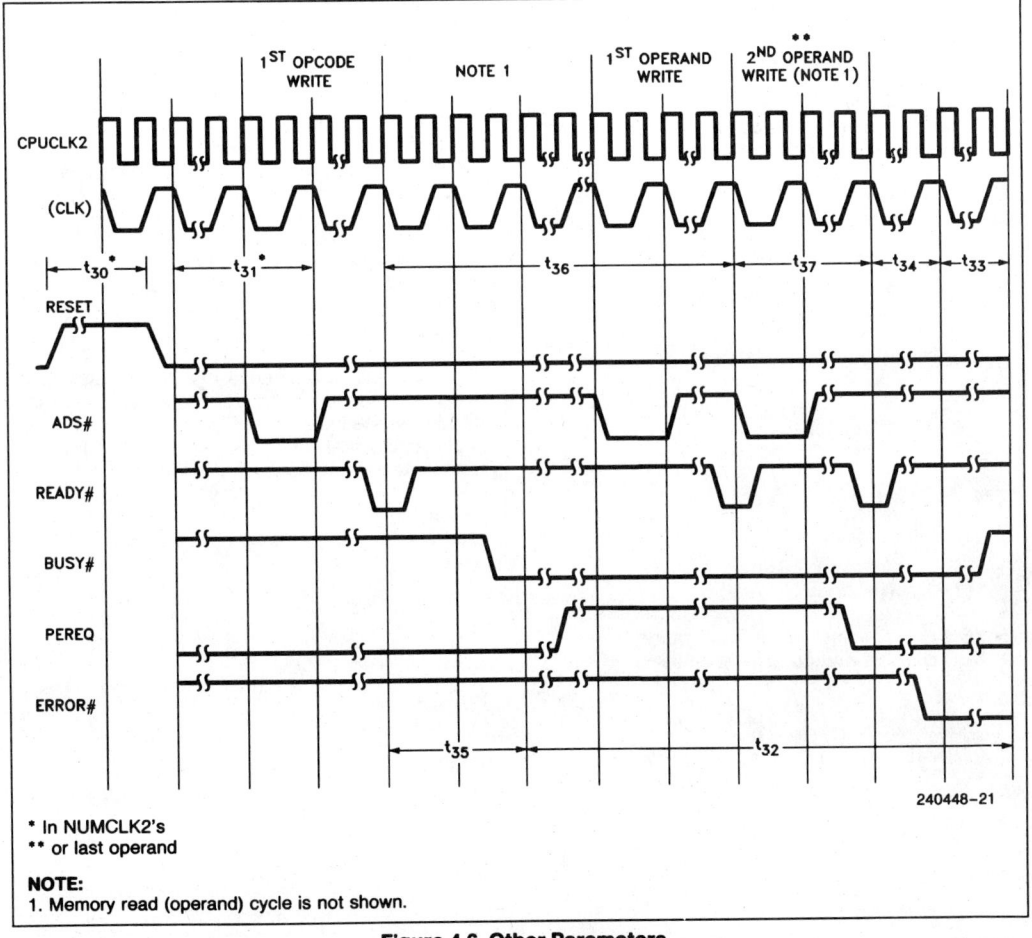

* In NUMCLK2's
** or last operand

**NOTE:**
1. Memory read (operand) cycle is not shown.

**Figure 4.6. Other Parameters**

| Instruction | | | | | | | | Optional Fields | |
|---|---|---|---|---|---|---|---|---|---|
| First Byte | | | Second Byte | | | | | | |
| 11011 | OPA | 1 | MOD | 1 | OPB | R/M | | SIB | DISP |
| 11011 | MF | OPA | MOD | | OPB | R/M | | SIB | DISP |
| 11011 | d | P | OPA | 1 | 1 | OPB | ST(i) | | |
| 11011 | 0 | 0 | 1 | 1 | 1 | 1 | OP | | |
| 11011 | 0 | 1 | 1 | 1 | 1 | 1 | OP | | |
| 15–11 | 10 | 9 | 8 | 7 | 6 | 5 | 4 3 2 1 0 | | |

(Row numbers at left: 1, 2, 3, 4, 5)

## 5.0 387™ DX NPX EXTENSIONS TO THE 386™ DX CPU INSTRUCTION SET

Instructions for the 387 DX NPX assume one of the five forms shown in the following table. In all cases, instructions are at least two bytes long and begin with the bit pattern 11011B, which identifies the ESCAPE class of instruction. Instructions that refer to memory operands specify addresses using the 386 DX CPU addressing modes.

OP = Instruction opcode, possible split into two fields OPA and OPB

MF = Memory Format
    00—32-bit real
    01—32-bit integer
    10—64-bit real
    11—16-bit integer

P = Pop
    0—Do not pop stack
    1—Pop stack after operation

ESC = 11011

d = Destination
    0—Destination is ST(0)
    1—Destination is ST(i)

R XOR d = 0—Destination (op) Source
R XOR d = 1—Source (op) Destination

ST(i) = Register stack element $i$
    000 = Stack top
    001 = Second stack element
        •
        •
        •
    111 = Eighth stack element

MOD (Mode field) and R/M (Register/Memory specifier) have the same interpretation as the corresponding fields of the 386 DX Microprocessor instructions (refer to *386™ DX Microprocessor Programmer's Reference Manual*).

SIB (Scale Index Base) byte and DISP (displacement) are optionally present in instructions that have MOD and R/M fields. Their presence depends on the values of MOD and R/M, as for 386 DX Microprocessor instructions.

The instruction summaries that follow assume that the instruction has been prefetched, decoded, and is ready for execution; that bus cycles do not require wait states; that there are no local bus HOLD request delaying processor access to the bus; and that no exceptions are detected during instruction execution. If the instruction has MOD and R/M fields that call for both base and index registers, add one clock.

## 387™ DX NPX Extensions to the 386™ DX CPU Instruction Set

| Instruction | Encoding | | | Clock Count Range | | | |
|---|---|---|---|---|---|---|---|
| | Byte 0 | Byte 1 | Optional Bytes 2–6 | 32-Bit Real | 32-Bit Integer | 64-Bit Real | 16-Bit Integer |
| **DATA TRANSFER** | | | | | | | |
| **FLD** = Load[a] | | | | | | | |
|   Integer/real memory to ST(0) | ESC MF 1 | MOD 000 R/M | SIB/DISP | 18 | 35–42 | 23 | 42 |
|   Long integer memory to ST(0) | ESC 111 | MOD 101 R/M | SIB/DISP | | 43–54 | | |
|   Extended real memory to ST(0) | ESC 011 | MOD 101 R/M | SIB/DISP | | 43 | | |
|   BCD memory to ST(0) | ESC 111 | MOD 100 R/M | SIB/DISP | | 69–97 | | |
|   ST(i) to ST(0) | ESC 001 | 11000 ST(i) | | | 12 | | |
| **FST** = Store | | | | | | | |
|   ST(0) to integer/real memory | ESC MF 1 | MOD 010 R/M | SIB/DISP | 43 | 62–76 | 44 | 63–76 |
|   ST(0) to ST(i) | ESC 101 | 11010 ST(i) | | | 11 | | |
| **FSTP** = Store and Pop | | | | | | | |
|   ST(0) to integer/real memory | ESC MF 1 | MOD 011 R/M | SIB/DISP | 43 | 62–76 | 44 | 63–76 |
|   ST(0) to long integer memory | ESC 111 | MOD 111 R/M | SIB/DISP | | 65–82 | | |
|   ST(0) to extended real | ESC 011 | MOD 111 R/M | SIB/DISP | | 52 | | |
|   ST(0) to BCD memory | ESC 111 | MOD 110 R/M | SIB/DISP | | 134–190 | | |
|   ST(0) to ST(i) | ESC 101 | 11011 ST (i) | | | 11 | | |
| **FXCH** = Exchange | | | | | | | |
|   ST(i) and ST(0) | ESC 001 | 11001 ST(i) | | | 17 | | |
| **COMPARISON** | | | | | | | |
| **FCOM** = Compare | | | | | | | |
|   Integer/real memory to ST(0) | ESC MF 0 | MOD 010 R/M | SIB/DISP | 25 | 45–52 | 27 | 58–62 |
|   ST(i) to ST(0) | ESC 000 | 11010 ST(i) | | | 21 | | |
| **FCOMP** = Compare and pop | | | | | | | |
|   Integer/real memory to ST | ESC MF 0 | MOD 011 R/M | SIB/DISP | 25 | 45–52 | 27 | 58–62 |
|   ST(i) to ST(0) | ESC 000 | 11011 ST(i) | | | 21 | | |
| **FCOMPP** = Compare and pop twice | | | | | | | |
|   ST(1) to ST(0) | ESC 110 | 1101 1001 | | | 21 | | |
| **FTST** = Test ST(0) | ESC 001 | 1110 0100 | | | 25 | | |
| **FUCOM** = Unordered compare | ESC 101 | 11100 ST(i) | | | 21 | | |
| **FUCOMP** = Unordered compare and pop | ESC 101 | 11101 ST(i) | | | 21 | | |
| **FUCOMPP** = Unordered compare and pop twice | ESC 010 | 1110 1001 | | | 21 | | |
| **FXAM** = Examine ST(0) | ESC 001 | 11100101 | | | 29–37 | | |
| **CONSTANTS** | | | | | | | |
| **FLDZ** = Load + 0.0 into ST(0) | ESC 001 | 1110 1110 | | | 17 | | |
| **FLD1** = Load + 1.0 into ST(0) | ESC 001 | 1110 1000 | | | 22 | | |
| **FLDPI** = Load pi into ST(0) | ESC 001 | 1110 1011 | | | 36 | | |
| **FLDL2T** = Load $\log_2(10)$ into ST(0) | ESC 001 | 1110 1001 | | | 36 | | |

Shaded areas indicate instructions not available in 8087/80287.

**NOTE:**
a. When loading single- or double-precision zero from memory, add 5 clocks.

**387™ DX NPX Extensions to the 386™ DX CPU Instruction Set** (Continued)

| Instruction | Encoding | | | Clock Count Range | | | |
|---|---|---|---|---|---|---|---|
| | Byte 0 | Byte 1 | Optional Bytes 2–6 | 32-Bit Real | 32-Bit Integer | 64-Bit Real | 16-Bit Integer |
| **CONSTANTS** (Continued) | | | | | | | |
| **FLDL2E** = Load $\log_2(e)$ into ST(0) | ESC 001 | 1110 1010 | | | 36 | | |
| **FLDLG2** = Load $\log_{10}(2)$ into ST(0) | ESC 001 | 1110 1100 | | | 35 | | |
| **FLDLN2** = Load $\log_e(2)$ into ST(0) | ESC 001 | 1110 1101 | | | 38 | | |
| **ARITHMETIC** | | | | | | | |
| **FADD** = Add | | | | | | | |
| Integer/real memory with ST(0) | ESC MF 0 | MOD 000 R/M | SIB/DISP | 21–29 | 41–56 | 26–34 | 53–64 |
| ST(i) and ST(0) | ESC d P 0 | 11000 ST(i) | | | 18–26[b] | | |
| **FSUB** = Subtract | | | | | | | |
| Integer/real memory with ST(0) | ESC MF 0 | MOD 10 R R/M | SIB/DISP | 21–29 | 41–56 | 26–34 | 53–64[c] |
| ST(i) and ST(0) | ESC d P 0 | 1110 R R/M | | | 18–26[d] | | |
| **FMUL** = Multiply | | | | | | | |
| Integer/real memory with ST(0) | ESC MF 0 | MOD 001 R/M | SIB/DISP | 24–32 | 50–71 | 28–53 | 63–74 |
| ST(i) and ST(0) | ESC d P 0 | 1100 1 R/M | | | 22–50[e] | | |
| **FDIV** = Divide | | | | | | | |
| Integer/real memory with ST(0) | ESC MF 0 | MOD 11 R R/M | SIB/DISP | 85 | 107–114[f] | 91 | 120–124[g] |
| ST(i) and ST(0) | ESC d P 0 | 1111 R R/M | | | 80[h] | | |
| **FSQRT**[i] = Square root | ESC 001 | 1111 1010 | | | 104–111 | | |
| **FSCALE** = Scale ST(0) by ST(1) | ESC 001 | 1111 1101 | | | 63–82 | | |
| **FPREM** = Partial remainder | ESC 001 | 1111 1000 | | | 60–140 | | |
| **FPREM1** = Partial remainder (IEEE) | ESC 001 | 1111 0101 | | | 78–168 | | |
| **FRNDINT** = Round ST(0) to integer | ESC 001 | 1111 1100 | | | 48–62 | | |
| **FXTRACT** = Extract components of ST(0) | ESC 001 | 1111 0100 | | | 57–63 | | |
| **FABS** = Absolute value of ST(0) | ESC 001 | 1110 0001 | | | 21 | | |
| **FCHS** = Change sign of ST(0) | ESC 001 | 1110 0000 | | | 23–24 | | |

Shaded areas indicate instructions not available in 8087/80287.

**NOTES:**
b. Add 3 clocks to the range when d = 1.
c. Add 1 clock to **each** range when R = 1.
d. Add 3 clocks to the range when d = 0.
e. typical = 52 (When d = 0, 46–54, typical = 49).
f. Add 1 clock to the range when R = 1.
g. 135–141 when R = 1.
h. Add 3 clocks to the range when d = 1.
i. $-0 \leq ST(0) \leq +\infty$.

## 387™ DX NPX Extensions to the 386™ DX CPU Instruction Set (Continued)

| Instruction | Encoding | | | Clock Count Range |
|---|---|---|---|---|
| | Byte 0 | Byte 1 | Optional Bytes 2–6 | |
| **TRANSCENDENTAL** | | | | |
| FCOS[k] = Cosine of ST(0) | ESC 001 | 1111 1111 | | 122–680 |
| FPTAN[k] = Partial tangent of ST(0) | ESC 001 | 1111 0010 | | 162–430[j] |
| FPATAN = Partial arctangent | ESC 001 | 1111 0011 | | 250–420 |
| FSIN[k] = Sine of ST(0) | ESC 001 | 1111 1110 | | 121–680 |
| FSINCOS[k] = Sine and cosine of ST(0) | ESC 001 | 1111 1011 | | 150–650 |
| F2XM1[l] = $2^{ST(0)} - 1$ | ESC 001 | 1111 0000 | | 167–410 |
| FYL2X[m] = $ST(1) * \log_2(ST(0))$ | ESC 001 | 1111 0001 | | 99–436 |
| FYL2XP1[n] = $ST(1) * \log_2(ST(0) + 1.0)$ | ESC 001 | 1111 1001 | | 210–447 |
| **PROCESSOR CONTROL** | | | | |
| FINIT = Initialize NPX | ESC 011 | 1110 0011 | | 33 |
| FSTSW AX = Store status word | ESC 111 | 1110 0000 | | 13 |
| FLDCW = Load control word | ESC 001 | MOD 101 R/M | SIB/DISP | 19 |
| FSTCW = Store control word | ESC 101 | MOD 111 R/M | SIB/DISP | 15 |
| FSTSW = Store status word | ESC 101 | MOD 111 R/M | SIB/DISP | 15 |
| FCLEX = Clear exceptions | ESC 011 | 1110 0010 | | 11 |
| FSTENV = Store environment | ESC 001 | MOD 110 R/M | SIB/DISP | 103–104 |
| FLDENV = Load environment | ESC 001 | MOD 100 R/M | SIB/DISP | 71 |
| FSAVE = Save state | ESC 101 | MOD 110 R/M | • SIB/DISP | 375–376 |
| FRSTOR = Restore state | ESC 101 | MOD 100 R/M | SIB/DISP | 308 |
| FINCSTP = Increment stack pointer | ESC 001 | 1111 0111 | | 21 |
| FDECSTP = Decrement stack pointer | ESC 001 | 1111 0110 | | 22 |
| FFREE = Free ST(i) | ESC 101 | 1100 0 ST(i) | | 18 |
| FNOP = No operations | ESC 001 | 1101 0000 | | 12 |

Shaded areas indicate instructions not available in 8087/80287.

**NOTES:**
j. These timings hold for operands in the range $|x| < \pi/4$. For operands not in this range, up to 76 additional clocks may be needed to reduce the operand.
k. $0 \leq |ST(0)| < 2^{63}$.
l. $-1.0 \leq ST(0) \leq 1.0$.
m. $0 \leq ST(0) < \infty$, $-\infty < ST(1) < +\infty$.
n. $0 \leq |ST(0)| < (2 - SQRT(2))/2$, $-\infty < ST(1) < +\infty$.

# APPENDIX A
# COMPATIBILITY BETWEEN
# THE 80287 AND THE 8087

The 80286/80287 operating in Real-Address mode will execute 8086/8087 programs without major modification. However, because of differences in the handling of numeric exceptions by the 80287 NPX and the 8087 NPX, exception-handling routines *may* need to be changed.

This appendix summarizes the differences between the 80287 NPX and the 8087 NPX, and provides details showing how 8086/8087 programs can be ported to the 80286/80287.

1. The NPX signals exceptions through a dedicated ERROR# line to the 80286. The NPX error signal does not pass through an interrupt controller (the 8087 INT signal does). Therefore, any interrupt-controller-oriented instructions in numeric exception handlers for the 8086/8087 should be deleted.

2. The 8087 instructions FENI/FNENI and FDISI/FNDISI perform no useful function in the 80287. If the 80287 encounters one of these opcodes in its instruction stream, the instruction will effectively be ignored—none of the 80287 internal states will be updated. While 8086/8087 containing these instructions may be executed on the 80286/80287, it is unlikely that the exception-handling routines containing these instructions will be completely portable to the 80287.

3. Interrupt vector 16 must point to the numeric exception handling routine.

4. The ESC instruction address saved in the 80287 includes any leading prefixes before the ESC opcode. The corresponding address saved in the 8087 does not include leading prefixes.

5. In Protected-Address mode, the format of the 80287's saved instruction and address pointers is different than for the 8087. The instruction opcode is not saved in Protected mode—exception handlers will have to retrieve the opcode from memory if needed.

6. Interrupt 7 will occur in the 80286 when executing ESC instructions with either TS (task switched) or EM (emulation) of the 80286 MSW set (TS = 1 or EM = 1). If TS is set, then a WAIT instruction will also cause interrupt 7. An exception handler should be included in 80286/80287 code to handle these situations.

7. Interrupt 9 will occur if the second or subsequent words of a floating-point operand fall outside a segment's size. Interrupt 13 will occur if the starting address of a numeric operand falls outside a segment's size. An exception handler should be included in 80286/80287 code to report these programming errors.

8. Except for the processor control instructions, all of the 80287 numeric instructions are automatically synchronized by the 80286 CPU—the 80286 automatically tests the BUSY# line from the 80287 to ensure that the 80287 has completed its previous instruction before executing the next ESC instruction. No explicit WAIT instructions are required to assure this synchronization. For the 8087 used with 8086 and 8088 processors, explicit WAITs are required before each numeric instruction to ensure synchronization. Although 8086/8087 programs having explicit WAIT instructions will execute perfectly on the 80286/80287 without reassembly, these WAIT instructions are unnecessary.

9. Since the 80287 does not require WAIT instructions before each numeric instruction, the ASM286 assembler does not automatically generate these WAIT instructions. The ASM86 assembler, however, automatically precedes every ESC instruction with a WAIT instruction. Although numeric routines generated using the ASM86 assembler will generally execute correctly on the 80286/80287, reassembly using ASM286 may result in a more compact code image.

The processor control instructions for the 80287 may be coded using either a WAIT or No-WAIT form of mnemonic. The WAIT forms of these instructions cause ASM286 to precede the ESC instruction with a CPU WAIT instruction, in the identical manner as does ASM86.

# PC/AT-Compatible 387™ DX Connection

F

# APPENDIX F
# PC/AT-COMPATIBLE 387™ DX CONNECTION

The PC/AT uses a nonstandard scheme to report 80287 exceptions to the 80286. When replicating the PC/AT coprocessor interface in 386™ DX-based systems, the PC/AT interface cannot be used in exactly the same way; however, this appendix outlines a similar interface that works on 386 DX/387™ DX systems and maintains compatibility with the nonstandard PC/AT scheme.

Note that the interface outlined here does not represent a new interface standard; it needs to be incorporated in AT-compatible designs only because the 80286 and 80287 in the PC/AT are not connected according to the standards defined by Intel. The standard 386 DX/387 DX connection recommended by Intel in the 387 DX Data Sheet functions properly; the 386 DX implementation has not been and will not be altered.

## F.1 THE PC/AT INTERFACE

In the PC/AT, the ERROR# input to the 80286 is tied inactive (high) permanently. The ERROR# output of the 80287 is tied to an interrupt port (IRQ13) (see Figure F-1). This interrupt replaces exception signaling via the 80286's ERROR# input. To guarantee (in the case of an 80287 exception) that INTR 13 will be serviced prior to the execution of any further 80287 instructions, an edge-triggered flip-flop latches BUSY# using ERROR# as a clock. The output of this latch is ORed with the BUSY# output of the 80287 and drives the BUSY# input of the 80286. This PC/AT scheme effectively delays deactivation of BUSY# at the 80286 whenever an 80287 ERROR# is signaled.

Since the 80286 BUSY# input remains active after an exception, the 80286 interrupt 13 handler is guaranteed to execute before any other 80287 instructions may begin. The interrupt 13 handler clears the BUSY# latch (via a write to a special I/O port), thus allowing execution of 80287 instructions to proceed. The interrupt 13 handler then branches to the NMI handler, where the user-defined numerics exception handler resides in PC-compatible systems.

The use of an interrupt guarantees that an exception from a coprocessor instruction will be detected. Latching BUSY# guarantees that any coprocessor instruction (except FINIT, FSETPM, and FCLEX) following the instruction that raised the exception will not be executed before the NMI handler is executed.

This PC/AT scheme approximates the exception reporting scheme between the 8087 and 8088 in the original PC.

## F.2 HOW TO ACHIEVE THE SAME EFFECT IN A 386™ DX SYSTEM

The 386 DX can use a PC/AT-compatible interface to communicate with an 387 DX provided that, when an NPX exception occurs, BUSY# active time is extended and PEREQ is reactivated only after 387 DX BUSY# has gone inactive. The 387 DX is left active (tying STEN high) at all times. Also, the 386 DX and 387 DX must be reset by the same RESET signal.

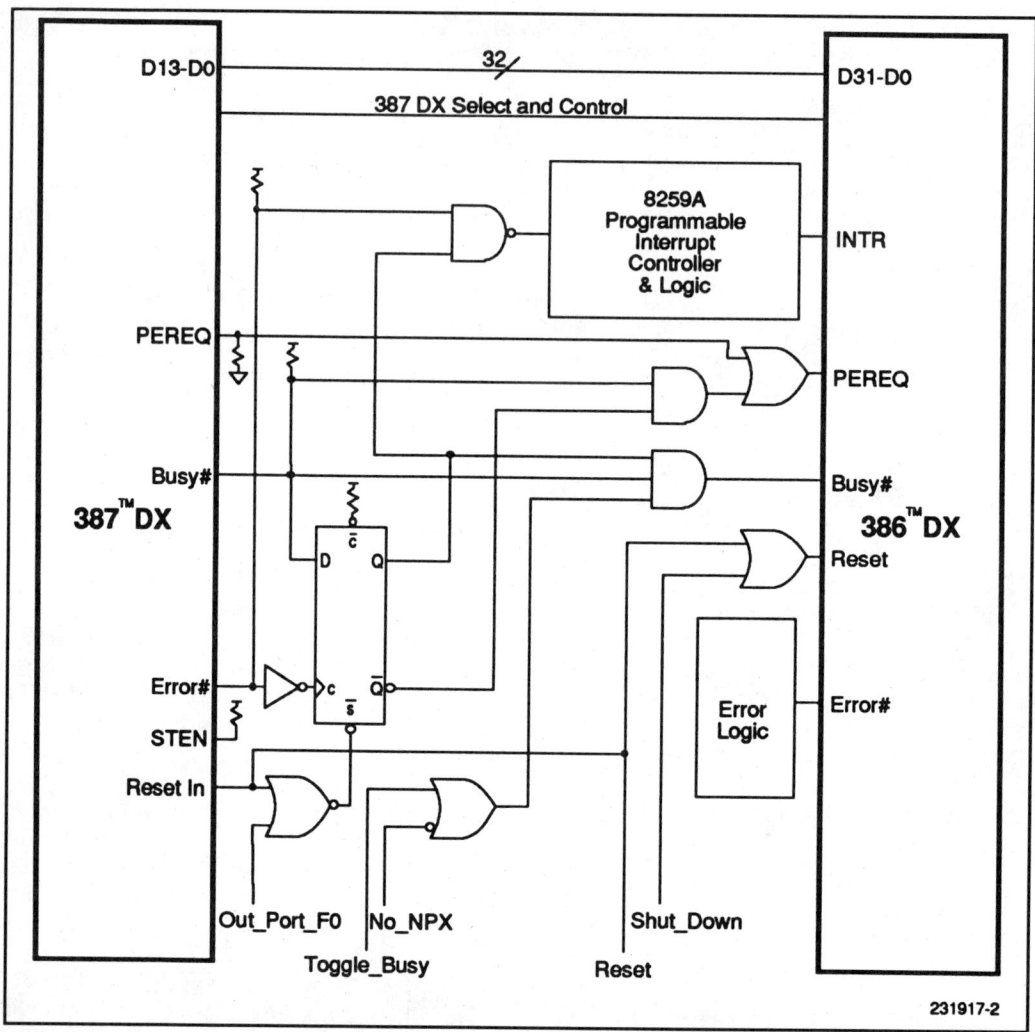

**Figure F-1. A Tested Example of the IBM PC/AT Compatible 386™ DX/387™ DX Interface**

The reactivation of PEREQ for the 386 DX is needed for store instructions (for example, FST *mem*) because the 387 DX drops PEREQ once it signals an exception. While the 386 DX has not yet recognized the occurrence of the exception, it still expects the data transfers to complete via PEREQ reactivation. It is permissible for the 386 DX to receive undefined data during such I/O read cycles. Disabling the 387 DX is not necessary, because the dummy data-transfer cycles directed to the 387 DX when PEREQ is externally reactivated for the 386 DX will not disturb the operation of the 387 DX. The interrupt 13 handler should remove the extension of BUSY# and reactivation of PEREQ via a write to PC/AT-compatible hardware at I/O port F0H.

Figure F-1 is a tested example of the IBM PC/AT-compatible 386 DX/387 DX interface.

# Glossary of 387™ DX and Floating-Point Terminology

# GLOSSARY OF 387™
# AND FLOATING-POINT TERMINOLOGY

This glossary defines many terms that have precise technical meanings as specified in the IEEE 754 Standard or as specified in this manual. Where these terms are used, they have been italicized to emphasize the precision of their meanings. In reading these definitions, you may therefore interpret any italicized terms or phrases as cross-references.

**Base:** (1) a term used in logarithms and exponentials. In both contexts, it is a number that is being raised to a power. The two equations (y = log base b of x) and ($b^y$ = x) are the same.

**Base:** (2) a number that defines the representation being used for a string of digits. *Base* 2 is the binary representation; *base* 10 is the decimal representation; *base* 16 is the hexadecimal representation. In each case, the *base* is the factor of increased significance for each succeeding digit (working up from the bottom).

**Bias:** a constant that is added to the true exponent of a real number to obtain the *exponent* field of that number's *floating-point* representation in the 387 DX. To obtain the true *exponent*, you must subtract the *bias* from the given *exponent*. For example, the *single real* format has a *bias* of 127 whenever the given *exponent* is nonzero. If the 8-bit *exponent* field contains 10000011, which is 131, the true *exponent* is $131 - 127$, or $+4$.

**Biased Exponent:** the *exponent* as it appears in a *floating-point* representation of a number. The *biased exponent* is interpreted as an unsigned, positive number. In the above example, 131 is the *biased exponent*.

**Binary Coded Decimal:** a method of storing numbers that retains a *base* 10 representation. Each decimal digit occupies 4 full bits (one hexadecimal digit). The hexadecimal values A through F (1010 through 1111) are not used. The 387 DX supports a *packed decimal* format that consists of 9 bytes of *binary coded decimal* (18 decimal digits) and one sign byte.

**Binary Point:** an entity just like a decimal point, except that it exists in binary numbers. Each binary digit to the right of the *binary point* is multiplied by an increasing negative power of two.

**C3 − C0:** the four "condition code" bits of the 387 DX *status word*. These bits are set to certain values by the compare, test, examine, and remainder functions of the 387 DX.

**Characteristic:** a term used for some non-Intel computers, meaning the *exponent* field of a *floating-point* number.

**Chop:** to set one or more low-order bits of a real number to zero, yielding the nearest representable number in the direction of zero.

**Condition Code:** the four bits of the 387 DX *status word* that indicate the results of the compare, test, examine, and remainder functions of the 387 DX.

**Control Word:** a 16-bit 387 DX register that the user can set, to determine the modes of computation the 387 DX will use and the exception interrupts that will be enabled.

**Denormal:** a special form of *floating-point* number. On the 387 DX, a *denormal* is defined as a number that has a *biased exponent* of zero. By providing a *significand* with leading zeros, the range of possible negative *exponents* can be extended by the number of bits in the *significand*. Each leading zero is a bit of lost accuracy, so the extended *exponent* range is obtained by reducing significance.

**Double Extended:** the Standard's term for the 387 DX's *extended format*, with more *exponent* and *significand* bits than the *double format* and an explicit *integer bit* in the *significand*.

**Double Format:** a *floating-point* format supported by the 387 DX that consists of a sign, an 11-bit *biased exponent*, an *implicit integer bit*, and a 52-bit *significand* — a total of 64 explicit bits.

**Environment:** the 14 or 28 (depending on addressing mode) bytes of 387 DX registers affected by the FSTENV and FLDENV instructions. It encompasses the entire state of the 387 DX, except for the 8 registers of the 387 DX stack. Included are the *control word*, *status word*, *tag word*, and the instruction, opcode, and operand information provided by interrupts.

**Exception:** any of the six conditions (invalid operand, denormal, numeric overflow, numeric underflow, zero-divide, and precision) detected by the 387 DX that may be signaled by status flags or by traps.

**Exception Pointers:** The data maintained by the 386 DX to help exception handlers identify the cause of an exception. This data consists of a pointer to the most recently executed ESC instruction and a pointer to the memory operand of this instruction, if it had a memory operand. An exception handler can use the FSTENV and FSAVE instructions to access these pointers.

**Exponent:** (1) any number that indicates the power to which another number is raised.

**Exponent:** (2) the field of a *floating-point* number that indicates the magnitude of the number. This would fall under the above more general definition (1), except that a *bias* sometimes needs to be subtracted to obtain the correct power.

**Extended Format:** the 387 DX's implementation of the Standard's *double extended* format. *Extended format* is the main *floating-point* format used by the 387 DX. It consists of a sign, a 15-bit *biased exponent*, and a *significand* with an explicit *integer bit* and 63 fractional-part bits.

**Floating-Point:** of or pertaining to a number that is expressed as base, a sign, a significand, and a signed exponent. The value of the number is the signed product of its significand and the base raised to the power of the exponent. *Floating-point* representations are more versatile than *integer* representations in two ways. First, they include fractions. Second, their *exponent* parts allow a much wider range of magnitude than possible with fixed-length *integer* representations.

**Gradual Underflow:** a method of handling the *underflow* error condition that minimizes the loss of accuracy in the result. If there is a *denormal* number that represents the correct result, that *denormal* is returned. Thus, digits are lost only to the extent of denormalization. Most computers return zero when *underflow* occurs, losing all significant digits.

**Implicit Integer Bit:** a part of the *significand* in the *single real* and *double real* formats that is not explicitly given. In these formats, the entire given *significand* is considered to be to the right of the *binary point*. A single *implicit integer bit* to the left of the *binary point* is always one, except in one case. When the *exponent* is the minimum (*biased exponent* is zero), the *implicit integer bit* is zero.

**Indefinite:** a special value that is returned by functions when the inputs are such that no other sensible answer is possible. For each *floating-point* format there exists one *quiet NaN* that is designated as the *indefinite* value. For binary *integer* formats, the negative number furthest from zero is often considered the *indefinite* value. For the 387 DX *packed decimal* format, the *indefinite* value contains all 1's in the sign byte and the uppermost digits byte.

**Inexact:** The Standard's term for the 387 DX's *precision exception*.

**Infinity:** a value that has greater magnitude than any *integer* or any *real* number. It is often useful to consider *infinity* as another number, subject to special rules of arithmetic. All three Intel *floating-point* formats provide representations for $+\infty$ and $-\infty$.

**Integer:** a number (positive, negative, or zero) that is finite and has no fractional part. *Integer* can also mean the computer representation for such a number: a sequence of data bytes, interpreted in a standard way. It is perfectly reasonable for *integers* to be represented in a *floating-point* format; this is what the 387 DX does whenever an *integer* is pushed onto the 387 DX stack.

**Integer Bit:** a part of the *significand* in *floating-point* formats. In these formats, the *integer bit* is the only part of the *significand* considered to be to the left of the *binary point*. The *integer bit* is always one, except in one case: when the *exponent* is the minimum (*biased exponent* is zero), the *integer bit* is zero. In the *extended format* the *integer bit* is explicit; in the *single format* and *double format* the *integer bit* is implicit; i.e., it is not actually stored in memory.

**Invalid Operation:** the exception condition for the 387 DX that covers all cases not covered by other exceptions. Included are 387 DX stack overflow and underflow, NaN inputs, illegal infinite inputs, out-of-range inputs, and inputs in unsupported formats.

**Long Integer:** an *integer* format supported by the 387 DX that consists of a 64-bit *two's complement* quantity.

**Long Real:** an older term for the 387 DX's 64-bit *double format*.

**Mantissa:** a term used with some non-Intel computers for the *significand* of a *floating-point* number.

**Masked:** a term that applies to each of the six 387 DX *exceptions* I,D,Z,O,U,P. An exception is *masked* if a corresponding bit in the 387 DX *control word* is set to one. If an exception is *masked*, the 387 DX will not generate an interrupt when the exception condition occurs; it will instead provide its own exception recovery.

**Mode:** One of the *status word* fields "rounding control" and "precision control" which programs can set, sense, save, and restore to control the execution of subsequent arithmetic operations.

**NaN:** an abbreviation for "Not a Number"; a *floating-point* quantity that does not represent any numeric or infinite quantity. *NaNs* should be returned by functions that encounter serious errors. If created during a sequence of calculations, they are transmitted to the final answer and can contain information about where the error occurred.

**Normal:** the representation of a number in a *floating-point* format in which the *significand* has an *integer bit* one (either explicit or *implicit*).

**Normalize:** convert a denormal representation of a number to a normal representation.

**NPX:** Numeric Processor Extension. This is the 387 DX, 80287, or 8087.

**Overflow:** an exception condition in which the correct answer is finite, but has magnitude too great to be represented in the destination format. This kind of overflow (also called numeric overflow) is not to be confused with stack overflow.

**Packed Decimal:** an *integer* format supported by the 387 DX. A *packed decimal* number is a 10-byte quantity, with nine bytes of 18 *binary coded decimal* digits and one byte for the sign.

**Pop:** to remove from a stack the last item that was placed on the stack.

**Precision:** The effective number of bits in the significand of the *floating-point* representation of a number.

**Precision Control:** an option, programmed through the 387 DX *control word*, that allows all 387 DX arithmetic to be performed with reduced precision. Because no speed advantage results from this option, its only use is for strict compatibility with the *standard* and with other computer systems.

**Precision Exception:** an 387 DX *exception* condition that results when a calculation does not return an exact answer. This exception is usually *masked* and ignored; it is used only in extremely critical applications, when the user must know if the results are exact. The *precision exception* is called *inexact* in the *standard*.

**Pseudozero:** one of a set of special values of the *extended real* format. The set consists of numbers with a zero *significand* and an *exponent* that is neither all zeros nor all ones. *Pseudozeros* are not created by the 387 DX but are handled correctly when encountered as operands.

**Quiet NaN:** a *NaN* in which the most significant bit of the fractional part of the *significand* is one. By convention, these *NaNs* can undergo certain operations without causing an exception.

**Real:** any finite value (negative, positive, or zero) that can be represented by a (possibly infinite) decimal expansion. *Reals* can be represented as the points of a line marked off like a ruler. The term *real* can also refer to a *floating-point* number that represents a *real* value.

**Short Integer:** an *integer* format supported by the 387 DX that consists of a 32-bit *two's complement* quantity. *short integer* is not the shortest 387 DX *integer* format—the 16-bit *word integer* is.

**Short Real:** an older term for the 387 DX's 32-bit *single format*.

**Signaling NaN:** a *NaN* that causes an *invalid-operation exception* whenever it enters into a calculation or comparison, even a nonordered comparison.

**Significand:** the part of a *floating-point* number that consists of the most significant non-zero bits of the number, if the number were written out in an unlimited binary format. The *significand* is composed of an *integer bit* and a *fraction*. The *integer bit* is implicit in the *single format* and *double format*. The *significand* is considered to have a *binary point* after the *integer bit*; the *binary point* is then moved according to the value of the *exponent*.

**Single Extended:** a *floating-point* format, required by the *standard*, that provides greater precision than *single*; it also provides an explicit *integer bit* in the *significand*. The 387 DX's *extended format* meets the *single extended* requirement as well as the *double extended* requirement.

**Single Format:** a *floating-point* format supported by the 387 DX, which consists of a sign, an 8-bit *biased exponent*, an *implicit integer bit*, and a 23-bit *significand*—a total of 32 explicit bits.

**Stack Fault:** a special case of the *invalid-operation* exception which is indicated by a one in the SF bit of the *status word*. This condition usually results from stack underflow or overflow.

**Standard:** "IEEE Standard for Binary Floating-Point Arithmetic," ANSI/IEEE Std 754-1985.

**Status Word:** A 16-bit 387 DX register that can be manually set, but which is usually controlled by side effects to 387 DX instructions. It contains condition codes, the 387 DX stack pointer, busy and interrupt bits, and exception flags.

**Tag Word:** a 16-bit 387 DX register that is automatically maintained by the 387 DX. For each space in the 387 DX stack, it tells if the space is occupied by a number; if so, it gives information about what kind of number.

**Temporary Real:** an older term for the 387 DX's 80-bit *extended format*.

**Tiny:** of or pertaining to a floating-point number that is so close to zero that its exponent is smaller than smallest exponent that can be represented in the destination format.

**TOP:** The three-bit field of the status word that indicates which 387 DX register is the current top of stack.

**Transcendental:** one of a class of functions for which polynomial formulas are always approximate, never exact for more than isolated values. The 387 DX supports trigonometric, exponential, and logarithmic functions; all are *transcendental*.

**Two's Complement:** a method of representing *integers*. If the uppermost bit is zero, the number is considered positive, with the value given by the rest of the bits. If the uppermost bit is one, the number is negative, with the value obtained by subtracting ($2^{\text{bit count}}$) from all the given bits. For example, the 8-bit number 11111100 is $-4$, obtained by subtracting $2^8$ from 252.

**Unbiased Exponent:** the true value that tells how far and in which direction to move the *binary point* of the *significand* of a *floating-point* number. For example, if a *single-format exponent* is 131, we subtract the Bias 127 to obtain the *unbiased exponent* $+4$. Thus, the *real* number being represented is the *significand* with the *binary point* shifted 4 bits to the right.

**Underflow:** an exception condition in which the correct answer is nonzero, but has a magnitude too small to be represented as a normal number in the destination *floating-point* format. The Standard specifies that an attempt be made to represent the number as a *denormal*. This denormalization may result in a loss of significant bits from the significand. This kind of underflow (also called numeric overflow) is not to be confused with stack underflow.

**Unmasked:** a term that applies to each of the six 387 DX *exceptions*: I,D,Z,O,U,P. An exception is *unmasked* if a corresponding bit in the 387 DX *control word* is set to zero. If an exception is *unmasked*, the 387 DX will generate an interrupt when the exception condition occurs. You can provide an interrupt routine that customizes your exception recovery.

**Unnormal:** a *extended real* representation in which the explicit *integer* bit of the *significand* is zero and the exponent is nonzero. Unnormal values are not supported by the 387 DX; they cause the invalid-operation exception when encountered as operands.

**Unsupported Format:** Any number representation that is not recognized by the 387 DX. This includes several formats that are recognized by the 8087 and 80287; namely: pseudo-NaN, pseudoinfinity, and unnormal.

**Word Integer:** an *integer* format supported by both the 386 DX and the 387 DX that consists of a 16-bit *two's complement* quantity.

**Zero divide:** an *exception* condition in which the inputs are finite, but the correct answer, even with an unlimited *exponent*, has infinite magnitude.

# DOMESTIC SALES OFFICES

**ALABAMA**

†Intel Corp.
5015 Bradford Dr., #2
Huntsville 35805
Tel: (205) 830-4010
FAX: (205) 837-2640

**ARIZONA**

†Intel Corp.
11225 N. 28th Dr.
Suite D-214
Phoenix 85029
Tel: (602) 869-4980
FAX: (602) 869-4294

Intel Corp.
1161 N. El Dorado Place
Suite 301
Tucson 85715
Tel: (602) 299-6815
FAX: (602) 296-8234

**CALIFORNIA**

†Intel Corp.
21515 Vanowen Street
Suite 116
Canoga Park 91303
Tel: (818) 704-8500
FAX: (818) 340-1144

†Intel Corp.
2250 E. Imperial Highway
Suite 218
El Segundo 90245
Tel: (213) 640-6040
FAX: (213) 640-7133

Intel Corp.
1510 Arden Way
Suite 101
Sacramento 95815
Tel: (916) 920-8096
FAX: (916) 920-8253

†Intel Corp.
9665 Chesapeake Dr.
Suite 325
San Diego 95123
Tel: (619) 292-8086
FAX: (619) 292-0628

†Intel Corp.*
400 N. Tustin Avenue
Suite 450
Santa Ana 92705
Tel: (714) 835-9642
TWX: 910-595-1114
FAX: (714) 541-9157

†Intel Corp.*
San Tomas 4
2700 San Tomas Expressway
2nd Floor
Santa Clara 95051
Tel: (408) 986-8086
TWX: 910-338-0255
FAX: (408) 727-2620

**COLORADO**

Intel Corp.
4445 Northpark Drive
Suite 100
Colorado Springs 80907
Tel: (719) 594-6622
FAX: (303) 594-0720

†Intel Corp.*
650 S. Cherry St.
Suite 915
Denver 80222
Tel: (303) 321-8086
TWX: 910-931-2289
FAX: (303) 322-8670

**CONNECTICUT**

†Intel Corp.
301 Lee Farm Corporate Park
83 Wooster Heights Rd.
Danbury 06810
Tel: (203) 748-3130
FAX: (203) 794-0339

**FLORIDA**

†Intel Corp.
6363 N.W. 6th Way
Suite 100
Ft. Lauderdale 33309
Tel: (305) 771-0600
TWX: 510-956-9407
FAX: (305) 772-8193

†Intel Corp.
5850 T.G. Lee Blvd.
Suite 340
Orlando 32822
Tel: (407) 240-8000
FAX: (407) 240-8097

Intel Corp.
11300 4th Street North
Suite 170
St. Petersburg 33716
Tel: (813) 577-2413
FAX: (813) 578-1607

**GEORGIA**

Intel Corp.
20 Technology Parkway, N.W.
Suite 150
Norcross 30092
Tel: (404) 449-0541
FAX: (404) 605-9762

**ILLINOIS**

†Intel Corp.*
300 N. Martingale Road
Suite 400
Schaumburg 60173
Tel: (312) 605-8031
FAX: (312) 706-9762

**INDIANA**

†Intel Corp.
8777 Purdue Road
Suite 125
Indianapolis 46268
Tel: (317) 875-0623
FAX: (317) 875-8938

**IOWA**

Intel Corp.
1930 St. Andrews Drive N.E.
2nd Floor
Cedar Rapids 52402
Tel: (319) 393-1294

**KANSAS**

†Intel Corp.
10985 Cody St.
Suite 140, Bldg. D
Overland Park 66210
Tel: (913) 345-2727
FAX: (913) 345-2076

**MARYLAND**

†Intel Corp.*
10010 Junction Dr.
Suite 200
Annapolis Junction 20701
Tel: (301) 206-2860
FAX: (301) 206-3677
      (301) 206-3678

**MASSACHUSETTS**

†Intel Corp.*
Westford Corp. Center
3 Carlisle Road
2nd Floor
Westford 01886
Tel: (508) 692-3222
TWX: 710-343-6333
FAX: (508) 692-7867

**MICHIGAN**

†Intel Corp.
7071 Orchard Lake Road
Suite 100
West Bloomfield 48322
Tel: (313) 851-8096
FAX: (313) 851-8770

**MINNESOTA**

†Intel Corp.
3500 W. 80th St.
Suite 360
Bloomington 55431
Tel: (612) 835-6722
TWX: 910-576-2867
FAX: (612) 831-6497

**MISSOURI**

†Intel Corp.
4203 Earth City Expressway
Suite 131
Earth City 63045
Tel: (314) 291-1990
FAX: (314) 291-4341

**NEW JERSEY**

†Intel Corp.*
Parkway 109 Office Center
328 Newman Springs Road
Red Bank 07701
Tel: (201) 747-2233
FAX: (201) 747-0983

†Intel Corp.*
280 Corporate Center
75 Livingston Avenue
First Floor
Roseland 07068
Tel: (201) 740-0111
FAX: (201) 740-0626

**NEW YORK**

Intel Corp.*
850 Cross Keys Office Park
Fairport 14450
Tel: (716) 425-2750
TWX: 510-253-7391
FAX: (716) 223-2561

†Intel Corp.*
2950 Expressway Dr., South
Suite 130
Islandia 11722
Tel: (516) 231-3300
TWX: 510-227-6236
FAX: (516) 348-7939

†Intel Corp.
Westage Business Center
Bldg. 300, Route 9
Fishkill 12524
Tel: (914) 897-3860
FAX: (914) 897-3125

**NORTH CAROLINA**

†Intel Corp.
5800 Executive Center Dr.
Suite 105
Charlotte 28212
Tel: (704) 568-8966
FAX: (704) 535-2236

Intel Corp.
5540 Centerview Dr.
Suite 215
Raleigh 27606
Tel: (919) 851-9537
FAX: (919) 851-8974

**OHIO**

†Intel Corp.*
3401 Park Center Drive
Suite 220
Dayton 45414
Tel: (513) 890-5350
TWX: 810-450-2528
FAX: (513) 890-8658

†Intel Corp.*
25700 Science Park Dr.
Suite 100
Beachwood 44122
Tel: (216) 464-2736
TWX: 810-427-9298
FAX: (804) 282-0673

**OKLAHOMA**

Intel Corp.
6801 N. Broadway
Suite 115
Oklahoma City 73162
Tel: (405) 848-8086
FAX: (405) 840-9819

**OREGON**

†Intel Corp.
15254 N.W. Greenbrier Parkway
Building B
Beaverton 97005
Tel: (503) 645-8051
TWX: 910-467-8741
FAX: (503) 645-8181

**PENNSYLVANIA**

†Intel Corp.*
455 Pennsylvania Avenue
Suite 230
Fort Washington 19034
Tel: (215) 641-1000
TWX: 510-661-2077
FAX: (215) 641-0785

†Intel Corp.*
400 Penn Center Blvd.
Suite 610
Pittsburgh 15235
Tel: (412) 823-4970
FAX: (412) 829-7578

**PUERTO RICO**

†Intel Corp.
South Industrial Park
P.O. Box 910
Las Piedras 00671
Tel: (809) 733-8616

**TEXAS**

Intel Corp.
8911 Capital of Texas Hwy.
Austin 78759
Tel: (512) 794-8086
FAX: (512) 338-9335

†Intel Corp.*
12000 Ford Road
Suite 400
Dallas 75234
Tel: (214) 241-8087
FAX: (214) 484-1180

†Intel Corp.*
7322 S.W. Freeway
Suite 1490
Houston 77074
Tel: (713) 988-8086
TWX: 910-881-2490
FAX: (713) 988-3660

**UTAH**

†Intel Corp.
428 East 6400 South
Suite 104
Murray 84107
Tel: (801) 263-8051
FAX: (801) 268-1457

**VIRGINIA**

†Intel Corp.
1504 Santa Rosa Road
Suite 108
Richmond 23288
Tel: (804) 282-5668
FAX: (216) 464-2270

**WASHINGTON**

†Intel Corp.
155 108th Avenue N.E.
Suite 386
Bellevue 98004
Tel: (206) 453-8086
TWX: 910-443-3002
FAX: (206) 451-9556

Intel Corp.
408 N. Mullan Road
Suite 102
Spokane 99206
Tel: (509) 928-8086
FAX: (509) 928-9467

**WISCONSIN**

Intel Corp.
330 S. Executive Dr.
Suite 102
Brookfield 53005
Tel: (414) 784-8087
FAX: (414) 796-2115

# CANADA

**BRITISH COLUMBIA**

Intel Semiconductor of
Canada, Ltd.
4585 Canada Way
Suite 202
Burnaby V5G 4L6
Tel: (604) 298-0387
FAX: (604) 298-8234

**ONTARIO**

†Intel Semiconductor of
Canada, Ltd.
2650 Queensview Drive
Suite 250
Ottawa K2B 8H6
Tel: (613) 829-9714
FAX: (613) 820-5936

†Intel Semiconductor of
Canada, Ltd.
190 Attwell Drive
Suite 500
Rexdale M9W 6H8
Tel: (416) 675-2105
FAX: (416) 675-2438

**QUEBEC**

Intel Semiconductor of
Canada, Ltd.
620 St. Jean Boulevard
Pointe Claire H9R 3K2
Tel: (514) 694-9130
FAX: 514-694-0064

†Sales and Service Office
*Field Application Location

# DOMESTIC DISTRIBUTORS

**ALABAMA**

Arrow Electronics, Inc.
1015 Henderson Road
Huntsville 35805
Tel: (205) 837-6955

†Hamilton/Avnet Electronics
4940 Research Drive
Huntsville 35805
Tel: (205) 837-7210
TWX: 810-726-2162

Pioneer/Technologies Group, Inc.
4825 University Square
Huntsville 35805
Tel: (205) 837-9300
TWX: 810-726-2197

**ARIZONA**

†Hamilton/Avnet Electronics
505 S. Madison Drive
Tempe 85281
Tel: (602) 231-5140
TWX: 910-950-0077

Hamilton/Avnet Electronics
30 South McKiemy
Chandler 85226
Tel: (602) 961-6669
TWX: 910-950-0077

Arrow Electronics, Inc.
4134 E. Wood Street
Phoenix 85040
Tel: (602) 437-0750
TWX: 910-951-1550

Wyle Distribution Group
17855 N. Black Canyon Hwy.
Phoenix 85023
Tel: (602) 249-2232
TWX: 910-951-4282

**CALIFORNIA**

Arrow Electronics, Inc.
10824 Hope Street
Cypress 90630
Tel: (714) 220-6300

Arrow Electronics, Inc.
19748 Dearborn Street
Chatsworth 91311
Tel: (213) 701-7500
TWX: 910-493-2086

†Arow Electronics, Inc.
521 Weddell Drive
Sunnyvale 94086
Tel: (408) 745-6600
TWX: 910-339-9371

Arrow Electronics, Inc.
9511 Ridgehaven Court
San Diego 92123
Tel: (619) 565-4800
TWX: 888-064

†Arrow Electronics, Inc.
2961 Dow Avenue
Tustin 92680
Tel: (714) 838-5422
TWX: 910-595-2860

†Avnet Electronics
350 McCormick Avenue
Costa Mesa 92626
Tel: (714) 754-6071
TWX: 910-595-1928

†Hamilton/Avnet Electronics
1175 Bordeaux Drive
Sunnyvale 94086
Tel: (408) 743-3300
TWX: 910-339-9332

†Hamilton/Avnet Electronics
4545 Ridgeview Avenue
San Diego 92123
Tel: (619) 571-7500
TWX: 910-595-2638

†Hamilton/Avnet Electronics
9650 Desoto Avenue
Chatsworth 91311
Tel: (818) 700-1161

†Hamilton Electro Sales
10950 W. Washington Blvd.
Culver City 20230
Tel: (213) 558-2458
TWX: 910-340-6364

Hamilton Electro Sales
1361B West 190th Street
Gardena 90248
Tel: (213) 217-6700

†Hamilton/Avnet Electronics
3002 'G' Street
Ontario 91761
Tel: (714) 989-9411

†Avnet Electronics
20501 Plummer
Chatsworth 91351
Tel: (213) 700-6271
TWX: 910-494-2207

†Hamilton Electro Sales
3170 Pullman Street
Costa Mesa 92626
Tel: (714) 641-4150
TWX: 910-595-2638

†Hamilton/Avnet Electronics
4103 Northgate Blvd.
Sacramento 95834
Tel: (916) 920-3150

Wyle Distribution Group
124 Maryland Street
El Segundo 90254
Tel: (213) 322-8100

Wyle Distribution Group
7382 Lampson Ave.
Garden Grove 92641
Tel: (714) 891-1717
TWX: 910-348-7140 or 7111

Wyle Distribution Group
11151 Sun Center Drive
Rancho Cordova 95670
Tel: (916) 638-5282

†Wyle Distribution Group
9525 Chesapeake Drive
San Diego 92123
Tel: (619) 565-9171
TWX: 910-335-1590

†Wyle Distribution Group
3000 Bowers Avenue
Santa Clara 95051
Tel: (408) 727-2500
TWX: 910-338-0296

†Wyle Distribution Group
17872 Cowan Avenue
Irvine 92714
Tel: (714) 863-9953
TWX: 910-595-1572

Wyle Distribution Group
26677 W. Agoura Rd.
Calabasas 91302
Tel: (818) 880-9000
TWX: 372-0232

**COLORADO**

Arrow Electronics, Inc.
7060 South Tucson Way
Englewood 80112
Tel: (303) 790-4444

†Hamilton/Avnet Electronics
8765 E. Orchard Road
Suite 708
Englewood 80111
Tel: (303) 740-1017
TWX: 910-935-0787

†Wyle Distribution Group
451 E. 124th Avenue
Thornton 80241
Tel: (303) 457-9953
TWX: 910-936-0770

**CONNECTICUT**

†Arrow Electronics, Inc.
12 Beaumont Road
Wallingford 06492
Tel: (203) 265-7741
TWX: 710-476-0162

Hamilton/Avnet Electronics
Commerce Industrial Park
Commerce Drive
Danbury 06810
Tel: (203) 797-2800
TWX: 710-456-9974

†Pioneer Electronics
112 Main Street
Norwalk 06851
Tel: (203) 853-1515
TWX: 710-468-3373

**FLORIDA**

†Arrow Electronics, Inc.
400 Fairway Drive
Suite 102
Deerfield Beach 33441
Tel: (305) 429-8200
TWX: 510-955-9456

Arrow Electronics, Inc.
37 Skyline Drive
Suite 3101
Lake Marv 32746
Tel: (407) 323-0252
TWX: 510-959-6337

†Hamilton/Avnet Electronics
6801 N.W. 15th Way
Ft. Lauderdale 33309
Tel: (305) 971-2900
TWX: 510-956-3097

†Hamilton/Avnet Electronics
3197 Tech Drive North
St. Petersburg 33702
Tel: (813) 576-3930
TWX: 810-863-0374

†Hamilton/Avnet Electronics
6947 University Boulevard
Winter Park 32792
Tel: (305) 628-3888
TWX: 810-853-0322

†Pioneer/Technologies Group, Inc.
337 S. Lake Blvd.
Alta Monte Springs 32701
Tel: (407) 834-9090
TWX: 810-853-0284

Pioneer/Technologies Group, Inc.
674 S. Military Trail
Deerfield Beach 33442
Tel: (305) 428-8877
TWX: 510-955-9653

**GEORGIA**

†Arrow Electronics, Inc.
3155 Northwoods Parkway
Suite A
Norcross 30071
Tel: (404) 449-8252
TWX: 810-766-0439

†Hamilton/Avnet Electronics
5825 D Peachtree Corners
Norcross 30092
Tel: (404) 447-7500
TWX: 810-766-0432

Pioneer/Technologies Group, Inc.
3100 F Northwoods Place
Norcross 30071
Tel: (404) 448-1711
TWX: 810-766-4515

**ILLINOIS**

Arrow Electronics, Inc.
1140 W. Thorndale
Itasca 60143
Tel: (312) 250-0500
TWX: 312-250-0916

†Hamilton/Avnet Electronics
1130 Thorndale Avenue
Bensenville 60106
Tel: (312) 860-7780
TWX: 910-227-0060

MTI Systems Sales
1100 W. Thorndale
Itasca 60143
Tel: (312) 773-2300

†Pioneer Electronics
1551 Carmen Drive
Elk Grove Village 60007
Tel: (312) 437-9680
TWX: 910-222-1834

**INDIANA**

†Arrow Electronics, Inc.
2495 Directors Row, Suite H
Indianapolis 46241
Tel: (317) 243-9353
TWX: 810-341-3119

Hamilton/Avnet Electronics
485 Gradle Drive
Carmel 46032
Tel: (317) 844-9333
TWX: 810-260-3966

†Pioneer Electronics
6408 Castleplace Drive
Indianapolis 46250
Tel: (317) 849-7300
TWX: 810-260-1794

**IOWA**

Hamilton/Avnet Electronics
915 33rd Avenue, S.W.
Cedar Rapids 52404
Tel: (319) 362-4757

**KANSAS**

Arrow Electronics
8208 Melrose Dr., Suite 210
Lenexa 66214
Tel: (913) 541-9542

†Hamilton/Avnet Electronics
9219 Quivera Road
Overland Park 66215
Tel: (913) 888-8900
TWX: 910-743-0005

Pioneer/Tec Gr.
10551 Lockman Rd.
Lenexa 66215
Tel: (913) 492-0500

**KENTUCKY**

Hamilton/Avnet Electronics
1051 D. Newton Park
Lexington 40511
Tel: (606) 259-1475

**MARYLAND**

Arrow Electronics, Inc.
8300 Guilford Drive
Suite H, River Center
Columbia 21046
Tel: (301) 995-0003
TWX: 710-236-9005

Hamilton/Avnet Electronics
6822 Oak Hall Lane
Columbia 21045
Tel: (301) 995-3500
TWX: 710-862-1861

†Mesa Technology Corp.
9720 Patuxent Woods Dr.
Columbia 21046
Tel: (301) 290-8150
TWX: 710-828-9702

†Pioneer/Technologies Group, Inc.
9100 Gaither Road
Gaithersburg 20877
Tel: (301) 921-0660
TWX: 710-828-0545

Arrow Electronics, Inc.
7524 Standish Place
Rockville 20855
Tel: 301-424-0244

**MASSACHUSETTS**

Arrow Electronics, Inc.
25 Upton Dr.
Wilmington 01887
Tel: (617) 935-5134

†Hamilton/Avnet Electronics
10D Centennial Drive
Peabody 01960
Tel: (617) 531-7430
TWX: 710-393-0382

MTI Systems Sales
83 Cambridge St.
Burlington 01803

Pioneer Electronics
44 Hartwell Avenue
Lexington 02173
Tel: (617) 861-9200
TWX: 710-326-6617

**MICHIGAN**

Arrow Electronics, Inc.
755 Phoenix Drive
Ann Arbor 48104
Tel: (313) 971-8220
TWX: 810-223-6020

Hamilton/Avnet Electronics
2215 29th Street S.E.
Space A5
Grand Rapids 49508
Tel: (616) 243-8805
TWX: 810-274-6921

Pioneer Electronics
4504 Broadmoor S.E.
Grand Rapids 49508
FAX: 616-698-1831

†Hamilton/Avnet Electronics
32487 Schoolcraft Road
Livonia 48150
Tel: (313) 522-4700
TWX: 810-282-8775

†Pioneer/Michigan
13485 Stamford
Livonia 48150
Tel: (313) 525-1800
TWX: 810-242-3271

**MINNESOTA**

†Arrow Electronics, Inc.
5230 W. 73rd Street
Edina 55435
Tel: (612) 830-1800
TWX: 910-576-3125

†Hamilton/Avnet Electronics
12400 Whitewater Drive
Minnetonka 55434
Tel: (612) 932-0600

†Pioneer Electronics
7625 Golden Triange Dr.
Suite G
Eden Prairi 55343
Tel: (612) 944-3355

**MISSOURI**

†Arrow Electronics, Inc.
2380 Schuetz
St. Louis 63141
Tel: (314) 567-6888
TWX: 910-764-0882

†Hamilton/Avnet Electronics
13743 Shoreline Court
Earth City 63045
Tel: (314) 344-1200
TWX: 910-762-0684

**NEW HAMPSHIRE**

†Arrow Electronics, Inc.
3 Perimeter Road
Manchester 03103
Tel: (603) 668-6968
TWX: 710-220-1684

†Hamilton/Avnet Electronics
444 E. Industrial Drive
Manchester 03103
Tel: (603) 624-9400

---

†Microcomputer System Technical Distributor Center

# DOMESTIC DISTRIBUTORS (Contd.)

**NEW JERSEY**

†Arrow Electronics, Inc.
Four East Stow Road
Unit 11
Marlton 08053
Tel: (609) 596-8000
TWX: 710-897-0829

†Arrow Electronics
6 Century Drive
Parsipanny 07054
Tel: (201) 538-0900

†Hamilton/Avnet Electronics
1 Keystone Ave., Bldg. 36
Cherry Hill 08003
Tel: (609) 424-0110
TWX: 710-940-0262

†Hamilton/Avnet Electronics
10 Industrial
Fairfield 07006
Tel: (201) 575-5300
TWX: 710-734-4388

†MTI Systems Sales
37 Kulick Rd.
Fairfield 07006
Tel: (201) 227-5552

†Pioneer Electronics
45 Route 46
Pinebrook 07058
Tel: (201) 575-3510
TWX: 710-734-4382

**NEW MEXICO**

Alliance Electronics Inc.
11030 Cochiti S.E.
Albuquerque 87123
Tel: (505) 292-3360
TWX: 910-989-1151

Hamilton/Avnet Electronics
2524 Baylor Drive S.E.
Albuquerque 87106
Tel: (505) 765-1500
TWX: 910-989-0614

**NEW YORK**

†Arrow Electronics, Inc.
3375 Brighton Henrietta
Townline Rd.
Rochester 14623
Tel: (716) 275-0300
TWX: 510-253-4766

Arrow Electronics, Inc.
20 Oser Avenue
Hauppauge 11788
Tel: (516) 231-1000
TWX: 510-227-6623

Hamilton/Avnet
933 Motor Parkway
Hauppauge 11788
Tel: (516) 231-9800
TWX: 510-224-6166

†Hamilton/Avnet Electronics
333 Metro Park
Rochester 14623
Tel: (716) 475-9130
TWX: 510-253-5470

†Hamilton/Avnet Electronics
103 Twin Oaks Drive
Syracuse 13206
Tel: (315) 437-0288
TWX: 710-541-1560

†MTI Systems Sales
38 Harbor Park Drive
Port Washington 11050
Tel: (516) 621-6200

†Pioneer Electronics
68 Corporate Drive
Binghamton 13904
Tel: (607) 722-9300
TWX: 510-252-0893

Pioneer Electronics
40 Oser Avenue
Hauppauge 11787
Tel: (516) 231-9200

†Pioneer Electronics
60 Crossway Park West
Woodbury, Long Island 11797
Tel: (516) 921-8700
TWX: 510-221-2184

†Pioneer Electronics
840 Fairport Park
Fairport 14450
Tel: (716) 381-7070
TWX: 510-253-7001

**NORTH CAROLINA**

†Arrow Electronics, Inc.
5240 Greensdairy Road
Raleigh 27604
Tel: (919) 876-3132
TWX: 510-928-1856

†Hamilton/Avnet Electronics
3510 Spring Forest Drive
Raleigh 27604
Tel: (919) 878-0819
TWX: 510-928-1836

Pioneer/Technologies Group, Inc.
9801 A-Southern Pine Blvd.
Charlotte 28210
Tel: (919) 527-8188
TWX: 810-621-0366

**OHIO**

Arrow Electronics, Inc.
7620 McEwen Road
Centerville 45459
Tel: (513) 435-5563
TWX: 810-459-1611

†Arrow Electronics, Inc.
6238 Cochran Road
Solon 44139
Tel: (216) 248-3990
TWX: 810-427-9409

†Hamilton/Avnet Electronics
954 Senate Drive
Dayton 45459
Tel: (513) 439-6733
TWX: 810-450-2531

Hamilton/Avnet Electronics
4588 Emery Industrial Pkwy.
Warrensville Heights 44128
Tel: (216) 349-5100
TWX: 810-427-9452

†Hamilton/Avnet Electronics
777 Brooksedge Blvd.
Westerville 43081
Tel: (614) 882-7004

†Pioneer Electronics
4433 Interpoint Boulevard
Dayton 45424
Tel: (513) 236-9900
TWX: 810-459-1622

†Pioneer Electronics
4800 E. 131st Street
Cleveland 44105
Tel: (216) 587-3600
TWX: 810-422-2211

**OKLAHOMA**

Arrow Electronics, Inc.
1211 E. 51st St., Suite 101
Tulsa 74146
Tel: (918) 252-7537

†Hamilton/Avnet Electronics
12121 E. 51st St., Suite 102A
Tulsa 74146
Tel: (918) 252-7297

**OREGON**

†Almac Electronics Corp.
1885 N.W. 169th Place
Beaverton 97005
Tel: (503) 629-8090
TWX: 910-467-8746

†Hamilton/Avnet Electronics
6024 S.W. Jean Road
Bldg. C, Suite 10
Lake Oswego 97034
Tel: (503) 635-7848
TWX: 910-455-8179

Wyle Distribution Group
5250 N.E. Elam Young Parkway
Suite 600
Hillsboro 97124
Tel: (503) 640-6000
TWX: 910-460-2203

**PENNSYLVANIA**

Arrow Electronics, Inc.
650 Seco Road
Monroeville 15146
Tel: (412) 856-7000

Hamilton/Avnet Electronics
2800 Liberty Ave.
Pittsburgh 15238
Tel: (412) 281-4150

Pioneer Electronics
259 Kappa Drive
Pittsburgh 15238
Tel: (412) 782-2300
TWX: 710-795-3122

†Pioneer/Technologies Group, Inc.
Delaware Valley
261 Gibralter Road
Horsham 19044
Tel: (215) 674-4000
TWX: 510-665-6778

**TEXAS**

†Arrow Electronics, Inc.
3220 Commander Drive
Carrollton 75006
Tel: (214) 380-6464
TWX: 910-860-5377

†Arrow Electronics, Inc.
10899 Kinghurst
Suite 100
Houston 77099
Tel: (713) 530-4700
TWX: 910-880-4439

†Arrow Electronics, Inc.
2227 W. Braker Lane
Austin 78758
Tel: (512) 835-4180
TWX: 910-874-1348

†Hamilton/Avnet Electronics
1807 W. Braker Lane
Austin 78758
Tel: (512) 837-8911
TWX: 910-874-1319

†Hamilton/Avnet Electronics
2111 W. Walnut Hill Lane
Irving 75038
Tel: (214) 550-6111
TWX: 910-860-5929

†Hamilton/Avnet Electronics
4850 Wright Rd., Suite 190
Stafford 77477
Tel: (713) 240-7733
TWX: 910-881-5523

†Pioneer Electronics
18260 Kramer
Austin 78758
Tel: (512) 835-4000
TWX: 910-874-1323

†Pioneer Electronics
13710 Omega Road
Dallas 75234
Tel: (214) 386-7300
TWX: 910-850-5563

†Pioneer Electronics
5853 Point West Drive
Houston 77036
Tel: (713) 988-5555
TWX: 910-881-1606

Wyle Distribution Group
1810 Greenville Avenue
Richardson 75081
Tel: (214) 235-9953

**UTAH**

Arrow Electronics
1946 Parkway Blvd.
Salt Lake City 84119
Tel: (801) 973-6913

†Hamilton/Avnet Electronics
1585 West 2100 South
Salt Lake City 84119
Tel: (801) 972-2800
TWX: 910-925-4018

Wyle Distribution Group
1325 West 2200 South
Suite E
West Valley 84119
Tel: (801) 974-9953

**WASHINGTON**

†Almac Electronics Corp.
14360 S.E. Eastgate Way
Bellevue 98007
Tel: (206) 643-9992
TWX: 910-444-2067

Arrow Electronics, Inc.
19540 68th Ave. South
Kent 98032
Tel: (206) 575-4420

†Hamilton/Avnet Electronics
14212 N.E. 21st Street
Bellevue 98005
Tel: (206) 643-3950
TWX: 910-443-2469

Wyle Distribution Group
15385 N.E. 90th Street
Redmond 98052
Tel: (206) 881-1150

**WISCONSIN**

Arrow Electronics, Inc.
200 N. Patrick Blvd., Ste. 100
Brookfield 53005
Tel: (414) 767-6600
TWX: 910-262-1193

Hamilton/Avnet Electronics
2975 Moorland Road
New Berlin 53151
Tel: (414) 784-4510
TWX: 910-262-1182

# CANADA

**ALBERTA**

Hamilton/Avnet Electronics
2816 21st Street N.E.
Calgary T2E 6Z3
Tel: (403) 230-3586
TWX: 03-827-642

Zentronics
Bay No. 1
3300 14th Avenue N.E.
Calgary T2A 6J4
Tel: (403) 272-1021

**BRITISH COLUMBIA**

†Hamilton/Avnet Electronics
105-2550 Boundary
Burmalay V5M 3Z3
Tel: (604) 437-6667

Zentronics
108-11400 Bridgeport Road
Richmond V6X 1T2
Tel: (604) 273-5575
TWX: 04-5077-89

**MANITOBA**

Zentronics
60-1313 Border Unit 60
Winnipeg R3H 0X4
Tel: (204) 694-1957

**ONTARIO**

Arrow Electronics, Inc.
36 Antares Dr.
Nepean K2E 7W5
Tel: (613) 226-6903

Arrow Electronics, Inc.
1093 Meyerside
Mississauga L5T 1M4
Tel: (416) 673-7769
TWX: 06-218213

†Hamilton/Avnet Electronics
6845 Rexwood Road
Units 3-4-5
Mississauga L4T 1R2
Tel: (416) 677-7432
TWX: 610-492-8867

Hamilton/Avnet Electronics
6845 Rexwood Rd., Unit 6
Mississauga L4T 1R2
Tel: (416) 277-0484

†Hamilton/Avnet Electronics
190 Colonnade Road South
Nepean K2E 7L5
Tel: (613) 226-1700
TWX: 05-349-71

†Zentronics
8 Tilbury Court
Brampton L6T 3T4
Tel: (416) 451-9600
TWX: 06-976-78

†Zentronics
155 Colonnade Road
Unit 17
Nepean K2E 7K1
Tel: (613) 226-8840

Zentronics
60-1313 Border St.
Winnipeg R3H 0l4
Tel: (204) 694-7957

**QUEBEC**

†Arrow Electronics Inc.
4050 Jean Talon Quest
Montreal H4P 1W1
Tel: (514) 735-5511
TWX: 05-25590

Arrow Electronics, Inc.
500 Avenue St-Jean Baptiste
Suite 280
Quebec G2E 5R9
Tel: (418) 871-7500
FAX: 418-871-6816

Hamilton/Avnet Electronics
2795 Halpern
St. Laurent H2E 7K1
Tel: (514) 335-1000
TWX: 610-421-3731

Zentronics
817 McCaffrey
St. Laurent H4T 1M3
Tel: (514) 737-9700
TWX: 05-827-535

†Microcomputer System Technical Distributor Center

CG/SALE/101789

# EUROPEAN SALES OFFICES

**DENMARK**

Intel Denmark A/S
Glentevej 61, 3rd Floor
2400 Copenhagen NV
Tel: (45) (31) 19 80 33
TLX: 19567

**FINLAND**

Intel Finland OY
Ruosilantie 2
00390 Helsinki
Tel: (358) 0 544 644
TLX: 123332

**FRANCE**

Intel Corporation S.A.R.L.
1, Rue Edison-BP 303
78054 St. Quentin-en-Yvelines
Cedex
Tel: (33) (1) 30 57 70 00
TLX: 699016

**WEST GERMANY**

Intel Semiconductor GmbH*
Dornacher Strasse 1
8016 Feldkirchen bei Muenchen
Tel: (49) 089/90992-0
TLX: 5-23177

Intel Semiconductor GmbH
Hohenzollern Strasse 5
3000 Hannover 1
Tel: (49) 0511/344081
TLX: 9-23625

Intel Semiconductor GmbH
Abraham Lincoln Strasse 16-18
6200 Wiesbaden
Tel: (49) 06121/7605-0
TLX: 4-186183

Intel Semiconductor GmbH
Zettachring 10A
7000 Stuttgart 80
Tel: (49) 0711/7287-280
TLX: 7-254826

**ISRAEL**

Intel Semiconductor Ltd.*
Atidim Industrial Park-Neve Sharet
P.O. Box 43202
Tel-Aviv 61430
Tel: (972) 03-498080
TLX: 371215

**ITALY**

Intel Corporation Italia S.p.A.*
Milanofiori Palazzo E
20090 Assago
Milano
Tel: (39) (02) 89200950
TLX: 341286

**NETHERLANDS**

Intel Semiconductor B.V.*
Postbus 84130
3099 CC Rotterdam
Tel: (31) 10.407.11.11
TLX: 22283

**NORWAY**

Intel Norway A/S
Hvamveien 4-PO Box 92
2013 Skjetten
Tel: (47) (6) 842 420
TLX: 78018

**SPAIN**

Intel Iberia S.A.
Zurbaran, 28
28010 Madrid
Tel: (34) (1) 308.25.52
TLX: 46880

**SWEDEN**

Intel Sweden A.B.*
Dalvagen 24
171 36 Solna
Tel: (46) 8 734 01 00
TLX: 12261

**SWITZERLAND**

Intel Semiconductor A.G.
Zuerichstrasse
8185 Winkel-Rueti bei Zuerich
Tel: (41) 01/860 62 62
TLX: 825977

**UNITED KINGDOM**

Intel Corporation (U.K.) Ltd.*
Pipers Way
Swindon, Wiltshire SN3 1RJ
Tel: (44) (0793) 696000
TLX: 444447/8

# EUROPEAN DISTRIBUTORS/REPRESENTATIVES

**AUSTRIA**

Bacher Electronics G.m.b.H.
Rotenmuehlgasse 26
1120 Wien
Tel: (43) (0222) 83 56 46
TLX: 31532

**BELGIUM**

Inelco Belgium S.A.
Av. des Croix de Guerre 94
1120 Bruxelles
Oorlogskruisenlaan, 94
1120 Brussel
Tel: (32) (02) 216 01 60
TLX: 64475 or 22090

**DENMARK**

ITT-Multikomponent
Naverland 29
2600 Glostrup
Tel: (45) (0) 2 45 66 45
TLX: 33 355

**FINLAND**

OY Fintronic AB
Melkonkatu 24A
00210 Helsinki
Tel: (358) (0) 6926022
TLX: 124224

**FRANCE**

Almex
Zone industrielle d'Antony
48, rue de l'Aubepine
BP 102
92164 Antony cedex
Tel: (33) (1) 46 66 21 12
TLX: 250067

Jermyn-Generim
60, rue des Gemeaux
Silic 580
94653 Rungis cedex
Tel: (33) (1) 49 78 49 78
TLX: 261585

Metrologie
Tour d'Asnieres
4, av. Laurent-Cely
92606 Asnieres Cedex
Tel: (33) (1) 47 90 62 40
TLX: 611448

Tekelec-Airtronic
Cite des Bruyeres
Rue Carle Vernet - BP 2
92310 Sevres
Tel: (33) (1) 45 34 75 35
TLX: 204552

**WEST GERMANY**

Electronic 2000 AG
Stahlgruberring 12
8000 Muenchen 82
Tel: (49) 089/42001-0
TLX: 522561

ITT Multikomponent GmbH
Postfach 1265
Bahnhofstrasse 44
7141 Moeglingen
Tel: (49) 07141/4879
TLX: 7264472

Jermyn GmbH
Im Dachsstueck 9
6250 Limburg
Tel: (49) 06431/508-0
TLX: 415257-0

Metrologie GmbH
Meglingerstrasse 49
8000 Muenchen 71
Tel: (49) 089/78042-0
TLX: 5213189

Proelectron Vertriebs GmbH
Max Planck Strasse 1-3
6072 Dreieich
Tel: (49) 06103/30434-3
TLX: 417903

**IRELAND**

Micro Marketing Ltd.
Glenageary Office Park
Glenageary
Co. Dublin
Tel: (21) (353) (01) 85 63 25
TLX: 31584

**ISRAEL**

Eastronics Ltd.
11 Rozanis Street
P.O.B. 39300
Tel-Aviv 61392
Tel: (972) 03-475151
TLX: 33638

**ITALY**

Intesi
Divisione ITT Industries GmbH
Viale Milanofiori
Palazzo E/5
20090 Assago (MI)
Tel: (39) 02/824701
TLX: 311351

Lasi Elettronica S.p.A.
V. le Fulvio Testi, 126
20092 Cinisello Balsamo (MI)
Tel: (39) 02/2440012
TLX: 352040

Telcom S.r.l.
Via M. Civitali 75
20148 Milano
Tel: (39) 02/4049046
TLX: 335654

ITT Multicomponents
Viale Milanofiori E/5
20090 Assago (MI)
Tel: (39) 02/824701
TLX: 311351

Silverstar
Via Dei Gracchi 20
20146 Milano
Tel: (39) 02/49961
TLX: 332189

**NETHERLANDS**

Koning en Hartman Elektrotechniek
B.V.
Energieweg 1
2627 AP Delft
Tel: (31) (0) 15/609906
TLX: 38250

**NORWAY**

Nordisk Elektronikk (Norge) A/S
Postboks 123
Smedsvingen 4
1364 Hvalstad
Tel: (47) (02) 84 62 10
TLX: 77546

**PORTUGAL**

ATD Portugal LDA
Rua Dos Lusiados, 5 Sala B
1300 Lisboa
Tel: (35) (1) 64 80 91
TLX: 61562

Ditram
Avenida Miguel Bombarda, 133
1000 Lisboa
Tel: (35) (1) 54 53 13
TLX: 14182

**SPAIN**

ATD Electronica, S.A.
Plaza Ciudad de Viena, 6
28040 Madrid
Tel: (34) (1) 234 40 00
TLX: 42477

ITT-SESA
Calle Miguel Angel, 21-3
28010 Madrid
Tel: (34) (1) 419 09 57
TLX: 27461

Metrologia Iberica, S.A.
Ctra. de Fuencarral, n.80
28100 Alcobendas (Madrid)
Tel: (34) (1) 653 86 11

**SWEDEN**

Nordisk Elektronik AB
Torshamnsgatan 39
Box 36
164 93 Kista
Tel: (46) 08-03 46 30
TLX: 105 47

**SWITZERLAND**

Industrade A.G.
Hertistrasse 31
8304 Wallisellen
Tel: (41) (01) 8328111
TLX: 56788

**TURKEY**

EMPA Electronic
Lindwurmstrasse 95A
8000 Muenchen 2
Tel: (49) 089/53 80 570
TLX: 528573

**UNITED KINGDOM**

Accent Electronic Components Ltd.
Jubilee House, Jubilee Road
Letchworth, Herts SG6 1TL
Tel: (44) (0462) 686666
TLX: 826293

Bytech-Comway Systems
3 The Western Centre
Western Road
Bracknell RG12 1RW
Tel: (44) (0344) 55333
TLX: 847201

Jermyn
Vestry Estate
Otford Road
Sevenoaks
Kent TN14 5EU
Tel: (44) (0732) 450144
TLX: 95142

MMD
Unit 8 Southview Park
Caversham
Reading
Berkshire RG4 0AF
Tel: (44) (0734) 481666
TLX: 846669

Rapid Silicon
Rapid House
Denmark Street
High Wycombe
Buckinghamshire HP11 2ER
Tel: (44) (0494) 442266
TLX: 837931

Rapid Systems
Rapid House
Denmark Street
High Wycombe
Buckinghamshire HP11 2ER
Tel: (44) (0494) 450244
TLX: 837931

**YUGOSLAVIA**

H.R. Microelectronics Corp.
2005 de la Cruz Blvd., Ste. 223
Santa Clara, CA 95050
U.S.A.
Tel: (1) (408) 988-0286
TLX: 387452

Rapido Electronic Components
S.p.a.
Via C. Beccaria, 8
34133 Trieste
Italia
Tel: (39) 040/360555
TLX: 460461

*Field Application Location

# INTERNATIONAL SALES OFFICES

**AUSTRALIA**

Intel Australia Pty. Ltd.*
Spectrum Building
200 Pacific Hwy., Level 6
Crows Nest, NSE, 2065
Tel: 612-957-2744
FAX: 612-923-2632

**BRAZIL**

Intel Semicondutores do Brazil LTDA
Av. Paulista, 1159-CJS 404/405
01311 - Sao Paulo - S.P.
Tel: 55-11-287-5899
TLX: 3911153146 ISDB
FAX: 55-11-287-5119

**CHINA/HONG KONG**

Intel PRC Corporation
15/F, Office 1, Citic Bldg.
Jian Guo Men Wai Street
Beijing, PRC
Tel: (1) 500-4850
TLX: 22947 INTEL CN
FAX: (1) 500-2953

Intel Semiconductor Ltd.*
10/F East Tower
Bond Center
Queensway, Central
Hong Kong
Tel: (5) 8444-555
TLX: 63869 ISHLHK HX
FAX: (5) 8681-989

**INDIA**

Intel Asia Electronics, Inc.
4/2, Samrah Plaza
St. Mark's Road
Bangalore 560001
Tel: 011-91-812-215065
TLX: 9538452875 DCBY
FAX: 091-812-215067

**JAPAN**

Intel Japan K.K.
5-6 Tokodai, Tsukuba-shi
Ibaraki, 300-26
Tel: 0298-47-8511
TLX: 3656-160
FAX: 029747-8450

Intel Japan K.K.*
Daiichi Mitsugi Bldg.
1-8889 Fuchu-cho
Fuchu-shi, Tokyo 183
Tel: 0423-60-7871
FAX: 0423-60-0315

Intel Japan K.K.*
Bldg. Kumagaya
2-69 Hon-cho
Kumagaya-shi, Saitama 360
Tel: 0485-24-6871
FAX: 0485-24-7518

Intel Japan K.K.*
Mitsui-Seimei Musashi-kosugi Bldg.
915 Shinmaruko, Nakahara-ku
Kawasaki-shi, Kanagawa 211
Tel: 044-733-7011
FAX: 044-733-7010

Intel Japan K.K.
Nihon Seimei Atsugi Bldg.
1-2-1 Asahi-machi
Atsugi-shi, Kanagawa 243
Tel: 0462-29-3731
FAX: 0462-29-3781

Intel Japan K.K.*
Ryokuchi-Eki Bldg.
2-4-1 Terauchi
Toyonaka-shi, Osaka 560
Tel: 06-863-1091
FAX: 06-863-1084

Intel Japan K.K.
Shinmaru Bldg.
1-5-1 Marunouchi
Chiyoda-ku, Tokyo 100
Tel: 03-201-3621
FAX: 03-201-6850

Intel Japan K.K.
Green Bldg.
1-16-20 Nishiki
Naka-ku, Nagoya-shi
Aichi 450
Tel: 052-204-1261
FAX: 052-204-1285

**KOREA**

Intel Technology Asia, Ltd.
16th Floor, Life Bldg.
61 Yoido-dong, Youngdeungpo-Ku
Seoul 150-010
Tel: (2) 784-8186, 8286, 8386
TLX: K29312 INTELKO
FAX: (2) 784-8096

**SINGAPORE**

Intel Singapore Technology, Ltd.
101 Thomson Road #21-05/06
United Square
Singapore 1130
Tel: 250-7811
TLX: 39921 INTEL
FAX: 250-9256

**TAIWAN**

Intel Technology Far East Ltd.
8th Floor, No. 205
Bank Tower Bldg.
Tung Hua N. Road
Taipei
Tel: 886-2-716-9660
FAX: 886-2-717-2455

# INTERNATIONAL DISTRIBUTORS/REPRESENTATIVES

**ARGENTINA**

DAFSYS S.R.L.
Chacabuco, 90-6 PISO
1069-Buenos Aires
Tel: 54-1-334-7726
FAX: 54-1-334-1871

**AUSTRALIA**

Email Electronics
15-17 Hume Street
Huntingdale, 3166
Tel: 011-61-3-544-8244
TLX: AA 30895
FAX: 011-61-3-543-8179

NSD-Australia
205 Middleborough Rd.
Box Hill, Victoria 3128
Tel: 03 8900970
FAX: 03 8990819

**BRAZIL**

Elebra Microelectronica S.A.
Rua Geraldo Flausina Gomes, 78
10th Floor
04575 - Sao Paulo - S.P.
Tel: 55-11-534-9641
TLX: 55-11-54593/54591
FAX: 55-11-534-9424

**CHILE**

DIN Instruments
Suecia 2323
Casilla 6055, Correo 22
Santiago
Tel: 56-2-225-8139
TLX: 240.846 RUD

**CHINA/HONG KONG**

Novel Precision Machinery Co., Ltd.
Flat D, 20 Kingsford Ind. Bldg.
Phase 1, 26 Kwai Hei Street
N.T., Kowloon
Hong Kong
Tel: 852-0-4223222
TWX: 39114 JINMI HX
FAX: 852-0-4261602

**INDIA**

Micronic Devices
Arun Complex
No. 65 D.V.G. Road
Basavanagudi
Bangalore 560 004
Tel: 011-91-812-600-631
011-91-812-611-365
TLX: 9538458332 MDBG

Micronic Devices
No. 516 5th Floor
Swastik Chambers
Sion, Trombay Road
Chembur
Bombay 400 071
TLX: 9531 171447 MDEV

Micronic Devices
25/8, 1st Floor
Bada Bazaar Marg
Old Rajinder Nagar
New Delhi 110 060
Tel: 011-91-11-5723509
011-91-11-589771
TLX: 031-63253 MDND IN

Micronic Devices
6-3-348/12A Dwarakapuri Colony
Hyderabad 500 482
Tel: 011-91-842-226748

S&S Corporation
1587 Kooser Road
San Jose, CA 95118
Tel: (408) 978-6216
TLX: 820281
FAX: (408) 978-8635

**JAPAN**

Asahi Electronics Co. Ltd.
KMM Bldg. 2-14-1 Asano
Kokurakita-ku
Kitakyushu-shi 802
Tel: 093-511-6471
FAX: 093-551-7861

C. Itoh Techno-Science Co., Ltd.
4-8-1 Dobashi, Miyamae-ku
Kawasaki-shi, Kanagawa 213
Tel: 044-852-5121
FAX: 044-877-4268

Dia Semicon Systems, Inc.
Flower Hill Shinmachi Higashi-kan
1-23-9 Shinmachi, Setagaya-ku
Tokyo 154
Tel: 03-439-1600
FAX: 03-439-1601

Okaya Koki
2-4-18 Sakae
Naka-ku, Nagoya-shi 460
Tel: 052-204-2916
FAX: 052-204-2901

Ryoyo Electro Corp.
Konwa Bldg.
1-12-22 Tsukiji
Chuo-ku, Tokyo 104
Tel: 03-546-5011
FAX: 03-546-5044

**KOREA**

J-Tek Corporation
6th Floor, Government Pension Bldg.
24-3 Yoido-dong
Youngdeungpo-ku
Seoul 150-010
Tel: 82-2-780-8039
TLX: 25299 KODIGIT
FAX: 82-2-784-8391

Samsung Electronics
150 Taepyungro-2 KA
Chungku, Seoul 100-102
Tel: 82-2-751-3985
TLX: 27970 KORSST
FAX: 82-2-753-0967

**MEXICO**

SSB Electronics, Inc.
675 Palomar Street, Bldg. 4, Suite A
Chula Vista, CA 92011
Tel: (619) 585-3253
TLX: 287751 CBALL UR
FAX: (619) 585-8322

Dicopel S.A.
Tochtli 368 Fracc. Ind. San Antonio
Azcapotzalco
C.P. 02760-Mexico, D.F.
Tel: 52-5-561-3211
TLX: 177 3790 Dicome
FAX: 52-5-561-1279

PSI de Mexico
Francisco Villas Esq. Ajusto
Cuernavaca – Morelos – CEP 62130
Tel: 52-73-13-9412
FAX: 52-73-17-5333

**NEW ZEALAND**

Email Electronics
36 Olive Road
Penrose, Auckland
Tel: 011-64-9-591-155
FAX: 011-64-9-592-681

**SINGAPORE**

Electronic Resources Pte, Ltd.
17 Harvey Road #04-01
Singapore 1336
Tel: 283-0888
TWX: 56541 ERS
FAX: 2895327

**SOUTH AFRICA**

Electronic Building Elements
178 Erasmus Street (off Watermeyet Street)
Meyerspark, Pretoria, 0184
Tel: 011-2712-803-7680
FAX: 011-2712-803-8294

**TAIWAN**

Micro Electronics Corporation
5/F 587, Ming Shen East Rd.
Taipei, R.O.C.
Tel: 886-2-501-8231
FAX: 886-2-505-6609

Sertek
15/F 135, Section 2
Chien Juo North Rd.
Taipei 10479, R.O.C.
Tel: (02) 5010055
FAX: (02) 5012521
(02) 5058414

**VENEZUELA**

P. Benavides S.A.
Avilanes a Rio
Residencia Kamarata
Locales 4 AL 7
La Candelaria, Caracas
Tel: 58-2-574-6338
TLX: 28450
FAX: 58-2-572-3321

---

*Field Application Location

CG/SALE/101789

# DOMESTIC SERVICE OFFICES

**ALABAMA**

*Intel Corp.
5015 Bradford Dr., Suite 2
Huntsville 35805
Tel: (205) 830-4010

**ALASKA**

Intel Corp.
c/o TransAlaska Data Systems
300 Old Steese Hwy.
Fairbanks 99701-3120
Tel: (907) 452-4401

Intel Corp.
c/o TransAlaska Data Systems
1551 Lore Road
Anchorage 99507
Tel: (907) 522-1776

**ARIZONA**

*Intel Corp.
11225 N. 28th Dr.
Suite D-214
Phoenix 85029
Tel: (602) 869-4980

*Intel Corp.
500 E. Fry Blvd., Suite M-15
Sierra Vista 85635
Tel: (602) 459-5010

**CALIFORNIA**

†Intel Corp.
21515 Vanowen St., Ste. 116
Canoga Park 91303
Tel: (818) 704-8500

*Intel Corp.
2250 E. Imperial Hwy., Ste. 218
El Segundo 90245
Tel: (213) 640-6040

*Intel Corp.
1900 Prairie City Rd.
Folsom 95630-9597
Tel: (916) 351-6143
          1-800-468-3548

Intel Corp.
9665 Cheasapeake Dr., Suite 325
San Diego 92123-1326
Tel: (619) 292-8086

**Intel Corp.
400 N. Tustin Avenue
Suite 450
Santa Ana 92705
Tel: (714) 835-9642

**Intel Corp.
San Tomas 4
2700 San Tomas Exp., 2nd Floor
Santa Clara 95051
Tel: (408) 986-8086

**COLORADO**

*Intel Corp.
650 S. Cherry St., Suite 915
Denver 80222
Tel: (303) 321-8086

**CONNECTICUT**

*Intel Corp.
301 Lee Farm Corporate Park
83 Wooster Heights Rd.
Danbury 06810
Tel: (203) 748-3130

**FLORIDA**

**Intel Corp.
6363 N.W. 6th Way, Ste. 100
Ft. Lauderdale 33309
Tel: (305) 771-0600

*Intel Corp.
5850 T.G. Lee Blvd., Ste. 340
Orlando 32822
Tel: (407) 240-8000

**GEORGIA**

*Intel Corp.
3280 Pointe Pkwy., Ste. 200
Norcross 30092
Tel: (404) 449-0541

**HAWAII**

*Intel Corp.
U.S.I.S.C. Signal Batt.
Building T-1521
Shafter Plats
Shafter 96856

**ILLINOIS**

**†Intel Corp.
300 N. Martingale Rd., Ste. 400
Schaumburg 60173
Tel: (312) 605-8031

**INDIANA**

*Intel Corp.
8777 Purdue Rd., Ste. 125
Indianapolis 46268
Tel: (317) 875-0623

**KANSAS**

*Intel Corp.
10985 Cody, Suite 140
Overland Park 66210
Tel: (913) 345-2727

**MARYLAND**

**†Intel Corp.
10010 Junction Dr., Suite 200
Annapolis Junction 20701
Tel: (301) 206-2860
FAX: 301-206-3677

**MASSACHUSETTS**

**†Intel Corp.
3 Carlisle Rd., 2nd Floor
Westford 01886
Tel: (508) 692-1060

**MICHIGAN**

*†Intel Corp.
7071 Orchard Lake Rd., Ste. 100
West Bloomfield 48322
Tel: (313) 851-8905

**MINNESOTA**

*†Intel Corp.
3500 W. 80th St., Suite 360
Bloomington 55431
Tel: (612) 835-6722

**MISSOURI**

*Intel Corp.
4203 Earth City Exp., Ste. 131
Earth City 63045
Tel: (314) 291-1990

**NEW JERSEY**

**Intel Corp.
300 Sylvan Avenue
Englewood Cliffs 07632
Tel: (201) 567-0821

*Intel Corp.
Parkway 109 Office Center
328 Newman Springs Road
Red Bank 07701
Tel: (201) 747-2233

*Intel Corp.
280 Corporate Center
75 Livingston Ave., 1st Floor
Roseland 07068
Tel: (201) 740-0111

**NEW YORK**

*†Intel Corp.
2950 Expressway Dr. South
Islandia 11722
Tel: (516) 231-3300

*Intel Corp.
Westage Business Center
Bldg. 300, Route 9
Fishkill 12524
Tel: (914) 897-3860

**NORTH CAROLINA**

*Intel Corp.
5800 Executive Dr., Ste. 105
Charlotte 28212
Tel: (704) 568-8966

**Intel Corp.
2700 Wycliff Road
Suite 102
Raleigh 27607
Tel: (919) 781-8022

**OHIO**

**†Intel Corp.
3401 Park Center Dr., Ste. 220
Dayton 45414
Tel: (513) 890-5350

*†Intel Corp.
25700 Science Park Dr., Ste. 100
Beachwood 44122
Tel: (216) 464-2736

**OREGON**

Intel Corp.
15254 N.W. Greenbrier Parkway
Building B
Beaverton 97005
Tel: (503) 645-8051

*Intel Corp.
5200 N.E. Elam Young Parkway
Hillsboro 97123
Tel: (503) 681-8080

**PENNSYLVANIA**

*†Intel Corp.
455 Pennsylvania Ave., Ste. 230
Fort Washington 19034
Tel: (215) 641-1000

†Intel Corp.
400 Penn Center Blvd., Ste. 610
Pittsburgh 15235
Tel: (412) 823-4970

Intel Corp.
1513 Cedar Cliff Dr.
Camp Hill 17011
Tel: (717) 761-0860

**PUERTO RICO**

Intel Corp.
South Industrial Park
P.O. Box 910
Las Piedras 00671
Tel: (809) 733-8616

**TEXAS**

Intel Corp.
8815 Dyer St., Suite 225
El Paso 79904
Tel: (915) 751-0186

*Intel Corp.
313 E. Anderson Lane, Suite 314
Austin 78752
Tel: (512) 454-3628

**†Intel Corp.
12000 Ford Rd., Suite 401
Dallas 75234
Tel: (214) 241-8087

*Intel Corp.
7322 S.W. Freeway, Ste. 1490
Houston 77074
Tel: (713) 988-8086

**UTAH**

Intel Corp.
428 East 6400 South, Ste. 104
Murray 84107
Tel: (801) 263-8051

**VIRGINIA**

*Intel Corp.
1504 Santa Rosa Rd., Ste. 108
Richmond 23288
Tel: (804) 282-5668

**WASHINGTON**

*Intel Corp.
155 108th Avenue N.E., Ste. 386
Bellevue 98004
Tel: (206) 453-8086

## CANADA

**ONTARIO**

Intel Semiconductor of
Canada, Ltd.
2650 Queensview Dr., Ste. 250
Ottawa K2B 8H6
Tel: (613) 829-9714
FAX: 613-820-5936

Intel Semiconductor of
Canada, Ltd.
190 Attwell Dr., Ste. 102
Rexdale M9W 6H8
Tel: (416) 675-2105
FAX: 416-675-2438

# CUSTOMER TRAINING CENTERS

**CALIFORNIA**

2700 San Tomas Expressway
Santa Clara 95051
Tel: (408) 970-1700
          1-800-421-0386

**ILLINOIS**

300 N. Martingale Road
Suite 300
Schaumburg 60173
Tel: (708) 706-5700
          1-800-421-0386

**MASSACHUSETTS**

3 Carlisle Road, First Floor
Westford 01886
Tel: (301) 220-3380
          1-800-328-0386

**MARYLAND**

10010 Junction Dr.
Suite 200
Annapolis Junction 20701
Tel: (301) 206-2860
          1-800-328-0386

# SYSTEMS ENGINEERING MANAGERS OFFICES

**MINNESOTA**

3500 W. 80th Street
Suite 360
Bloomington 55431
Tel: (612) 835-6722

**NEW YORK**

2950 Expressway Dr., South
Islandia 11722
Tel: (506) 231-3300

†System Engineering locations
*Carry-in locations
**Carry-in/mail-in locations

CG/SALE/1017